WHO SHOULD WE TREAT?

Who Should We Treat?

Law, Patients and Resources in the NHS

CHRISTOPHER NEWDICK
Reader in Health Law
University of Reading

CLARENDON PRESS · OXFORD
1995

Oxford University Press, Walton Street, Oxford OX2 6DP

Oxford New York
Athens Auckland Bangkok Bombay
Calcutta Cape Town Dar es Salaam Delhi
Florence Hong Kong Istanbul Karachi
Kuala Lumpur Madras Madrid Melbourne
Mexico City Nairobi Paris Singapore
Taipei Tokyo Toronto
and associated companies in
Berlin Ibadan

Oxford is a trade mark of Oxford University Press

Published in the United States
by Oxford University Press Inc., New York

British Library Cataloguing in Publication Data
Data available

Library of Congress Cataloging in Publication Data
Newdick, Christopher
Who should we treat?: law, patients, and resources in the NHS/
Christopher Newdick.
p. cm.
Includes bibliographical references.
1. Great Britain. National Health Service. 2. National health
insurance—Law and legislation—Great Britain. 3. Medical care—Law
and legislation—Great Britain. 4. Medical care—Great Britain.
I. Title.
KD3210.N49   1995
344.41'02—dc20
[344.1042]   95–9156
ISBN 0–19–825924–7
ISBN 0–19–825925–5 (Pbk.)

1 3 5 7 9 10 8 6 4 2

Typeset by Cambrian Typesetters, Frimley, Surrey
Printed in Great Britain on acid-free paper by
Bookcraft Ltd., Midsomer Norton, Avon

Contents

Table of Cases

Table of Cases

MALAYSIA

NEW ZEALAND

UK

Table of Legislation

Guidance Notes

List of Abbreviations

ACHCEW	Association of Community Health Councils of England and Wales
All ER	All England Law Reports
BMLR	Butterworths Medico-Legal Reports
CHC	community health council
CL	Current Law
CSAG	Clinical Standards Advisory Group
DGM	district general manager
DHA	district health authority
DLR	Dominion Law Reports
DNR	'do not resuscitate' orders
DRG	diagnosis related groups
ECR	extra contractual referral
EL	Executive Letter
FCE	finished consultant episode
FHSA	family health service authority
GPFH	GP Fund-holder
HSG	Health Service Guidelines
IRLR	Industrial Relations Law Reports
Med LR	Medical Law Rports
NAHAT	National Association of Health Authorities and Trusts
NHS	National Health Service
NHSE	National Health Service Executive
NHSME	National Health Service Management Executive (renamed in 1994 'National Health Service Executive')
NLJ	New Law Journal
OECD	Organization for Economic Co-operation and Development
QALY	quality adjusted life year
QUANGO	quasi-autonomous non-governmental organisation

RHA	regional health authority
SHA	special health authority
Sol Jo	Solicitors' Journal
UGM	unit general manager

Introduction

Lawyers have long been concerned with the personal rights and duties which exist between doctor and patient. Recent tensions in our system of health care, however, have drawn attention to the impact of the National Health Service on their relationship. In any system of public health care, medical resources—doctors, nurses, ancillary staff, buildings, equipment, and so on—need to be managed. Management should ensure that resources are not allowed to lie idle, or be diverted to pointless use. Its purpose is to make optimum use of staff and facilities for the benefit of patients. Paradoxically, just when new systems of management have been introduced and the influence of managers expanded, the concern for the welfare of patients has become most intense.

Previously, the issue of management caused no particular anxiety. Little difference was perceived between the relationship of individual doctors and their patients, and the NHS as an institution and its patients. It made no difference which way one looked at it because doctors enjoyed the respect of patients and health service managers. Doctors had the lion's share of power within the system and, therefore, it was said, clinical priorities prevailed and patients considered themselves to be in safe hands. This perception may never have been entirely accurate, and it seems unlikely that all patients always received all the treatment they needed, but it offered a degree of reassurance that the service was doing all it could. In the modern system, however, doctors are no longer pre-eminent because aspects of their authority are shared with health service managers and resources are not at their complete disposal. When resources are under strain, a lack of co-ordination and planning could lead to patients being overlooked, or being offered inadequate care. Thus, managers have been given more authority to organize and promote the service.

At the same time, there has been concern that our original perceptions about the basic objective of the NHS, to promote the clinical well-being of patients, are being threatened. When responsibility for management is shared between doctors and managers the centre of gravity changes. Apart from their patients, doctors have to consider a variety of other matters. Clinical decisions may be subject to medical audit; business plans may have to be agreed; financial budgets and targets may be imposed. This means that clinical discretion may now involve considerations which differ from those of the past. There may be occasions when the best possible clinical care is compromised in order to spread resources over as many patients as possible. In truth this may always have happened, but the issue is now more visible and contentious than ever before.

This is why medical law must address the system within which health care is provided. Otherwise, it tells a detached and one-sided story. It means that we have to understand where demands for health care come from, the most appropriate ways of maximizing the benefits the system can offer, and who is responsible for balancing the conflicting demands made upon it: doctors, managers, government, or patients. We must understand how the system is organized, who is responsible for running it, and their legal obligations in doing so. These questions are addressed in Chapters 1, 2 and 5 of this book.

Obviously, there will be argument as to the standards of care the system ought to achieve. When resources are finite, is it better to treat two patients with second-best care, or only one with the best, most expensive, care? This question becomes more pressing as medical and pharmaceutical technology advances. Increasingly, we will be forced to consider those who will not have access to care when money is devoted to one category of patients at the expense of others. Ought some patients be excluded from care altogether on the grounds that they are 'uneconomic'? Both common law and statute have made contributions to these issues, which are raised in Chapters 3, 4, and 8.

One of the techniques for making those who purchase health care more sensitive to the cost and quality of care offered to patients has been the introduction of a system of managed competition for resources. Money is allocated to 'purchasers' (health authorities and GP fund-holders) who may select hospitals for their patients on the basis of value for money. Hospitals that offer poor quality will be encouraged to improve their standards, or risk being starved of resources. How does the system hold these bodies responsible for their use of NHS resources and how effective is it in doing so? These questions are raised in Chapter 6.

When there is dissatisfaction with the standards achieved by doctors or health service managers, what professional supervision of doctors and managers is available which enables complaints to be made about their conduct? This is considered in Chapter 7.

Lastly, Chapter 8 looks to the future for medical ethics as the pressures imposed by scarce resources become increasingly difficult to conceal and are more openly discussed at every level within the system. To what extent can we continue to hold to the principle of the Hippocratic Oath that doctors owe allegiance to their patients? Doctors have hundreds of patients. How should his or her allegiance be divided between them? This suggests the need for a more candid relationship between doctor and patient which takes account of expensive alternatives that may become unavailable.

This is a book about pressing questions in the National Health Service, but it does not provide a list of treatments or patients which ought to take precedence over others. English law provides no such list and lawyers have no particular expertise in suggesting one, though they may say who should not be excluded altogether. Philosophers, ethicists, and economists have attempted to answer the question, and lawyers and judges ought to be sensitive to their contribution as a source of guidance. Where appropriate, I have attempted to do so here.

Common law permits both doctors and health service managers a very broad measure of discretion in deciding how to discharge their responsibilities. It permits them to issue their own guidelines and recommendations, both as to matters of NHS management and as to the ways in which patients should be treated. These I have included in the discussion wherever they are relevant. Countless doctors, health service managers, and administrators from the NHS Executive and elsewhere have made time to explain these matters and send me their reports and guidelines. I express my sincere thanks to them all.

Andrew Grubb and Ian Kennedy of King's College, London; and John Appleby of the Health Services Management Centre at Birmingham University read a number of chapters of the book and I am grateful to them for their extremely helpful advice. My colleagues David Jabbari and Paul Jackson spent hours discussing with me the issues raised and provided many valuable insights. My wife Lyn read every word of the book. Without her it would have been less digestible and coherent. My son provided ample opportunity for reflection and contemplation. The book is for Lyn and Harry.

The book was submitted to the publishers at the end of February 1995, although a small number of amendments to the text were possible in the following months.

1

Resources in the NHS

Criticism of the National Health Service has always been endemic. Almost as soon as it began treating patients in 1948, it became clear that the cost of providing care would greatly exceed the resources allocated to it by the Treasury. As a consequence, prescription charges were introduced in 1951 and Aneurin Bevan, the first Secretary of State for the NHS, resigned in protest. This was perhaps the first crisis of spending in the system,[1] but the story has remained the same ever since: of demand exceeding supply, and reform succeeding reform both to improve patient care and to control costs. An ex-Minister of State for Health wrote in 1966: 'One of the most striking features of the National Health Service is the continual, deafening chorus of complaint which rises day and night from every part of it, a chorus only interrupted when someone suggests that a different system altogether might be preferable, which would involve the money coming from some less (literally) palpable source'.[2]

Similarly, in 1980 a judge of the Court of Appeal, in a case concerning a decision to withhold resources from an orthopaedic unit in Birmingham, said that it was 'a matter of common knowledge' that: 'the health service currently falls far short of what everyone would regard as the optimum desirable standard. This is very largely a situation brought about by lack of resources,

---

[1] See M. Foot, *Aneurin Bevan, vol. 2* (Davis-Poynter, London, 1973), ch. 8; and J. Campbell, *Nye Bevan and the Mirage of British Socialism* (Weidenfeld and Nicolson, 1973), ch. 12. Today the vast majority of prescriptions are issued free. Only 20% of those who require them are subject to charges. Most prescription medicines cost the NHS less than the amount of the prescription charge. The charge is levied, not to defray the cost of the medicine, but as 'a contribution to the NHS'. See the reply of Mr. B. Mawhinney, Minister for Health, to the House of Commons Health Committee, *Priority Setting in the NHS: The NHS Drug Budget* (HC 80–vii, Session 1993–94), para. 878. For the modern powers enabling charges to be imposed for medicines, see ss. 77–83 of the National Health Service Act 1977.

[2] J. Enoch Powell, *A New Look at Medicine and Politics* (Pitman Medical, 1966) 16.

lack of suitable equipment, lack of suitably qualified personnel, and above all lack of adequate finance.'[3]

Over the last decade these anxieties have been heightened. Why is there, half a century after its creation, so much concern about the NHS? This chapter considers (I) spending dilemmas in the service and (II) the proposals made by some health economists to resolve the tension.

I. SPENDING DILEMMAS IN THE NHS

There are a number of reasons why resources in the NHS will continue to present a serious challenge to any government.

A. NHS Expenditure and Inflation

Bare statistics suggest that the government has lavished unparalleled generosity on the NHS. Since its creation it has received an increased level of funding almost every year. Even when allowing for inflation, 'the NHS in 1990 still has well over four times the resources available to it in 1949. As a result, the NHS absorbed a greater share of the Gross Domestic Product (GDP), growing from 3.5% to 5.2% between 1949 and 1990.'[4] In addition, the Service has become increasingly efficient. Modern nursing practice and technology treat more patients, more effectively, more quickly, and at less cost per patient than ever before. In 1951 the number of in-patient cases treated in the UK, as measured by the numbers of discharges and deaths (the finished consultant episode, or FCE) was 3.8 million. In 1990–91 that figure had risen to 9.1 million. This corresponds to more than a threefold increase in the use of hospital beds: from seven to twenty-seven discharges per bed during the same period.[5]

Given the increase in the proportion of the nation's resources

---

[3] Bridge LJ in *R* v. *Secretary of State* ex parte *Hincks* (1992) 1 BMLR 93, 96 (the case was decided in 1980). See also *In a Terminal Condition—A Report on the State of London's Health Service* (Association of London Authorities, 1991).

[4] R. Chew, *Compendium of Health Statistics* (Office of Health Economics, 8th edn, 1992), section entitled 'Cost of the NHS'.

[5] Ibid., section entitled Hospital Services, 5. See also J. Perrin, 'Administrative and financial management of health care services', in E. Beck, S. Lonsdale, *et al.* (eds.), *In the Best of Health* (Chapman Hall, 1992) ch. 11.

made available to the service why is there so much dissatisfaction with the NHS? Inflation is a major factor. For a number of reasons inflation in the NHS has exceeded that in the general economy. Consequently, the NHS has needed consistently larger contributions from the Treasury simply to stand still. Salaries and wages have contributed significantly to this problem because they account for around 80 per cent of the costs of health authorities.[6] In particular, nurses' salaries account for a substantial proportion of that sum and they have, to unanimous applause, slowly improved their conditions of service by achieving wage settlements in excess of inflation.[7] But these increases have not been matched by additional funding from the Treasury. Hospital and community health services absorb around 60 per cent of the entire health service budget and received an increase of 16 per cent in real terms between 1971 and 1990. Allowing, though, for the cost of the improved salaries and conditions offered to doctors and nurses: 'Hospital Services in the UK have been experiencing a shortfall in cash allocations every financial year since 1981/82, amounting to a cumulative deficit in net revenue expenditure of £1,600 million by the end of 1990/91.'[8]

A second explanation concerns the reduction of the percentage of funds made available to hospital services in order to increase the funding of preventive and primary care. Hospitals are a visible and sensitive part of the NHS—particularly when waiting lists lengthen, vital operations are cancelled, and accident and emergency departments are unable to accommodate patients. Today, however, greater attention is being paid to the need to keep patients out of hospital. In 1979 the Royal Commission on the National Health Service commented on the belief that the NHS was a 'sickness service' rather than a health service, and that more should be invested in preventive medicine and keeping people out of hospital.[9] This view has continued to gain ground.

---

[6] Ibid., section entitled 'Costs of the NHS'. This compares to 69% in 1953.

[7] See K. Bloor and A. Maynard, *Expenditure on the NHS During and After the Thatcher Years: Its Growth and Utilisation* (Centre for Health Economics, University of York, 1993) 16.

[8] *Compendium of Health Statistics*, *supra* note 4, section entitled 'Hospital Services'.

[9] *Royal Commission on the National Health Service* (Cmnd. 7615, 1979), para. 4.23. The Commission had reservations about this view.

Between 1979 and 1992 the proportion of NHS expenditure devoted to hospital funding decreased from 60.9 per cent to 55.8 per cent. By contrast, spending on community health services increased from 6 per cent to 8.8 per cent.[10] The result is that a very conspicuous aspect of the service has suffered difficulties which have not been experienced to the same extent in the community.

B. Expanding Demand for Health Care

Another factor which gives rise to concern is our expanded perception of the conditions for which a visit to the doctor is appropriate.[11] Consider our ideas of 'illness' and 'health' in 1946 when the health service was created. Medicine had recently undergone very rapid development. The treatment of sexual disease became possible with the discovery of sulfanomides during the 1930s; and during the 1940s, penicillin was put to astonishingly effective use in the treatment of those who fought in the War. High expectation was generated based on our successes with opportunistic infections and acute illnesses. Originally, it may have been hoped that the creation of a National Health Service would tend to diminish the need for health care by reducing the incidence of ill-health in society. Any such optimism soon gave way. With immense foresight, the first Committee of Enquiry into health service costs observed in 1956:

The growth of medical knowledge adds continually to the number and expense of treatments and, by prolonging life, also increases the incidence of slow-killing diseases. No-one can predict whether the speeding of therapy and the improvement of health will ultimately offset this expense; there is at present no evidence that it will; indeed, current trends seem to be all the other way . . . [T]here is no reason at present to suppose that demands on the service as a whole will be reduced thereby so as to stabilise (still less reduce) its total cost in terms of finance and the absorption of real resources.[12]

Since then the pharmaceutical industry, despite some catastrophic set-backs, (most infamous of which was the protracted

---

[10] Bloor and Maynard, *supra*, note 7, 6.

[11] Our faith in medicine and the medical profession is severely criticised in I. Illich, *Limits to Medicine* (Pelican, reprinted 1988).

[12] *Report of the Committee of Enquiry into the Costs of the National Health Service* (Cmnd. 9663, 1956), para. 95.

dispute surrounding Thalidomide) has provided an increasing range of medicines capable of achieving extremely effective results which save patients from expensive and dangerous surgery, or enable them to lead more active, productive, or peaceful lives. Nevertheless, as forecast by the Enquiry of 1956, the cost of the NHS steadily rises. Medicine no longer focuses on opportunistic and acute illness. It routinely deals with chronic conditions such as the diseases of the cardio-vascular system, of the respiratory system, the gastrointestinal system, the central nervous system, and joint diseases such as arthritis. Treatments for these conditions are usually long-term and often last many years. Combined together, they accounted for some 63.6 per cent of the total drugs bill in England in 1992.[13] These are the diseases associated with relative affluence and old age which, for the moment, are likely to put increasing pressure on resources. As a result of these pressures, some treatments are not routinely provided by the NHS. For example, tattoo removal is often not offered by hospitals, and many health authorities have restricted the availability of in vitro fertilization, gender reassignment, reversal of sterilisation, cosmetic surgery, and complementary medicine.[14]

Matters will soon become more complicated still. The pharmaceutical industry stands on the edge of a new generation of medicines which will revolutionize our ideas about sickness and health. But they may be so expensive that health service providers will be forced to reassess the question of priorities. 'Just the past year has seen a paradigm shift in modern biology because it is revealing so much information about the basic mechanisms of disease for which drugs can be developed. In the past, pharmaceutical firms relied on serendipity to find new drugs. In future that is not the way to go if the idea is to produce medicines of value.'[15]

Today, as a result of the Human Genome Project, we have sufficient knowledge of the basic structures of DNA in the human

[13] See *Priority Setting in the NHS: The NHS Drugs Budget* (HC 80–vii, Session 1993–94), statistics at 261. Their total cost was £1,817 million.

[14] See the responses of the health authorities to the questionnaire issued by the House of Commons Health Committee in *Priority Setting in the NHS: Purchasing* (HC 227, Session 1993–94).

[15] Comment of Sir Richard Sykes, chief executive of Glaxo Pharmaceuticals PLC in 'Engineering Health', *The Economist*, 19 Mar. 1994 13.

body to consider genetic treatments for chronic conditions of illness which were hitherto entirely beyond the reach of doctors and medicines. We may soon be in a position to attack the genetic causes of chronic illness. Cystic fibrosis, for example, is being treated in this way.[16] Similar developments are occurring in the field of medical devices and technology, in both diagnosis and treatment of illness. Such techniques offer the potential for considerable savings on conventional, long-term treatment of conditions such as heart and liver disease, diabetes, and cancer and may be attractive on health and financial grounds. On the other hand, their cost may be so prohibitive as to threaten the availability of other, less expensive treatments. They also raise fundamental questions about the meaning of the words 'health' and 'illness'. Curative treatment may become available for a range of conditions which are explained in societal or personal terms, rather than as illnesses. Obesity, alcoholism, cigarette smoking, and drug addiction provoke arguments of this nature. Should they qualify for care in the same way as other conditions? These issues raise questions about the very purpose of a 'health' service.

Could the boundaries of the NHS be defined more clearly? Unfortunately the idea of 'health' is so broad and flexible that it almost defies definition. Health may be described in medical (or biological) terms or in social (or functional) terms. Take the examples of infertility, arthritis in the elderly and dwarfism. Should they be defined in *biological* terms, meaning the absence of illness, or in *functional* terms, as departures from normal physiological function? If the latter, who is to define what is 'normal'? Infertility and dwarfism are not illnesses. Are they 'abnormal' on the functional test? Before the Mental Health Act 1957, sexual promiscuity was used as evidence of mental illness. That judgment was clearly not driven by clinical considerations. Arthritis may qualify on both the biological and functional tests, but in elderly people is it an example of illness, or abnormality, or simply one of the natural, normal impediments we may all suffer in later life? The point is that there is no complete definition of words like 'health' and 'illness'. The concepts are liable to change both with advances in medical science and developments in social attitudes.

The World Health Organisation describes 'health' as: 'a state of

[16] See *Report of the Committee on the Ethics of Gene Therapy* (Cm. 1788, 1992).

complete physical, mental and social well-being and not merely the absence of disease or infirmity.'[17] This, however, says nothing about the question of the proper responsibility of a health service. It is statement of an ideal condition of human happiness to which we all might aspire. Such a condition would depend on a good system of education, sanitation, decent living accommodation, family and friends, and a holiday each summer. These are not, however, the concerns of medicine, which has a dramatically more limited area of responsibility. In addition, in so far as the phrase is used to describe the role of doctors it seems to place unwarranted, and perhaps unwanted, power in the hands of the medical profession. Doctors receive training in medicine, in the diagnosis of disease and prognosis for care or cure. They claim no particular expertise with respect to 'social well-being' (whatever that may mean). Definitions which appear to describe society's problems in terms of ill health must be treated with great caution.[18]

Also, in determining which demands on the health service are legitimate, we need to remind ourselves that good health and a good health service may have very little in common. Many of the most significant improvements in health have come about not by virtue of the health service or doctors, but from improvements in our environment and our diet.[19] 'The combined death rate from scarlet fever, diphtheria, whooping cough and measles among children up to fifteen shows that nearly 90% of the total decline in mortality between 1860 and 1965 had occurred before the

---

[17] More obscurely, it has been suggested that health can be thought of as 'a responsive functional state where inappropriate responsiveness and maladjustment to change are evidence of an unhealthy state even if scientifically and medically defined pathology do not result. It is this dynamic and socially sensitive quality which makes health a mirage; it will vary with the complexity of each macrosystem and with the nature and frequency of deterioration in the ecology that produces equilibrium.' See R. Kohn and K. White, *Health Care: An International Study* (Oxford University Press, 1976) 58.

[18] See D. Callahan, 'The WHO Definition of "Health" ', in T. Beauchamp and L. Walters, *Contemporary Issues in Bioethics* (Wadsworth, 1982) 80: 'it is important to keep clear and distinct the roles of different professions, with a clearly circumscribed role for medicine limited to those domains of life where the contribution of medicine is appropriate. Medicine can save lives; it cannot save society.'

[19] See T. McKeown, *The Modern Rise of Population and the Role of Medicine: Dream, Mirage or Nemesis?* (Nuffield Provincial Hospital Trust, 1976).

introduction of antibiotics and immunization . . . by far the most important factor was a higher host-resistance due to better nutrition.'[20]

These considerations show the wide scope for disagreement both as to the meaning of the word 'health' and as to the proper responsibilities of a public health service. In the absence of any objective yardstick of this nature, there is reason to suspect that public expectations of the health service are likely to increase.

C. An Ageing Population—Health Care or Community Care?

Patterns of demography also help to explain our increased demand for health care. The very success of the NHS tends to increase the demands put upon it, particularly in the way in which it assists survival into old age. Between 1991 to 2031 the population of England and Wales is expected to grow by 8 per cent. However, those aged between 45 and 59 are projected to increase by 15 per cent; those between 60 and 74 by 43 per cent; and those aged between 75 and 84 will expand by 138 per cent.[21] Just when larger numbers of us will be able enjoy our old age, the proportion of the productive population on whom we depend for support is declining.

Perhaps the most important contributor to the financial expansion of the NHS has been the growing proportion of the old and very old in the population. Not only is their frequency of demand for health care higher, but also each period of treatment tends to last longer than for younger patients. . . . It may be calculated that the very elderly population (aged 75 and over) who account for about 7 per cent of the total population, absorbed approximately 25 per cent of the overall NHS expenditure in the financial year 1989/90. In 1973/74, the equivalent figure was 21 per cent.[22]

This imposes a strain on the system which it has not yet succeeded in resolving. There have been some extreme proposals to ease the expected pressure caused by our increasing longevity.

---

[20] I. Illich, *supra*, note 11, 24.

[21] *The Health of the U.K.'s Elderly People* (Medical Research Council, 1994) 17.

[22] *Compendium of Health Statistics. supra* note 4, section entitled 'Cost of Health Care'. Our contributions to the service in times of health may be regarded as the insurance premium which assures our care when we are old.

[23] See D. Callahan, *Setting Limits: Medical Goals in an Aging Society* (Simon and Schuster, New York, 1990). For those elderly patients who have enjoyed good

One is that patients over a certain age should simply not be treated and should receive community and palliative care only.[23] Treating people in the community is a less expensive way of providing care and there has been a movement away from institutional to community care,[24] with residential care considered only as a last resort. What is not yet clear, however, is when elderly people should be in hospital, at home, or in a nursing home; and wherever they are, who should be responsible for the cost of their treatment and support. Largely by default, the costs have increasingly been borne by relatives so that about one adult in seven in Britain (some six million people) is a carer, in the large majority of cases, of an elderly relative. Further, when care is provided in a residential nursing home, it is increasingly paid for by the individuals themselves. 'It is apparent that there has been a disengagement of the NHS from responsibilities in this area. Moreover, this move has entailed a redrawing of the boundaries of entitlement to free health care, with increased individual responsibility for arranging and financing long term nursing care in old age.'[25]

This has become one of the major questions concerning the role of the NHS. The prospect of retired people having to accept financial and nursing responsibility for their own parents may be resisted both by the parents themselves and their (sic) children. In addition, since the majority of carers are women who are increasingly likely to remain in work, the number of people available to fulfil the role is declining. This poses a problem which has not yet been clearly addressed.

Although attention has been given to the managerial structures in which care for elderly people is provided,[26] little has been done to distinguish the responsibilities of the NHS and the Department

health and made no previous demands on the health service, this will appear unreasonable; as it will to those who require relatively inexpensive care to return them to full health.

[24] See *Caring for People: Community Care in the Next Decade and Beyond* (Cm. 849, 1989, HMSO). In para. 1.11, the government says it wishes 'people to live in their own homes wherever feasible and sensible . . . In future, the government will encourage the targeting of home-based services on those people whose need for them is greatest.'

[25] M. Henwood, *Through a Glass Darkly: Community Care and Elderly People* (King's Fund Institute, 1992) 42.

[26] See Audit Commission, *Making a Reality of Community Care* (HMSO, 1986), National Audit Office, *Community Care Developments* (HMSO, 1987), Sir Roy Griffiths, *Community Care: Agenda for Action* (HMSO, 1988).

of Social Services. In this situation of uncertainty, shortages of resources exert a number of pressures on the manner in which care is provided to elderly patients. First, there is a powerful disincentive for hospitals to provide continuing care for long periods since each bed is capable of generating additional revenue from other NHS contracts. Secondly, there is a strong incentive for private nursing homes to attract fee-paying patients into their care, but there is a weak incentive for them to supply the specialist orthopaedic care (available under the NHS) which might enable elderly people to regain their independence, both because it is expensive to provide and because it could result in a fall in revenue. Lastly, financial pressure creates a weak incentive on social services departments to co-operate with the NHS by undertaking responsibility for more patients and committing themselves to additional expenditure. What happens, then, to hospital patients in need of long-term, continuing care? Evidence from the Association of Community Health Councils suggests that the supply of continuing NHS care for elderly people is falling well short of the demand and is often of poor quality. In addition: 'Pressure is too often placed on elderly patients and their relatives to move out of hospital into private nursing homes with little or no consultation, choice, or information. Once they are receiving private nursing care, many residents experience financial difficulties and consequent distress.'[27]

Precisely this issue was considered by the Health Service Ombudsman in the case of a man who in 1989 suffered a stroke and serious damage to his brain. In 1991, when he was 55, the hospital in which he had been receiving treatment told his wife that his condition had stabilized, that nothing more could be done for him, and that the bed was needed for other patients. Nevertheless, he still needed a medical bed in a nursing home because he continued to need nursing care. He was discharged into a private nursing home which was able to provide the care needed at a net cost (deducting social security benefits) of £6,000 per year. His wife complained to the Ombudsman on the ground that since he needed such intensive nursing care, he met the criteria justifying

[27] Association of Community Health Councils of England and Wales, *NHS Continuing Care of Elderly People* (ACHCEW, 1990), quoted in M. Henwood, *supra* note 25.

care either in an NHS hospital or in a nursing home paid for the health authority.[28]

The health authority replied to the complaint by saying that it could not meet every need. Its policy was for shorter in-patient stays with continuing care to be provided in the community. For this reason, the authority provided no long-stay beds in hospital, nor did it have contractual arrangements under which such care could be provided by a nursing home. It said that if it were obliged to provide such care it would soon be financially overstretched. In any case, the chief executive of the NHS Management Executive had said that the duty to provide care on clinical grounds was always subject to the duty to remain within available resources and, accordingly, to distinguish between patients. This is what the Ombudsman said of the case.

The patient was a highly dependent patient in hospital . . . ; and yet, when he no longer needed care in an acute ward but manifestly still needed what the National Health Service is there to provide, they regarded themselves as having no scope for continuing to discharge their responsibilities to him because their policy was to make no provision for continuing care. . . . In my opinion the failure to make available long-term care within the NHS for this patient was unreasonable and constitutes a failure in the service provided by the Health Authority.[29]

Thus, the complaint was upheld and the health authority agreed to make a payment to the complainant to cover her out-of-pocket expenses incurred by way of fees for the private nursing home and to pay for the future cost of her husband's care. The case illustrates the pressures being imposed on the NHS by those needing long-term, continuing care and the difficulty of drawing a clear line between medical and community care. The Ombudsman recommended a review of the policy which attempted to exclude patients in this condition from NHS care, the implications of which are considered in Chapter 4.

---

[28] *Health Service Commissioner, Second Report for Session 1993-94. Failure to provide long term NHS care for a brain-damaged patient* (HC 197, 1994). The Ombudsman's powers are considered at p. 247 *infra.*

[29] Ibid, para. 22. Subsequently, the Chief Executive of the NHS, Mr Alan Langlands, told the House of Commons Health Committee: 'if a similar case were to crop up . . . tomorrow then the expectation would be that there should be a continuing commitment from the NHS. So, in other words, we accept that the Ombudsman was right in his judgment.' (*Priority Setting in the NHS: Purchasing* HC 134–II, Session 1994–95 161.)

D. The Cost of Medical Negligence

As resources in the system become more strained, the risk of things going wrong increases. Claims for medical negligence in 1989 were estimated to cost the NHS £40 million.[30] For 1991–2 the figure was put at £58 million.[31] In 1994, it was £75 million, and in 1995, £125 million.[32] It is likely that both the numbers and the value of claims will increase.[33] Costs of this magnitude clearly restrict the provision of services to patients. There is little evidence about the claims because information based on common statistics has not been collected and no records of claims exist which enable useful comparisons, either over time or between districts. Consequently, the evidence tends to be anecdotal. One survey of claims found that of the twenty-eight areas of medical specialty, four were responsible for over 60 per cent of the total claims notified; they were general surgery, orthopaedics, accident and emergency, and obstetrics and gynaecology.[34] The latter area is particularly vulnerable to high-value claims. Clearly, such major financial obligations are a significant factor in health service expenditure.

Successful compensation claims must be met by the hospital responsible for the negligence and the costs will inevitably result in increased prices to future purchasers of care. The burden has to be borne by the relevant clinical unit, or units, alone rather than by the whole service, in order to encourage high-risk units to introduce effective systems of risk management[35] and reduce their exposure to negligence claims. Once an award has been made,

---

[30] See *Just Finance in Medical Negligence Claims* (National Association of Health Authorities and Trusts, 1992) 2.

[31] Tom Sackville, Under-Secretary of State for Health, *Hansard*, 18 May 1993, vol. 225, col. 149 (WA).

[32] *Clinical Negligence: Proposed Creation of a Central Fund in England* (NHSME Consultation Document, 1994), para. 4 and parliamentary answer by the Minister of State for Health, Mr. Gerald Malone: *Hansard*, 6 Mar. 1995, vol. 256, cols. 41–2 (WA).

[33] Unofficially, the Department of Health considers that over the past eight years the total cost of claims against it has quadrupled.

[34] *First and Second Wave Trust Clinical Negligence Claim Liabilities: A Report for the NHS Trust Federation* (Health Care and Risk Management and the Medical Defence Union, 1993), app. 6. The statistic concerned claims reported against first wave fund-holders.

[35] See *NHS Trust Finance Manual*, pt. 3, section 7, 'Risk management, the role of insurance and clinical negligence' (FDL(93)84; NHSME, 1993).

damages must be paid immediately and it is often impossible for hospitals to meet the costs incurred by substantial claims against them. Thus, arrangements have been introduced in which the first tranche of a claim, or claims, must be met by the responsible hospital, after which a loan will be made available from the Department of Health to cover the outstanding portion. The loan must be repaid, with interest, according to the following scale:

Award	*Repayment period*
£100,000 or less	1 year
£100,001–£300,000	1–3 years
£300,001–£500,000	3–5 years
£500,001–£700,000	5–7 years
£700,001–£900,000	9–7 years
£900,000 or more	10 years.

These arrangements assume that hospitals are able to assess their exposure to risk and to make a general prediction as to what loans will be required to meet claims in any year. The evidence so far, however, suggests that prediction will be very difficult. From year to year the numbers of claims rises, but the rate of increase is not consistent. More importantly, there is a wide variation in the financial severity of the claims from year to year, both within and between hospitals.[36] This poses a problem of stability in the system, because individual hospitals will find that the payment of damages imposes such a severe strain on resources that services to patients are prejudiced, particularly when the unit is involved in several cases. That instability will make it increasingly difficult for health authorities to plan for the future. Prices will be difficult to forecast and entire units may cease to be viable. 'Healthcare commissioners express the concern that their role in assessing health needs, and commissioning care to provide for those needs, will be dramatically skewed by the unknown and potentially massive costs that providers might have to meet to cover medical negligence payments.'[37]

A number of proposals have been made to manage these difficulties. The first is the use of the structured settlement, in

---

[36] See *First and Second Wave Trust Clinical Negligence Claim Liabilities*, *supra* note 34.
[37] *Just Finance in Medical Negligence Cases*, *supra* note 30, 4.

which annual payments, rather than a capital sum, are made to the plaintiff during the remainder of his or her life. The settlement may be financed either from within the hospital's own revenue or by the purchase of an annuity on the life of the plaintiff to ensure a steady income.[38] The first such settlement reported was arranged in 1991, for the benefit of a plaintiff who suffered brain damage and paralysis following the use of forceps at her birth in 1984. A lump sum of £557,000 was paid as a contingency fund from which the following payments were made: £59,000 became payable immediately with an equal sum to be paid annually for the duration of the plaintiff's life (which was uncertain, but expected to be into her thirties); an annual pension of £15,351 became payable after five years; an additional annual pension of £32,578 became payable after ten; and five yearly lump sums of £50,000 will be paid, indexed to the retail price index, for the purpose of replacing equipment.[39] Such an arrangement has a number of advantages for both plaintiff and defendant. Management of one enormous lump sum obviously presents difficulties for the plaintiff which structured settlements avoid without any financial penalty. Equally, the ability of the defendant to distribute payment over a number of years enables the impact of a large award to be absorbed more easily.

The second measure has been to introduce a scheme under section 21 of the National Health Service and Community Care Act 1990, by which the Secretary of State with the consent of Treasury, may 'establish a scheme whereby [health authorities and NHS Trusts] may make provision to meet . . . liabilities to third parties for loss, damage or injury arising out of the carrying out of the functions of the bodies concerned.'

Under section 21 a special health authority, supervised by the Medical Protection Society, has been created to operate the

---

[38] See *Structured Settlements in Clinical Negligence Claims* (FDL(92)28, NHSME), para. 6: 'The self-financed option will usually be the best value for money for the public sector and the NHS as a whole as it avoids paying the profit element to a life office, and perhaps commission for intermediaries. It involves the NHS taking its own risks in terms of life expectancy of Plaintiffs but taken across the NHS risks should even out.'

[39] See R. Lewis, 'Health Authorities and the Payment of Damages by Means of a Pension', 56 *Modern Law Review* 844 (1993). The total cost to the defendants was estimated at £1.6 m., which was about £100,000 less than a comparable lump sum award of damages.

scheme as an internal insurance policy.[40] One of its purposes will
be to provide an incentive to those hospitals which reduce risk and
the incidence of claims against them by offering them discounted
premiums. Some types of NHS business, such as acute care, carry
higher risks than others and will accordingly attract higher
premiums. The scheme serves a number of functions. It will
smooth the burden imposed by large claims against NHS Trusts,
encourage good risk management, and create a national database
from which hospitals may learn how to minimize risk. The scheme
comes into operation in 1995 and will seek to set premiums
sufficient only for the current level of claims. Reserves will not be
built up for the future. This means that premiums will be relatively
low in the early years of the scheme and build up to a steady level
over a period of eight or ten years. Insurance in the scheme works
on the principle that responsibility for the costs incurred by claims
is divided three ways. The NHS Trust concerned will carry an
excess and bear responsibility for the first tranche of any claim
unassisted. The second tranche of the claim will be shared between
the NHS Trust (20 per cent) and the Special Health Authority (80
per cent). For the last tranche, involving the largest claims, the
SHA will bear 100 per cent of the burden.

The scheme is entirely voluntary and its success will depend on
whether Trusts believe that their own exposure to risk warrants
the payment of annual premiums into the scheme.

E. Priorities in Health Care

Inevitably, as demand for resources increasingly exceeds supply,
the need to identify health care priorities becomes more urgent. In
1979 the Royal Commission on the National Health Service said
that: 'the demand for health care is always likely to outstrip supply
and . . . the capacity of health services to absorb resources is
almost unlimited. Choices have therefore to be made about the
use of available funds and priorities have to be set. The more
pressure there is on resources, the more important it is to get the
priorities clear.'[41]

---

[40] The scheme is explained in *Clinical Negligence Scheme for Trusts*, published
jointly by NHS Executive, Touche Ross, Medical Protection Society, and Willis
Corroon, 1995.
[41] *Royal Commission on the National Health Service*, *supra* note 9, para. 6.1.

Who should have priority? There is no agreed measure by which priorities can be assessed. The simple view is that those in most need should receive priority in the allocation of scarce resources, but there is no generally agreed criterion on which the notion of 'need' can be assessed. Central government is inclined to promote a policy of 'preventive' medicine as a means of tackling the incidence of ill-health and keeping people out of hospital.[42] However, a district health authority responsible for large numbers of elderly patients might wish to concentrate its resources on the treatment of arthritis, or providing hip replacements. By contrast, parents whose baby needs an urgent operation to repair a hole in the heart will say that there can be no greater need than to save a child's life. On what basis should 'need' be assessed? We are as yet very far from being able to provide any consistent principles on which the question can be answered. Discussions within the Department of Health prompted the observation that: 'Despite the frequent use of the term "needs" there is little agreement even on what is meant by the term. Furthermore, there is very little work which explicitly assesses population needs in a way that is useful to health service managers, purchasers and planners.'[43]

Nor have we developed a reliable system for measuring the effectiveness of treatment once need has been established. Both need and effectiveness are extremely difficult to assess against an objective yardstick because they are so influenced by our perceptions of illness and health which vary not only from person to person but also in the same person, from time to time.[44] The question is particularly pertinent to the assessment of highly sophisticated and hugely expensive medical equipment, capable of achieving the most dramatic results for a relatively small number of patients. When there is a choice between achieving huge improvements in the conditions of those in very poor health (say cancer or transplant patients), or more modest preventive measures

---

[42] See *The Health of the Nation* (Department of Health, 1992). A similar, if less specific, recommendation was made by the *Royal Commission on the Health Service* in 1979, ch, 5. The same view has been adopted by the Labour Party, see *Health 200* (The Labour Party, 1994), ch. 4.

[43] *Assessing Health Care Needs—A DHA project discussion paper* (NHSME, 1991) 3. See also A. Stevens and J. Gabbay, 'Needs Assessment needs assessment', 23 *Health Trends* 20 (1991).

[44] See C. Orchard, 'Comparing Health Care Outcomes', 308 *British Medical Journal* 1493 (1994).

designed to encourage the preservation of good health amongst larger numbers of people, how ought choices to be made? The question is complicated by the need for hospitals, particularly specialist hospitals, to be conscious of their public image in order to attract doctors and patients; facilities which enhance the international reputation of a unit may attract patients, and therefore revenue. American commentators have said: 'we are doing more and more for fewer and fewer people, at higher and higher cost, for less and less benefit . . . it is a fact that we have yet to develop an effective method to assess technology and have no methods for determining whether or not new or existing technologies are useful and appropriate for inclusion in any reasonable health insurance scheme.'[45]

Internationally, there is pressure to encourage both doctors and health service managers to reconsider the ways in which money is spent. A specialist committee in The Netherlands has made two radical recommendations. It says, first, that some forms of treatment ought expressly to be excluded from the public health service (for example dental care for adults). Secondly, and even more controversially, it proposes 'restrictions on the freedom of the doctor to assist the individual patient as he/she sees fit.'[46] Clearly, this approach to the problem would involve a major shift of power from doctors to politicians and health service managers. Who would decide what treatments should be excluded? The Dutch report considered that health policy and priorities require hard choices to be made between competing demands but that the matter should be considered as follows: (i) at the 'macro' or aggregate level, between government departments (e.g. education, social services, and health); (ii) at the 'meso' or intermediate level, between the numerous groups which compete for resources within the health service, and (iii) at the 'micro' or individual level, between patients. It attempted to identify a hierarchy amongst

---

[45] G. Annas, S. Law, R. Rosenblatt, and K. Wing, *American Health Law*, (Little Brown & Co., 1990) 293. Similar concern has been expressed by the Department of Health. See *Assessing the Effects of Health Service Technologies* (Department of Health, 1992).

[46] See *Choices in Health Care* (Ministry of Welfare, Health and Cultural Affairs, The Netherlands, 1992) 22. Note also that the Department of Health in the UK looks forward to an 'era of knowledged-based care [in which] diversity of approach in routine practice will be increasingly difficult to defend unless supported by a sustainable and convincing rationale.' *Research for Health* (Department of Health, 1993) 1.

these approaches as follows: 'The community approach rules
decision-making at the macro level; the professional approach
rules—within the limits of the community approach—at the meso
level; and the individual approach—within the limits of the
professional approach—at the micro level.'[47]

By contrast, the UK government has consistently avoided the
use of the word 'rationing'. It prefers the phrase 'priority setting'.
In some areas of health care, however, the government has
already restricted the service. Doctors are no longer at liberty to
prescribe the medicines of their choice but must choose from a
limited list.[48] Optical examinations are no longer universally
provided under the NHS. Dental care too, though provided under
the aegis of the NHS, is largely financed directly by patients.[49]
Thus, financial decisions which restrict access to care are not new
to the health service, indeed they have become commonplace, but
when patients have been refused treatment, there has often been
very little candour about the real reasons for failing to offer
treatment. The matter was commented upon in 1989 by the Social
Services Committee of the House of Commons. It said:

At any one time, wards can be closed ostensibly because they need
refurbishing, or through inability to recruit staff, neither of which would
necessarily be true. Theatres can be closed on rotation, asbestos can be
discovered in essential parts of the hospital etc. . . . Doctors too have
participated in this implicit rationing of health care, by accepting that they
can only afford to provide a certain level of care and have rationed by
choosing the more appropriate patients and either putting the others on to
waiting lists or not informing them that such treatments are available.
Two obvious examples are renal replacement and angioplasty.[50]

---

[47] *Choices in Health Care*, ibid., 55.

[48] The list is contained in the NHS (General Medical Services) Regs. 1992, SI
1992, No. 635, sched. 10.

[49] 'In terms of all charges collected by the NHS, the general dental services input
rose from 30 per cent of the total to 51 per cent during [1980–1990].' *Compendium
of Health Service Statistics*, *supra*, note 4, section entitled 'Cost of the NHS'.
Increasingly, dentists appear to be withdrawing their services from the NHS
altogether. See *A Survey of BDA members in general practice* (British Dental
Association, 1993).

[50] *Resourcing the National Health Service: the Government's Plans for the Future
of the National Health Service* (Social Services Committee, 8th Report, HC 214–III,
1989), para. 2.65. See also A. Wing, 'Why don't the British treat more patients with
kidney failure', 287 *British Medical Journal* 1157 (1983); and R. Brook, R. Park *et
al.*, 'Diagnosis and Treatment of Coronary Disease: Comparison of Doctors'
Attitudes in the USA and the UK' [1988] *The Lancet* 750.

This method of resource allocation, however, tends to reduce the process of planning to chance and to crisis management, and makes the formation of strategy in the health service very difficult. Inevitably, unless we are prepared to invest in our system of health sums of money which successive governments have found unsustainable,[51] we must accept that 'judgments often have to be made about accepting a level of health care which is far from ideal.'[52] In that case the process must be managed and planned sensibly and fairly, and it must be more amenable to public scrutiny.

II. ECONOMIC LOGIC IN HEALTH CARE

Health economists have begun to make a significant contribution to the way in which we consider these matters. Economics has been described as: 'the study of how men and society end up choosing, with or without the use of money, to employ scarce productive resources that could have alternative uses, to produce various commodities and distribute them for consumption among various people and groups in society. It analyses the costs and benefits of improving patterns of production.'[53]

The question is entirely pertinent to the health service. Health economists start with the proposition that health service resources are scarce and that hard decisions between patients are unavoidable. Given the scarcity of those resources, economists ask, for example, should priority be given to the elderly, rather than the mentally ill and what criteria should be used in deciding? Should more surgical patients be treated as day patients? Should a new hospital be built? Is prevention 'better' than cure, always or just sometimes?[54] Economics encourages us to consider an uncomfortable truth.

---

[51] See the comments of the Secretary of State for Health in response to the Black Report on *Inequalities in Health*, published in M. Whitehead, *The Health Divide* (Pelican, 1988) 305.

[52] *Royal Commission on the National Health Service*, *supra* note 9, para. 2.2.

[53] P.A. Samuelson, *Economics* (McGraw-Hill, 1976) 5, quoted in G. Mooney, *Economics, Medicine and Health Care* (2nd edn., Harvester Wheatsheaf, 1992) 5.

[54] These questions are posed by G. Mooney, ibid. 6. See also A. Culyer, *Need and the National Health Service* (Martin Robertson, London, 1976).

It is all too easy in considering 'need' to assume that if a treatable condition exists, therefore (1) it should be treated and (2) it should be treated in the 'best' possible way. . . . If this were accepted, this would mean that all need should be treated and only the most effective treatments should be used. Both of these ignore the facts that resources are scarce and an overall better use of resources may be obtained from employing less effective but cheaper policies.[55]

A. Allocating Scarce Resources

Economics analyses the cost–benefit implications of our decisions about treatment. Common sense says we should not always try to preserve all lives for as long as possible. In some cases it would simply be cruel to do so.[56] What is misleadingly called 'heroic' treatment is often frowned upon for this reason. It may extend the quantity of a patient's life but, in doing so, leave him or her with such an impoverished quality of life that we would not wish upon ourselves. It is also criticized simply as a waste of money. It may deny treatment to others who could benefit from it. But the question is also asked of those for whom treatment could be effective. What about cases in which the patient could indeed benefit from treatment, but the expense involved in provding it would be so great as to deprive other patients from care? One screening test for cancer of the bowel is reported to have cost $47 million per case detected![57] Despite the small number for whom the test would have been beneficial, many would agree that such a procedure should not be routine. Precisely the same question has been put by a senior administrator of a London hospital, who considered a case concerning

a lady who had a bowel disorder requiring total parenteral nutrition at a cost of £25,000 per annum. She was not from my district so we were cross-charging another district for it, otherwise we would not have allowed her

---

[55] G. Mooney, *Economics, Medicine and Health Care*, *supra* note 53, 70.

[56] A number of cases have offered doctors the opportunity of withdrawing treatment on grounds of compassion. The subject is dealt with in more detail in Chapter 8.

[57] D. Neuhauser and A. Lweicki, 'What do we gain from the sixth stool guaiac?', 293 *New England Journal of Medicine* 226 (1975). The example is cited by R. Gillon, 'Ethics, Economics and General Practice', in G. Mooney and A. McGuire (eds.), *Medical Ethics and Economics in Health Care* (Oxford University Press, 1988) 127.

to start treatment. She was in her early thirties, decided she wished to get pregnant so was sent to our IVF unit which made her pregnant with twins. She was admitted for the whole of her pregnancy to ensure the foetus had optimal growth, went into labour and her twins each spent six months in the neonatal intensive care unit before discharge. One died shortly after. We costed the complete episode and it totalled almost £300,000. That meant, in effect, that one of the wards we had closed last year, which would have treated a thousand patients, could have remained open if that had not taken place. I . . . am certain that many cases like this arise with the various new technologies available.[58]

One cannot know to what extent decisions of this nature are typical. But it demonstrates the inevitable fact that decisions to treat one patient, or one category of patients, may mean that others are denied care. The cause for concern is that some of the routine decisions which dramatically affect access to health care are made at random. The arguments at the extremes are easy. But they suggest that, although an individual patient may derive benefit from treatment, overall resources may still be wasted if that treatment is focused on too few people, or applied to procedures producing little clinical benefit. This is wasteful in the sense that others, with more to gain, may be denied access to care. Thus one needs to state a principle by which different forms of treatment and types of patient may be distinguished. Health economists have assisted this process by applying the notion of 'opportunity cost' to health service spending, that is, the loss of benefits which results from using finite resources for one purpose rather than another.

As resources are limited, not all that is desirable can be done. If resources are used in one way (for example, providing more physiotherapy for handicapped people) they cannot be used in other ways (such as screening for Down's syndrome or providing more hip replacements). Thus, in this example, providing benefit for handicapped people means giving up the chance to give benefits to pregnant women or elderly people. Whatever the best alternative use is judged to be, it is the benefits given up in that use that represent the 'opportunity cost'.[59]

---

[58] K. Grant, 'The balance of care provision in the National Health Service', in H. L'Etang (ed.), *Health Care Provision Under Financial Constraint: A Decade of Change* (Royal Society of Medicine, 1990) 138.

[59] G. Mooney, K. Gerard and C. Donaldson, *Priority Setting in Purchasing— Some Practical Guidelines* (National Association of Health Authorities and Trusts, 1992) 7.

In other words, in allocating priorities amongst patients, who do we decide not to treat? When should our natural compassion give way to the cold logic of economic analysis?

B. Economics and the QALY Principle

Many would agree that if resources are being used without accounting for opportunity costs, then an element of planning is missing; and if it is unplanned then it is arbitrary and devoid of social policy. This is where health economists have made an important contribution to the debate. Prominent amongst a number of economic approaches to the determination of priorities is that of the 'quality adjusted life year' (QALY).[60] This approach attempts to evaluate healthcare outcomes according to a generic scale. It asks (i) to what extent, and for how long, will a treatment improve the quality of a patient's life and (ii) how much does the treatment cost. In this way it seeks to compare the costs of generating QALYs, regardless of the particular treatment in question. In this theory, there is a sliding scale on which each year of full health counts as one, and each year of declining health counts as less than one; death scores 0. Thus, if the improvement in health after treatment is both significant and long-lasting, the patient accumulates units and scores high on the quality of life measure. If the treatment is relatively inexpensive, then the cost per unit of quality is low. The theory favours treatments which achieve the greatest increase in the quality of life, over the longest period, for the least cost. Conversely, if the cost of medical intervention is high, and the relative improvement in the condition of the patient is small, or capable of being enjoyed over a short period of time only, then the cost per QALY will be relatively high. On this basis, the adoption of health policies which produce the largest number of QALYs will be those which spend money most efficiently. A comparison of a number of treatments reveals the following results.[61]

---

[60] See e.g. A. Williams, 'The Economics of Coronary Artery Bypass Grafting', 291 *British Medical Journal* 326 (1985); A. Maynard, 'Logic in Medicine', 295 *British Medical Journal* 1537 (1987). Other measures have also been developed. See e.g. L. Fallowfield, *The Quality of Life: The Missing Measurement in Health Care* (Souvenir Press, London, 1990) and R. Rosser, M. Cottee et al., *Measures of the Quality of Life* (Royal College of Physicians, 1992).

[61] C. Gudex, *QALYs and their use by the Health Service* (Centre for Health Economics, University of York, 1986) 14.

Table 1 Cost/QALY Data for Each Procedure

	QALYs gained per patient (discounted at 5%)	Annual cost per patient	Total cost (discounted at 5%)	Cost per QALY
Continuous ambulatory peritoneal dialysis (4 years)	3.4	£12,866	£45,676	£13434**
Haemodialysis (8 years)	6.1	£8,569	£55,354	£9075**
Treatment of cystic fibrosis with ceftazidime (over 22 years)	0.4	£250	£3.290	£8225**
Kidney transplant (10 years)	7.4	£10.452	£10,452	£1413*
Shoulder joint replacement (10 years)	0.9	£533	£533	£592*
Scoliosis surgery				
– idiopathic adolescent	1.2	£3,143	£3,143	£2619*
– neuromuscular illness	16.2	£3,143	£3.143	£194*

* Represents one-off costs per case, and benefits discounted over life of case
** Represents recurring annual costs and annual QALYs per case

Consider also the following example.[62] Medical technology has made significant advances in neonatal intensive care. It has led to vast improvements in the treatment of premature babies by use of total intravenous feeding and transcutaneous monitoring of blood gasses. The number of babies born weighing less than 750 grams who survive has increased from none until 1983, to between 30 per cent and 67 per cent in 1991. These successes have brought their ethical dilemmas. A percentage of low birth-weight babies will die irrespective of any efforts to save them. Some will live but with varying degrees of disability. Others will thrive and develop into perfectly healthy children. It is difficult to distinguish one group from another. Should we always do everything for every premature infant, in the hope that he or she will thrive? Or should we decide to withdraw treatment in some cases? And if treatment may be withdrawn, on what basis?

This is the economists' point; 'the average total cost of a

Table 2 Neonatal, postnatal, and life-time costs of care for
109 VLBW* infants—1984 pay and prices.
(Discounted at 5 per cent)

Birthweight (g)	Total cost (£)	Average cost of a survivor (£)	Average cost of a QALY (£)
500–599	1,188	–	–
600–699	33,000	16,500	16,500
700–799	146,012	146,012	584,048
800–899	140,267	23,278	24,394
900–999	114,187	38,062	50,750
1000–1099	235,836	21,440	23,584
1100–1199	210.472	21,047	22,155
1200–1299	276,746	27,675	33,545
1300–1399	275,011	15,278	16,667
1400–1499	61,890	7,736	7,736

* Very low birth weight.

[62] J. Griffin, *Born Too Soon* (Office of Health Economics, 1993).

survivor ranged from between £146,012 for an infant weighing 700–799 grams, and £7,736 for an infant weighing 1,400–1,499 grams (1984 pay and prices).'[63] Also, '. . . the cost to the NIIS of neonatal intensive care for infants whose birthweight was less than 1,500 grams, put into 1990 prices, would be between £42 and £70 million per annum.'[64] Measured in terms of QALYs, the result is reflected in Table 2:[65]

Thus, although babies weighing 700–799 are not the most expensive group to treat in total, their cost per QALY is highest because, despite intensive care, their life expectancy is relatively short. This analysis prompts the question of whether this money could more advantageously be directed to other patients.

C. QALY Folly?

For the moment, the scheme has had little practical impact.[66] Although health service managers are said to be interested in applying the idea,[67]

Health authorities appear to accept that there is as yet no readily applicable and agreed scientific method ör choosing between priorities: there is no use, consequently, of QALYs or of cost-effectiveness techniques which relate expenditure to outcomes. . . . 'Health gains' therefore remains a somewhat vague and elusive concept. . . .

In practice, many [health authority] purchasers appear to solve their dilemma by not choosing. A detailed analysis of the priorities in individual [health authority] plans suggests a widespread strategy of 'spreading the money around'. . . . In short, the aim appears to be to keep as many people as possible happy by giving them at least some funds, even if only token amounts are involved.[68]

---

[63] Ibid. 45　　　　　　　[64] Ibid.　　　　　　　[65] Ibid. 52.

[66] But see e.g. A. Culyer, R. Lavers and A. Williams, 'Social Indications of Health', *Social Trends: No. 2* (HMSO, 1971); '. . . the Minister should attach explicit *valuations* to a variety of levels of the state indicator: increments in these could then be compared with the incremental social cost of attaining any given level.' Cited in G. Mooney, *Economics, Medicine and Health Care*, *supra* note 53, 71.

[67] See M. Dean, 'Is your treatment economic, effective, efficient?' 302 *British Medical Journal* 1253 (1991).

[68] R. Klein and S. Redmayne, *Patterns of Priorities—A Study of the Purchasing and Rationing Policies of Health Authorities* (National Association of Health Authorities and Trusts, 1992) 19.

Proponents of QALYs are not alone in attempting to evaluate health outcomes on the basis of economics. There are reasons, however, for doubting whether any outcome measure of this kind will be able to do more than provide general support for decisions which have already been made on other grounds. How, in practical terms, can one measure in numbers the degree of improvement in a patient's health after treatment? Is this a matter which can be objectively analysed? The question could be decided by democratic opinion, but illness manifests itself with infinite degrees of severity and, in the same patient, in infinite combinations of diseases. How could the scale be sufficiently sensitive to distinguish, for example, between intensive care units for premature babies, hip replacements for those over fifty-five, and a patient with haemophilia complicated by liver disease and blindness? And how could it accommodate the subtle shifts over time in social attitudes to the concepts of 'health' and 'illness'?[69] Consider a patient who is confined to a wheelchair and who now needs treatment in hospital for an unrelated condition. Compared to a patient without disability, should he be put at a disadvantage by the QALY system which attaches value to the degree of improvement after treatment? If the disabled patient could never expect the same mobility as the able-bodied one, and would score lower on the QALY scale, does the system not discriminate against those with pre-existing diseases or disabilities? Many strong and healthy people dependent on wheelchairs would say that such a system was unfair and that they derive just as much benefit from treatment as the able-bodied.[70] Indeed, they might say that such a judgment could only be made by those in a similar position, not by able-bodied administrators with no understanding of life in a wheelchair.

Much the same argument applies to elderly patients. Naturally, their expectation of life after treatment is shorter than that of younger patients. Should they, as a category, be disfavoured on the 'outcome' scale, on the basis that they have fewer years ahead of them in which QALYs (or comparable units of measurement)

---

[69] See R. Carr-Hill, 'Assumptions of the QALY Procedure', 29 *Social Science and Medicine* 469 (1989).

[70] This point was made most persuasively by a wheelchair-dependent postgraduate student of mine.

could accumulate?[71] There is evidence that clinical decisions are often influenced by the patient's age rather than his or her clinical prognosis, and that strong and vigorous elderly patients may be disfavoured, even by comparison with less healthy younger patients whose outlook is less good.[72] This may be both unwise and extremely expensive. Many elderly patients will derive terrific benefit from medical treatment and lead full and independent lives thereafter. Thus, a fit elderly person with a life expectancy of ten years might score (say) $10 \times 0.8 = 8$ QALYs. Compare this to a younger person with a serious illness and a life expectancy of thirty years, for whom medical intervention will have limited value. Such a patient might score $30 \times 0.5 = 15$ QALYs. Too narrow an application of a theory which automatically favoured the maximization of QALYs would increase the level of disability in society and inflate the costs of health care. Even if a convincing case could be made for using numbers to measure quality, the logic of the system is questionable. Particularly in relation to elderly patients, a more sensitive measure of the benefits of care must be found.

Quite apart from practical concerns, to what extent is the theory itself ethically acceptable?[73] In one sense, it is entirely egalitarian as between patients; it favours none since it seeks only to maximize the number of QALYs and makes no attempt to say which categories of patient, or types of illness, ought to be given priority. As between a large number of patients with minor ailments and a smaller number with more serious complaints, it does not judge which should be given treatment, as long as the total number of outcome units produced from each group is the same. It also reflects the fact that decisions of one sort or another are already being made and that it is unethical to waste money and so deprive deserving patients from access to care. When doctors have insufficient resources with which to treat all their patients,

---

[71] J. Avron, 'Benefit and Cost Analysis in Geriatric Care: Turning Age Discrimination into Health Policy' (1984) 310 *New England Journal of Medicine* 1294. Forthright support for such 'ageist' discrimination is provided by D. Callahan, *What Kind of Life: the Limits of Medical Progress* (Simon and Schuster, New York, 1990).

[72] See I. Fentiman, U. Tirelli, S. Monfandi *et al.*, 'Cancer in the Elderly: Why so Badly Treated?', 335 *The Lancet* 1020 (1990) and the discussion in *The Health of the U.K.'s Elderly People, supra* note 21.

[73] See A. Williams, 'Cost-effectiveness analysis: is it ethical?', 18 *Journal of Medical Ethics* 18 (1992).

compromise is inevitable. To this extent, the QALY approach has the support of a reputable international body. When a decision to treat one patient may deny treatment to others with similar need, consideration of opportunity costs is an appropriate ethical concern.[74]

No one will argue that considerations of cost and efficiency are irrelevant. If they become the dominant or only concern, however, can they be described as ethical? The momentum in the theory would erode the traditional view of the relationship between doctor and patient. The idea of the doctor promoting the best interests of the patient would have to be replaced by the view that the interests of the individual ought generally to be secondary to those of the group.[75] The notion of clinical freedom would be eroded so that doctors would have no primary duty to individual patients. Rather, the duty would be to achieve efficiency and the greatest good for the greatest number. The matter is starkly put as follows:

medical ethics, particularly in the form of clinical freedom, tends to breed inefficiency. Indeed, it seems that it sometimes provides a convenient escape mechanism for the romantic member of the medical profession neither to pursue efficiency nor to attempt any rationalisation at all of the potential for pursuing efficiency in health care.[76]

Those [doctors] who advise on equity and efficiency ought to do so from a standpoint which is much wider than either the individual patient or indeed the individual practitioner and his patients. There has to be a strong case for those who proffer such advice being separated from the demands and prejudices of patient care.

Hence emerges the role of the community physician. . . . It can be argued that [issues of equity and efficiency] are not the province of the medical profession, outside community medicine, *except* as doers of

---

[74] 'Decisions to forego life-sustaining treatment under conditions of scarcity', from *The Appleton International Conference—Developing Guidelines for Decisions to Forego Life-Prolonging Medical Treatment*, reproduced in 18 *Journal of Medical Ethics* 16 (1992).

[75] G. Mooney, *Economics, Medicine and Health Care*, *supra* note 53, 87.

[76] Ibid. 84. See also A. Williams, 'Ethics, Clinical Freedom and the Doctors' Role', in A. Culyer, A. Maynard and J. Posnett (eds.), *Competition in Health Care—Reforming the NHS* (Macmillan Press, 1990) 188: '. . . refusing to accept responsibility for the efficient use of the resources which are committed by your own clinical decisions is tantamount to rejecting the principle "do no harm", since using resources wastefully harms the patients who might have benefitted from them.'

society's will. In terms of equity and efficiency, clinicians need to be advised not the advisers.[77]

The weakness of this view as an ethical theory lies in its diluted concern for the individual. No one could know of their rights to care until a calculation had been undertaken on the scale. Some for whom we might have great sympathy and compassion could score rather badly on such a calculation. For example, pure economic logic does not see a return in treating pain, say in a patient suffering cancer, particularly if there is little chance of that patient being cured.[78] Where does a consideration of the individual needs of such a patient fit into the priorities identified by QALYs?

More broadly, outcome measurements equate the idea of health 'need' with the ability to benefit from treatment,[79] or health 'gain'. But it is equally plausible to consider 'need' more broadly. One might ask instead: where is suffering most severe, or which illnesses are the major causes of death and disease? Take the example of a young child with cerebral palsy. Inevitably, that child requires more expensive treatment than others of the same age, and both the quality and quantity of his life may be more limited. Measured by means of a QALY, the returns on the money invested in that child may be smaller than those achieved by equivalent sums spent on other groups of children in need of care. Many, however, would say that to deny the care which enables that child to realize his potential would be wrong. No doubt, the allocation of priorities on this basis would not produce the most QALYs and, to that extent, would not be the most efficient, but it might correspond more closely to the sorts of values and goals with which most people would identify.[80] Indeed, some would say that our health service as a whole would be impoverished for

---

[77] G. Mooney, *Economics, Medicine and Health Care, supra* note 53, 118. At 150 he says: 'Given their involvement with individual patients, members of the caring professions might have to be excluded from acting as society's agents in these matters.' One doubts, however, whether there is such a thing as 'society's will', particularly with respect to the new and relatively unexplored field of health service priorities.

[78] See F. Stoll, 'Choosing Between Cancer patients', 6 *Journal of Medical Ethics* 71 (1990).

[79] G. Mooney, K. Gerard and C. Donaldson, *Priority Setting in Purchasing—Some Practical Guidelines* (National Association of Health Authorities and Trusts, 1992) 10.

[80] One survey suggests that people do not sympathize with the logic of the QALY. Rather they adopt a view which favours treatment for the 'needy', and give

attempting such a judgment. 'Quality of life decisions made on behalf of those who are sick or disabled have no place in rigorous ethical thought . . . any grading of human beings according to value or worth is both repugnant and highly dangerous, since once one human life is judged worthless or expendable, all are inevitably reduced from an infinite to a relative value.'[81]

Economists, of course, will say that judgments of this nature are made every day; that the decision is inescapable and that the only difference is that QALYs, or other tests, attempt to perform the task on a rational and open basis. It may be, however, that the cold logic of efficiency is not the only criterion on which decisions should be made. The concept of the outcome measurement has most value when it forms one of the many clinical, moral, and compassionate considerations which motivate medical care. It informs, but does not decide, how money ought to be spent. As one economist has put it: 'Cost and QALY values should be viewed as a way of asking questions about the resource consequences of interventions and their contribution to length and quality of life, not as the sole basis of decision-making.'[82]

Economic measurements (of which QALYs are only one) are statements of general goals that might be pursued by health service planners dealing with issues of 'macro-allocation'. Economic principles may well provide guidance to planners at central, regional or district level. But they are often too blunt to guide those who must distinguish between patients waiting for treatment in hospital.

D. The Oregon Experiment

A variation of the principle of spreading scarce health service resources across the largest number of patients has been proposed

---

less emphasis to the question of cost. See E. Nord, 'The Relevance of Health State After Treatment in Prioritising Between Patients', 19 *Journal of Medical Ethics* 37 (1993).

[81] Evidence from the Handicap Division of the Society for the Protection of the Unborn Child, quoted in the House of Lords' *Report of the Select Committee on Medical Ethics* (HL 21–I, 1994), para. 167.

[82] M. Drummond, 'Output Measurement for Resource Allocation Decisions in Health Care', in A. McGuire, P. Fenn and K. Mayhew (eds.), *Providing Health Care: the Economics of Alternative Systems of Finance and Delivery* (Oxford University Press, 1991) 118.

in Oregon, USA. For those who are too poor to obtain health service insurance, Oregon receives funding from central government under the Medicaid system (like almost every other state in the Nation). However, the Medicaid grant is insufficient to cover the health care requirements of all those who fall below the relevant level of income (the federal poverty level). Rather than axe entire categories of treatment, such as dentistry and prescription medicines, a policy was devised which attempted to compile 'a list of health services ranked by priority, from the most important to the least important, representing the comparative benefits of each service to the population to be served.'[83] A Health Service Commission was established to undertake the task. The Commission listed services by reference to specific treatments and specific conditions (e.g. appendicitis and appendectomy). The list comprised 709 condition-treatments[84] subdivided into seventeen general service categories which distinguished acute and chronic illness, illnesses from which complete, or only partial recovery would be expected, illnesses which cause death or disability, effective and ineffective treatment, preventive and comfort care.

The categories reproduced in Table 3 below were developed in which numbers 1–9 were considered 'essential' and 10–13 were designated 'very important'.[85]

A separate ranking process took place within each category according to the 'net benefit' gained from specific treatment which produced a final list of over 700 procedures. The net benefit was assessed by reference to treatment outcomes and, in a very general way, public opinion as to the value of different attributes of health care. The Health Service Commission also felt obliged to add its own preference for priority treatments after it found that the results of the first list seemed perverse (e.g. obstetrical care was ranked low on the list and infertility treatment high.) The treatment-conditions were given a score from one to zero,

[83] *Evaluation of the Oregon Medicaid Proposal*, (Congress of the US, Office of Technology Assessment, 1992) 4.

[84] The list was complied by reference to the World Health Organisation, *International Classification of Diseases* (9th revn; Ann Arbor, MI, Edwards Bros Inc, 1980), which contains over 10,000 diagnoses. The list originally ran to 1,680 treatment-conditions and was reduced by a process of exclusion and consolidation.

[85] Taken from F. Honigsbaum, *Who Shall Live? Who Shall Die?—Oregon's Health Financing Proposals* (King's Fund College, 1993) 25.

Table 3

Rank of treatment Condition and effects	Examples
1 Acute fatal, prevents death, full recovery	appendectomy, medical therapy for myocarditis
2 Maternity care, including disorders of the newborn	obstetric care of pregnancy; medical therapy for low birth-weight babies
3 Acute fatal, prevents death, without full recovery	medical therapy for bacterial meningitis; reduction of open fracture of joint
4 Preventive care for children	immunizations; screening for vision or hearing problems
5 Chronic fatal, improves life span and patient's well-being	medical therapy for diabetes mellitus and asthma; all transplants
6 Reproductive services	contraceptive management, vasectomy
7 Comfort care	palliative therapy for conditions in which death is imminent
8 Preventive dental care	cleaning and fluoride
9 Proven effective preventive care for adults	mammograms; blood pressure screening
10 Acute nonfatal, treatment causes return to previous health state	Medical therapy for vaginitis; restorative dental service for dental caries
11 Chronic nonfatal, one-time treatment improves quality of life	hip replacement; medical therapy for rheumatic fever
12 Acute nonfatal, treatment without return to previous health state	relocation of dislocated elbow; repair of corneal laceration
13 Chronic nonfatal, repetitive treatment improves quality of life	medical therapy for migraine and asthma
14 Acute nonfatal, treatment expedites recovery of self-limiting conditions	Medical therapy for diaper rash and acute conjunctivitis
15 Infertility services	in-vitro fertilization, micro-surgery for tubular disease
16 Less effective preventive care for adults	dipstick urinalysis for haematuria in adults under age 60; sigmoidoscopy for persons under age 40
17 Fatal or nonfatal, treatment causes minimal or no improvement in quality of life	medical therapy for end stage HIV disease; life support for extremely low birthweight babies (under 500 gm)

representing the difference between perfect health and death on the basis of the following equation:[86]

Table 4 The Oregonian Formula of the QALY

$$Y * [\sum_{i=1}^{5} (P_{i1} * QWB_{i1}) \quad - \quad \sum_{i=1}^{5} (P_{i2} * QWB_{i2})]$$

[With treatment]   [Without Treatment]

with $QWB_{ik} = 1 + \sum_{i=1} d_{ijk}w_j$

where

B_n = the net benefit value ratio for the nth condition/treatment pair to be ranked. This value will be used in determining the actual rankings of health services from highest (0) to lowest ($^{-\infty}$).

c = cost *with* treatment, including all medications and ancillary services as well as the cost of the primary procedure.

Y = the years for which the treatment can be expected to benefit the patient with this condition. This may be the remainder of the patient's lifetime or some shorter amount of time.

P_{i1} = the probability that the ith outcome will occur five years hence · *with* treatment.

d_{ij1} = an indicator variable denoting the presence (= 1) or absence (= 0) of the jth health limitation (MOB, PAC or SAC) or chief complaint for the ith outcome *with* treatment.

w_j = the weight given by Oregonians to the jth health limitation or chief complaint ranging from 0 = no significant effect to −1 = death.

P_{i2} = the probability that the ith outcome will occur five years hence *without* treatment.

d_{ij2} = an indicator variable denoting the presence or absence of the jth health limitation or chief complaint for the ith outcome *without* treatment.

On this basis, given the Medicaid funds made available to provide for those without health insurance, only the first 587 treatment-conditions could be provided under the scheme. The remainder would not be made available under Medicaid. A selection of the conditions and treatments to which priority was assigned is provided as follows:[87]

[86] Ibid. at 44.   [87] Ibid. at 30.

Table 5 Ranking of Selected Condition—Treatment Pairs

Condition	Treatment	Category	Rank
pneumonia	medical	1	1
appendicitis	appendectomy	1	5
ischaemic heart disease	cardiac by-pass op	3	149
HIV disease	medical	5	158
imminent death	comfort care	7	164
cancer of uterus	medical and surgical	5	186
end stage renal disease	medical including dialysis	5	319
cataract	extraction	11	337
osteoarthritis	hip replacement	11	399
wisdom teeth	surgery	11	480
tonsils and adenoid disease	tonsillectomy and adenoidectomy	11	494
hernia without obstruction	repair	11	504
back pain (spondylosis)	medical and surgical	13	586
all below 587 may not be funded			
varicose veins	stripping/sclerotherapy	11	616
bronchitis	medical	13	643
cancer where treatment will not result in 10% of patients surviving 5 years	medical and surgical	17	688
tubal disfunction	in-vitro fertilisation GIFT	15	696
haemmorrhoids, uncomplicated	haemmorrhoidectomy	17	698
AIDS, end stage HIV disease	medical	17	702
extemely low birthweight (under 500 gm)	lift support	17	708

The Oregon scheme presents a number of major problems which have yet to be resolved. First, despite the list of 709 treatment-conditions and a spectacular equation, the system is often too crude to differentiate sensibly between individuals. Many conditions are not included in the list and patients often present themselves with more than one condition. A patient with two conditions, only one of which was funded under the scheme, could not sensibly be treated for that complaint alone, particularly if the untreated disease were the more serious. In such a case, either both complaints should be dealt with or neither. Equally, given the various forms in which illness may manifest itself, it seems absurd categorically to preclude treatment which will afford certain benefit to a patient. Conversely, for a condition above the line, it would be foolish to raise a presumption that treatment will be provided if the responsible doctor believes it will be futile. In both cases, clinical discretion must still play a part. As one of the framers of the plan said, 'intuition is as important as mathematical formulas.'[88]

Secondly, there is some doubt as to how serious a contribution the public can be expected to make to the debate about health service priorities. In Oregon some 1,000 people were canvassed for their views, but the community meetings were attended mainly by those employed in the health care system. Very few of those whom the scheme was intended to benefit participated in the debate.[89] In any case, the issues often involve very sensitive and delicate ethical questions in which conflicting demands may best be considered over a period of time with a particular strategy in mind. They may be ill-suited to ranking on the basis of single questionnaires or discussions with random groups. The truth may be that lay people cannot be expected to contribute constructively to the question unless they also understand what has been achieved, whether further savings are possible, where medical services are least effective, how resources might be used more effectively, who would gain and by how much, and so on. For the cynically minded: 'A concern must be that many of those championing public involvement are not in fact truly seeking to empower people in order to enable them to participate effectively but rather may be seeking a superficial legitimacy—a veneer for management decisions about priorities.'[90]

[88] Quoted in F. Honnigsbaum, ibid. 45.

[89] Similarly, in England, interest has been expressed in the idea of letting people influence the allocation of health care. See L. Moore, *Purchasing Health Care: Involving Local People in the Process of Explicit Priority Setting* (London School of Hygiene and Tropical Medicine, 1991), written for North West Thames Regional Health Authority. See also *Local Voices: The views of local people in purchasing for health* (NHSME, 1992).

[90] D. Hunter, *Rationing Dilemmas in Health Care* (National Association of Health Authorities and Trusts, 1993) 27. See also the view of M. Rigge, 'Involving Patients and Consumers' (*Health Service Journal: Health Management Guide*, 1993) 3: 'There is a danger that such forms of consumer participation may be a kind

As the experiment in Oregon showed, it is difficult to involve a representative cross-section of people in the exercise. Often, particular groups will be involved and some will effectively lobby for funds, but one wonders who will speak up for the less articulate groups such as the mentally handicapped, the elderly, and those with 'unpopular' diseases.[91] Of course, if sufficient numbers of people could be involved then the highest common denominator, or lowest common factor, of opinions could be used to guide health care policy making for the present. But people have widely differing and inconsistent views about the concepts of health, illness and disease[92] which will vary over time and between, for example, the young, the old, the disabled. This means that it would be impossible to define the overall objectives of the system, or to distinguish problems of health from those concerning the broader issues of life and society. And long-term planning would become very difficult.[93]

Thirdly, the whole process of putting patients into categories disguises the fact that doctors would retain a considerable measure of discretion in deciding how to treat a patient. Is the condition acute or chronic; is the patient likely to make a full, or partial recovery; if the condition is fatal, is it in its terminal stages (for palliative care, rather than active treatment)? All these are matters for individual clinical discretion which is flexible enough to include more patients within the scheme than the available funds were intended to support. In this case, if doctors were to react in a compassionate way and tend to include, rather than exclude, patients then the numbers of treatment-conditions covered by the plan could be larger than anticipated. Thus, given the same quantity of resources, the number of treatment-conditions might have to be reduced and the difficult question presents itself all over again.

of tokenism when people are allowed to feel involved in decision-making up to a point, but in fact little more than lip-service is paid to their views.'

[91] See e.g. *AIDS: The Challenge for Health Authorities* (National Association of Health Authorities, 1988), which estimated that in 1988/9, £515 m. would be required to maintain standards of service to those suffering HIV and AIDS.

[92] See E. Campbell, J. Scadding, R. Roberts, 'The Concept of Disease' [1979] 2 *British Medical Journal* 757.

[93] Thus, this approach was rejected as an general solution by a committee of enquiry in The Netherlands in *Choices in Health Care, supra* note 46, 51.

E. International Comparisons

Are we spending enough on health care? One way of approaching the question is by comparing our investment with that of other countries. Measured as a percentage of gross national product, the USA spends the most on health care (around 13 per cent of GNP) and the UK ranks twentieth (at around 6 per cent) amongst the modern industrialised nations. Only Spain, Portugal, Greece, and Turkey spend less.[94] 'What is unclear from these comparisons, however, is whether the lower spending in the UK should be a cause for congratulation, or dissatisfaction.'[95] The statistic measures quantity, not quality. It fails to record that 30 million Americans have no health insurance at all and many others have insurance which specifically excludes the very illness that most concerns the patient. Also, statistics are not compiled in the same way from country to country. Some may include elements which others exclude, or attach different significance to them in a way that makes direct comparison impossible. Allowance must also be made for differing national levels of inflation in order to compare the real purchasing power of money. It would be meaningless to say that health investment in one country had increased four-fold over ten years if that growth had been matched by inflation which eroded any expansion in services in real terms. Similarly, the transaction costs associated with running some systems are higher than others. For example, comparing two sets of statistics: 'the USA goes from being the highest spender per capita if health-care expenditures are corrected to a comparative base using exchange rates, to the eighth highest spender if international differences in the price of medical care is taken into account.'[96]

More difficult still are the socio-economic and cultural variations between nations as to the notion of what counts as health and disease, the patterns of 'illness' which have developed over many years, and the different health priorities which have been

[94] See *Compendium of Health Statistics*, *supra* note 4, figure 2.6.

[95] R. Robinson, D. Evans, and M. Exworthy, *Health and the Economy* (National Association of Health Authorities and Trusts, 1994) 26, discussing the connection between a strong economy and a healthy work-force.

[96] J. Appleby, *Financing Health Care in the 1990s* (Open University Press, 1992) 73. The UK goes from 13th to 10th on the same measures. See table in D. Parkin, *infra*, note 98.

identified from place to place.[97] Obviously, then, there will be disagreement about what ought to be measured and how. And after that, there will be disagreement about what it all means anyway. So what if The Netherlands spends more than Italy, but less than Norway? This is descriptive, but not prescriptive. It tells us nothing about what we ought to do. 'The simple recitation of findings seems to show that very little can be said on the basis of them about efficiency, or indeed much else! Ambiguities abound, and the choice of interpretation is largely a matter of taste rather than judgement. . . . Not only are there problems in the data, there is no really useful framework for analysing them.'[98]

Indeed, even within one country, it is difficult to compare like with like. In America, for example, hospital activities are vetted and improved by the Joint Commission on the Accreditation of Healthcare Organisations. But some hospitals operate in areas of far greater social deprivation than others, and allowance has to be made for different regional levels of unemployment, alcoholism, disease from factory dust, and so on. Similar difficulties of comparison apply at an international level. For the moment, therefore, there is so much subjectivity in both the compilation and interpretation of international health statistics that they do not assist our understanding of the quantity of investment which is prudent or desirable.

[97] See L. Payer, *Medicine and Culture* (Victor Gollancz, 1989).
[98] D. Parkin, 'Comparing Health Service Efficiency Across Countries', in A. McGuire, P. Fenn, and K. Mayhew (eds.), *Providing Health Care: The Economics of Alternative Systems of Finance and Delivery* (Oxford University Press, 1991), 179.

2

Managed Competition in the NHS

Pressure to reform the National Health Service developed during the 1980s, no doubt, partly due to the factors discussed in Chapter 1. Hospitals were given powers to generate revenue for themselves and health authorities were expected to invite tenders from private business for the provision of certain services[1] In 1987, however, during a television interview the Prime Minister, Margaret Thatcher, announced her intention to chair a working party to reconsider the funding of the NHS. The announcement coincided with the publicity which surrounded a child with a heart defect who was refused intensive care facilities because of shortages of staff and other resources.[2] The Prime Minister's statement came as a surprise because less than a week beforehand the Secretary of State for Social Services, John Moore, had delivered a major speech on the future of the NHS in the House of Commons in which no reference to such a review was made.[3] There was nothing new about talk of financial crisis in the NHS. 'The rhetoric of imminent disaster was almost as old as the system itself.'[4] On the other hand, the NHS was (and still is) facing increasing demands on its resources and the decision to review its operation was consistent with similar reassessments of health care systems elsewhere in the world. This chapter considers how the National Health Service was reorganized following the review and how the internal market for health care reformed the system.

---

[1] The power to raise money is provided by the Health and Medicines Act 1988, s. 7. No specific powers were required to encourage health authorities to invite private tenders.

[2] The case is that of *R* v. *Central Birmingham Health Authority, ex parte Collier* (unreported, reproduced in part in I. Kennedy and A. Grubb, *Medical Law—Text with Materials* (Butterworths, 1994) 428). The case is discussed in Chapter 4.

[3] See J. Butler, 'Origins and Early Development', in R. Robinson and J. Le Grand (eds.), *Evaluating the NHS Reforms* (King's Fund Institute, 1994) 16.

[4] Ibid, citing Enoch Powell, *A New Look at Medicine and Politics* (Pitman Medical, 1966).

I. COMPONENTS OF THE NATIONAL HEALTH SERVICES

The NHS is organized in accordance with the National Health Service Act 1977 and the National Health Service and Community Care Act 1990. The 1977 Act gives the Secretary of State wide powers to fulfil his or her statutory obligations and a duty to establish regional health authorities (RHAs),[5] district health authorities (DHAs),[6] family health service authorities (FHSAs)[7] and special health authorities (SHAs)[8] in order to promote these purposes. The major functions of these authorities are to advance the policies adopted by the Secretary of State[9] and to commission care on behalf of patients by means of 'NHS contracts' with hospitals.[10]

Two further health service bodies were introduced by the 1990 Act known as 'NHS Trust hospitals',[11] and 'GP fund-holding practices'.[12] NHS Trust hospitals differ from hospitals under the direct management of a health authority in that they have greater operational independence. They are responsible for generating their own business strategy and revenue by offering their services to purchasers of health care. Some 90 per cent of all hospitals are now NHS Trusts.[13] GP fund-holding practices have analogous freedom in the management and provision of primary care by means of their own fund. Around one-third of GPs and of general practices, are now fund-holders.

---

[5] See the National Health Service Act 1977, s. 8(1A)(a), substituted by the Health Services Act 1980, ss. 1, 2, and sched. 1, Part 1, para. 28.

[6] Ibid, as amended by the National Health Service and Community Care Act 1990, ss. 1(1), 66(2) and sched. 10.

[7] See the National Health Service Act 1977, s. 19, as amended by the National Health Service and Community Care Act 1990, s. 2(1) and (3)(a).

[8] See the National Health Service Act 1977, s. 11 as amended by the Health Services Act 1980, ss. 1, 2, and sched. 1, Part 1, para. 31 and the National Health Service and Community Care Act 1990, s. 2(1). There are three types of SHA: (i) non-hospital SHAs e.g. those which provide services for the NHS, (ii) hospital SHAs which provide postgraduate education and training and (iii) special hospitals for those suffering serious mental illness requiring high security accommodation.

[9] Explained in *Priorities and Planning Guidance 1994–95* (EL(94)55, NHSME, 1994).   [10] See text accompanying footnotes 88–100 below.

[11] See ss. 5–11 and sched. 2, 1990 Act. 9.

[12] See ss. 14–17, 1990 Act.

[13] NHS Trust hospitals are discussed below.

One of the purposes of the 1990 reforms was to increase sensitivity with respect to the costs and benefits of treating patients by introducing an 'internal market' for health care. This mechanism[14] tends to devolve decision-making power down the chain of authority towards GPs and hospitals so that many of the supervisory and administrative functions of RHAs to set objectives and monitor performance have declined.[15] The Secretary of State has proposed that (subject to Parliamentary approval) RHAs be abolished from 1996, that the numbers of DHAs should be reduced, and that FHSAs and DHAs should merge their responsibilities for commissioning primary and secondary care.[16] Legislation amending the 1977 Act will be required before these reforms can be introduced.[17] The following sections are based on the present system.

II. REFORMING THE NATIONAL HEALTH SERVICE

Two features of expenditure in the NHS prompted the government to reconsider its system of funding. The first was a method of distributing financial resources to hospitals largely according to the perceived 'needs' of a resident population, to its mortality and morbidity, without considering the 'efficiency' of the hospitals responsible for providing treatment. This became known as the 'efficiency trap'. Those hospitals which reduced their unit costs and became more efficient were unable to admit more patients because they were limited by their financial allocation. Arguably, hospitals which are funded simply according to the requirements of their population's needs may feel no incentive to manage their funds as effectively as those whose funding is performance-related. Indeed, when there is no relationship between the amount of

---

[14] The 'internal market' for health is discussed below.

[15] See *Their Health, Your Business: The Role of District Health Authorities* (Audit Commission, 1993).

[16] See *Managing the New NHS* (Department of Health, 1993). Also *Practices Make Perfect: The Role of Family Health Service Authorities* (Audit Commission, 1993). The reforms are contained in the Health Authorities Bill; see discussion in the Postscript below.

[17] For practical purposes, the succession of amendments, deletions, and substitutions to the 1977 Act make it inaccessible. The Secretary of State should take the opportunity to introduce a consolidating Act with her proposed reforms.

money allocated to a district and the number of patients it is able to treat, the more efficient hospital appears to suffer a penalty. By treating more patients it spends its allocation more quickly and exhausts its funds before the end of the financial year. One commentator, who influenced the eventual shape of the health service reforms, wrote of the NHS in 1984:

> The NHS runs on the ability and dedication of the many people who work in it. . . . But other than the satisfaction of a job well done—which I do not wish to minimise—the system contains no serious incentives to guide the NHS in the direction of better quality care and service at reduced cost. . . In the non-competitive NHS, the manager who attempts to implement efficiency-improving changes is more likely to be seen as a cause of problems.

In fact, the structure of the NHS contains perverse incentives. For example, a District that develops an excellent service in some specialty that attracts more referrals is likely to get more work without getting more resources to do it. A District that does a poor job will 'export' patients and have less work, but not correspondingly less resources, for its reward . . . management and consultants in a District risk weakening the case for a new hospital wing they have been campaigning for by solving their waiting list problem by referring patients to other districts with excess capacity . . . [and] GPs have weak or no incentives to reduce referrals. They have neither the incentives nor the resources to make extra efforts to keep people out of hospital.[18]

One solution to this trap is to enable efficient hospitals with spare capacity to offer their services to larger numbers of patients. Obviously, an incentive is required for such a hospital to fund the additional work and logic suggests that the money ought to come from those hospitals which work below full capacity. Those hospitals which achieve most, at least cost and at highest quality, ought to receive more funding than those that do less.

The second feature of the system which gave cause for concern was that those responsible for spending had no direct interest in controlling costs.[19] The argument was: so long as GPs and

[18] A. Enthoven, *Reflections on the Management of the National Health Service— An American looks at incentives to efficiency in health services management in the UK* (Nuffield Provincial Hospitals Trust, 1985) 13–15.

[19] Economists refer to this feature, rather inscrutably, as 'moral hazard'. See C. Donaldson and K. Gerard, *Economics of Health Care Financing: The Visible Hand* (Macmillan, 1994), chs 6, 7; and A. McGuire, P. Fenn, and K. Mayhew, *Providing Health Care: The Economics of Alternative Systems of Delivery* (Oxford University Press, 1991) 14.

consultants are not asked to account for the medicines they prescribe or the procedures they recommend, there may be a tendency to over-treat patients. Why refuse to prescribe anti-biotics to a patient who mistakenly expects that they will cure his cold, or anti-depressants to the patient who, for entirely non-medical reasons, has good reason to be depressed?[20] Not only might it cause the patient upset and distress, but also doctors are increasingly concerned about the time, expense, and anxiety caused by patients' complaints. On one view, it makes more sense to satisfy patient's misplaced expectations than to spend time trying to explain the medical risks associated with pointless treatment.

A. The Internal Market

Both features were thought to work against efficient use of resources. The solution proposed was the creation of an 'internal market'[21] for the National Health Service, in order to enable purchasers of health care (DHAs, GPs and patients) to choose freely between providers (the hospitals), who would thus be forced to compete with one another on price, quality, and value for money. The advantage of a 'market' in goods and services for health care is that:

well-managed [hospitals] will have incentive to improve efficiency and perceived quality in order to attract more 'sales' of services to purchasers, thus increasing their share of funding but also consequently exerting pressure on less successful competitors who, in turn, improve their own efficiency and quality so as to avoid cut-backs or possible redundancies or closures. In theory all this should result in a larger volume of low-cost, good quality care being delivered to the public.[22]

---

[20] Over-prescribing of medicines is discussed in *A Prescription for Improvement: Towards More Rational Prescribing in General Practice* (Audit Commission, 1994).

[21] Although it rejects the application of pure market principles to health care, the Labour Party has said that: 'It is important to examine how to implement a system of rewards for those units which demonstrate high quality and increased productivity. Budgetary flexibility within the overall finance and service objectives would permit the necessary freedom to adapt to demand and to innovate in the provision of public service.' *Health 2000* (The Labour Party, 1994), para. 6.5.

[22] J. Perrin, 'Administrative and financial management of health care services', in E. Beck, S. Lonsdale *et al.* (eds.), *In the Best of Health* (Chapman Hall, 1992) 266.

Competition in the internal market is introduced by separating those who purchase or commission health care from those who provide it. In England and Wales, DHAs, FHSAs, and GP fund-holders are primarily responsible for commissioning health care. By contrast, health care is provided by NHS Trust hospitals, the small number of hospitals under the supervision of DHAs, and FHSAs. Momentum is achieved in the market by enabling GP fund-holders to compete on quality by using their funds in the ways they consider most appropriate in the interests of their patients. Similarly, NHS Trust hospitals are obliged to attract custom by providing a high-quality, low-cost service to patients. Contracts between commissioners and providers are negotiated at local level and, subject to national policy constraints, the assessment of health needs will be dominated by local influences. The same logic appealed to the Royal Commission in 1979 which noted that 'large organisations are most efficient when problems are solved and decisions taken at the lowest effective point',[23] but whether the transaction costs involved in setting up and operating an internal market will be less than the cost of the large bureaucracy it replaces remains to be seen.[24]

This incentive to attract more customers has no doubt enabled some hospitals to do more work than others. It has not, however, entirely resolved the problem of the efficiency trap. One would expect the major part of a hospital's revenue to arise from block contracts, in which a lump sum payment is agreed by a DHA purchaser for a category of work. In this case, even the most efficient hospitals with the greatest income will face the prospect of exhausting their revenue before the end of the financial year because the money available to purchasers remains limited. A critic of the system has commented:

When hospitals increase throughput all that happens is that the purchaser runs out of money before the end of the year. We start to read the familiar stories of ward closures and idle operating theatres . . . which the reforms were supposed to eliminate. To tell hospital managers that they should have paced themselves to spread the money over the full year is a denial of

---

[23] *Royal Commission on the National Health Service* (Cmnd. 7615, 1979), para. 1.9.

[24] See the discussion in J. Le Grand and W. Bartlett (eds.), *Quasi-Markets and Social Policy* (Macmillan, 1993).

all the theoretical advantages of a free market. In 1988 the money ran out because of 'inefficiency' and 'bad management'. . . . This year the same problem has arisen as a result of 'overtrading'.[25]

Also, GP fund-holding practices who manage their own budgets have a clear incentive to reduce spending, and some appear to have done so. But the pressures imposed on non-fund-holders have been less effective. So, for the moment at least, the introduction of an internal market for health has not had a profound effect on prescribing practice.[26]

B. Impact of the Internal Market

In the early days of the reforms the commitment to open competition between providers of health care was largely un-qualified.[27] The internal market for health was promoted by the slogan 'money follows the patient', implying that patients and their doctors would be able to choose when and where treatment would be given. Today, however, it is recognised that market principles have limitations in practice. It is more accurate to think of the internal market for health as a 'mixed economy', in which the effects of unrestricted competition will often be inappropriate and occasionally unlawful. Thus, the government has said that regula-tion of the market is necessary to promote the aspirations of the NHS. 'Without a regulatory framework the internal market in health services, like markets in other sectors, is likely to develop anti-competitive features, such as monopolies (of purchasers as well as providers), barriers to entry, poor information, inappro-priate pricing, and collusion.'[28]

In the current system it is more accurate to say that purchasers of health care decide how and when to spend resources, and therefore that the patient follows the money. Research so far

---

[25] 'Letter to Mrs Bottomley', 306 *British Medical Journal* 702 (1993).

[26] See H. Glennerster, M. Matsaganis *et al.*, 'GP Fund-holding: Wild Card or Winning Hand?', in R. Robinson and J. Le Grand, *Evaluating the NHS Reform* (King's Fund Institute, 1994), ch. 4; and *A Prescription for Improvement*, supra note 20.

[27] See J. Butler, *Patients, Policies and Politics* (Open University Press, 1992).

[28] *Managing the New NHS: Functions and Responsibilities in the New NHS* (NHS Executive, 1994), para. 10.

suggests that the internal market for health has not significantly expanded the choices available to patients and doctors.[29] However, patterns of activity appear to have changed to the benefit of fund-holders' patients. Inevitably, with significant purchasing power in the hands of general practices, there has been a shift in power away from consultants and toward fund-holders. Waiting times for treatment are reduced, for example, because a consultant has spent a day a week in the fund-holder's own clinic, or the provider has extended its facilities. In addition, laboratory testing has improved by competition from private services, and GPs have generally been able to exercise more influence over hospital services.[30] Further, there appears to be no evidence that fund-holders have attempted to make unwarranted savings from their funds, for example by refusing to refer patients for treatment in hospital, or by increasing the number of referrals to private clinics so the cost is borne by the patient's private insurance.[31] On the other hand, some of the pressures imposed by market principles were mitigated by the goodwill of fund-holders themselves, some of whom 'consciously ignored attractive business propositions from the private sector for the benefit of a longer term relationship, based on trust, with a local hospital.'[32] In the future, with stiffer competition between fund-holders and less money available to promote the scheme, there may be less reluctance to smooth over the ethical conflicts thrown up by the system.

Similarly, DHAs have not introduced dramatic changes to their patterns of purchasing from hospitals. To some extent decisions are influenced by the pressures exerted by established customs, but this should not conceal the fact that decisions are, none the

[29] See A. Mahon, D. Wilkin and C. Whitehouse, 'Choice of Hospital for Elective Surgery: GPs' and Patients' Views', in *Evaluating the NHS Reforms, supra* note 26, ch. 5. The slight trend, however, appears to be towards more choice, see ibid. 118.

[30] See the discussion in H. Glennerster, M. Matsaganis, P. Owens, *A Foothold for Fund-holding—A preliminary report on the introduction of GP fund-holding* (King's Fund Institute, 1992), ch. 5.

[31] See 'Effect of the NHS Reforms on General Practitioners Referral Patterns', 306 *British Medical Journal* 433 (1993).

[32] *A Foothold for Fund-holding*, supra note 30, 32. See also the reasons suggested for the lack of change in 'Effect of the NHS Reforms on General Practitioners Referral Patterns', 306 *British Medical Journal, supra* note 31.

less, being made to preserve the *status quo*.[33] One reason for this apparent inertia is the absence of an equation which enables particular categories of health care, or patient, to be given priority. Rather, there is a: 'multiplicity of policy objectives in the NHS . . . there is no master formula or methodology which allows purchasers to prioritise between the many competing priorities—national, regional and local—which are crowding in on them.'[34]

One should not underestimate the potential of market pressures, however. The problem is illustrated by the Tomlinson Report on *London's Health Service*, which found that the costs associated with running the prestigious hospitals in London were higher than those of hospitals elsewhere. This is attributable to a number of factors, including the large quantity of teaching and research conducted there and the high proportion of specialist centres of excellence. Now that NHS contracts are placed by purchasers concerned chiefly with value for money, DHAs and GP fund-holders are less inclined to pay a premium, when comparable treatment is available less expensively outside central London. The Report discovered that many inner London health authorities would no longer purchase from inner London hospitals, especially for routine surgery.[35]

Our analysis of the future need for acute beds in inner London demonstrates that the capacity of the inner London hospitals must, over time, be brought into balance with the demands that will henceforth be made upon them. A reduction in capacity on the scale needed cannot be achieved by piecemeal bed closures and efficiency savings in each hospital. . . . We recommend that whole sites should be taken out of service altogether, and the essential services within them relocated; the capital stock involved should be sold or turned to alternative use; and the staff concerned should be redeployed.[36]

This is the power of the market. Its only strategy is to increase short-term efficiency and value for money. On one analysis, the closure of a hospital ward, indeed the closure of the entire

---

[33] R. Klein and S. Redmayne, *Patterns of Purchasing* (National Association of Health Authorities and Trusts, 1992) 19.

[34] S. Redmayne and R. Klein, *Sharing Out Resources: Purchasing and Priority Setting in the NHS* (National Association of Health Authorities and Trusts, 1993) 30.

[35] *Report of the Inquiry into London's Health Service, Medical Education and Research* (HMSO, 1992) 23.　　　　　　　　　　　　　　　　[36] Ibid. 26.

hospital, may represent the finest example of market forces in action. If the cost of its procedures is higher than those of other hospitals, its income will decline as GPs and DHAs purchase less expensively elsewhere. Patients, however, may hold that the same hospital in the highest regard. To them, its closure might be considered a disaster. A 'pure market' cannot take into account, as Tomlinson recommended, how and when the adjustments should occur. For this reason, the effects of the market in health care must be regulated to preserve continuity and standards, and to implement strategy. Additional funding is needed to plan the adjustments which market forces introduce. To maintain consistency and reliability, funds must always be reserved for the purpose of allowing services to be phased in or out over a reasonable period of time.

C. Limitations of Market Principles

As applied to health care, market principles have limitations. For a number of reasons unrestricted competition in the NHS could never be a complete solution.[37] Markets are driven by consumers, but the use of patients and doctors as 'consumers' presents problems. One of the most serious difficulties concerns the quantity of information needed in an effective market place.

Real markets are hard to create in health care. Patients want a local and immediate service, whilst hospitals come in multi-million pound lumps, not in packets like soap powder, and are, therefore, very few and far between. And while real competition depends on generally available information, well informed participants—whether patients, doctors, nurses or managers—are in very short supply. Though everyone wants better outcomes, who knows how to measure them? And just what is the role of local managers in health care when most serious data on the performance of their institutions are lacking?[38]

The most serious difficulties, therefore, concern (1) inadequate information, (2) NHS strategy in the internal market, and (3) the danger of a 'two-tier' health service.

---

[37] *Economics of Health Care Financing, supra* note 19, chs. 2, 3; and *Providing Health Care: The Economics of Alternative Systems of Delivery, supra* note 19, ch. 1.

[38] P. Strong and J. Robinson, *The NHS Under New Management,* (Open University Press, 1990) 191.

1. Inadequate Information

Effective markets require that consumers are able to assess and compare the value of the goods and services supplied, and to alter their purchasing behaviour accordingly. But such comparisons and assessments are often impossible in the health service. It is true that, at an intuitive level, patients are now more able to choose between GPs. Those practices which leave patients feeling that they have received a good service are more likely to attract custom than others. But objective data on the rates of success and failure of hospitals, which would assist in promoting high achievers, is largely unavailable. Although there is crude information about activity in the National Health Service; e.g. expenditure per age group, the numbers of patients to have received treatment as in-patients and out-patients, the duration of treatment, the occupancy of hospital beds and so on,[39]

there remains one basic blind spot . . . there is little or no information on the impact of health care services on the health of individual patients or the community at large. Indeed such is the design of hospital information systems that no real distinction is made between patients who leave hospital alive and those who die there.'[40]

Statistics which simply record the numbers of patients treated in hospital are clearly inadequate, in that they fail to assess the quality of the care provided, e.g. whether the treatment was successful.[41] Indeed, if a patient has to be readmitted after discharge because the initial treatment is unsuccessful, this would appear in such statistics as being counted more than once.[42] Clinicians are not routinely monitored for the purposes of comparison, nor is information available to patients as to the hospitals with the least attractive records of surgical success. Thus, both patients and doctors are often wholly ignorant of the relative

[39] See e.g. *Compendium of Health Statistics* (Office of Health Economics, 8th edn. 1992).

[40] P. Kind, *Hospital Deaths—The Missing Link: Measuring Outcome in Hospital Activity Data* (Office of Health Economics, 1988) 1. See also J Appleby and S. Boyle, 'Finding the Facts', *Health Service Journal* 3 Feb. 1994 24.

[41] 'Finished consultant episodes' (FCEs) are doubted as a measure of hospital efficiency in A. Clarke and M. McKee, 'The consultant episode: an unhelpful measure', 305 *British Medical Journal* 1307 (1992).

[42] See the helpful discussion in *Hospital Deaths—The Missing Link*, *supra* note 40.

advantages and disadvantages of the service-providers available. There has been some interest in making patients more critical of the standards achieved, and consequently more selective in their choice of doctor, by giving them more information about the outcome of treatments in hospital. The Department of Health has said with respect to health technology: 'Outcomes which patients themselves would find interesting and important include clinical outcomes, such as survival rates, symptoms and complications; health status and "quality of life". Other outcomes include the costs and use of resources, and the wider social, ethical, legal and organisational impacts of technologies.'[43]

Conceivably, if information of this nature were available then patients could become purchasers by being given a 'health voucher'[44] to spend on their health as they saw fit. In this case, in theory, if not in practice, patients would then have real power to choose between hospitals, and the insoluble debate about how to allocate health service resources could be handed to patients themselves. But it is difficult to see how reliable any such comparisons, between hospitals or between doctors, could be. As between hospitals, allowance would have to built in to the system for the different degrees of mortality and morbidity between, say, the region of retired patients on the South coast and the industrialized conurbations of the Midlands and North East. Similarly, as between doctors, case-mixes will vary. A larger percentage of one surgeon's patients may have died following surgery, but that is not necessarily due to incompetence. It may be that this doctor accepts the most difficult cases because he or she is the best in that field, or that more of those patients are elderly. As one comparison of American hospitals showed, most of the differences of outcomes were accounted for by differences in 'inputs', i.e. the conditions of the patients admitted for treatment.[45]

---

[43] *Assessing the Effects of Health Technologies—Principles, Practice, Proposals* (Department of Health, 1992) 10.

[44] For precisely such a suggestion see M. Bassett, *A Health Cheque for All: Proposals for a Mixed Market in Health Care* (Health Service Management Unit, University of Manchester, 1993). The voucher would be weighted according to age and other relevant criteria to reflect a patient's needs, but the precise quantification of patients' 'needs' is not explained. What of those who remained healthy and had no use of such a health cheque, or those whose treatment was so expensive as to exceed the funds made available by the voucher?

[45] W. Knaus and D. Nash, 'Predicting and Evaluating Patient Outcomes', 109 *Annals of International Medicine* 521 (1988).

To make matters more complicated it is difficult to measure the extent to which a modern health service can be responsible for improved levels of health. Proxy measures of quality have been used but none are free from ambiguity, and the evidence which they present is equivocal. For example, a number of indices show how our standards of health have increased. Infant mortality has declined steadily and morbidity and mortality statistics demonstrate that we are in general living longer and healthier lives than ever before. But the extent to which these improvements may be attributed to the health service is difficult to assess because other factors have significant effects. As the Royal Commission said in 1979, we need to recognize that many of the main improvements in the health of the nation have come about not from advances in medical treatment, or the existence of the NHS, but from public health measures, better nutrition, and improvements in the economic, social, and natural environments.

The provision of a clean water supply, an efficient sewerage system and better standards of food hygiene in the nineteenth century virtually eliminated cholera and greatly reduced enteric fever which until then had been endemic in the UK. Medical advances made little impact on mortality rates until the introduction of immunisation and the sulpha drugs in the 1930s, and the antibiotics of the 1940s.[46]

Amongst all those external factors, reliable and unambiguous information in this field will probably always be unobtainable.

2. NHS Strategy in the Internal Market

A separate difficulty concerns the extent to which a market for health is consistent with the development of clear strategy in the NHS. Before the implementation of the reforms, NHS resources were distributed from the top downwards from the Secretary of State, through the regions, to the districts. In principle, national policy could be imposed at local level. With the introduction of GP fund-holders and NHS Trusts, however, decision-making power has shifted towards GPs and local hospitals. Strategic decisions must now be made at local level. Of course, this is the idea of the market, and may bring advantages for doctors and patients, but it is not clear how the planning and objectives of the Secretary of

---

[46] *Royal Commission on the Health Service* (Cmnd.7615, 1979), para. 5.3.

State, or the overall stability of hospitals, are promoted by such a system. The point was made by a House of Commons Committee:

The twin objectives of the [re]organisation of the NHS are, on the one hand, to delegate as much decision-making as possible down to the lowest possible tier of health services, and on the other, to strengthen accountability up through the service to the centre. Both are laudable in intention, but there may be incompatibility between these objectives.[47]

Clearly, the Secretary of State will continue to be responsible for the promotion of the NHS and may not simply abandon her duty to buyers and sellers in the internal market. As she has said with respect to health service resources: 'the first step in a strategic approach must be the establishment of clear priorities so that action and resources can be directed to best effect. This is necessary because if everything is regarded as a "priority" then there is, in effect, no priority at all.'[48]

There are a number of reasons for retaining control at the centre, both over specific policy objectives and operational matters. Thus, greater priority has been given to primary care,[49] emphasizing prevention rather than cure, by means of screening and by education about the dangers of certain forms of behaviour. A crucial aspect of 'policy' is the need for a reasonably consistent long-term strategy. 'Key areas' have been selected for attention on the basis of three principles, namely (i) the area should be a major cause of premature death or avoidable ill-health; (ii) effective interventions should be possible, offering significant scope for improvement in health; and (iii) it should be possible to set objectives and targets, and monitor progress towards them.[50] Specific attention has been given to coronary heart disease and stroke, cancers, mental illness, HIV and AIDS, and accidents. In each case targets for reduction have been set, to be achieved

---

[47] *Resourcing the National Health Service: The Government's Plans for the Future of the National Health Service* (Social Services Select Committee, 8th Report, HC 214–III, 1989), para. 5.2.

[48] *The Health of the Nation* (Department of Health, 1992) 8. See also the annual statement of *Priorities and Planning Guidance for the NHS* in EL(92)47 (NHSME, 1992), EL(93)54 (NHSME, 1993) and EL(94)55 (NHSE, 1994).

[49] See *The Health of the Nation* ibid. A similar, if less specific, recommendation was made by the *Royal Commission on the Health Service* in 1979, ch. 5. The same view has been adopted by the Labour Party, see *Health 2000*, *supra* note 21, ch. 4.

[50] *The Health of the Nation*, ibid. 8.

before a specific date. Without clear leadership from the centre, these objectives would probably not be given the same emphasis by local doctors and health managers.

Equally, with regard to operational matters within hospitals, the market may be too slow or ineffective to deal with lapses in standards of treatment. For example, there are wide variations between the standards of care achieved by different hospitals which are difficult to explain. The National Audit Office has noted that there are major differences in mortality rates between hospitals. Standardized mortality rates for chronic rheumatic heart disease ranged from nil to approximately six times the 'expected' rate in different districts.[51] Similar variations appear in the treatment of cancer.[52] Given the difficulty of obtaining information of this nature, market principles are not always helpful to patients and it is proper for the Secretary of State to intervene with measures to improve the levels of care made available to patients, say, by concentrating expertise in fewer hospitals. In addition, as the Tomlinson Report demonstrates, the market may operate too quickly and threaten the smooth running of hospitals in a particular area. Contrary to market trends, it may be necessary for the Department of Health to insist that the centres of excellence continue to provide long-term care for patients, and not be tempted to close expensive units on the ground that the facilities could generate more revenue by being put to other uses.

There is another serious concern. Markets work best when there are large numbers of buyers and sellers. When demand is small, the number of suppliers declines and competition plays a smaller part in effecting price and quality. How does this apply to relatively uncommon illnesses in the internal market? Take patients with cystic fibrosis, of whom the average RIIA has around 350 patients.[53] The illness presents the system with demand for hi-tech, high-cost, low-volume specialist care. Hospitals, however, often cannot afford the investment in staff or equipment necessary to provide a satisfactory service for such a small number of patients. Similarly, the obligation to purchase care is agreed by

---

[51] See *Quality of Clinical Care in National Health Service Hospitals* (National Audit Office, HC 736, 1988) 9.

[52] See *A Policy Framework for Commissioning Cancer Services* (Department of Health, 1994).

[53] See *Cystic Fibrosis* (Clinical Standards Advisory Group, HMSO, 1993).

means of 'block contracts' which do not expressly refer to the needs of such patients because it is extremely difficult to price such open ended procedures accurately. The result is that many units never treat the critical mass of patients needed to acquire and retain the specialists skills necessary for the treatment of cystic fibrosis. Consequently, there is a danger of some patients receiving inadequate care by inexperienced staff,[54] while others obtain excellent treatment from a small number of specialist units.

When demand is so limited it is inappropriate and inefficient for non-specialist hospitals to compete with one another. Instead, there is a need for a regional strategy to select centres of excellence in order for proper standards to be maintained. The Clinical Standards Advisory Group (CSAG) has said with respect to cystic fibrosis: 'there was clearly a problem before the NHS reforms, but there is some evidence that the situation has worsened, particularly in prescription of essential maintenance medicine.'[55] The same problem also applies to the intensive care facilities available to new-born babies, which vary from district to district.[56] Market principles operating at district level cannot guarantee a proper mechanism for providing adequate care in these circumstances.[57] The Department of Health accepts these observations and recommends that, for specialist services, co-ordination between districts is needed, for example by making one 'lead' district responsible for purchasing services on behalf of other districts from a single centre of excellence.[58] In these cases co-operation, rather than competition, is the best way to maintain quality.

---

[54] Patients or their families report that they often feel they know more about cystic fibrosis than their GPs and hospital doctors. This increased their sense of dissatisfaction. See ibid., ch. 6.   [55] Ibid. para. 9.13.

[56] See *Neonatal Intensive Care* (CSAG, HMSO, 1993), ch. 9. The British Paediatric Association and the Royal College of Obstetricians had recommended one intensive care cot per 1,000 live births, see *Recommendations for the Improvement of Infant Care During the Perinatal Period in the UK* (British Paediatric Association and Royal College of Obstetricians and Gynaecologists, 1977).

[57] See T. Pope and N. Wild, 'Putting the Clock Back 30 Years: Neonatal Services Since the 1991 NHS Reforms' 62 *Archives of Disease in Childhood* 879 (1992).

[58] See *Government Response to the Reports of the Clinical Standards Advisory Group* (Department of Health, 1993) and *Contracting for Specialist Services* (NHSME, 1993).

'Managed' competition, therefore, is about balance. Health authorities and NHS Trusts are not entirely free to merge with one another, or engage in collusive behaviour because such activity would weaken the benefits that competition may bring. The Government has issued detailed guidance on the principles governing such ventures which confirms that 'the purpose of the National Health Service is to improve health and to provide comprehensive and high quality care on the basis of clinical need.'[59] As it acknowledges, however:

> The internal market itself does not, and was not expected to, achieve all the goals of the National Health Service. . . . A strategic perspective will always be important, especially where we are faced with continuing change as a result of medical and technological advance. We need constructive co-operation between different parts of the NHS as well as the beneficial impact of competition.[60]

3. A Two-tier Health Service?

The tension between central and local objectives is well illustrated by fund-holding practices. Some GP fund-holders have been able to bargain aggressively with hospital providers by combining to form consortia. While individual practices cannot have less than 7,000 patients, some have many more. By combining in consortia of five or six practices, the number of patients represented becomes substantial. Such a consortium could represent almost as many patients as the district itself, but with no corresponding obligations with respect to policy laid down centrally. No contracts manager in a hospital can afford to lose the custom of doctors with the potential buying power of perhaps 50,000 patients. Inevitably, pressure will be exerted on hospitals to alter their practices to reflect the new demands made upon them by fund-holders. In some respects this may be an excellent thing; that hospitals and consultants become more sensitive to the demands of their patients is laudable.[61] But those demands have no necessary connection with the strategic aspirations of the Secretary of State for Health.

---

[59] *The Operation of the NHS Internal Market: Local Freedoms, National Responsibilities* (NHSE, 1994) 1.   [60] Ibid., Foreword.
[61] *A Foothold for Fund-holding, supra* note 30, 30. The report stated that 'the planning case does not seem to us a decisive one against fund-holding', ibid.

DHAs and fund-holders may emphasize different aspects of policy. Districts might be expected to plan services for whole populations over the long term, perhaps with a view to minimizing inequalities in their provision, and to adhere to the strategy adopted by the Secretary of State. By contrast, fund-holders are encouraged to promote their practices on the basis of an annual allocation of funds and are more remote from central planning. For example, some fund-holding practices have achieved savings from their funds, from which they have made lump-sum gifts of money to local hospitals to improve specific services.[62] This shows great public spirit, but it is an extremely random and haphazard way of distributing resources which does nothing to promote a co-ordinated approach to health care planning.

Precisely this question has arisen with respect to waiting lists. Fund-holding practices can use their bargaining power aggressively on behalf of their patients, and some have demanded that their patients be given hospital appointments ahead of the patients of non-fundholding practices. This has led to allegations that fund-holding has created a 'two-tier' health service. Of course, there is nothing new about a two-tier system; private care has always offered patients greater flexibility as to the timing and location of their treatment than under the NHS. Indeed, even within the NHS there may be unintended variations in the standards of care provided in different parts of the country owing to the complicated formulas by which regions are funded. On the other hand, before the introduction of the internal market for health the system did not encourage distinctions between NHS patients. What is new in fund-holding is the idea that doctors should be more enterprising in promoting their patients' interests. As the Department of Health said, unlike non-fundholding GPs: 'Fund holding GPs will be able to choose the hospital to which they send their patients and pay the hospitals directly for certain services provided for their patients. This will mean that those . . . who join the scheme will have a direct and personal influence on the way in which hospital services are delivered.'[63]

---

[62] See *General Practitioner Fundholding in England* (HC 51, Session 1994–95, National Audit Office), para. 4.13.

[63] *Funding General Practice* (Department of Health, 1989), section 1.

Thus, fund-holders may decide to pay consultants to provide a specialist out-patient clinic for their patients at the practice surgery, instead of putting them on hospital waiting lists. Also, some hospitals appear to offer preferential treatment to the patients of fund-holding practices.[64] Waiting times may be systematically shorter for patients of fund-holders, hospitals may agree to provide separate out-patient clinics for fund-holders' patients, 'hotel' care may be more comfortable and, toward the end of the financial year, hospitals may only accept for non-urgent care referrals from fund-holders. Arguably, if one accepts the advantages to be gained from competition, one must also accept that some will inevitably do less well than others. This will encourage an improvement in standards.

To what extent is this acceptable? The government has been keen to stress that there is a limit to the differences between patients who are, and those who are not, from fund-holding practices. Thus, as regards accident and emergency care, the Department of Health advocates that 'every patient attending an accident and emergency department should be seen immediately and their need for treatment clinically assessed by an appropriately qualified person.'[65] Whether or not the referring doctor happens to be a fund-holder should not influence the care offered to patients with urgent requirements. It takes the same view of seriously ill patients and advises that:

[i] 'common waiting lists should be used by provider units [i.e. hospitals] for urgent and seriously ill patients and for highly specialised diagnosis and treatment'; [and ii] 'waiting time specifications offered by provider units should consequently provide sufficient flexibility to allow for relativities in clinical need.'[66]

[64] See *Fundholding and Access to Hospital Care* (Association of Community Health Councils for England and Wales, 1994); *College Survey of Activity in the NHS* (Royal College of Surgeons, 1994); and 'Clerical error exposes fundholder privilege', *Health Service Journal* 12 May 1994 4.

[65] See *The Patient's Charter News* (Issue 1, March 1992).

[66] *Joint Guidance (NHSME/JCC) to hospital consultants on GP fundholding* (EL(91)84, NHSME, 1991). See also *Clinical Priority on Waiting Lists* (EL(94)19, NHSME), para. 3: 'It is particularly important that urgent cases on waiting lists, for whom delay in investigation or treatment would pose an unacceptable risk to life or risk morbidity, are treated promptly. *DHA and GP Fundholder purchasers, in discussion with their providers and the clinicians involved, should seek to ensure that this objective is met within available resources*' (original emphasis).

With respect to those already in hospital, it says: 'It is not acceptable for patients to be accorded differing standards of clinical care whilst undergoing hospital treatment by virtue of the contracts covering their care.'[67]

In a *national* health service, this must be right. Say an operation for which a patient has been waiting is cancelled in order to make way for a non-urgent patient of a fund-holder. The cancellation causes the patient to suffer additional complications. Such a patient would have legitimate cause for complaint. The common law would also insist that, unless there were compelling reasons to the contrary, a *system* of management which attached more weight to the status of the referring doctor than the urgency of clinical needs would be arbitrary and unreasonable.[68] The most compelling way of organizing waiting lists is on the basis of clinical need.[69] Patients awaiting treatment in accident and emergency units are owed a duty of care in the law of negligence,[70] and the same must be true of those admitted routinely, whose need for care has become urgent. Thus, for example, Slade LJ agreed in the case of *Bull* v. *Devon Area Health Authority* that the hospital staff owed a duty of care to a mother and her child in a maternity unit: 'The duty of a hospital is to provide a woman admitted in labour with a reasonable standard of skilled obstetric and paediatric care, in order to ensure as far as reasonably practicable the safe delivery of the baby or babies and the health of the mother and offspring thereafter.'[71]

The urgency with which such patients must be treated can never depend on the status of their GP. What about non-urgent patients? Fund-holders enjoy a freedom to use financial savings

---

[67] *Joint Guidance (NHSME/JCC) to hospital consultants*, ibid.

[68] The *Patient's Charter*, supra note 65, 8 provides that 'Every citizen has the right . . . to receive health care on the basis of clinical need, regardless of ability to pay.'

[69] See *Guidelines for the Management of Surgical Waiting Lists* (Royal College of Surgeons, 1991).

[70] See *Barnett* v. *Chelsea and Kensington Hospital Management Committee* [1969] 1 QB 428, which concerned the admission of a man to an A&E unit with serious stomach pains. He was discharged without being seen and advised to see his doctor if things did not improve. He died soon thereafter. It was held that he ought to have been seen and that the defendants were in breach of their duty of care in failing to do so. (On the facts, however, it was decided that he had been fatally poisoned and that no intervention by the hospital could have saved him. Thus, the defendants were exonerated from blame for his death.)

[71] [1993] 4 Med LR 117, 126.

made during the year for other purposes, such as physiotherapy sessions, or out-patient appointments with a consultant at the surgery. No comparable freedom exists for non-fundholders who have no funds with which to transfer savings. At best, they will have to seek the permission of their FHSA to divert funds in this way. Why should its patients be at a disadvantage by comparison to those of the fund-holder; why should all patients not be entitled to the same flexibility regardless of the status of their GP?[72] Here, the Department of Health has not issued guidance, nor is the common law likely to intervene. The principle of equality between NHS patients may be desirable,[73] but there is no such legal entitlement. Clearly, non-urgent cases may become urgent and deserve priority treatment. Until that time, however, hospitals and health authorities may seek to fulfil different objectives and differ in their approaches to fund-holders.[74]

III. FUNDING THE NATIONAL HEALTH SERVICE

The government remains responsible for providing resources in the NHS. The NHS spent almost £30 billion pounds in England in 1992/3. Of this, around £5.2 billion (19 per cent) went toward General Practitioner Services, £21.4 billion (77 per cent) went to Hospital and Community Health Services, and £1.0 billion (4 per cent) was devoted to central health services and administration.[75] How are these resources distributed in the internal market? We examine the position of (A) those who purchase health care and (B) those who provide health care.

A. Funding Purchasers of Health Care

The Department of Health allocates money to (1) health authorities and (2) GP fund-holders to enable them to purchase

[72] This question is discussed in *Priority Setting in the NHS: The NHS Drug Budget* (HC 80–vii, Session 1993–94) 309–311.

[73] See M. Whitehead, 'Who Cares About Equity in the NHS?', 308 *British Medical Journal* 1284 (1994).

[74] Subject to *The Patient's Charter*, which guarantees 'admission for treatment by a specific date no later than two years from the day when your consultant places you on a waiting list'. *Patient's Charter*, *supra* note 65, 10. See also *Implementing the Patient's Charter* (HSG(92)4, NHSME). These standards do not confer legal rights on patients.

[75] *A Formula for Distributing NHS Revenues Based on Small Area Use of Hospital Beds* (University of York, 1994), para. 2.2.

(or commission) health care from hospitals on behalf of patients. Each is considered in turn.

1. Health Authorities

The National Health Service Act 1977 provides that it is the Secretary of State's duty to pay in respect of each financial year: 'to each Regional Health Authority . . . sums not exceeding the amount allotted by him to the Authority for that year towards meeting the expenditure attributable to the performance by the Authority of their functions in that year.'[76]

Correspondingly, it is the duty of each RHA to pay to each of its DHAs and FHSAs the amount allotted by it to meet the expenditure incurred by their functions;[77] and FHSAs must pay GP fund-holding practices an 'allotted sum' representing the fund for which they have accepted responsibility.[78] The small minority of hospitals remaining within a district health authority continue to receive their funding from that source.

The distribution of NHS resources is calculated on the basis of a weighted capitation formula[79] which assesses health needs according to: (i) the projected size of the population concerned, (ii) the numbers of elderly people in the population, (iii) the health needs of the population measured by 'standardised mortality ratios' as an indication of the extent of morbidity, and (iv) an allowance for the higher costs of the Thames Regions. Weighting for age allows more for those who are 75 and over. Some say that such a

[76] National Health Service Act 1977, s. 97(1)(a) as substituted by Health Services Act 1980, s. 6(1) and (5) and amended by the Health and Social Security Act 1984, s. 24, sched.8, para. (aa) and the National Health Service Act 1990, ss. 13 and 19(2). Slightly different provisions apply to Wales, in which there are no RHAs.

[77] See 1977 Act, s. 97(2) as amended by 1990 Act, s. 19(3). RHAs, DHAs, and FHSAs are under a duty to remain within the limits of funding, see 1977 Act, ss. 97A and 97B (added by the Health Services Act 1980 s. 6 and the Health and Social Security Act 1984, s. 5, sched. 3, para. 10 respectively).

[78] See 1990 Act, s. 15(1) as amended by the National Health Service (Fund-holding Practices) Regulations 1993 (SI 1993, No. 567), reg. 26(3), discussed below.

[79] See R. Carr-Hill, 'RAWP is Dead: Long Live RAWP', in A. Culyer, A. Maynard, J. Posnett (eds.), *Competition in Health Care—Reforming the NHS* (Macmillan, 1990) 192.

weighting in favour of elderly people is illogical, because it attributes too much significance to age, and insufficient weight to social deprivation.

Because mortality rates are consistently higher for poorer occupational classes among both men and women, areas that have higher proportions of the population in manual occupational classes have 'younger' age profiles because they are less healthy, i.e. more people die at a younger age. Under the national capitation formula such areas are discriminated against. . . .

[T]he national formula automatically works against poor districts because affluent districts tend to survive longer than deprived populations . . . and experience lower levels of ill health.[80]

Some of these criticisms have been accepted by the Government, which proposes to reform the system in order to shift the allocation of resources from the South to the North of the country.[81] No doubt there will be misgivings, no matter what formula of allocation is used. However, it is difficult to conceive of circumstances in which the reforms could be successfully challenged, for example by a region which considered it had received inadequate funding. An analogous issue arose concerning expenditure guidance issued by the Secretary of State for the Environment to local authorities, which was challenged as being unreasonable. Lord Scarman dealt with the claim as follows:

We are in the field of public financial administration and we are being asked to review the exercise by the Secretary of State of an administrative discretion which inevitably requires political judgment on his part. . . . I cannot accept that it is constitutionally appropriate, save in very exceptional circumstances, for the courts to intervene on the ground of 'unreasonableness' to quash guidance framed by the Secretary of State and by necessary implication approved by the House of Commons, the guidance being concerned with the limits of public expenditure by local authorities and the incidence of the tax burden as between taxpayers and ratepayers . . . these are matters of political judgment for him and for the

---

[80] See *A Fairer Way of Funding the NHS: A Closer Look at Weighted Capitation Funding* (Association of Community Health Councils, 1992) 4.

[81] See *HCHS Revenue Resource Allocation: Weighted Capitation Formula* (NHSE, 1994). The report is based on *A Formula for Distributing NHS Revenues Based on Small Area Use of Hospital Beds* (University of York, 1994). See also 'A New Approach to Weighted Capitation' 309 *British Medical Journal* 1031 (1994).

House of Commons. They are not matters for the judges. . . . I refuse in this case to examine the detail of the guidance or its consequences.[82]

On the other hand, different arguments could arise if the Secretary of State were to change the basis on which funds were distributed during the course of the financial year in a way that prejudiced the efficient management of the health service. In this unlikely event, an action for judicial review could be considered on the ground that the Secretary of State was estopped from going back on his word,[83] or that the health authority had a legitimate expectation that funds would be forthcoming.[84]

2. GP Fund-holders

Purchasing power in the system is said to be increased and refined if GPs are given their own health service resources to manage because they, rather than a remote health authority, are able to make the arrangements with hospitals which best suit the practice and its patients. This has been made possible by the introduction of GP fund-holding. Fund-holding practices are allotted funds annually, as determined by the RHA.[85] Inevitably, fund-holding gives GPs a much more explicit role in the management of NHS resources. For the moment, no precise formula exists by which the allotment can be made and the process allows for reference to past referral patterns, mortality and morbidity statistics, and a good deal of hard bargaining.[86]

Practices must satisfy a number of conditions in order to become eligible to apply for fund-holding status,[87] and their funds are

---

[82] *R* v. *Secretary of State for the Environment,* ex p. *Nottinghamshire County Council* [1986] AC 240, 247. And see the consideration of the case in *R* v. *Secretary of State for the Environment,* ex p. *Hammersmith and Fulham London Borough Council* [1991] 1 AC 521.

[83] *Laker Airways* v. *Department of Trade* [1976] QB 643.

[84] See *R* v. *Secretary of State for Health* ex p. *United Tobacco International Inc* [1992] 1 QB 353, *R* v. *Secretary of State for the Home Department,* ex p. *Asif Mahmood Khan* [1984] 1 WLR 1337.

[85] National Health Service and Community Care Act 1990, s.15(1) as amended by the National Health Service (Fund-holding Practices) Regulations 1993 (SI 1993, No. 567), reg.26(3), under the powers made available in s. 17 of the 1990 Act.

[86] See *General Practitioner Fundholding in England, supra* note 62, ch. 3.

[87] See s.14, 1990 Act and the National Health Service (Fund-holding Practices) Regulations 1993 (SI 1993, No.567), Part II and sched.1. A detailed appeal procedure to the Secretary of State is available to those whose applications are refused, see ibid. reg. 7.

closely regulated by FHSAs. These matters are discussed in Chapter 6 below.

B. Funding Providers of Health Care

The providers of health care are mainly hospitals. The following considers (1) NHS 'contracts', (2) NHS Trust hospitals, (3) competition from private hospitals, and (4) raising revenue from patients.

1. NHS 'Contracts'

What are 'NHS contracts' and to what extent do they resemble contracts at common law? We consider (i) the parties to NHS contracts, (ii) the contracts, and (iii) resolving disputes concerning NHS contracts.

(i) The Parties

The new system of contract funding in the NHS requires hospitals to earn their revenue by selling goods and services to purchasers of health care by entering 'NHS contracts': 'the phrase "NHS contract" means an agreement under which one health service body ("the acquirer") arranges for the provision to it by another health service body ("the provider") of goods and services which it reasonably requires for the purposes of its functions.'[88]

'Health service body' means any of the following:

(a) a health authority;
(b) a health board;
(c) the Common Services Agency for the Scottish Health Service;
(d) a Family Health Services Authority;
(e) an NHS Trust;
(f) a recognised fund-holding practice;
(g) the Dental Practice Board or the Scottish Dental Practice Board;
(h) the Public Health Laboratory Service Board; or
(i) the Secretary of State.[89]

NHS contracts are intended to enable the parties to agree on matters of quality, quantity, and cost. They introduce pressures

---

[88] S. 4(1), 1990 Act.   [89] Ibid. s. 4(2).

common to ordinary business contracts between commercial parties. Parties may have to make compromises between competing objectives. Perhaps the quantity of a particular service ought to be reduced to expand facilities elsewhere; or prices ought to be reduced to attract more custom. Similarly, there is the need to balance administrative and transaction costs (the costs of setting up, operating, and monitoring the service) with the money devoted to the services themselves. However, the matter 'should not be approached as a legalistic or adversarial exercise but as an opportunity to discuss and agree how improvements to patient care can be secured and over what time'.[90] Clearly, NHS contracts will force the parties to be explicit about the services which they wish to provide and, by implication, those which they do not. In this respect, they make more visible than ever before the decisions made about which patients should be treated when demand for health care exceeds the resources available.

(ii) The Contracts

An average hospital works with around 30 NHS contracts.[91] Parties to NHS contracts may undertake such obligations as they see fit, but three models of contract have been suggested as the suitable means of commencing the process: i.e. 'block contracts', 'cost and volume contracts', and 'cost per case contracts'.

Block contracts. These are agreements in which hospital units undertake to provide an unlimited or a maximum, number of facilities, over a specified period of time. Under these arrangements DHAs may commit resources to a hospital provider irrespective of the actual usage of the facilities, and will consequently have difficulty in being precise with respect to quality. The block contract in its most simple form, should be replaced by more sophisticated agreements in which standards of performance are monitored more accurately and terms may be adjusted according to agreed maxima and minima.[92] Thus, a single contract may

---

[90] *Contracts for Health Services: Operating Contracts* (EL(90)MB/24, NHSME, 1990) 1.

[91] See J. Appleby, *Developing Contracting—A National Survey of District Health Authorities, Boards and NHS Trusts* (NAHAT, 1994) 10.

[92] See J. Appleby, P. Smith *et al.*, 'Monitoring Managed Competition', in R. Robinson and J. Le Grand (eds.), *Evaluating the NHS Reforms* (King's Fund Institute, 1994), ch. 2. See also *Developing Contracting, supra* note 91, 27.

guarantee a range of out-patient services for a price to be paid at monthly intervals. Block contracts for patients treated in the hospital may be distinguished by the department in which treatment is given. For example, radiology services may be provided for £20,000 on the assumption that 800 patients will be referred. The contract may provide that if the department is able to exceed an 'indicated workload', and deal with more than a specified number of patients, then additional treatments will be provided at a discounted rate. On the other hand, if it fails to provide a stated minimum of treatments by a certain date, the contract may be deemed to have been broken and be made subject to renegotiation by the purchaser.

Cost and volume contracts. These set out agreements for the provision of a particular service or services for a specific price. The emphasis is on output, in that the parties agree to a specific requirement for an exact price. 'The various advantages to both contracting parties—the opportunity for DHAs to link payment with activity; and for units to match funding to workload and deploy their resources more flexibly—suggest that cost and volume contracts are likely to be widely used as negotiating skills improve and more detailed information becomes available.'[93]

Depending on the size of the contract, some latitude may be included to allow for slight over- or under-performance, so that performance of between 97 per cent and 103 per cent will not give rise to adjustment of the terms originally agreed. Modification as to price may be agreed outside these limits. Arrangements of this nature may enable quality to be monitored by reference to, for example, waiting times, admission and discharge procedures, the facilities provided to patients, out-patients clinics, correspondence with referring doctors, and the provision of performance data to DHAs.[94] For the moment, data which compares the quality of clinical care and outcomes is not available.

Cost per case contracts. Individually agreed contracts may be used most frequently by fund-holding GPs. Because they inevitably carry larger transaction costs they will be less commonly used by DHAs, although they will often be the basis on which extra

---

[93] *Contracts for Health Services, supra* note 90, para. 3.38.
[94] See *The Patient's Charter: Hospital and Ambulance Services—Comparative Performance Guide 1993–94* (NHS Executive, 1994).

contractual referrals are priced, in which patients are referred to hospitals with which the DHA has no existing NHS contract. In general, purchasers may be reluctant to enter cost per case contracts on a day by day basis, for fear of losing control over their resources. The alternative is to use the contract as a means of negotiating entire episodes of care, with the emphasis on the provider to assess the average cost of each episode, allowing for occasional complications, or to refine cost and volume contracts after specified threshold targets have been achieved. For some categories of care it is impossible to predict for how long a patient will require treatment, for example the intensive care of new-borns and the treatment of cystic fibrosis.[95] A cost per case agreement in cases of this nature can expose one or other of the parties to considerable risk. Some hospitals have had to return to DHAs to renegotiate the costs involved in providing expensive treatments over extended periods of time.

No matter what the type of contract, there is a serious problem in costing the care provided. As a rule, hospital prices should be based on actual costs and there should be no cross-subsidization from one (profitable) contract to another.[96] However, the process of pricing is complex and entirely new. Parties to NHS contracts have had to learn how to assess the value of their agreements very quickly. Given the shortage of reliable information about costs and prices, accurate costing of hospital activity is extremely difficult.[97] For the present, the majority of hospitals charge according to the specific procedure, or programme of procedures, provided to patients.[98] For the future, however, there is interest in a method of costing developed in America based on what are known as diagnosis related groups (DRGs). As statistical information about large groups of patients accumulates, it may be possible to divide patients between clinical categories which accurately predict the type and duration of care which will be required. In America, some twenty-three major diagnostic categories have been used, sub-divided into 468 DRGs, depending on such factors

---

[95] See *Access and Availability of Specialist Services* (Clinical Services Advisory Group, 1993).

[96] See *Costing and Pricing Contracts: Cost Allocation Principles* (EL(90)173, NHSME, 1990).

[97] See *Markets and NHSME Guidelines—Costs and Prices in the NHS Internal Market* (University of York, Centre for Health Economics, 1994).

[98] See *Developing Contracting, supra* note 91, 14.

as age, need for surgery, and secondary diagnoses, which reflect the relative intensity of the services required.[99] Prices may then be fixed, according to the DRG to which the patient is assigned. Patient idiosyncrasies mean that some will cost more, others less. Total overall costs, however, should be covered by the average cost of each patient. A modified version of the idea is being considered in the UK, referred to as 'Healthcare Resource Groups'.

The theory is attractive, but the practice is more difficult. As the case of *Wickline*[100] suggests, DRGs may lead to under-treatment or premature discharge, because hospital revenue is fixed and not dependent on the exceptional treatment required by one individual. It may also cause over-treatment by the phenomenon of 'DRG creep'. Patients may be assigned to more expensive categories of care which they do not require in order that they may be discharged early and generate greater revenue for the hospital. These shortcomings could be managed by sophisticated systems of oversight. On the other hand, the costs involved in setting up and supervising the system are likely to be extremely high. The advantages of DRGs will have to be clear and significant before the benefits will be seen to justify the cost.

(iii) Resolving Disputes

In commerce, it is perfectly legitimate to exploit weaknesses in another party's position to achieve financial advantage so that the gain of one is at the expense of the other. NHS contracts cannot be understood in this way. They are agreements between partners in a common enterprise, with identical objectives.[101] Disputes, therefore, ought to be rare.[102] Nevertheless, parties to NHS contracts will be keen to ensure that the terms of their agreements are adhered to. DHAs and GP fund-holders will monitor the performance of the hospitals to which patients have been sent with a view to encouraging improvements in standards, or a change of hospital if performance is unsatisfactory. And hospitals themselves

---

[99] See A. Vladeck, 'Medicare Hospital Payment by Diagnosis Related Groups', 100 *Annals of Internal Medicine* 576 (1984).

[100] Discussed in Chapter 3.

[101] There is anecdotal evidence that this lesson is still being learned by health managers from the commercial sector.

[102] In an incomplete national survey, 15 per cent of providers had used arbitration in 1992/3. See *Developing Contracting*, *supra* note 91, 16.

may make 'tertiary referrals' of patients who need specialist treatment to other hospitals with particular expertise. They too will want to safeguard quality. Each will want to receive the goods and services paid for in the right quantity and quality, and at the right time. In cases of dispute, what action may be taken if an amicable settlement between the parties is impossible?

The 1990 Act removes the possibility of disputes over NHS contracts from proceeding to the courts. It provides:

Whether or not an arrangement which constitutes an NHS contract would, apart from this subsection, be a contract in law, it shall not be regarded for any purposes as giving rise to contractual rights and liabilities, but if any dispute arises with respect to such an arrangement, either party may refer the matter to the Secretary of State for determination.[103]

An adjudication may: 'contain such directions (including directions as to payment) as the Secretary of State or, as the case may be, the person appointed under subsection (5) . . . considers appropriate to resolve the matter in dispute; and it shall be the duty of the parties to the NHS contract in question to comply with any such directions.'[104]

The adjudicator also has authority to vary the terms of an NHS contract, or bring it to an end.[105] In addition to these rules, a procedure is available to negotiators who consider that:

(a) the terms proposed by another health service body are unfair by reason that the other party is seeking to take advantage of its position as the only, or the only practicable, provider of the goods and services concerned or by reason of any other unequal bargaining position as between the prospective parties to the proposed arrangement, or

(b) that for any other reason arising out of the relative bargaining position of the prospective parties any of the terms of the proposed arrangement cannot be agreed . . . [106]

The procedure by which disputes should be resolved is set down in regulations,[107] but no substantive guidelines have been suggested

---

[103] National Health Service and Community Care Act 1990, s. 4(3). The matter may be determined either by the Secretary of State, or by his appointee. See s. 4(5), 1990 Act. [104] See s. 4(7), 1990 Act.
[105] See s. 4(8), 1990 Act. [106] See s. 4(4), 1990 Act.
[107] See the National Health Service Contracts (Dispute Resolution) Regulations 1991 (SI 1991, No.725).

as a means of settlement. The explanatory notes state, rather ambiguously, that the adjudicator's decisions 'will not constitute precedents for the determination of other disputes, but they will be useful learning tools for all parties in reaching a shared understanding of the ways contracts might develop.'[108]

The Act does not exclude the right to natural justice, and judicial review is available to parties who consider they have been dealt with unfairly. Both parties must be heard in order for the adjudicator to have a balanced view of the dispute[109]; and the adjudication must be fair, in the sense that it must be truly independent of the parties.[110] Given that one of the parties to an NHS contract may be the Secretary of State, particular care will be required by the courts to ensure independence. There is a 'presumption . . . that the outcome will give effect to the agreement which was originally reached, rather than a new agreement which the parties should have reached.'[111] Some measure of consistency ought to exist between adjudications. If similar cases were treated inconsistently, the matter could be referred to judicial review.[112] In this way a common stock of responses to NHS contractual disputes might accumulate for the benefit of the parties.

Some have suggested that, although the courts are excluded from intervening in the substance of NHS contracts, there remains the possibility of a party avoiding the law of contract by pursuing a remedy in the law of restitution.[113] Such an action does not depend on the existence of a contract but it is capable of achieving similar objectives: the payment of money for the value of goods or services which the other party has received and from which he has taken benefit. Common law dislikes one party being unjustly

---

[108] See *NHS Contracts: Arrangements for Resolving Disputes*, HO 302/6 and EL (91)11 (NHSME, 1991).

[109] *Ridge* v. *Baldwin* [1964] AC 40, *Schmidt* v. *Secretary of State* [1969] 2 Ch 149.

[110] *R* v. *Kent Police Authority*, ex p *Gooden* [1971] 2 QB 662, *Metropolitan Properties Co (FGC) Ltd* v. *Lannon and Others* [1969] 1 QB 577.

[111] *NHS Contracts: Arrangements for Resolving Disputes*, *supra* note 108. Presumably, such an inflexible presumption would not apply if it effected the services made available to patients.

[112] See *Metropolitan Properties Ltd.* v. *Lannon* [1969] 1 QB 577, which concerned consistency between levels of rent established by rent assessment committees.

[113] J. Jacob, 'Lawyers go to Hospital', [1991] *Public Law* 255, 274.

enriched at the expense of another. Even when the legislation has precluded the existence of a contract, courts have sympathized with the plaintiff and provided a remedy in restitution.[114] Arguably therefore, assuming NHS contracts to be contracts at common law,[115] the exclusion from litigation of 'contractual rights' does not exclude other remedies available to the parties.[116]

On the other hand, the policy promoted by the Act is to exclude the courts from resolving disputes between parties to NHS contracts. It would be strange if, given two identical disputes, one alone were actionable simply by reason of the plea of restitution, rather than breach of contract, in the statement of claim. Such a ploy would undermine the intention of the Act and, incidentally, exclude complaints based on executory contracts (i.e. those to be performed in the future) and who had yet to confer benefit on the other party. This seems arbitrary. Thus, the courts will be reluctant to enable the intention of the Act to be bypassed in this way and will allow the internal system to operate 'provided they are satisfied that such claims can be enforced in another way; and provided they retain the ultimate power to review statutory arbitration decisions which are irrational, or beyond the powers of the arbitrator'.[117]

2. Competition from Private Hospitals

Private hospitals are free to offer their services to Health authorities and GP fund-holders, and so add to the competition in the market for health care. Private hospitals are not 'health service bodies',[118] and therefore cannot enter into NHS contracts. Nevertheless, they make a significant contribution to the work of

---

[114] See the Australian case of *Pavey & Mathews* v. *Paul* [1986] 162 CLR 221. See also *Delgman* v. *Guaranty Trust Co of Canada* [1954] 3 DLR 785.

[115] Arguably, NHS contracts are not contracts at common law, in which a fundamental requirement is the freedom of the parties to enter the contract and negotiate terms. Complete freedom does not exist in relation to NHS contracts because the parties have to enter agreements in order to fulfil their responsibilities. See *Pfizer* v. *Minister of Health* [1965] AC 512.

[116] See *Metropolitan Film Studios Ltd* v. *Twickenham Film Studios Ltd* [1962] 1 WLR 1315, 1323, and *Allen* v. *Thorn Electrical Industries Ltd* [1968] 1 QB 487.

[117] See K. Barker, 'NHS Contracts, Restitution and the Internal Market', 56 *Modern Law Review* 832, 840 (1993).

[118] Under s. 4, 1990 Act.

the NHS. Nearly a tenth of the UK's health care is provided by the independent sector.[119] In the past, its main contribution has been in the provision of nursing homes for the elderly and hospices. Arrangements made with private hospitals have often been short-term, designed to relieve occasional pressure on NHS institutions. In 1986, however, the government introduced the Waiting List Initiative under which sums of money were made available annually to ease pressures caused by long lists[120] and there has been an increase in private elective care, a development which has been actively encouraged by the government.[121]

NHS care may be provided by private hospitals and providers as follows: 'The Secretary of State may, where he considers it appropriate, arrange with any person or body (including a voluntary organisation) for that person or body to provide, or assist in providing, any service under this Act.'[122]

Facilities, including goods, materials, plant, apparatus, and premises may be made available for this purpose on such terms as may be agreed, including the making of payments by or to the Secretary of State.[123] In future, the traditional split between public and private providers will be more difficult to recognize. NHS patients may receive treatment in private hospitals, and staff engaged by private health companies may provide NHS care. The government has encouraged the use of private providers because external competition is thought to enhance quality by increasing the range of options available to patients and their GPs, as well as enabling different institutions to learn from one another.[124] The National Audit Office analysed Waiting List cases in the private sector in 1987–9 and found that the average cost per case for independent sector deals was 94 per cent higher than that for NHS deals.[125] The higher cost may represent good value in the sense

---

[119] *NHS Made Easy* (NHSME, 1992), para.35.

[120] See *The NHS and Independent Hospitals* (National Audit Office, HC 106, 1989).

[121] In 1988, some 17 per cent of all elective surgery was carried out by the independent sector at a cost of around £50 m. to the NHS. Ibid. paras. 2(3) and 2(8). [122] See National Health Service Act 1977, s. 23(1).

[123] See s. 23(2) and (3), 1977 Act .5

[124] See *Working for Patients* (Cm. 555, 1989), ch. 9.

[125] *The NHS and Independent Hospitals, supra* note 120, para. 2.19. The average cost per case was: NHS, £218.76; independent sector, £423.42. See ibid. Table 5.

that patients are treated more quickly, but as the National Audit Office has said: 'For longer term arrangements, there is a risk to value for money if private sector proposals are not subject to full evaluation against alternatives, including the use of facilities in other health authorities.'[126]

To date, these arrangements have had little or no impact on overall strategy in the health service. Interest has been shown, however, in schemes in which the capital cost and use of expensive equipment could be shared, joint ventures could be undertaken to pay for new hospital developments, and screening services could be purchased from independent laboratories. Clearly, agreements of this nature could introduce an entirely new form of relationship between the NHS and the private sector. One reason to encourage this collaboration is 'because it relieves pressure on the NHS'.[127] On the other hand, if the private hospitals were to undergo significant expansion, it would be natural for a government to reconsider the funding needed by the NHS. Presumably, a unit in a hospital which found itself unable to compete with a service provided by a private facility would find it difficult to sustain funding. Purchasers would send their patients to the less expensive alternative and the revenue to the NHS unit would decline.[128] The logic of this development is that a significant quantity of NHS care could be purchased from private providers whose hospital services have tended to exclude those with chronic illnesses, and over whom the government, and the *Patient's Charter*, have no power. In this sense, although private services may reduce pressure on the NHS in the short term, the longer-term threat ought to be recognized.

Manpower is also a consideration. Nearly all the basic pre-qualification training undertaken by doctors and nurses is provided and paid for by the NHS. This training costs around £450 million for nurses and £300 million for doctors. The private sector

---

[126] Ibid. para. 6.

[127] *Working for Patients, supra* note 124, para. 9.4.

[128] Obviously, much of the activity of the private sector will be designed for profit. It will not, therefore, tend to be involved in the care of those with chronic ill health (i.e. long-term and resistant to treatment). There has been 'no consideration of the problem of the relationship between a private sector concentrating on the potentially lucrative and easier elective surgery and a public sector which has to deal with priority care services and the elderly.' See *Resourcing the National Health Service, supra* note 47, para. 2.38.

is heavily dependent on the expertise of nurses and doctors drawn from the NHS. It depends on the work of some 12,000 NHS consultants (85 per cent) for specialist work,[129] but there is no requirement for the private sector to contribute to the cost of training.[130] If the private sector continues to expand in the future, and absorbs larger numbers of medical staff from the NHS, it may be expected to pay a proportion of the cost of their training, in return for its access to NHS patients.

3. Raising Revenue from Patients

Quite apart from the funds generated from NHS contracts with health authorities and GP fund-holders, hospitals in the NHS may raise revenue from (i) private patients and (ii) NHS patients.

(i) Private Care in NHS Hospitals

As a general rule services provided to patients in the NHS 'shall be free of charge except in so far as the making and receiving of charges is expressly provided for by or under any enactment.'[131] However, private fee-paying care may be provided in NHS hospitals. Thus, to such extent as it may determine:

a District or Special Health Authority may make available at a hospital or hospitals for which they have responsibility accommodation and services for patients who give undertakings (or for whom undertakings are given) to pay, in respect of the accommodation and services made available, such charges as the Authority may determine . . . on any basis that the Authority considers to be the appropriate commercial basis.[132]

Similarly, under arrangements made with medical or dental practitioners, a health authority may allow accommodation and services to be made available for the treatment of private patients

---

[129] See *The NHS and Independent Hospitals*, *supra* note 120, para. 3.22.
[130] Ibid. para. 2.47.
[131] S. 1(2), 1977 Act. See also ss. 25, 63, 65, 77–83, and sched. 12 for circumstances in which fees may be charged.
[132] See s. 65(1) 1977 Act, as amended by the Health and Medicines Act 1988, s. 7(10) and the National Health Service and Community Care Act 1990, s. 25(2). Agreements may also be entered into with respect to goods, land, and other services 'in order to make income available for improving the health service . . .' See Medicines Act 1988, s. 7(2).

of the practitioner.[133] Beds may be used for private fee-paying patients in a way that is indistinguishable from normal NHS facilities; or whole wards or wings may be dedicated to private use. Beds, wards, or units utilized in this way are a source of revenue for hospitals, and the Secretary of State has power to direct that activities of this nature are undertaken.[134] For the moment, the numbers of complete units dedicated to private care is relatively small. At the beginning of 1994 there were believed to be seventy dedicated NHS pay-bed units in NHS hospitals with a total of 1,328 beds.[135] The units are generally managed by the hospitals themselves, although they may have private staffing arrangements. Total income from this source amounted to £164 million in the year 1992/3.[136] In the past, private hospital care has tended to concentrate on acute (curable) conditions, rather than chronic (long-term) ones. If an NHS hospital[137] were to allow its resources to be substantially turned over to private care, it would risk compromising the care of those with intractable conditions. This is not necessarily serious provided that purchasers of care are able to refer such patients for treatment elsewhere.

The power of a district health authority to use facilities for private care is restricted. It can permit facilities to be used in this way only if and to the extent that the Authority is satisfied that to do so:

(a) will not to a significant extent interfere with the performance by the Authority of any function conferred on the Authority under [the 1977] Act to provide accommodation or services of any kind; and

(b) will not to a significant extent operate to the disadvantage of persons seeking or afforded admission or access to accommodation or

---

[133] S. 65(2) 1977 Act, as amended by the Health and Medicines Act 1988, s. 7(2) and the National Health Service and Community Care Act 1990, s. 25(5).

[134] See the Health and Medicines Act 1988, s. 7(3).

[135] See *Laing's Review of Private Health Care* (Laing and Buisson, London, 1994) 112. Previously, section 75 of the National Health Service Act 1977 required a register of private use to be kept. The provision was repealed by the Health Services Act 1980. No other central record of private use of NHS facilities appears to have been kept.

[136] Ibid. 99.

[137] For the comparable power to generate revenue in relation to NHS Trust hospitals see the National Health Service and Community Care Act 1990, sched. 2, para. 14.

services at health service hospitals (whether as resident or non-resident patients) otherwise than under this section.[138]

No identical restriction exists concerning NHS Trust hospitals,[139] which make up the vast majority of all NHS hospitals. Given their obligation to 'ensure that [their] revenue is not less than sufficient, taking one financial year with another, to meet outgoings properly chargeable to revenue account',[140] there may be an incentive for them to use fee-paying patients as a means of balancing their books.[141] Conceivably, commercial incentives could induce an NHS Trust to allocate its resources to fee-paying patients in a way that interfered with the duty imposed on the Secretary of State to provide a 'comprehensive health service'[142] and this may create concern. However, each NHS Trust has a duty to: 'comply with any directions given to it by the Secretary of State with respect to . . . compliance with guidance or directions given (by circular or otherwise) to health authorities, or particular descriptions of health authorities.'[143] This enables the Secretary of State to interfere with the strategy adopted by an NHS Trust hospital, but it is not at all clear to what extent he or she may be inclined to undermine the natural pressures of the market.

(ii) Revenue from NHS Care

The Secretary of State may authorize certain accommodation to be made available for patients: 'and recover such charges as he may

---

[138] S. 65(1) 1977 Act, as substituted by the Health and Medicines Act 1988 s. 7, and amended by the National Health Service and Community Care Act 1990, s. 25(2). If the powers are exercised by the Secretary of State, the same restrictions apply; see the Health and Medicines Act 1988, s. 7(8)(a).

[139] See s. 65(4), 1977 Act, added by the National Health Service and Community Care Act 1990, s. 66(1), sched. 9, para. 18(4).

[140] See National Health Service and Community Care Act 1990, s. 10.

[141] Spending by NHS Trust hospitals on private health care rose by 265 per cent between 1991–2 and 1992–3, i.e. from around £12 m. to £44 m. The comparable increase by district health authorities was 17 per cent, from around £160 m. to £187 m. See 'NHS Trust Spending on Private Care up by 265% in a Year', *News Release* (The Labour Party, 22 Dec. 1993).

[142] See s. 1, 1977 Act, discussed in chapter 4.

[143] National Health Service and Community Care Act 1990, Sched. 2, para. 6(2)(f). But see also the National Health Service Act 1977, s. 72 in relation to private, non-resident patients, with respect to whom permission to treat must be sought from the Secretary of State and is subject to restrictions.

determine in respect of such accommodation and calculate them on any basis that he considers to be the appropriate commercial basis.'[144] In this way, income may be generated from NHS patients who choose, for example, to be treated in a private room or a small ward, not otherwise needed by any patient on medical grounds. Income from the use of NHS beds for paying patients has increased steadily, from around £78 million in 1988–9, to £157 million in 1992–3.

[144] S. 63(1), 1977 Act, as amended by the Health and Medicines Act 1988, s. 7(9).
[145] A full break-down of statistics by year and by region is supplied by the Secretary of State in a Parliamentary written answer at *Hansard, House of Commons*, 31 Jan. 1994, vol. 236, col. 532 (WA). This form of business activity may work against private hospitals.

3

Common Law Regulation of Standards

'Value for money' has become a catch-phrase of the market place. The logic of the internal market for health is to drive prices down and quality up. In theory, those hospitals whose prices are uncompetitive, or whose quality standards are poor, will tend to lose customers. Accordingly, there is pressure on hospitals to understand the nature of the products and services which they provide, as well as those of their competitors. If their costs appear high, hospital managers will want to know why, and also how they might be reduced. As we saw in Chapter 2, however, 'pure' market principles are impossible in health care. There is insufficient knowledge amongst 'consumers' for informed judgments to be made and, in any case, there may be good political, economic, or health reasons to modify or reverse market trends. Even when changes in working practices do bring about improvements, the logic of competition discourages hospitals from sharing their knowledge with others. The prospect of enabling a competitor to improve its performance and threaten one's own position has a contrary effect. Although the Department of Health encourages altruism between providers for the benefit of the service as a whole,[1] anecdotal evidence suggests that hospitals are reluctant to practise it. This suggests that the market may encourage activity intended to preserve financial stability, but it cannot guarantee high standards for patients. There is, therefore, a continuing need to understand the problems which scarcity brings.

I. CONCERN FOR QUALITY IN THE NHS

There has long been concern for quality in the NHS. In 1988, for example, the National Audit Office noted the increasing awareness of the need to monitor, appraise, and review in a positive way

---

[1] See *Working Together for Better Health* (Department of Health, 1993).

the quality of care provided by the National Health Service. However, it said 'there is no widely recognised definition of "quality of care", and within local initiatives there have been marked differences in approach and coverage.'[2] A variety of recent reports have illustrated precisely how patients may suffer when facilities, or staff, cannot be made available. The British Paediatric Association, for example, reported that:

Every children's intensive care unit in the UK reported having refused admission to critically ill children in the period 1991–1992. The reason most commonly given for refusing admissions was a shortage of both beds and nursing staff. . . . [M]any units informed us that one or more of their beds are, in effect, permanently closed, because of lack of staff. Even those beds which were open were often grossly understaffed.[3]

Similarly, in its comprehensive annual report, the *Confidential Enquiry into Perioperative Deaths* for 1987 established that although the number of patients who die following anaesthesia and surgery is low (out of an estimated 485,850 operations, 4,034 patients died within thirty days of surgery, most of whom were elderly) many are avoidable. Surgeon assessors considered that in 22 per cent of deaths examined there were avoidable factors in the management of the patient which might have affected the outcome.

The enquiry team identified: (a) differences between the regions in the overall mortality rates and marked variations in the levels of 'avoidable' mortality reported in the different districts; (b) important differences in clinical practice between the three regional health authorities; (c) examples of surgeons operating for conditions for which they were not trained or performing operations outside their field of primary expertise, and some instances of moribund or terminally ill patients having operations that would not improve their condition; (d) important differences in the consultants' supervision of trainees, for example deaths occurred where junior surgeons or anaesthetists had not sought the advice of their consultants or senior registrars at any time before, during or after

---

[2] *Quality of Clinical Care in National Health Service Hospitals* (National Audit Office, HC 736, 1988) 6.

[3] *The Care of the Critically Ill* (British Paediatric Association, 1994) 40. The cost of paediatric intensive care is significantly less than neonatal intensive care in which low birth-weight babies need care for months, rather than days; for which see *Neonatal Intensive Care: Access to and Availability of Services* (Clinical Services Advisory Group, 1993).

the operations; (e) the pre-operative assessment and resuscitation of patients by doctors was sometimes compromised by undue haste to operate.[4]

Concern has also been expressed about the standard of care in some accident and emergency units. In a survey of the treatment of skeletal trauma following serious accidents, the British Orthopaedic Association studied 800 patients selected at random. Medical assessors were asked to decide how many patients suffered morbidity following treatment and whether it would have been preventable using proper methods of management. Their results were as follows.

50% of patients had no morbidity at all, often as a result of good treatment. 30% were judged to have morbidity which was inevitable regardless of facilities, treatment etc. However, in some 20% of patients the assessors judged that the morbidity could have been less with ideal treatment and in 12% this was of significant proportions affecting the quality of their life, work, independence etc.

The assessors were asked to judge how treatment could have been improved. . . . Of the 98 patients (12%) with severe preventable morbidity, our assessors felt that 55 patients had been treated by people with inadequate training and special interest to obtain a good result.[5]

The report notes that 'the figures from our survey suggest that some 900,000 injuries occur each year of sufficient severity to require referral to a fracture department and if 12% of these have significant preventable disability this amounts to 108,000 [patients] per year, which gives some insight into the level of unnecessary and avoidable expenditure [caused by remedial treatment and lost earnings].'[6] The major causes of these failings were identified as inadequacies with respect to staffing,[7] workload,[8] facilities,[9] and organisation.[10] (Footnotes 8–10 appear on page 80).

---

[4] This summary is taken from *Quality of Clinical Care in National Health Service Hospitals*, *supra* note 2, 10. See also *Anaphylactic Reactions Associated with Anaesthesia* (Association of Anaesthetists of Great Britain and Ireland, 1990).

[5] *The Management of Skeletal Trauma in the United Kingdom* (British Orthopaedic Association, 1993) 33.

[6] Ibid. at 36.

[7] 'The overall level of staffing is too low to provide a satisfactory level of service. . . . Many units which were obliged to provide a 24 hour trauma service for all comers are frequently too small to sustain an adequate standard [and] duty rosters

Similarly, some ambulance services often find it difficult to reach the scene of an emergency within the period specified by the *Patient's Charter*, namely fourteen minutes for urban areas, and nine minutes in rural areas.[11] In one instance an ambulance arrived 53 minutes after the initial 999 call from a young girl suffering a serious kidney condition. By the time she arrived in hospital her condition had become irretrievable and she died early the next morning. The failure was made the subject of the *Report on the London Ambulance Service*[12] which noted serious failings in the systems of management adopted by the service. There was no procedure for prioritizing calls, indeed the nature of the information taken over the telephone did not enable priorities to be determined. Ambulances were often despatched to calls that could not be described as emergency cases at the expense of those in genuine need of emergency care. Standards of call-taking were poor so that the information supplied to those responsible for allocating and despatching ambulances was inadequate. Amongst those working in the emergency room, no single person was responsible for linking the several 999 calls made in this case. The report made a number of recomendations for improving the management and organization of the service.

Obviously, in all these cases improved levels of care could be provided if additional resources were made available. Responsible medical experts will often be prepared to say that the level of services provided by a unit was unacceptable. However, in the current and foreseeable circumstances, more has to be achieved with relatively fewer resources. In the light of these circumstances,

---

for consultants were too onerous to be in the interests of the surgeon concerned or his patients.' Ibid. 56.

[8] There are 'grossly over-crowded fracture clinics and congestion of operating lists with an unnecessary number of operations being undertaken outside normal working hours for no other reason than lack of operating theatre availability during the day. Such operations were therefore frequently performed under sub-optimal conditions by inexperienced staff.' Ibid.

[9] 'Many units offering a full fracture service lack the necessary range of essential supporting specialties and equipment.' Ibid. 57.

[10] 'There was little evidence of any local organisation or co-ordination of trauma care and in particular there was little onward referral of serious or difficult cases as is commonplace in reconstructive orthopaedics.' Ibid.

[11] *Patient's Charter* (Department of Health, 1991) 14.

[12] *Report to the Secretary of State following the death of Nasima Begum* (South Thames RHA, 1994).

we will examine the law of negligence as it applies to doctors and
health authorities, and ask whether legal standards of care ought
to be affected by scarce resources.

II LIABILITY OF THE DOCTOR

Every action in negligence requires the plaintiff to show: that the
defendant owed the plaintiff a duty of care, that the defendant
failed to achieve a standard of care demanded by law, and that it
was this failure which caused the plaintiff's injuries. An award of
damages depends on proof of fault; it has nothing at all to do with
the mere fact that the plaintiff has suffered terrible injury and
grief. Unless each one of these elements is satisfied the plaintiff
will fail to recover compensation. Under these principles, many
who suffer the most tragic and catastrophic damage are left to cope
alone on the contributions made by the social security system.[13]

A. Medical Negligence[14]

Once a doctor accepts responsibility for a patient, he or she will
usually owe them a duty of care.[15] The duty is imposed because the
GP or hospital doctor is able to foresee that carelessness on their
part could cause damage to the patient and that they ought
therefore to take reasonable care. In the majority of cases,
therefore, the difficulty faced by the patient who issues proceedings in negligence is not to establish the existence of a duty of care,
but rather to prove that, in treating the patient, the doctor failed to
achieve a satisfactory standard of care. The complaint may be that

[13] Sometimes judges are moved to remark at the harshness of such a system
which pays so little regard to the needs of patients who suffer injury in the absence
of negligence. See e.g. *Whitehouse* v. *Jordan* [1981] 1 WLR 246. In New Zealand
and Sweden compensation for accidents is awarded not on the basis of the
defendant's fault but on that of the claimant's need. Such a system of no-fault
compensation has much to recommend it.

[14] See I. Kennedy and A. Grubb, *Medical Law—Text With Materials* (Butterworths, 2nd edn., 1994), ch. 5; M. Jones, *Medical Negligence* (Sweet & Maxwell,
1991).

[15] In a small number of cases a more restricted duty arises, see *Medical Ethics
Today: Its Practice and Philosophy* (British Medical Association, 1993), ch. 9; most
notable amongst which concerns doctors who simply examine patients on behalf of
others, e.g. an employer, or a local authority. See also *M* v. *Newham LBC* [1994] 2
WLR 554.

the doctor failed to tell the patient about the risks or side-effects associated with the treatment, made a wrong diagnosis or prognosis, or that the treatment caused more harm than good because it was not performed carefully.

Cases which do not concern the exercise of professional judgment are assessed according to the objective standards of the 'man on the street'. The question of whether an employer is responsible for exposing an employee to an unsafe system of work, or the driver of a car for injuries caused to a pedestrian, can be considered by the judge who applies common sense to the question of the standard of care which ought to have been achieved. But cases concerning professionals cannot always be judged in this way. The considerations which ought to have been borne in mind, or the exploratory tests which should have been conducted by a doctor during diagnosis, or the measures which ought to have been taken to deal with it, are matters requiring professional judgment. Thus, in assessing the standard of care owed to patients, medical negligence has been generous to doctors, and to a slightly lesser extent to professionals generally. The standard of care is normally assessed by reference to standards expected by a reasonable body of practitioners in that area of practice. It is very broadly expressed because medicine is often as much an art as a science and permits many differences of professional opinion as to appropriate treatment. The point was made in the Scottish case of *Hunter* v. *Hanley*[16] in which it was said:

In the realm of diagnosis and treatment there is ample scope for genuine difference of opinion, and one man clearly is not negligent because his conclusion differs from that of other professional men, nor because he has displayed less skill or knowledge than others would have shown. The true test for establishing negligence in diagnosis or treatment on the part of a doctor is whether he has been proved to be guilty of such failure as no doctor of ordinary skill would be guilty of acting with ordinary care.

In England and Wales this principle has become known as the *Bolam* test of medical negligence, derived from the case of *Bolam* v. *Friern Hospital Management Committee*.[17] The case concerned a patient who was receiving electro-convulsive treatment. The shock

[16] 1955 SLT 213, 217.   [17] [1957] 2 All ER 118

administered during the procedure was sufficient to make limbs flex violently and doctors had to decide on the best way of reducing the risk of patients being damaged by such a convulsion. Some doctors in similar cases administered relaxant drugs to patients. But others considered the risks of doing so unnecessary. Some simply tucked their patients up in bed to prevent them falling to the ground. The defendant doctor in this case took no precautionary measures and his patient suffered serious damage to his thighs and hips when the shock of the treatment propelled him from the hospital bed on to the floor. McNair J instructed the jury as follows.

A doctor is not guilty of negligence if he has acted in accordance with a practice accepted as proper by a responsible body of medical men skilled in that particular art. . . . [A] doctor is not negligent if he is acting in accordance with such a practice merely because there is a body of opinion that takes a contrary view. At the same time, that does not mean that a medical man can obstinately and pig-headedly carry on with some old techniques if it has been proved to be contrary to what is really substantially the whole of informed medical opinion.[18]

This approach to medical malpractice has been adopted to questions of diagnosis,[19] prognosis,[20] and (possibly) consent to treatment[21] and may vary according to the degree of skill and expertise of the particular doctor concerned, so that more is expected of a consultant than a junior house officer.[22] It is a generous rule designed to protect doctors from a constant fear of

[18] *Bolam* v. *Friern Hospital Management Committee* [1957] 2 All ER 118, 122. However, unless it was considered to present unreasonable risk to the patient, it is not clear why the precaution of tucking a blanket around the patient should not have been required as a matter of common sense (no clinical expertise needed) and well within the competence of the court to decide (like the need to remove swabs).

[19] *Maynard* v. *West Midlands Regional Health Authority* [1985] 1 All ER 635 and *Hinfey v Salford HA* [1993] 4 Med LR 143. But contrast *Sa'd* v. *Robinson* [1989] 1 Med LR 41, (failure to diagnose burns to a child's throat and trachea, as opposed to her mouth, after sucking on the spout of a pot of tea) and *Bova* v. *Spring* [1994] 4 Med LR 120 (failure to diagnose pneumonia).

[20] *Whitehouse* v. *Jordan* [1981], *supra* note 13, 267.

[21] *Sidaway* v. *Royal Bethlem Hospital* [1985] 1 All ER 643. The subject of consent to treatment and the obligation to disclose risks to patients is discussed in Chapter 8.

[22] See *Sidaway* ibid., 660, *per* Lord Bridge. Indeed, if the individual specialist can be shown to have greater knowledge of risks and dangers than the average specialist, he may be held to his own, higher, standard. See *Stokes* v. *Guest, Keen and Nettlefold (Bolts & Nuts) Ltd* [1968] 1 WLR 1776, 1783, *per* Swanwick J.

litigation whenever things go wrong, which, it is feared would tend stifle initiative and prejudice the interests of patients.[23]

B. The Courts: Rubber Stamp or Independent Review?

The law must to be clear about when it will be prepared to criticize clinical decision making, and when it will not. How inclined are the courts to defer to medical judgment in cases of medical negligence?

1. Matters of Common Sense

Some clinical activities are so much matters of common sense that they are entirely amenable to independent assessment by the courts. 'Thus an accepted practice is open to censure . . . (no expert testimony required) at any rate in matters not involving diagnostic or clinical skills, on which an ordinary person may presume to pass judgment sensibly, like failure to remove a sponge.'[24]

For example, doctors generally are sometimes criticized for having poor hand-writing. It could not be argued that illegible prescriptions ought to be excused on the ground that the handwriting conformed to the standards achieved by reasonable doctors. This was the issue in a case in which a prescription was misread by a pharmacist who dispensed the wrong medicine to a patient who suffered brain damage as a result. The court dealt with the matter on common sense principles and held both the doctor and the pharmacist liable for failing to take proper care of the patient.[25] In the same way, when responsibility for a patient is passed from one doctor to another, determination of the duty to give the new doctor a full and accurate history of the patient's condition is within the court's own competence.[26] Similarly, a

---

[23] See the comments of Lord Denning in *Roe* v. *Minister of Health* [1954] 2 QB 66 and *Hatcher v Black* (1954) *The Times* 2 July.

[24] *Hucks* v. *Cole* [1993] 4 Med LR 393, 394, *per* Lord Denning MR. See *Mahon* v. *Osborne* [1939] 2 KB 14 on a failure to remove swabs. Reconsider the example of the precaution of loosely tucking ECT patients in bed to prevent their falling to the ground, as in *Bolam, supra* note 18.

[25] See *Prendergast* v. *Sam & Dee Ltd* [1989] 1 Med LR 36.

[26] *Chapman* v. *Rix* [1994] 5 Med LR 239. Lord Goddard said 'I hardly regard this as a medical question at all . . .', 245.

doctor who failed to read a patient's notes before prescribing drugs to which she was allergic was dealt with by reference to the standards of the reasonable person,[27] as was a psychiatrist who formed an emotional relationship with a vulnerable patient,[28] and a doctor who performed untested cosmetic surgery on a child which disfigured her face.[29]

Inevitably, the distinction between matters within and without the court's competence is a matter of degree, and depends on the sympathies of the court and the circumstances of the case. However, it becomes increasingly difficult for the court to impose its own common sense on the dispute when medical experts are available to both parties. To what extent does the court retain discretion in these circumstances to declare that medical opinion is unreasonable? Outside the field of medical practice, the courts have shown a willingness to question for themselves the reasons on which skilled and professional people have adopted a particular practice. Specialist employers have been criticized as a class for failing to maintain a reasonably safe place of work for their employees,[30] as have the practices adopted by solicitors,[31] surveyors,[32] architects,[33] bankers,[34] and the captains of cross-channel ferries.[35] The question was raised with respect to doctors in *Hucks* v. *Cole*.[36] The patient presented the doctor with an infected finger. The doctor failed to prescribe penicillin and the patient subsequently suffered puerperal septicaemia. The patient sued in negligence. Sachs LJ was satisfied that if penicillin had been administered the infection would not have occurred and the patient could have avoided a very serious illness. Thus, he said, unless there was a good cause for not administering it:

the onset was due to a lacuna between what could easily have been done and what was in fact done. According to the defence, that lacuna was

[27] See *Chin Keow* v. *Government of Malaysia* [1967] 1 WLR 813.
[28] See *Landau* v. *Werner* (1961) 105 SJ 1008.
[29] See *Doughty* v. *North Staffordshire HA* [1992] 3 Med LR 81.
[30] See *Stokes* v. *Guest, Keen and Nettlefold (Bolts & Nuts) Ltd.*, *supra* note 22 and *Thompson* v. *Smith's Shiprepairers (North Shields) Ltd* [1984] QB 405.
[31] See *Edward Wong Finance Co Ltd* v. *Johnstone, Stokes and Masters* [1984] AC 296 (PC). [32] *Smith* v. *Eric S Bush* [1990] 1 AC 831.
[33] *Greaves & Co* v. *Baynham Meikle & Partners* [1974] 1 WLR 1261.
[34] See *Lloyds Bank* v. *Savory & Co.* [1933] AC 201.
[35] *Re. The Herald of Free Enterprise The Independent*, 18 Dec. 1987.
[36] *Hucks* v. *Cole* [1993], *supra* note 24 (decided in 1968).

consistent with and indeed accorded with the reasonable practice of others with obstetric experience. When the evidence shows that a lacuna in professional practice exists by which risks of grave danger are knowingly taken, then, however small the risks, the Courts must anxiously examine that lacuna—particularly if the risks can be easily and inexpensively avoided. If the Court finds, on analysis of the reasons given for not taking those precautions that, in the light of current professional knowledge, there is no proper basis for the lacuna, and that it is definitely not reasonable that those risks should have been taken, its function is to state the fact and where necessary to state that it constitutes negligence. In such a case the practice will no doubt thereafter be altered to the benefit of patients. On such occasions the fact that other practitioners would have done the same thing as the defendant practitioner is a very weighty matter to be put in the scales on his behalf; but it is not . . . conclusive. The Court must be vigilant to see whether the reasons given for putting a patient at risk are valid. . . .

[T]his is not apparently the case of 'two schools of thought'; it appears to be a case of doctors who said in one form or another that they would have acted or might have acted in the same way as the defendant did for reasons which on examination do not really stand up to analysis.[37]

The risk of failing to treat was septicaemia and, ultimately, death. Given that penicillin presented no serious danger and was readily available to the doctor, he ought to have administered it to his patient. Thus, despite the support of his colleagues, the defendant was held liable for his failure. The logic of the duty requires the court to examine the substance and rationale of the decision, not merely the fact that others can be found to support it. Sometimes the court will find it impossible to criticize clinical practice, particularly if it involves technical considerations beyond its competence. In other cases, however, the doctor's decision may have included non-clinical concerns which are well within the competence of the court. The test applied to distinguish the excusable from the inexcusable difference of opinion depends on

[37] Ibid. 397. See also *Helling* v. *Carey* ((1974) 519 P.2d 981, Wash Sup Ct). An optician failed to test the plaintiff's eyes for glaucoma. She was 32 and the incidence of the disease in people of a similar age is around one in 25,000. The professional standard did not offer routine testing for those under the age of 40 because it was not thought cost-effective to do so. The court held that the matter was not governed by the medical standard because, as a matter of law, the relevant test was so simple and inexpensive that it ought in all the circumstances to have been offered to the plaintiff.

the judgment of a responsible body of doctors. How do the courts recognize such a body?

2. A Responsible Body of Opinion

For many years the case of *Hucks* received almost no recognition in the courts[38] and in the meantime was overtaken by a number of decisions of the House of Lords which tended to insulate doctors from liability and so exposed the *Hucks* judgment to doubt. The doubt arises from the very proper observation that judges are not in a good position to criticize the opinions of specialists in a field of medicine. Does this mean, however, that the courts ought to be slow to condemn the decision of a doctor when they are supported by others, or that they should *never* do so?

In *Maynard* v. *West Midlands RHA*[39] the deferential approach was adopted. The plaintiff presented with symptoms which suggested she was suffering either Hodgkin's disease or tuberculosis. Given the additional dangers presented by the former, two doctors advised her to undergo a test (a mediastinoscopy), the side-effects of which damaged her vocal chords. She sued for her loss. At the trial, the plaintiff offered evidence showing that the likelihood of her symptoms being Hodgkin's disease were so small, and the diagnosis of her condition so improbable, that it could never justify exposing her to the risk of damage by the exploratory procedure. The more likely explanation was 'almost certainly tuberculosis from the outset',[40] which she was indeed found to be suffering. The judge was persuaded by this evidence. He found that the defendants' explanation for their action was unconvincing and that the tests exposed her to an unreasonable risk. He upheld the plaintiff's claim. The case was appealed to the House of Lords, in which Lord Scarman said:

. . . a judge's preference for one body of distinguished medical opinion to another also professionally distinguished is not sufficient to establish negligence in a practitioner whose actions have received the seal of approval of those whose opinions, truthfully expressed, honestly held, were not preferred. . . . For in the realm of diagnosis and treatment

---

[38] It was resurrected in I. Kennedy and A. Grubb, *Medical Law: Cases and Materials* (Butterworth, 1989).

[39] [1985] 1 All ER 635. [40] Ibid. 638.

negligence is not established by preferring one respectable body of professional opinion to another.[41]

Thus, the House of Lords reversed the decision of the judge and found for the defendant on the basis that the court was precluded from judging the matter for itself.[42] This provokes the question of the current status of *Hucks* and the authority of the courts to scrutinize doctors' decisions, notwithstanding that they have the support of other reasonable doctors.

C. Excusable and Inexcusable Differences of Opinion

Reason suggests that the courts must reserve some power of review in order to deal with those who refuse to move with the times, and whose use of medicine or surgical techniques exposes patients to unreasonable dangers because improved standards render the old practices redundant.[43] The same applies to medicines or practices which have yet to be proved safe.[44] Blind faith, even if it is held in good faith, will not be sufficient to excuse these practices.[45] Also, doctors candidly report that they some-times make clinical decisions for reasons which have nothing to do

---

[41] *Maynard* v. *West Midland Regional Health Authority* [1985] *supra* note 19, 639. And see, to the same effect, his opinion in *Sidaway*, *supra* note 21. *Hucks* v. *Cole* was cited in neither case.

[42] Even if the court had conducted a *Hucks* examination of the medical evidence, the result would probably have been the same because 'the defence had called a formidable number of distinguished experts . . . all of whom . . . approved the course of action taken in deferring diagnosis and performing the operation.' Ibid. 639 *per* Lord Scarman.

[43] See *Crawford* v. *Charing Cross Hospital*, *The Times* 8 December 1953, in which an article in *The Lancet* had contra-indicated a form of treatment some six months earlier. The court exonerated the defendants from blame on the ground that it would be asking too much to expect doctors to keep abreast of all the contemporary medical literature. On the other hand, if the impact of a new finding was dramatic and well publicized, one would expect most doctors to be familiar with it within a shorter period.

[44] See 'Cancer expert attacks "cowboy" doctors', *The Independent*, 1 Dec. 1993 26, in which a professor of oncology alleged that 'there are two many clinicians with biased, ill-informed opinions of what constitutes optimal care . . . Cowboys up and down the country are giving cytotoxic [cell killing] drugs and patients are having the most extraordinary experiences, which are costing money. We must find ways of stopping inappropriate treatment.'

[45] See *Halushka* v. *University of Saskatchewen* (1965) 53 DLR (2d) 436, concerning the testing of an experimental anaesthetic on a volunteer which proved to be unsafe.

with the illness of the patient. It would be very strange if the law excluded itself from matters of this nature. One influential study exposed the extent to which doctors chose not to tell parents that their children were suffering asthma, and declined to treat the condition for fear of upsetting the parents with an unwelcome diagnosis. It seems likely that children were put at additional risk as a result.[46] Others may expose the patient to unnecessary tests and procedures, not strictly in the patient's interests but in the practice of 'defensive medicine'.[47] Indeed, there may be no compelling clinical reason for a decision, other than the fact that it is in common practice at the moment.[48] Conversely, treatment may be denied when questions of cost confuse the issue of clinical need.[49] Of course, doctors may (and probably will) be found to support all these decisions, but does that necessarily make them reasonable and logical? The question is raised in its clearest form when a plaintiff's experts are prepared to say not merely that they disagree with the defendant doctor, but that the defendant's decision was so unreasonable, so devoid of logical foundation, that no *reasonable* doctor would have done the same. Who is then the judge of whether a decision is 'reasonable', doctors or the courts?

1. Complete Freedom to Differ?

Precisely this issue arose in *Bolitho* v. *City and Hackney HA*[50]. The plaintiff, a two-year-old boy called Patrick, was being treated in hospital for breathing difficulties caused by patent ductus arteriosus, a condition of the heart. The staff responsible for his care knew of his condition and the danger it presented. He

---

[46] A. Speight *et al.*, 'Underdiagnosis and Undertreatment of Asthma in Childhood', 286 *British Medical Journal* 1253 (1986). Of such a practice, Lord Denning once said 'I can understand that a medical man may sometimes feel justified in giving misleading information to a patient so as not to worry him. But if he does, he must be very careful to give the true information to his relatives and those about him' See *Chapman* v. *Rix, supra* note 26, 248. With respect, however, these words spoken in 1960 must surely be wrong today.

[47] M. Ennis, A. Clark, J. Grudzinskas, 'Change in Obstetric Practice in response to fear of litigation in the British Isles', 338 *British Medical Journal* 616 (1991).

[48] J. Burnum, 'Medical Practice à la Mode: How Medical Fashions Determine Medical Care', 317 *New England Journal of Medicine* 1220 (1987).

[49] T. Hope, D. Sprigings and R. Crisp, ' "Not Clinically Indicated": Patients' Interest or Resource Allocation?', 306 *British Medical Journal* 379 (1993)

[50] *Bolitho* v. *City and Hackney HA* 13 BMLR 111 (1993).

suffered an episode of breathlessness and, in breach of their duty
of care, the doctors responsible for his care failed to respond and
attend to him. He suffered a cardiac arrest and severe brain
damage. The defendants admitted negligence in failing to attend
the patient. Their defence, however, was that even if they had
attended him, they would probably not have assisted his breathing
by intubation, and, therefore their negligence did not cause the
damage, which he would have suffered in any event. Their case
was that his condition in the past had improved spontaneously and
that, since intubation involved the risk associated with the use of
anaesthetic, they would have decided against it.

The plaintiffs, on the other hand, said that no reasonable doctor
would have failed to intubate the patient. Of course there was a
risk in so doing but it was acceptably small. By contrast, its great
benefit would have been to avoid the tragedy which occurred: a
cardiac arrest and brain damage. As Simon Brown LJ put it: 'It
was . . . the defendants' case that it would have been positively
wrong for an attending doctor to intubate. But that is surely an
impossible contention having regard not least to the agreed fact
that intubation alone would have averted this tragedy.'[51]

Weighing together the risks and the benefits presented by
intubation, the plaintiff alleged that 'it was unreasonable and
illogical not to anticipate the recurrence of a life-threatening event
and take the step which it was acknowledged would probably have
saved Patrick from harm'.[52] Thus, it was argued, the principle in
Hucks v. *Cole* permitted the court to examine and condemn a
practice which exposed the patient to such an unreasonable and
avoidable danger.

The trial judge rejected the claim. Taking an entirely passive
view of his function in the case, he said:

> It is not for me to make a choice between [the plaintiffs' and
> defendants' experts], one of whom is convinced that any competent
> doctor would, the other that she would not, have undertaken that
> procedure. Plainly, in my view, this is one of those areas in which there is
> a difference of opinion between two distinguished and convincing medical
> witnesses, as to what as a matter of clinical judgment proper treatment
> requires.[53]

---

[51] *Bolitho* v. *City and Hackney HA* per Simon Brown LJ, dissenting, 128.
[52] Ibid. 122. This was described by the judge as 'a powerful argument—which I
have to say, as a layman, appealed to me . . .'.   [53] Cited in ibid. 122.

No question arose of requiring the defendant to satisfy the judge of the reasonableness of her opinion; it was deemed reasonable by virtue of the support it attracted from another specialist. One is prompted to ask: is there no threshold of evidence, other than the support of an expert, which the court must insist on to satisfy itself of the logical foundation for the doctor's decision? Significantly, on appeal, the Court of Appeal endorsed the judgment of Sachs LJ in *Hucks* v. *Cole*. It said:

There is no inconsistency between the decisions in *Hucks* v. *Cole* and *Maynard's* case. It is not enough for a defendant to call a number of doctors to say that what he had done or not done was in accord with accepted clinical practice. It is necessary for the judge to consider that evidence and decide whether that clinical practice puts the patient unnecessarily at risk.[54]

Understandably, it was cautious before reassessing the weight of the evidence adduced on behalf of the defendant. A court will only criticize a doctor if, fully conscious of its own lack of medical and clinical experience, it is clearly satisfied that 'the views of that group of doctors were *Wednesbury* unreasonable, i.e. views which no reasonable body of doctors could have held.'[55] On this approach, the court should be amenable to persuasion that, despite the support of colleagues, a medical practice is unreasonable and consequently negligent. This clarification of the law by the Court of Appeal is most important. Curiously, however, having heard the judge refuse to assess the substance of the defendants explanation for the accident on the grounds that it was not his business to choose between the experts, the Court of Appeal said: 'Once it is shown that the judge took the criticism into account there is no basis upon which this court could interfere.'[56]

The findings by the judge are inconsistent with the suggestion that the approach of [the defendant's medical expert] put Patrick unnecessarily at risk. The judge clearly concluded that [his] evidence did constitute 'a responsible body of medical opinion' . . .[57]

---

[54] Ibid., *per* Farquharson LJ.   [55] Ibid. 132 *per* Dillon LJ.
[56] Ibid. 118, *per* Farquharson LJ.
[57] Ibid. 119. Dillon LJ appeared prepared to undertake a substantive review of the reasons for the decision, but was not prepared to describe them as *Wednesbury* unreasonable, (see 132). With respect, in doing so he considered the defendant's explanations for their decision, but not their reasonableness.

Thus, the majority[58] refused to require the defendant to explain why she preferred to expose the child to the risk of catastrophe rather than the small risk of intubation, or to assess the logic on which such an opinion could have been held. With respect, however, the Court was wrong to say the judge had concluded this question; this is precisely what he declined to do. The rightness of the decision may be questioned because, contrary to the reasoning in *Hucks*, no one seemed to have been satisfied of the threshold question of the sufficiency of the medical evidence which contra-indicated intubation. *Bolitho* leaves the impression that the courts appreciate their duty to judge the propriety of some clinical decisions, but that they have severe reservations about doing so.

2. Courts' Reluctance to Criticise

Much the same reluctance to examine the logic of a decision occurred in *Defreitas* v. *O'Brien*[59]. The plaintiff suffered severe discomfort in her back which affected her mobility. Despite being seen by a number of specialists, no firm diagnosis of the cause of the complaint could be made. The defendant decided to undertake exploratory surgery of the plaintiff's spine. The operation carried an unavoidable risk of infection which materialized in damage.[60] Her experts argued said that spinal surgery was unavoidably hazardous. Given the inescapable risk of serious harm, doctors would never be justified in undertaking spinal surgery for exploratory reasons only; a clear diagnosis was always a pre-requisite. By contrast, the defendant's experts said that they constituted a sub-group of 'specialist' specialists, amounting to some four or five out of 250 neurosurgeons in the United Kingdom, who dealt exclusively with the spine and that they had additional expertise in spinal surgery.[61] In the right hands, they said, the risks associated with an exploratory operation were acceptable, given the severity of the plaintiff's condition, at around 15–20 per cent.

The court found that the defendant's decision to operate was supported by a responsible body of medical opinion and accepted

---

[58] Ibid., Simon Brown LJ dissented and decided for the plaintiff.

[59] [1993] 4 Med LR 281, decided in the Mayor's and City Court.

[60] The plaintiff's spinal fluid became infected. She alleged that, although such a risk was an unavoidable part of the surgery in question, it was unreasonable to have exposed her to such a risk in the first place.   [61] See ibid. 291.

their judgment that exploratory spinal surgery was justified even in the absence of a firm diagnosis.[61a] The most worrying thing about this approach to experts is the entirely passive acceptance by the court of the statistics advanced by the defendant's experts. What was the evidence of a '15–20%' incidence of risk? (Recall that there were only four or five such specialists practising in the UK.) The judge appeared to accept the statistic as a fact, but how can such a precise figure, from such a small sample of doctors, be considered reliable? On how many patients, what cross-section of patients, over how many years, with what medical facilities and with what severity of injuries was the figure based? Such a figure ought to have been substantiated. One should not be surprised by the fact of disagreement between doctors, and the need for judgment is endemic. But if the statistics were really a reflection of someone's personal opinion, they ought to be as open to challenge as the decision to operate itself.[62]

Of course, there is often substantial agreement about the choices available to doctors because there is 'agreement about disagreement', that is, about the various merits and demerits of different forms of treatment. In such cases the court should naturally be inclined to accept the judgment of doctors that the differences of opinion are reason-able. This is what McNair J meant in *Bolam* when he referred to 'a *practice* accepted as proper by a responsible *body* of responsible men' [My italics]. However, if, as in *Defreitas*, the practice is condemned as wrong, and supported only by an extremely small number of specialists, the court should be the more anxious to examine the reasons behind the defendant's actions in order to be satisfied that they are responsible. The point was made in 1960 by Lord Goddard.[63] He said that it would not be sufficient for a doctor simply to present the court with two colleagues prepared to support his action if there was evidence the other way. In such a case the judge would still be entitled to find negligence.[64] The more substantial the

---

[61a] The Court of Appeal dismissed the appeal on the ground that the defendant was supported by a reasonable body of medical opinion. See [1995] 6 Med LR 108. *Hucks* was not cited.

[62] See D. Eddy, 'Variations in Physician Practice: The Role of Uncertainty', 3 *Health Affairs* 74 (1984) who doubts the value of precise statistics in these matters.

[63] In *Chapman* v. *Rix*, *supra* note 26, 247.

[64] And Lord Donaldson said in *Sidaway* v. *Royal Bethlem Hospital*, *supra* note

more substantial the criticism from medical colleagues, the more satisfied the court should be of the logical steps on which the decision was based. Forensic scientists have become accustomed to greater analysis of their use of statistics.[65] Particularly in circumstances such as these, doctors should be prepared for the same. Judges are entirely familiar with cases involving technical evidence of which they have no previous expertise and many are extremely adept at assimilating and analysing large quantities of information at great speed. Defendants from other professions are required to satisfy the judge of the internal logic and consistency of the facts argued in their defence. There is no reason why the same approach should not apply to defendant doctors for the benefit of patients.

III. LIABILITY OF HEALTH AUTHORITIES AND NHS TRUSTS

To what extent may a health authority or an NHS Trust be held responsible for damage caused to a patient?[66] Liability may be imposed on the basis of (A) vicarious liability for the negligence of employees, or (B) the primary liability of the authority itself.

21, 1028 (CA): 'I think that, in an appropriate case, a judge would be entitled to reject a unanimous medical view if he were satisfied that it was manifestly wrong and that the doctors must have been misdirecting themselves as to their duty in law.' See also the comments of Lord Bridge in the House of Lords, [1985] 1 All ER 643 at 662. The same view was taken in the Canadian case of *Reibl* v. *Hughes* (1980) 114 DLR (3d) 1 13.

[65] See *R* v. *Gordon, The Independent* 9 June 1994, on the reliability of statistics concerning DNA testing.

[66] See generally *Medical Negligence, supra* note 14, ch. 7. Generally, actions in negligence should be taken against the relevant health authority or NHS Trust and not the Secretary of State for Health, see National Health Service Act 1977, sched. 5, para. 15(1). Exceptionally, however, it may be proper to join the Secretary of State as a defendant. Ralph Gibson LJ has said of the provision: 'the Secretary of State should not be vicariously liable in respect of the exercise of a function by an authority on behalf of the Secretary of State. I accept that if, in respect of any delegated function, it could be shown that the Secretary of State was independently in breach of the relevant duty, the [provision] does not provide any protection. In other words . . . if there is a duty upon the Secretary of State for breach of which there is a civil remedy, the fact of delegation of the exercise of the function would not by itself provide a defence if it could be shown that, notwithstanding the delegation, the duty was breached.' (In *Re HIV Haemophiliac litigation* (CA, [1990] NLJR 1349).

A. Vicarious Liability for Employees

Employers are generally liable for the negligence of their employees committed during the course of their employment under the principle of vicarious liability. In the cases discussed above, in which the doctors were employees of the relevant health authority, the general rule of the vicarious liability of employers for their employees would have applied.[67] Consultant employees are covered by exactly the same rule.[68] The rule as to the vicarious liability of health authorities for the negligence of their staff, whether clinical or non-clinical, will not usually be in doubt.

B. Primary Liability for Management and Policy

A more awkward issue concerns the theory of primary liability. Common law recognizes that public authorities often operate with scarce resources and have to make difficult choices. There is always more that could be done to improve a public service than there is money available to pay for it, whether in respect of maintaining standards in hospitals, or schools, or the quality of roads and public transport. In matters of this nature it is mistaken to think in terms of right and wrong solutions. Different people may identify different priorities. In the end, however, a decision has to be made about a suitable course of action based on a democratic expression of feeling, or some other means of breaking the deadlock. This is a problem faced by health authorities. How do the courts deal with the matter?

1. The General law

Understandably, the courts are extremely slow to allow themselves to become embroiled in decisions of this kind, since their own opinions could not be expected to be more informed than

---

[67] See the discussion in *Cassidy* v. *Ministry of Health* [1951] 1 All ER 574.

[68] See *Razzel* v. *Snowball* [1954] 1 WLR 1382 at 1386, *per* Denning LJ: 'the term consultant does not denote a particular relationship between a doctor and a hospital. It is simply a title denoting his place in the hierarchy of the hospital staff. He is a senior member of staff but nevertheless just as much a member of staff as the house surgeon. Whether he is called a specialist or a consultant makes no difference.'

those of the executive concerned, particularly if the latter have
long experience of the area. On the other hand, the courts
recognize equally that public authorities are not solely concerned
with the difficult problems of making policy and assessing
priorities. They also undertake matters of day-to-day routine
about which it is possible to expect minimum standards of care. In
this respect the courts feel perfectly able to apply the usual
principles of negligence since the matter is within the competence
of reasonable people. This distinction is often expressed by
reference to the 'policy' and the 'operational' spheres of decision
making, but it is crucial to understand that the two elements
cannot be separated as if they were black and white. The issue is
better considered as a spectrum in which decisions will usually
involve aspects of both. The matter was considered by Lord
Wilberforce who said:

> Most, indeed probably all, statutes relating to public authorities or
> public bodies, contain in them a large area of policy. The courts call this
> 'discretion' meaning that the decision is one for the authority or body to
> make, and not for the courts. Many statutes also prescribe or at least
> presuppose the practical execution of policy decisions: a convenient
> description of this is to say that in addition to the area of policy or
> discretion, there is an operational area. Although this distinction between
> the policy area and the operational area is convenient, and illuminating, it
> is probably a distinction of degree; many 'operational' powers or duties
> have in them some element of 'discretion'. It can safely be said that the
> more 'operational' a power or duty may be, the easier it is to superimpose
> upon it a common law duty of care.[69]

Thus, at each end of the spectrum the decision of the court
about whether to intervene may be relatively straightforward.
But as the decision under review approaches the centre, the matter
becomes increasingly one of judicial instinct, about which reasonable judges may differ. In one case the courts accepted a Home
Office *policy* designed to rehabilitate juvenile offenders by
allowing them to live in relatively open conditions in Borstal.

---

[69] *Anns* v. *Merton London Borough Council* [1978] AC 728, 753. This part of the
ratio of the case, based on *Dorset Yacht Co* v. *Home Office* [1970] AC 1004,
survived the reappraisal of the law of negligence made in *Murphy* v. *Brentwood DC*
[1991] 1 AC 398 (HL). See Bingham LJ in *Re HIV Haemophiliac litigation, supra,*
note 66.

However, when a number of boys escaped and damaged neigh-bouring property because their supervisors had fallen asleep the House of Lords had no hesitation in holding the Home Office responsible for negligence in the *operation* of the policy, rather than in the policy itself.[70] How has the distinction been made in health service cases?

2. Operational Management in the Health Service

Complaints concerning operational matters in a hospital may concern its system of management. Here the plaintiff alleges that the way in which a particular service was organized was negligent. Such a complaint against a provider was made in *Wilsher* v. *Essex Area Health Authority*,[71] in which a baby born prematurely received improper treatment due, in part, to the failure to supervise an inexperienced doctor who shared responsibility for his care. In the Court of Appeal the Vice-Chancellor, Sir Nicolas Browne-Wilkinson, would have been prepared to exonerate the junior doctor from responsibility for the damage caused, on the ground that he was simply not to blame for it. On the other hand, rather than deprive the plaintiff of any form of remedy, he advised that action be considered against the Health Authority for its failure to provide hospital staff with sufficient skill to undertake the duties assigned to them. He said: 'In my judgment, a hospital authority which so conducts its hospital that it fails to provide doctors of sufficient skill and experience to give the treatment offered at the hospital may be directly liable in negligence to the patient.'[72]

Thus, a failure to ensure that experienced staff were available to provide supervision to junior doctors could be negligent. An application of this principle seems to have occurred in *Bull* v. *Devon Health Authority*[73] in which the defendant's *system* for summoning a consultant urgently to an obstetrics unit broke down. As a result the plaintiff suffered brain damage during birth. The system intended to provide the assistance of a consultant within twenty minutes of his being summoned. In the event, however,

---

[70] See *Dorset Yacht*, ibid.   [71] [1986] 3 All ER 801.
[72] Ibid. 833. Glidewell agreed with this proposition: 831.
[73] (1993) 4 Med LR. 117 (decided in 1989).

there was an interval of about an hour before the consultant arrived during which time the baby suffered asphyxia and brain damage. The defendants explained the failure by saying that the hospital operated on two sites and that there would inevitably be occasions when senior staff would be required in both places; the system for summoning consultants from one site to another was 'par for the course' by comparison with other hospitals, and that to require anything else was unrealistic. Mustill LJ rejected this defence. He said:

> I see nothing ideal about a system which would have given the mother and child the protection against emergencies when it was needed. . . . The system should have been set up so as to produce a registrar or consultant on the spot within twenty minutes, subject to some unforeseeable contingency. In the present case there was an interval of about an hour during which the mother and child were at risk, with nobody present who could do anything if an emergency were to develop. The trend of the evidence seems to me manifestly that this interval was too long. Either there was a failure in the operation of the system, or it was too sensitive to hitches which fell short of the kind of major breakdown against which no system is invulnerable.[74]

Thus, the defendants were held liable for the failure of the system to provide the plaintiff with an acceptable standard of care. The distinction between operational and policy issues was made for the benefit of plaintiffs in *Department of Health and Social Security* v. *Kinnear*, who complained that they had suffered brain damage following the administration to them of pertussis vaccine when they were babies.[75] The plaintiffs made a number of allegations against the Secretary of State for Health and Social Security and the relevant health authorities. They said, *inter alia*, that since the risk of suffering a severe form of whooping cough was very small, and because the dangers presented by the vaccine were so high, the policy of mass immunization of babies was misconceived. This allegation was struck out at a preliminary hearing to test whether the action should proceed to trial, on the ground that the policy of vaccination was within the discretion of the Secretary of State and beyond the jurisdiction of the court. However, another allegation was allowed to go forward, namely

[74] Ibid. 141.
[75] *Department of Health and Social Security* v. *Kinnear* 134 NLJ 886 (QBD, 1984).

that doctors and parents ought to have been warned that some children were much more vulnerable to damage by the vaccine than others and that their suffering was easily avoidable. Stuart Smith J said the foundation of the plaintiff's case was that:

they advised how and in what circumstances the treatment should be administered, but this advice was misleading and negligent because it did not indicate that a respiratory disease was a contra-indication for vaccination. [Counsel for the plaintiff] submits that, in giving advice on these matters, the DHSS were acting in the operational sphere and were no longer protected by the limits of discretion. . . . To my mind it is at least arguable, in giving such advice, that the DHSS has entered the operational area.[76]

Thus the courts have been willing to criticize matters of day-to-day operation and decisions about the ways in which policies should be put into effect.

3. Purchasing Policy in the Health Service

As the decision under attack contains greater elements of policy, so it becomes more difficult for the courts to involve themselves in its review. This problem is often faced by those who wish to challenge the purchasing policies of health authorities. Purchasers are primarily concerned with deciding large-scale questions of resources; for example what proportion of finances should be used to purchase neonatal, paediatric, or orthopaedic care? How much ought to go on preventive medicine? These are questions which require the exercise of judgment and the courts have always been reluctant to become involved in matters of this nature. On the other hand, if the very policy under review is negligent, perhaps because it exposes people to unreasonable and avoidable risk of harm, then such a policy may be actionable. Clearly, the circumstances would have to be extreme but such an issue arose in Re *HIV Haemophiliac litigation*.[77] The question arose in the

---

[76] 'Arguable' because the Secretary of State might have said that the matter was still within his discretion. The inclusion of too many warnings and notices of contra-indications could have alarmed parents and doctors to such an extent that the entire policy of vaccination would have been undermined and rendered ineffective. See *Bonthrone* v. *Secretary of State for Scotland* (1987) SLT 34 and *Ross* v. *Secretary of State for Scotland* [1990] Med LR 235. This aspect of the Scottish law may not be identical to that in England and Wales.   [77] [1990] NLJR 1349.

context of another group action taken on behalf of 962 haemophiliac patients and their relatives who suffered damage after
patients had been transfused with a blood product (Factor VIII)
which was contaminated with HIV. The plaintiffs alleged negligence on the part of the Secretary of State, the health authorities of
England and Wales, and the Committee on the Safety of
Medicines based on their purchasing policy for blood products.
Salient amongst the plaintiffs' complaints were the allegations that
(i) the then current knowledge about the human immuno-
deficiency virus was such that the defendants ought to have
become self-sufficient in blood and blood products rather than
purchasing them from America where blood donors are paid and
the system tends to attract categories of donor whose blood is
more likely to be contaminated; and (ii) since the blood
transfusion service was not self-sufficient, more ought to have
been done to warn and inform patients of the dangers presented by
HIV, to screen donors in this country, and to introduce a system of
heat-treatment of blood to minimize the risks of contamination.[78]
   In reply, the defendants argued that matters such as these
concerning the allocation of health service resources were exclusively in the discretion of the Secretary of State; the claim was not
justiciable by individual patients. Accordingly, they said, no duty
of care was owed by the defendants because there was insufficient
proximity between the plaintiffs and defendants, and it would not
be fair and reasonable to impose a duty of care between the
parties.[79] The Court of Appeal allowed the case to proceed to
trial. The court was persuaded that the plaintiffs had presented an
arguable case that the defendants' policy of continuing to import
blood and failing to use heat treatment was unreasonable and
amenable to an action in negligence. The court was influenced by
the fact that the dangers threatened patients' lives[80] and that the
catastrophe could largely have been avoided had measures been
introduced at an earlier date. Ralph Gibson LJ appeared to agree

[78] The matter is now the subject of Health Service Guidelines. See *Provision of
haemophilia treatment and care* (HSG(93)30, NHSME, 1993).
   [79] These arguments were based on *Rowling* v. *Takaro Properties Ltd* [1988] AC
473 and *Hill* v. *Chief Constable of West Yorkshire* [1989] 1 AC 53.
   [80] Bingham LJ said: 'where, as here, foreseeability by a defendant of severe
personal injury to a person such as the plaintiff is shown and the existence of a
proximate relationship between plaintiff and defendant is accepted, the plaintiff is
well on his way to establishing the existence of a duty of care.'

with the submission of counsel for the plaintiffs that '. . . the fact that the decision attacked is a matter of discretion or policy-making does not make the decision immune in law. If it is *ultra vires* or wholly unreasonable the authority will be liable in negligence if the decision is shown to be negligent by reference to proximity and foreseeability. His Lordship said

. . . if it is proved that the information as to the nature and gravity of the risk, and of the steps available to eliminate or reduce it, was supplied to those who were required to make the decisions, then, in my judgment, the plaintiffs would have a *prima facie* case for asserting that the decisions were such that no reasonable or responsible person could properly make them.[81]

In the end the Government settled the case before it reached trial, but His Lordship recognized the extreme difficulty for plaintiffs of establishing negligence when questions concerning resources are central to the case. The case demonstrates that actions against purchasers are not doomed to failure, but they raise the most difficult and intractable issues in negligence. It is probably true to say that, in order to succeed in negligence, the court would have to be persuaded that the decision was *Wednesbury* unreasonable, i.e. so unreasonable that no health authority ought to have made it. Given the difficult choices that have to be made routinely with scarce health service resources, this will always be extremely difficult to prove. This raises the question of the minimum obligations imposed on the Secretary of State to provide a 'comprehensive health service' under the National Health Service Act 1977. This issue is addressed in Chapter 4.

C. Services Contracted to Private Companies

Increasingly, hospitals and health authorities are required to ask private companies to tender for the provision of hospital goods

---

[81] Bingham LJ agreed saying: 'While the court cannot review the merits of a decision taken by a public authority if it fell within the area of discretion conferred by Parliament, it may do so even in a common law action for damages for negligence if satisfied that the decision in question for any of the recognised reasons fell outside the area of such discretion. Whether the plaintiffs can discharge that considerable burden on the facts here I cannot at present determine.' On the facts, however, Ralph Gibson LJ considered it more probable that 'such an error [of] failing to act appropriately upon available information, was the result of failure at some level within the Department to pass that available information to those who were required to make decisions.'

and services in order to give them the opportunity to compete for the business. The principle behind the policy is to encourage providers of health care to reassess the quality of the services they provide in the light of competition from private companies.[82] Until relatively recently services put out to tender to private companies were limited to the non-clinical sector and concerned catering, domestic services, and laundry. 'For 1992/93 [the NHSME had] returns covering 3,700 contracts worth over £900 million. They show that approx 40% by value were contracted out and the remaining 60% were retained in-house through service agreements with the staff concerned.'[83]

In future hospitals will also be expected to ask the private sector to tender for clinical services. This poses a question of a different order. The circumstances discussed above concerned the manner in which health authorities organize themselves. The future question is whether NHS patients who receive services from an independent provider retain a right of action against the NHS Trust or health authority with whom the arrangement was made. Say a private caterer failed to maintain proper standards of hygiene so that patients were poisoned, or a private clinical screening service failed to alert a hospital that a blood sample had tested positive for a disease, or a privately run hospital unit was so badly managed that patients were given inadequate care. Would a patient who suffered damage by the negligence of a private contractor be able to sue the hospital by whom it was engaged? Or would the action be limited to the private contractor responsible for providing the service concerned? The same problem arises for GP fund-holders. If they engage a consultant from a local hospital on a private basis to take out-patient clinics in the surgery, who is liable if the consultant is negligent?

The common law puts the question as follows. Do hospitals and GPs bear a non-delegable responsibility for independent contractors engaged to perform functions on their behalf, so that they will be held liable for the negligence of the contractor even

---

[82] See *Market Testing in the NHS. Revised Guidance* (HMSO, 1993). The policy is encouraged throughout the public services, see *Competing for Quality—Buying Better Public Services* (Cm. 1730, 1991). It has been formally introduced by the Deregulation and Contracting Out Act 1994, discussed in Chapter 6.

[83] R. Schofield, 'Do You Need to Market Test?', Norwich Systems and Accounting Conference, 17 Feb. 1994. (Mr Schofield spoke as Head of the Operational Policy Unit at the NHSME.)

without negligence on their own part? Or is the duty limited to taking reasonable care when appointing and retaining them to ensure that they are competent to perform their duties, in which case liability lies against the contractor alone? The general rule of vicarious liability of an employer for an employee does not apply to those who engage independent contractors.[84] Is the position between NHS Trust/health authority and patient governed by the same rule? A number of influential cases have said that hospitals do owe a non-delegable duty to their patients so that it is irrelevant whether the consultant is the hospital's employee or not. In 1951 Lord Denning said:

the hospital authorities accepted the plaintiff as a patient for treatment, and it was their duty to treat him with reasonable care. They selected, employed and paid all the surgeons and nurses who looked after him. He had no say in their selection at all. If those surgeons and nurses did not treat him with proper care and skill, then the hospital authorities must answer for it, for it means that they themselves did not perform their duty to him. I decline to enter into the question whether any of the surgeons were employed only under a contract for services [i.e. independent consultants], as distinct from a contract of service [i.e. employees] . . . the liability of the hospital authorities should not, and does not, depend on nice considerations of that sort. The plaintiff knew nothing of the terms on which they employed staff: all he knew was that he was treated in the hospital by people whom the hospital had appointed; and that the hospital must be answerable for the way in which he was treated.[85]

Although His Lordship repeated this view in another case,[86] all the doctors concerned appear to have been employees for whom the defendant's were vicariously liable. In the hospital context, therefore, the point has not yet arisen in this country on its own merits.[87] In addition, the issue today may be more complicated

---

[84] *Rivers* v. *Cutting* [1982] 1 WLR 1146. Liability may be imposed in exceptional circumstances, e.g. if the contractor was authorised or condoned the tort, see *Ellis* v. *Sheffield Gas Consumers Co* (1853) 2 E & E 767, *D & F Estates Ltd* v. *Church Commissioners for England* [1988] 2 All ER 992.

[85] *Cassidy* v. *Ministry of Health*, *supra*, note 67, 365. His Lordship excluded from this rule cases in which the patient had chosen and engaged his own private doctor: 362.

[86] In *Jones* v. *Manchester Corporation* [1952] 2 All ER 125, 132 and *Roe* v. *Ministry of Health*, *supra*, note 23, 82.

[87] Authorities abroad are divided on the point. Compare *Yepremian* v. *Scarborough General Hospital* (1980) 110 DLR (3d) 513 (Canada) and *Ellis* v. *Wallsend District Hospital* [1989] Med LR 567 (Australia).

than that envisaged by Lord Denning because negligence may be committed by a contractor away from the hospital premises, or in wards of the hospital over which the hospital has retained no day-to-day control. Such a situation is common within the NHS in relation to 'tertiary referrals'. For example, a baby is transferred from a general hospital to a special care baby unit in another hospital. The second hospital fails to take proper care of the baby who suffers damage. Which of the two hospitals should be held responsible? It is most improbable that the first hospital would be liable if it was entirely free from blame for the damage. Should the position be different with respect to private suppliers of health services which provide care on behalf of the NHS, either in their own premiscs or those of an NHS hospital? Ought the NHS hospital to be held directly liable to the patient under a non-delegable duty for someone else's negligence?

The Courts are slow to impose liability on one party for damage caused by the negligence of another[88] unless there is an especially close relationship between the two,[89] or the first is under a duty to exercise control over the second.[90] Outside hospitals there has been an occasional willingness to extend the boundary of non-delegable duties to relations between employer and employee, so that one employer retains responsibility for the safety of employees who have been 'borrowed' by another. Even though the employer has no reason to suspect that the 'borrower' will expose the employee to danger, he will retain responsibility if the employee is injured by unsafe working practices.[91] Exceptionally, the same approach was adopted in relation to an agency providing a taxi service to the public, even though it engaged its drivers as independent contractors and not employees. In that case a person

---

[88] See e.g. *Hill* v. *Chief Constable of West Yorkshire* [1989] AC 53, *Perl Exporters Ltd* v. *Camden LBC* [1984] QB 342, *Lamb* v. *Camden LBC* [1981] QB 625.

[89] See *Smith* v. *Littlewoods Organisation* [1988] AC 241, 272 *per* Lord Goff.

[90] *Dorset Yacht, supra,* note 69, *Vicar of Writtle* v. *Essex County Council* (1979) 77 LGR 656.

[91] *McDermid* v. *Nash Dredging Ltd* [1987] 2 All ER 878. Lord Hailsham said (at 887): 'The essential characteristic of the [non-delegable] duty is that, if it is not performed, it is no defence for the employer to show that he delegated its performance to a person, whether his servant or not his servant, whom he reasonably believed to be competent to perform it. Despite such delegation the employer is liable for the non-performance of the duty.'

injured by the negligence of a taxi driver was held to have an action against the booking agency.[92] However, the most recent application of these cases suggests that the non-delegable duty is simply one of reasonable care of employees and that the employer will not be liable unless he ought to have known that the employee would be exposed to unreasonable risk.[93] The law in this area is unsettled, but instinct suggests that the courts will be slow to impose liability on NHS Hospitals when the real cause of the injury is a third party. This will be particularly likely when the costs involved in imposing a non-delegable duty on hospitals may be the closure of a children's ward, or the inability to purchase essential equipment.

Patients should be troubled by this situation. They remain NHS patients and will often have no role in choosing the private contractor responsible for their injuries. Why should they suffer if the private company to whom they have been referred fails to arrange proper insurance to cover its risks, or goes out of business and is unable to honour its responsibilities? After all, although GPs remain in private practice their rights and obligations within the NHS are comprehensively controlled through their Terms of Service with FHSAs, which are statutory regulations requiring Parliamentary approval.[94] Private hospitals and other providers who wish to work in the NHS should be expected to agree to their own Terms of Service established by Parliament under similar principles which preserve the rights of patients and ensure that they are not disadvantaged by the arrangements entered into on their behalf by DHAs and NHS Trusts. In the meantime, no contract entered into by a DHA should restrict any such right and, as a minimum, such arrangements should insist that the private contractor maintains insurance cover sufficient to meet foreseeable claims against it. Indeed, an action in negligence could be contemplated against an NHS body which entered such a contract without first ensuring that its patients would be covered adequately in the event of mishap.

Thus, at common law, public authorities which contract out

---

[92] See *Rogers* v. *Night Riders (A Firm)* [1983] RTR 324.
[93] See *Square D Ltd* v. *Cook* [1992] IRLR 34, in which the Court of Appeal considered *McDermid* v. *Nash Dredging* to be binding on the issue of vicarious liability only. See also *R* v. *Swan Hunter Ship Builders Ltd* [1982] 1 All ER 264.
[94] GP's Terms of Service with FHSAs are discussed in chapter 4.

services may not be responsible for the negligence of the private provider. However, there is support for a contrary view of the liability of public authorities in the Deregulation and Contracting Out Act 1994, which authorizes the contracting out of public authority functions to 'authorized persons', i.e. private contractors. With respect to failures on the part of private contractors, the Act provides that 'anything done or omitted to be done by or in relation to the authorised person (or an employee of his) in, or in connection with, the exercise or purported exercise of the function shall be treated for all purposes as done or omitted to be done . . . by or in relation to the Minister or office-holder in his capacity as such.'[95] As long as negligence can be established against the private contractor, the Act will hold the public authority liable for the failure, even though the common law on vicarious liability might hesitate to do so. The Deregulation and Contracting Out Act 1994 is discussed further in Chapter 6.

IV. STANDARDS OF CARE AND SCARCE RESOURCES

Until now the analysis of the cases has assumed that the standards required by the law of negligence have been set by reference to a mixture of standards set by the profession and the courts, but not by reference to resources. Increasingly, however, the central issue will be whether questions of cost should be allowed to compromise the standard of care reasonably to be expected of doctors and hospitals. Relatively few cases have yet considered the point. The following section considers the arguments for and against the proposition that the standard of care ought to be adjusted according to the available resources.

A. A Variable Standard of Care?

The law of medical malpractice has traditionally imposed a uniform standard of care on doctors, characterised by the *Bolam* standard of care which is assessed according to the standards of reasonable doctors. Could a patient's right to such a reasonable

---

[95] Section 72(2).

standard of care be compromised by an NHS contract? Given the need to spread resources across as many patients as possible, there may be a temptation for contracts to allow for standards which fall short of those currently required by reasonable doctors and by the law of negligence. In a commercial environment a seller may be prepared to lower his prices, provided that the buyer accepts the risk that the quality of the goods or services may be reduced. Hospitals, after all, have to tread a fine line between the need to treat as many patients as possible and the need to ensure that patients receive adequate care.[96]

Reductions in standards of care would be disadvantageous in that they would compromise the care which patients are currently entitled to expect. However, their advantage is that they could make available treatment which would otherwise have been denied altogether because of fear of litigation by the minority for whom the procedures were unsuccessful. Ultimately, the choice is between treating limited numbers of patients with optimum standards of care, or maximum numbers with limited care. In America, where large numbers of people have no health care insurance, the argument in favour of maximizing *access* to health care has been put as follows:

if reality is allowed to supplant myth, the folly of the unitary standard becomes clear. This is not a nation where all can afford the best that medicine has to offer. Instead, the medical profession must serve at least two very different populations, one reasonably well-insured and able to afford a relatively high standard of care and the other poor and uninsured, wholly dependent on direct and indirect forms of charity for the care it receives. . . . To blink in the face of this painful reality and judge the medical care provided to the indigent under a standard of care derived to protect the well-off makes little more sense than would a foreign policy insisting that the humanitarian medical care this country supplies to impoverished nations like Ethiopia or Bangladesh match that provided by Massachusetts General Hopsital.[97]

---

[96] In America, entire contracts have been drafted attempting to limit the standard of care owed to the patient, e.g. by excluding liability for personal injury except in cases of *gross* negligence. See *Tunkl* v. *Regents of the University of California* 383 P.2d 441 (Cal.Sup.1963) (clause excluding remedies based on vicarious liability declared void). See also s. 2, Unfair Contract Terms Act 1977.

[97] J. Siliciano, 'Wealth, Equity and the Unitary Medical Standard', 77 *Virginia Law Review* 439, 466 (1991).

On the other hand:

if quality is defined in a collective sense—in terms, for example, of the number of lives saved or ailments relieved—rather than through a mechanistic comparison of treatment received by different individuals [i.e. the rich and the poor], the inadequacy of the unitary standards seems clear. To be sure, the standard may ensure that a few of the indigent are treated very well, but this comes at the expense of the many. In practice, the operation of the standard resembles a lottery, where most go empty-handed so that a lucky few may be showered with riches.[98]

From the 'macro' point of view such an approach might spread resources across more people. Although the cost would be unsatisfactory results for a minority, economists might argue that the health system would operate with greater efficiency as a whole if such a compromise of standards were possible.[99] There has been some support for this point of view in the English law of negligence. In *Knight* v. *Home Office*,[100] an inmate was held in the hospital wing of Brixton Prison. He suffered serious mental illness and was a recognized suicide risk. Owing to lack of staff and facilities he was treated in a way which would not have been considered adequate by a mental hospital outside prison. He was not provided with counselling and interactive support, or given continuous observation, treatments which would have been expected in a non-prison setting. Instead he was confined alone for long periods of time and succeeded in hanging himself from the bars of his cell. On behalf of the deceased, it was said that his management had fallen below the standard required of reasonable doctors under the *Bolam*[101] test. It was no defence that the standard was as good as in other prisons because that was not the relevant test. The hospital facilities in the prison were inadequate with reference to what ought reasonably to have been available to patients suffering this form of mental illness in prison.

The court rejected the defendant's contention that, since prison

---

[98] Ibid. 468.

[99] For a defence of such an approach in the American system see also Rex O'Neal, 'Safe Harbor for Health Care Cost Containment' 43 *Stanford Law Review* 399 (1991). For the contrary view see Mark A. Hall, 'Institutional Control of Physician Behaviour: Legal Barriers to Health Care Cost Containment' 137 *Pennsylvania Law Review* 431 (1988).   [100] [1990] 3 All ER 237

[101] *Bolam, supra,* note 18.

funding depended on the Home Office and ultimately the Treasury, the plaintiff had no claim in negligence and that his only remedy was a political one. Pill J said:

It is for the court to consider what standard of care is appropriate to the particular relationship and in the particular situation. It is not a complete defence for a government department . . . to say that funds are not available for additional safety measures. . . . To take an extreme example, if the evidence was that no funds were available to provide any medical facilities in a large prison there would be a failure to achieve the standard of care appropriate to prisoners.[102]

On the other hand, His Lordship gave no indication of the means by which the courts could provide remedies to those who had suffered injury from decisions of this nature. Rejecting the plaintiff's claim, he said simply:

In making the decision as to the standard to be demanded the court must . . . bear in mind as one factor that resources available for the public service are limited and that the allocation of resources is a matter for Parliament. . . . I am unable to accept . . . that the law requires the standard of care in a prison hospital to be as high as the standard of care for all purposes in a psychiatric hospital outside prison. There may be circumstances in which the standard of care in a prison falls below that which would be expected in a psychiatric hospital without the prison authority being negligent.[103]

On this analysis resources are relevant to the standard of care expected of public authorities. Perhaps the medical standard is measured by a sliding scale, depending on what ought to be expected from reasonable doctors, or reasonable hospitals, *in the circumstances*, given the limited available funds, but subject to a minimum obligation.[104] Regrettably, on this crucial point no such

---

[102] *Knight* v. *Home Office* [1990] 3 All ER 237, 243.

[103] Ibid. For a consideration of health care in one prison see *Health Care of Prisoners in HM Prison Wandsworth* (Wandsworth Community Health Council, 1992) which is critical of health care in that institution.

[104] The general rule is to the contrary. Negligence does not consider the idiosyncrasies of the particular defendant (*Glasgow Corp.* v. *Muir* [1943] AC 448, 457, *Nettleship* v. *Weston* [1971] 2 QB 691). But a small number of cases have enabled the standard of care to vary. See e.g. *Goldman* v. *Hargrave* [1967] 1 AC 645, *Watt* v. *Hertfordshire CC* [1954] 1 WLR 835 (duty of emergency authorities hurrying to site of accident) and R. Kidner, 'The variable standard of care, contributory negligence and *volenti*' 11 Leg Stud 1 (1991).

principle was discussed, nor were the reasons to justify diminished standards in this case explained.[105] One is left wondering precisely on what basis the court was satisfied that a reasonable standard of care had been achieved and that no breach of duty had occurred.

Is the argument persuasive? Bear in mind that many of the most modern treatments have been adopted precisely because they are most effective in economic and clinical terms. This is why the average number of days which patients spend in hospital steadily decreases, while the number of patients treated increases.[106] Increasingly sophisticated medical intervention makes it possible to discharge in a single day a patient whose treatment would previously have required a week in hospital.[107] In many cases, therefore, it would not make financial sense to adopt out-dated regimes of treatment because they would often require longer stays in hospital. On the other hand, the provision and staffing of expensive medical equipment, such as intensive care units and magnetic resonance imagery, imposes a drain on resources which could be put to better use elsewhere. There may be circumstances when the hospital has to offer treatment which falls short of what it would acknowledge as the best available, because the alternative is to offer nothing at all and turn the patient away.

B. Argument for a Unitary Standard

These arguments possess a certain economic logic, but their legal logic is dubious. Once the standard of care is allowed to slip, how

---

[105] His lordship said at p. 243: '[e]ven in a medical context outside prison, the standard of care will vary with the context. The facilities available to deal with an emergency in a general practitioner's surgery cannot be expected to be as ample as those available in the casualty department of a general hospital.' With respect, however, this precisely misses the point. Of course the facilities differ, but the GP has a continuing duty to his patient to take reasonable steps to safeguard his welfare (e.g. by transferring him to hospital) which is not affected by the issue of resources. Why should a similar duty not also apply for the benefit of prisoners?

[106] *Compendium of Health Service Statistics* (8th edn. Office of Health Economics, 1992), section 5. See also K. Bloor and A. Maynard, *Expenditure on the NHS During and After the Thatcher Years: Its Growth and Utilisation* (York Centre for Health Economics, 1993).

[107] Modern techniques of 'key-hole' surgery have the potential for reducing the need for complicated operations and lengthy periods spent in recuperation. There is evidence, however, that these new techniques have been used without proper training and understanding by surgeons. Patients have been killed or damaged as a result. See *Minimal Access Surgery: Implications for the NHS* (Edinburgh HMSO, 1993).

will the courts set a benchmark against which to measure liability? Say a hospital routinely required junior staff to work in specialist units without proper training or supervision, or habitually reused 'once only' medical equipment because it could not afford to replace it, or shut its accident and emergency unit on a Friday evening, or failed to staff or equip its ambulance service adequately. Without a test by which to measure the propriety of such actions, each could be excused on grounds of lack of resources. Such an incoherent approach to the well-being and rights of patients is unacceptable. The position in law is by no means settled, but a number of authorities have been reluctant to allow the standard of care to fluctuate in this way.

1. Inadequate Facilities and Treatment

To what extent is the question of resources relevant to the standard of care which the patient is entitled to expect? This issue was raised by the British Orthopaedic Association in respect of the facilities available in many accident and emergency units.[108] A similar issue was raised in the case of *Bull* v. *Devon Area Health Authority* discussed above,[109] when the hospital system failed to provide adequate consultant cover. The defendants argued that limited resources precluded their being able to offer an 'ideal' solution, which might have been expected in a centre of excellence; '[t]hey could not be expected to do more than their limited best, allocating their limited resources as favourably as possible.'[110] The defendant's experts refused to accept that there was anything wrong with the system, or that the standards in the hospital compared unfavourably with those in other split-site hospitals. As one defence expert stated, it was 'par for the course', and as Mustill LJ stated: 'it seems to have been assumed by the experts that if this was so, the patient would have nothing to complain about.'[111]

In the face of this evidence, the court might have been deferred to the judgment of the experts responsible for the management of

---

[108] *Supra*, note 5 and associated text.
[109] *Supra*, note 73. This question was posed, but unanswered, by Browne-Wilkinson VC in *Wilsher* v. *Essex Area Health Authority* [1986] 3 All ER 801, 834.
[110] Ibid. 141 *per* Lord Mustill LJ, representing the gist of the defence.
[111] Ibid.

the hospital. It might have adopted a variation of the *Bolam* test of medical negligence in relation to managerial issues, and said that the matter lay within the judgment of reasonable hospital managers. But the judges were reluctant to do so.[112] With reference to the argument based on scarce resources, Mustill LJ said:

it is not necessarily an answer to allegations of unsafety that there were insufficient resources to enable the administrators to do everything which they would like to do. I do not for a moment suggest that public medicine is precisely analogous to other public services, but there is perhaps a danger in assuming that it is completely *sui generis*, and that it is necessarily a complete defence to say that even if the system in any hospital was unsatisfactory, it was no more unsatisfactory than those in force elsewhere.[113]

Thus, the court was able to examine for itself the adequacy of the system of providing obstetric care in this case. It described the system as being so delicately balanced that it was 'obviously operating on a knife edge'[114] since it could only provide an acceptable level of care if it was operated with supreme efficiency.[115] The doctors knew that the mother was expecting twins, that any undue delay between the delivery of each would be very dangerous, and that she would probably need skilled assistance in delivering them. According to its own standards, the hospital ought to have been able to provide care within twenty minutes at most. But as a result of the failure of the system, the mother had to wait over an hour.[116] The failure to provide her with the prompt care that she needed was attributable to 'the negligence of the defendants in implementing an unreliable and essentially unsatisfactory system for calling for the registrar.'[117]

An analogous issue arose in the American case of *Wickline* v. *State of California*.[118] The plaintiff was admitted to hospital suffering arteriosclerosis, requiring an operation to the arteries of her leg. Her doctors recommended that she be detained in hospital

---

[112] If this is right, the decision in *Knight* v.*Home Office*, *supra*, note 102, which reduced the *Bolam* standard, may be doubted as soon as prisoners in the hospital wing are considered to be in receipt of clinical treatment.

[113] *Bull* v.*Devon AHA*, *supra*, note 73, 141.

[114] Ibid. 131, *per* Slade LJ.   [115] Ibid. 137, *per* Dillon LJ.

[116] Ibid. 142.   [117] Ibid. 138, *per* Dillon LJ.

[118] 228 Cal Rptr 661 (1986).

for eight days after surgery in case the wound became infected. The insuring purchaser of the treatment, Medi-Cal, permitted only a four-day extension of stay, after which the plaintiff was discharged. Her condition deteriorated and by the time she was later re-admitted to hospital it was necessary to amputate the leg, which had become gangrenous. Her doctors claimed that if she had remained in hospital for eight days her leg could have been saved. The plaintiff proceeded against the defendant purchasing insurer for *inter alia* negligence in refusing the funds which would have enabled her to remain in hospital. On appeal it was held that:

it is essential that cost limitation programs not be permitted to corrupt medical judgment. . . .[119]

Third party payers of health care services can be held legally accountable when medically inappropriate decisions result from defects in the design or implementation of cost containment mechanisms as, for example, when appeals made on a patient's behalf for medical or hospital care are arbitrarily ignored or unreasonably disregarded or overridden.[120]

The standard has been held steady even in cases of emergency. Occasionally, large scale catastrophes such as a railway accident or motorway pile-up completely overwhelm reasonably staffed and equipped accident and emergency units. In these circumstances 'full allowance must be made for the fact that certain aspects of treatment may be carried out in . . . "battle conditions". An emergency may overburden available resources and, if an individual is forced by circumstances to do too many things at once, the fact that he does one of them incorrectly should not lightly be taken as negligence.'[121] The law has been expounded as follows:

This does not mean that a different standard of care is applied in an emergency situation, simply that reasonable care takes into account the circumstances in which a doctor has to operate. If the error is one which a reasonably competent doctor could have made in the circumstances the doctor is not negligent. Conversely, if a reasonably competent doctor

---

[119] Ibid. 672. Compare the contrary view, limited to the prison context, in *Knight* v.*Home Office*, *supra*, note 102.

[120] Ibid. 670. On the facts, the court blamed the doctors for failing to represent to the insurers the gravity of the patient's situation and exonerated the defendants from blame. See also *Wilson* v.*Blue Cross of Southern California* 222 Cal App 3d (1990) for a similar response to a mental patient whose insurers denied him the care prescribed by doctors.

[121] *Per* Mustill LJ in *Wilsher*, *supra*, note 109, 812.

would not have made that error the defendant will be liable, notwithstanding the fact that it occurred in the course of an emergency.[122]

What about the costs of medicines?[123] English courts have not yet been invited to consider the point in relation to the costs incurred by GPs in their prescription of medicines. There is much concern about this matter and a number of incentives have been developed aimed at reducing the rate of increase in spending on drugs. None, however, have suggested that patients ought to be given less effective medicines; indeed, that may be inefficient and more expensive. If the risks attached to the use of the inexpensive product mean that some will not be assisted by treatment and will have to be admitted to hospital (which is vastly more expensive), it may be counter-productive to insist on the saving. The question has arisen with respect to the medicines recommended by hospital consultants. Once the patient has been discharged from hospital, should the GP continue with the consultant's regime, even if it will increase the GP's spending on medicine? In principle, the doctor responsible for the patient's care is responsible for the consequences of treatment and if the patient needs expensive treatment, it ought not to be withheld. The General Medical Council puts it as follows: 'doctors responsible for the continuing management of the patient must be fully competent to exercise their share of clinical responsibility and have a duty to keep themselves informed of the drugs that are recommended for their patients . . . doctors should have no inhibitions about prescribing on the basis of the patient's need.'[124]

The same must be true in reverse, when a consultant prescribes low-cost medicine and more effective but more expensive treatment is available. The GP could not hide behind the recommendations of the consultant in denying responsibility for the patient if the GP follows the consultant's unreasonable decision and things go wrong. The GP's duty is to prescribe the treatment which he or

[122] *Medical Negligence, supra,* note 14, 92, citing *Cattley* v.*St John's Ambulance Brigade* (1988, unreported). Note the argument, however, that 'resources' are very much part of 'the circumstances in which a doctor has to operate'.

[123] This question is considered in more detail in Chapter 5 with respect to the duty of FHSAs to impose 'indicative prescribing amounts' on GPs.

[124] *Resource Constraints and Contracting: Professional Responsibilities in Relation to the Clinical Needs of Patients* (General Medical Council, 1992), para. 12.

she considers most appropriate. This is the common law position[125] and the Audit Commission have said that concern for the individual patient must remain the doctor's paramount concern.[126] Rather than simply adopting a policy of cheaper, and perhaps less effective prescribing, GPs should seek to rationalize their prescribing habits, for example by using less expensive drugs as a first course of action, with the intention of substituting others if the patient's condition so demands. Thus, each practice should agree a policy which sets out their choice of first, second, and third line drugs for key areas of prescribing, so that a range of drugs is always available which is sufficient to respond to the patient's clinical needs.[127]

2. Inexperienced Staff

What if an accident occurs by reason of the inexperience of the doctors treating the patient? Lord Denning addressed the question as long ago as 1952 in a case in which a simple error by junior doctors in their use of anaesthetics killed a patient. The Court of Appeal decided that the hospital authorities had to share responsibility for the accident.

It would be in the highest degree unjust that hospital authorities, by getting inexperienced doctors to perform their duties for them, without adequate supervision, should be able to throw all responsibility on to those doctors as if they were fully experienced practitioners . . . [Hospitals] should not leave patients in inexperienced hands without proper super-vision.[128]

More recently, the question arose in *Wilsher* v. *Essex Area Health Authority* in which an accident occurred owing to the

---

[125] Consider by analogy the duty of solicitors in respect of advice received from counsel. See *Locke* v. *Camberwell HA* [1991] 2 Med LR 249, 254: 'For a solicitor without specialist experience in a particular field to rely on counsel's advice is to make normal and proper use of the bar. However, he must not do so blindly but must exercise his own independent judgment. If he reasonably thinks counsel's advice is obviously or glaringly wrong, it is his duty to reject it.' See also *Davy-Chiesman* v. *Davy-Chiesman* [1984] Fam 48.

[126] See *A Prescription for Improvement: Towards More Rational Prescribing in General Practice* (Audit Commission, 1994), para.79.

[127] Ibid., para. 44.

[128] *Jones* v. *Manchester Corporation, supra,* note 86, 133. Given the hospital's fault, the health authority's claim to an indemnity against the doctor for the damages it had paid to the deceased's widow was disallowed.

inexperience of a junior doctor newly appointed to a neonatal unit. A baby born prematurely was given excessive oxygen which was implicated as one of the causes for his becoming blind. Being new to the post, the doctor was not blamed personally for the error. It was argued in his defence that he ought to be judged against a standard which required of him only so much as it would be reasonable to expect from a junior doctor and, therefore that he ought not to be considered negligent for his failure. Mustill LJ balanced the argument in the following way. On the one hand he accepted that all doctors learn their expertise on the job, by practising medicine. This is inevitable and desirable. Hospitals make their contribution to medical practice by training young doctors in the subject; they derive some benefit since they are able to employ many more doctors than would be possible if all were expected to be fully qualified before they could practise. Patients are well served by this arrangement. On the other hand, if the standard of care to be expected from doctors was tailored to the individual concerned, with his or her own degree of experience and training, the rights of patients would to a large extent:

vary according to the chance of recruitment and rostering. The patient's right to complain of faulty treatment will be more limited if he has been entrusted to the care of a doctor who is a complete novice in the particular field (unless he can point to some fault of supervision in a person up the hierarchy) than if he has been in the hands of a doctor who has already spent months on the same ward.

This he found unacceptable. '[I]t would be a false step to subordinate the legitimate expectation of the patient that he will receive from each person concerned with his care a degree of skill appropriate to the task which he undertakes to an understandable wish to minimize the psychological and financial pressures on hard-pressed young doctors.'[129]

On this basis he decided that negligence ought to be assessed according to the post which the doctor occupies, rather than the skill which could be expected of him individually. Many doctors will ask, however, why they should be exposed to liability in

[129] *Wilsher, supra*, note 109, 813. Glidewell LJ took the same view. He said 'the law requires the trainee or learner to be judged by the same standard as his more experienced colleagues. If it did not, inexperience would frequently be urged as a defence to an action for professional negligence.' Ibid. 831.

negligence for failing to achieve a standard which no one expects of them? The reason is demonstrated by a case involving a learner driver. Obviously, the learner could not be expected to drive with the same standard of care as an experienced driver. However, when she drove in a way which injured her instructor (and a lamp-post) the Court of Appeal decided that she must be judged according to the standard of an experienced and competent driver. The duty arose from the relationship between the driver and those likely to suffer damage by his or her bad driving, and does not allow for the inexperience of the individual.[130] To make such an allowance would cause so much uncertainty as to the standard to be expected from defendants that it would be unfair to those damaged by such conduct.

One wonders, however, how durable this approach will be. In a dissenting judgment, Sir Nicolas Browne-Wilkinson VC preferred the contrary view and said that the standard of care ought to be assessed according to the skill and expertise to be expected from the individual doctor. He acknowledged that doctors should not usually be allowed to say that their failure was due to inexperience, because their fault would often lie in giving treatment which they ought to have known was beyond their competence. But, he said, some junior doctors might lack even this degree of understanding:

the position of the houseman in his first year after qualifying . . . who has just started in a specialist field in order to gain the necessary skill in that field is not capable of such an analysis. The houseman takes up his post in order to gain full professional qualification. . . . In my judgment such doctors cannot in fairness be said to be at fault if, at the start of their time, they lack the very skills which they are seeking to acquire.[131]

Like the other members of the court, he exonerated the junior doctor from blame in this case because he did indeed take the reasonable step of asking for the assistance of a senior colleague. Instead, he blamed the registrar responsible for supervising the work, who was called to check the patient and failed to notice the error. Nevertheless, junior doctors will prefer the judgment of the Vice-Chancellor to that of the majority of the Court of Appeal. Arguably, the reasoning in the case of the learner driver is not

---

[130] *Nettleship* v. *Weston, supra,* note 104. See also *Glasgow Corporation* v. *Muir* [1943] AC 448, 457.   [131] Ibid. 833.

analogous to the position of junior doctors.[132] If they are obliged
to work unsupervised in areas in which they lack necessary skills,
the action ought to be directed against the health authority. Take
the example of doctors who have been on duty without proper rest
for 90 hours, as required by their contracts of employment with the
hospital or DHA. Clearly, close supervision is required in these
circumstances. If they make an error of judgment which is
explicable entirely by fatigue, which other reasonable but exhausted doctors could also have been expected to make, ought
they to be held personally liable? In *Johnstone* v. *Bloomsbury
Health Authority,*[133] the Court of Appeal was sympathetic to a
claim in negligence by a junior doctor against a health authority
that his own health was being damaged by stress and over-work
and allowed his action for damages to proceed. Subsequently, a
local authority employer was held liable to its employee in
negligence for exposing him to such stress at work as to cause him
to suffer a second mental breakdown.[134] These cases acknowledge
that the employee may not simply refuse to perform the duties
assigned to him. Who is really to blame if a patient is injured by
reason of the doctor's fatigue or by lack of adequate supervision?
When the circumstances are within the control of the employer
and the risk to patients from inexperience and fatigue is entirely
foreseeable, it may be better to exonerate the doctor from blame
and hold the employer responsible.

---

[132] The case of *Nettleship* v. *Weston, supra,* note 104, was reconsidered in *Cook*
v. *Cook* (1986) 162 CLR 376, which proposes a more sophisticated approach to the
relationship between learner driver and instructor. The case was prepared to
modify the standard of care required of the driver in the light of the 'special
relationship' with the instructor. Such an approach could be extended to junior
doctors working under supervision in hospital.

[133] [1991] 2 All ER 293.

[134] See *Walker* v. *Northumberland CC, The Independent* 17 Nov. 1994.

4

Statutory Regulation of Standards

Common law enables patients who have been injured by negligent treatment to recover compensation for their loss. Negligence usually concerns itself with individual incidents rather than with the organization of the National Health Service as a whole. Although it is capable of criticizing the system by which care is delivered to patients, it makes incidental rather than systematic contributions to the standards achieved by the service. In order to understand what the NHS itself intends to achieve, we must examine the statutes by which it is governed, namely the National Health Service Act 1977 and the National Health Service and Community Care Act 1990.

I. THE NATIONAL HEALTH SERVICE ACT 1977

The National Health Service Act 1977 imposes on the Secretary of State a 'duty to continue the promotion in England and Wales of a comprehensive health service designed to secure improvement (a) in the physical and mental health of the people of those countries, and (b) in the prevention, diagnosis and treatment of illness, and for that purpose to provide or secure the effective provision of services in accordance with this Act.'[1]

This duty was first created by the National Health Service Act 1946 and was discussed in the White Paper of 1944 entitled *A National Health Service*, on which it was based. Discussing the meaning and scope of a 'comprehensive' service, it said:

The proposed service must be 'comprehensive' in two senses—first, that it is available to all people and, second, that it covers all necessary forms of health care. . . . The service designed to achieve it must cover the whole field of medical advice and attention, at home, in the consulting room, in the hospital or the sanatorium, or wherever else is appropriate—from the

---

[1] Section 1.

personal or family doctor to the specialists and consultants of all kinds, from the care of minor ailments to the care of major diseases and disabilities. It must include ancillary services of nursing, of midwifery and of the other things which ought to go with medical care. It must ensure that everyone can be sure of a general medical advisor to consult as and when the need arises, and then that everyone can get access—beyond the general medical advisor—to more specialized branches of medicine or surgery.[2]

A. A 'Comprehensive Health Service'

In considering what a 'comprehensive health service' means, a starting point is to ask whether there are any hospital services so basic to a health service that they should be described as priority or 'core' services. Recall that the approach taken in Oregon was to list categories of treatment in order of priority and to put at the top of the list 'acute fatal', meaning treatment that prevents death and leads to full recovery. The State of Oregon, therefore, asks the question: what forms of treatment are most important from the patient's point of view? Originally, in considering the shape of its proposed reforms, the Government seemed to be taking a similar approach. It said:

there are many services to which patients need guaranteed access. These 'core' services can be divided into five broad categories [1] accident and emergency (A and E) departments; [2] immediate admissions to hospital from an A and E department, including a significant proportion of general surgery; [3] other immediate admissions, such as most general medicine and many geriatric and psychiatric services; [4] out-patient and other support services which are needed in support of the first three categories, either on site or immediately available [and, 5] public health, community-based services and other hospital services which need to be provided on a local basis . . . for example services for elderly mentally ill people . . . or district nursing and health visiting.[3]

Subsequently, however, a different approach was adopted, in which the phrase 'designated services' replaced that of 'core services', 'because the latter term has been misunderstood as implying that core services are more important than others not so

---

[2] *A National Health Service* (Cmd.6502, 1944) 9.
[3] *Working for Patients* (Cm. 555, 1989), para. 4.15. These were not the only services contemplated. Other services are discussed at para. 4.19.

described'.[4] Designated services are regarded as those 'identified by a DHA as necessary for local provision to a specific population'.[5] The reason for the change of emphasis is not clear, since it is natural to consider that some services are indeed more important than others and that hospitals and district health authorities ought to understand which are considered so basic that no reasonable authority should be without them. In the end, no services are given priority, or identified as 'core', although the 1977 Act sets out a number of 'specified health service functions'[6] which health authorities shall provide on behalf of the Secretary of State. Failing a list of priority services, it is necessary to examine the Secretary of State's statutory duty. The duty is not limited to the provision of secondary care and is described in section 3(1) of the 1977 Act as follows:

It is the Secretary of State's duty to provide . . . to such extent as he considers necessary to meet all reasonable requirements
(a) hospital accommodation;
(b) other accommodation for the purpose of any service provided under this Act;
(c) medical dental, nursing and ambulance services;
(d) such other facilities for the care of expectant mothers and nursing mothers and young children as he considers are appropriate as part of the health service;
(e) such facilities for the prevention of illness, the care of persons suffering from illness and the after-care of persons who have suffered from illness as he considers are appropriate as part of the health service;
(f) such other services as are required for the diagnosis and treatment of illness.[7]

In addition, every regional health authority shall provide, on behalf of the Secretary of State 'accident and emergency services, including ambulance services provided in connection with those

---

[4] *Working for Patients: Contracts for Health Services: Operating Contracts* (NHSME, 1990), para. 3.17.

[5] Ibid. para. 3.18.

[6] The phrase is used to describe the functions in the National Health Service Functions (Directions to Authorities and Administrative Arrangements) Regs., 1991, SI 1991, No. 554, reg. 2(1), and in the Schedule.

[7] Section 3(1) of the 1977 Act. See also Sched. 8, concerning mothers and young children; prevention and after-care; and home help.

services,[8] . . . [except that the regulations] do not include any subsequent treatment connected with the provision of those services.'[9]

We shall examine what this means in the context of care in hospital, before considering claims to resources under alternative rights and the boundary between health care and community care.

1. Care in Hospital

The provisions of the 1977 Act are not intended to describe 'core' services. Rather, they set out a broad cross-section of services which should be provided by the National Health Service. Is it possible to describe in any more detail the services, or patients, which ought to be given priority? To a limited extent, this question has been tested in the courts, but judges have been extremely reluctant to become involved in the assessment of priorities and the allocation of health service resources. Section 3(1) was first considered in *R* v. *Secretary of State for Social Services,* ex parte *Hincks*,[10] in which plans for a new orthopaedic unit in Birmingham, approved by the Secretary of State in 1971, were postponed by him in 1973 and 'virtually abandoned'[11] in 1978. He did not deny the need for improving and extending orthopaedic facilities in Birmingham but considered that 'in the light of the resources likely to be available for capital developments' the scheme did 'not command sufficient regional priority to start within the next ten years'.[12] The applicants alleged that the Secretary of State had

---

[8] National Health Service Functions (Directions to Authorities and Administrative Arrangements) Regs., *supra*, note 6, reg. 3(1)(b)(i).

[9] Ibid. reg.2 (3).

[10] (1992) 1 BMLR 93 (decided in 1980). Action should normally be taken against the health authority in question, and not the secretary of state. The National Health Service Act 1977, Schedule 5, para. 15(1) provides: 'An authority shall, notwithstanding that it is exercising any function on behalf of the Secretary of State or another authority . . . be liable in respect of any liabilities incurred (including liabilities in tort) in the exercise of that function, in all respects as if it were acting as principal.

Proceedings for the enforcement of such rights and liabilities shall be brought, and brought only by, or as the case may be against the authority in question in its own name.'

However, in *Re HIV Haemophiliac Litigation* (CA, 1990, unreported) Ralph Gibson LJ said 'if . . . it could be shown that the Secretary of State was independently in breach of the relevant duty, the wording of paragraph does not provide any protection'.   [11] Ibid. 95, *per* Lord Denning MR.

[12] Ibid.

failed in his duty to provide a comprehensive health service in their area. Since he had approved the plans to build the unit and acknowledged the need for the facility, section 3(1) required him to set aside the funds to fulfil his duty. The argument was that, since no limitation was placed on the statutory duty: 'If the Secretary of State needs money to do it, then he must see that Parliament gives it to him. Alternatively if Parliament does not give it to him, then a provision should be put in the statute to excuse him from his duty.'[13]

The Court of Appeal decided, however, that section 3(1) cannot be interpreted to impose an absolute duty to provide services irrespective of economic decisions taken at national level. The provision has to be read subject to the implied qualification that the Secretary of State's duty was 'to meet all reasonable requirements such as can be provided within the resources available',[14] which 'must be determined in the light of current Government economic policy.'[15] In addition, however, given the fact that there were twelve hospitals competing for resources in this particular area, Lord Denning approved the opinion of the judge at first instance that 'I doubt very much whether under s.3(1) it is permissible to put the spotlight, as it were, upon one particular department of one hospital and to say that conditions there are unsatisfactory'.[16] This view demonstrates the difficulty of succeeding in a claim of this nature.

Much the same response has been given to those awaiting treatment in hospital. In *R* v. *Secretary of State,* ex parte *Walker*[17] the health authority was satisfied that a premature baby required an operation to repair his heart. The authority said it was unable to perform the procedure as a result of a decision not to staff all the intensive care units in its neonatal ward. Nursing staff were available for only four of the six beds which were occupied by

[13] Ibid. *per* Lord Denning MR summarizing the 'attractive argument' of Mr. Blom-Cooper, counsel for the applicants.

[14] See *R* v. *Secretary of State* ex parte *Hincks* (decided 1980) (1992) 1 BMLR 93, 95 per Lord Denning MR. Contrary to the aspirations of its founders, investment in the NHS has not reduced demand for health care. Compare *A National Health Service* (Cmd. 6502, 1944) 5, with *The Government's Expenditure Plans, 1989–90 to 1991–92* (Cm. 614, 1989) ch. 14, table 14.1.

[15] *Hincks, supra,* note 14, 97, *per* Bridge LJ.   [16] Ibid.

[17] (1992) 3 BMLR 32 (decided 1987).

more urgent cases. The plaintiff alleged that her baby had been
denied the surgical care which the hospital acknowledged he
needed. Rejecting the application for an order that the operation
be performed, Macpherson J said:

I say at once that I find it quite impossible to say there is in the decision
made by the health authority, or by the surgeons who act on their behalf,
any illegality, nor any procedural defect, nor any such unreasonableness.
The fact that the decision is unfortunate, disturbing and in human terms
distressing, simply cannot lead to a conclusion that the court should
interfere in a case of this kind . . .

. . . I detect a general criticism of the decisions as to staffing and
financing of the National Health Service and of those who provide its
funds and facilities. It has been said before, and I say again, that this court
can no more investigate that on the facts of this case than it could do so in
any other case where the balance of available money and its distribution
and use are concerned . . . they are questions to be raised, answered and
dealt with outside this court.[18]

Dismissing the appeal, the Master of the Rolls, Sir John
Donaldson, said:

It is not for this court, or indeed any court, to substitute its own judgment
for the judgment of those who are responsible for the allocation of
resources. This court could only intervene where it was satisfied that there
was a *prima facie* case, not only of failing to allocate resources in the way
in which others would think that resources should be allocated, but of a
failure to allocate resources to an extent which was *Wednesbury* . . .
unreasonable.[19]

In *Walker*, Macpherson J stressed that 'at present the evidence
establishes that there is no danger to the baby' and that, were an
emergency to arise, the operation would have been performed.[20]
What is the position when facilities are not made available to
patients whose health will be damaged, or whose lives are put in
danger, as a result? The matter was considered in *R* v. *Central
Birmingham Health Authority*, ex parte *Collier*,[21] which concerned
a four-year-old boy suffering from a hole in the heart. In

---

[18] Ibid. 34.
[19] *R* v. *Secretary of State for Social Services*, ex p *Walker* (decided, 1987) (1992) 3
BMLR 32, 35. The concept of '*Wednesbury*' unreasonable is discussed below.
[20] Ibid. 34.
[21] Unreported, 1988, reproduced in part in I. Kennedy and A. Grubb, *Medical
Law—Text with Materials* (Butterworths, 1994) 428.

September 1987 his consultant said that 'he desperately needed open heart surgery' and placed the boy at the top of the waiting list, expecting that intensive care facilities would be made available by the hospital within a month. By January 1988 the operation had been arranged and cancelled on three occasions and had still not been carried out. No intensive care bed could be made available. The Court of Appeal was invited to order that, given that the boy would probably die unless the operation were performed, the operation should be carried out. It said, however, that:

even assuming that [the evidence] does establish that there is immediate danger to health, it seems to me that the legal principles to be applied do not differ from the case of Re *Walker*. This court is in no position to judge the allocation of resources by this particular health authority . . . there is no suggestion here that the hospital authority have behaved in a way which is deserving of condemnation or criticism. What is suggested is that somehow more resources should be made available to enable the hospital authorities to ensure that the treatment is immediately given.

Taken alone, therefore, these decisions give scant encouragement to those thousands of patients whose curable conditions are untreated because beds, wards, or entire units are closed for reasons associated with cost.[22] Their effect appears to be that the National Health Service Act creates no direct right to health service resources and that the duty should be considered from the perspective of the various health authorities who must do their reasonable best with scarce resources, subject only to the lightest supervision from the courts.[23] This raises the question of what is 'reasonable' in cases of this kind, and who is to be the judge?

2. What is *Wednesbury* Unreasonable?

There is no doubt that the decisions to be made between deserving patients are extremely delicate and difficult to make and that

---

[22] See *In a Terminal Condition: A Report on the State of London's Health Service* (Association of London Authorities, 1991).

[23] Some American courts have shown similar reluctance to interfere, e.g. *Boone* v. *Tate* 286 A.2d 26 (1972). Others have adopted a more active approach by demanding persuasive evidence that the hospital could not have provided the service, e.g. *Doe* v. *General Hospital of the District of Columbia* 434 F.2d 427 (1970) and *Greater Washington DC Area Council of Senior Citizens* v. *District of Columbia Government* 406 F.Supp 768 (1975).

judges have no particular expertise to do so. But it is wrong to think that they have no role in the exercise. In theory, they have reserved for themselves the right to review the decisions of managers and administrators if they are *Wednesbury* unreasonable,[24] i.e. so unreasonable that no reasonable person addressing himself to the issue in question could have come to such a decision. Lord Diplock has described the power of review as follows:

It applies to a decision which is so outrageous in its defiance of logic or of accepted moral standards that no sensible person who had applied his mind to the question to be decided could have arrived at it. Whether a decision falls within this category is a question that judges by their training and experience should be well equipped to answer, or else there would be something badly wrong with our system.[25]

In theory, the court is not entitled to substitute its own judgment for that under review and there may be cases in which the court will uphold it even if, had the court been responsible for making the decision, it would have decided otherwise.[26] Its function is limited to considering whether the decision-maker was unreasonable and, particularly in matters concerning the allocation of scarce resources, is most reluctant so to find.[27] In practice, however, this distinction is sometimes blurred and in suitable cases the courts have intervened even when there are arguments to support both sides to the dispute, so that neither party, perhaps, should be described as wholly unreasonable, simply because they feel strongly inclined to do so.[28]

With respect to the difficulties presented by the question of health service resources, however, there has been no such inclination. Thus, in *Collier*, the Court said: 'This is not the forum in which a court can properly express opinions upon the way in

---

[24] Following the case of *Associated Provincial Picture Houses Ltd* v. *Wednesbury Corporation* [1948] 1 KB 223.

[25] In *Council of Civil Service Unions* v. *Minister for the Civil Service* [1985] AC 374, 410.

[26] See e.g. *R* v. *Secretary of State for the Environment*, ex parte *Knowsley Metropolitan BC* (1991) *The Independent* 11 June 1991.

[27] See *Rowling* v. *Takaro Properties Ltd* [1988] AC 473, 501, *per* Lord Keith.

[28] See J. Jowell and A. Lester, 'Beyond *Wednesbury*: Substantive Principles of Administrative Law', [1987] PL 368. See also *West Glamorgan County Council* v. *Rafferty* [1987] 1 WLR 457, in which the Court of Appeal held a local authority unreasonable for seeking a possession order against gypsies occupying its land despite the fact that 'there are admissible factors on both sides of the question' (*per* Ralph Gibson LJ, 477).

which national resources are allocated or distributed.' Under-standably, the courts are extremely careful about telling hospital managers which cases should take priority over others. After all, during litigation involving the claim of an individual patient, who will speak for the large numbers of patients who are not parties to the dispute? Who will speak for those particular patients whose operations will have to be cancelled if someone else is treated first? The point was made subsequently in the Court of Appeal by Balcombe LJ who said:[29]

I would stress the absolute undesirability of the court making an order which may have the effect of compelling a doctor or health authority to make available scarce resources (both human and material) to a particular child, without knowing whether or not there are other patients to whom those resources might more advantageously be devoted.

In the case of *Collier*, however, we are presented with a child who, as everyone agreed, was in need of common, if not routine, life-saving cardiac surgery, yet the hospital was unable to make facilities available. How could this have happened? The district health authority would have had long experience of the annual demand for paediatric intensive care. The condition would probably have been top of the list of priorities, listed in Oregon as 'acute fatal' treatment, capable of saving a life and restoring the patient to full health. On what system of priorities was such a refusal to provide care based? The astonishing thing about the case is that no one seemed to know exactly why intensive care facilities could not be made available to the patient. Counsel for the boy accepted that, on the evidence, he simply did not know why the surgery had been cancelled; as he said, 'it may be good reason or bad reason.' And, in the absence of an explanation, Ralph Gibson LJ commented, somewhat wistfully: 'No doubt the health authority would welcome the opportunity to deal with such matters so that they could explain what they are doing and what their problems are.'

[29] *Re J (a minor)* [1992] 4 All ER 614, 625. Precisely this point has been made in the housing context. In *R* v. *Bristol Corporation, ex p. Hendy* [1974] 1 All ER 1047, 1051, Scarman LJ said ' . . . if there is evidence that a local authority is doing all that it honestly and reasonably can to meet the statutory obligation, and that its failure . . . arises out of circumstances over which it has no control, then I would think it would be improper for the court to make an order of *mandamus* compelling it to do that which it cannot do or which it can do at the expense of others not before the court.'

One sympathizes with the courts' reluctance to become organizers of hospital waiting lists—clearly they would not be able or competent to do so. However, this has nothing to do with asking a court to determine whether the reasons for denying care to such a patient are reasonable and defensible. Was the authority attending to other patients in greater need of care? Was there a temporary shortage of staff owing to sickness? Had there been unexpected demand for intensive care? Could an alternative unit not have been found in another hospital? Was it impossible to borrow staff from elsewhere? Indeed, had anyone made any serious effort to resolve the problem? In all the circumstances, ought matters of this nature to be beyond the scope of judicial review?

3. How much *Wednesbury* Review?

The problem with *Hincks*, *Walker*, and *Collier* is the blandness of the assertions of the courts' incompetence to supervise cases of this kind. On one view of the judgments, with respect to health service resources, the courts have effectively excluded any possibility of a review. But this is open to doubt. In the internal market of the NHS, business managers must set and meet financial targets and pressures may be imposed which are capable of diverting attention from the clinical merits of individual cases. Suppose a health authority defends a decision to refuse treatment to a patient on the ground that it is too expensive. Perhaps the case has arisen at the end of the financial year when funds are short. Say it refuses long-term clinical care to all elderly patients with chronic conditions of illness on the ground that they represent an inefficient use of bed space. The essential question is this: ought the *Wednesbury* test of reasonableness to insist upon health service managers taking account of, as a minimum, the clinical merits of cases in coming to decisions about the allocation of scarce resources?

Decisions based exclusively on financial considerations may be perfectly reasonable from a purely managerial perspective. But are they reasonable in the context of the duties imposed by the National Health Service Act 1977? Arguably, if individuals or categories of patients are excluded from care on this ground on a random basis, which would differ from area to area and from year to year, the Secretary of State would fail in her duty to provide a 'comprehensive health service'. The issue of reasonableness 'must always begin by examining the nature of the statutory power which the administrative authority . . . has purported to exercise, and asking . . . what were, and what were not, relevant considerations for the authority to take into account in deciding to exercise that power.'[30] It must be right that decisions concerning the allocation of health service resources should always give proper weight to the clinical advice of doctors, and not confine itself to the financial advice of accountants. Otherwise, there would be a failure to take into account a relevant consideration. The point was made by Lord Donaldson MR that, when there is agreement amongst doctors about a proper course of treatment with respect to an individual, it would be unreasonable for managers to take a different view. He said:

Health authorities are supported by medical and administrative staff. In the context of medical decisions, it would be perverse for it to act otherwise than in accordance with the advice of its medical staff when the advice was unanimous.[31]

Both the Health Service Ombudsman and the Department of Health appear to have taken a similar view of the weight to be given to clinical considerations. We discuss later in this Chapter the Ombudsman's criticism of the health authority which adopted a policy excluding from hospital chronically ill patients in need of long-term care (criticism which was formally accepted in subsequent NHS guidelines). The Department of Health advises that with respect to patients whose needs have not been provided for by means of NHS contracts, and who require to be referred for treatment to a hospital on an extra contractual basis, '[i]t is not acceptable . . . to refuse authorisation solely on the grounds of the proposed cost of the treatment'.[32] Authorities must keep funds aside, therefore, to cater for expensive cases of this nature. Nor, as we saw in Chapter 3 in *Bull* v. *Devon Area Health Authority*, will the law of negligence pardon systems of management inherited from the past which fail to provide patients with reasonable

---

[30] *Gillick* v. *West Norfolk Area Health Authority* [1985] 3 All ER 402, 426 *per* Lord Bridge.

[31] Re *J (a minor)*, *supra*, note 29, 619. The case concerned the *withdrawal* of treatment from a child, but this ought not to effect the general principle.

[32] See *Guidance on Extra Contractual Referrals* (NHSME, 1993), para.51.

standards of care, notwithstanding the severe pressure which such a duty imposes on health service managers. These examples suggest that the limits of the courts' reluctance to exercise its powers of *Wednesbury* review have yet to be tested.

Of course, there will always be differences of clinical opinion as to who should be placed where on the list of priorities and in many cases the courts will be understandably slow to intervene. But there will also be the case about which there is general agreement and which 'cries out for reasons'.[33] In these exceptional cases, there is an argument that hospitals and health authorities should be more explicit about their reasons for failing to provide treatment. The duty to give reasons has developed from natural justice cases concerning the exercise of adjudicatory authority and was used in Re *HIV Haemophiliac Litigation* in favour of patients who were granted discovery of documents after having been contaminated with HIV. Ralph Gibson LJ said in that case: 'It seems to me to be necessary for the fair and proper disposal of the case that there should be known to both sides the actual grounds for the various decisions which led to the continued use of imported and other blood products capable of infecting a patient with HIV.'[34] Subsequently, Lord Mustill has said 'I find in the more recent cases on judicial review a perceptible trend towards an insistence on greater openness, or . . . "transparency" in the making of administrative decisions'.[35] Consider the facts of *Collier*; the case was urgent, a child's life was in danger, doctors had given the case clinical priority, and the proposed treatment had good prospects of success. Ought the court to have been told exactly why the patient could not be offered treatment?[36]

Support for the idea that the court should be so satisfied was

---

[33] Per Sedley J in *R* v. *Higher Education Funding Council, ex p Institute of Dental Surgery* [1994] 1 All ER 651, 666. See also *R* v. *Civil Service Appeal Board, ex p Cunningham* [1991] 4 All ER 310.

[34] See Re HIV Haemophiliac Litigation (CA, 1990, unreported) granting discovery of documents against the Department of Health during the course of the litigation. The Department resisted the application, *inter alia*, on grounds of the need to make decisions with respect to scarce resources.

[35] *Doody* v. *Secretary of State for the Home Department* [1993] 3 All ER 92, 107: He also said 'The law does not at present recognise a general duty to give reasons for an administrative decision. Nevertheless, it is equally clear that such a duty may in appropriate circumstances be implied', 110.

[36] Lord Denning has said (referring to *Padfield* v. *Minister of Agriculture, Fisheries and Food* [1968] AC 997) that there are cases in which 'a Minister should

offered by the High Court in *R* v. *Cambridge DHA,* ex p *B*,[37] which concerned a ten-year-old girl with leukaemia who had been in the care of the authority since 1990. By 1995 her prognosis was very poor. Without treatment, her doctors expected she would die within a matter of months. Her health authority refused to provide her with remedial (as opposed to palliative) treatment that might have prolonged her life. One of the factors it had in mind was the availability of resources, since the treatment was expected to cost up to £75,000. Laws J was uncomfortable with the trite assertion that resources present difficulties in the National Health Service. He said:

> . . . merely to point to the fact that resources are finite tells one nothing about the wisdom, or . . . the legality of a decision to withhold funding in a particular case. . . . Where the question is whether the life of a ten year-old child might be saved, by however slim a chance, the responsible Authority must do more than toll the bell of tight resources. They must explain the priorities that have led them to decline to fund the treatment.[38]

Thus, he referred the matter back to the authority to reconsider the evidence on which its refusal to provide care was based. The case was taken to the Court of Appeal who on the same day reversed the judgment of Laws J and upheld the decision of the health authority. The evidence on which the Court based its decision was as follows: (i) The doctors responsible for treatment considered it to be so untested that it was 'experimental'; (ii) its prospects of success were very small: i.e. 10–20 per cent for the first stage of treatment, and *if* that were successful, 10–20 per cent for the second stage of treatment; i.e. between 1 per cent and 4 per cent overall; (iii) it would have debilitating side-effects which, given the patient's prospects, were not in her best interests; and (iv) given her prospects, the total cost of the two stages of procedures could not be justified. The unanimous clinical view of the doctors was that the procedure should not be carried out and they advised the authority accordingly. The authority accepted

---

give reasons, and if he gives none the court may infer that he had no good reasons . . . in particular in cases which affect life, liberty or property . . . ' See *Secretary of State for Employment* v. *ASLEF* [1972] 2 QB 455, 493.

[37] Q.B.D. unreported, 1995.
[38] Ibid.

their opinions, confirming at the same time that the decision had been taken in the light of 'all the clinical and other relevant matters . . . and not on financial grounds.'[39] Put this way (and in stark contrast to the case of *Collier*), there was sufficient clinical evidence to persuade the court that it was within the authority's discretion to refuse treatment in the circumstances. The Court of Appeal heard in detail the precise medical evidence on which the decision to withhold care was based, after which the Master of the Rolls, Sir Thomas Bingham, found it 'impossible to fault that process of thinking . . .'[40] He also observed that: 'Difficult and agonizing judgments have to be made as to how a limited budget is best allocated to the maximum advantage of the maximum number of patients. That is not a judgment the court can make. In my judgment, it is not something that a health authority . . . can be fairly criticized for not advancing before the court.'[41]

This addresses a slightly different question. Certainly, it is asking too much to require the courts to become familiar with the principles (if there are any) which seek to ensure that maximum numbers of patients receive maximum benefits, i.e. the 'macro' policies of resource allocation. Matters concerning the general distribution of funds between different hospitals, categories of patients, medical research, new equipment, staffing, and so on are largely unjusticiable, and the observation of the Master of the Rolls confirms the decision in *Hincks*. Our present concern, however, is whether the courts are competent to hear evidence as to why a *particular* patient has been refused care, i.e the 'micro' issue. *Ex parte B* demonstrates that it is entirely possible for health authorities to present evidence on which individual decisions have been based. For the court to review the reasons for such a decision does not require it to substitute its own decision. A requirement to adduce such evidence is necessary to enable the court to ascertain whether a decision was taken in the light of relevant considerations, and excluded irrelevant ones. Naturally, given the limitations of its expertise in the area, a fairly low threshold of

[39] *R* v. *Cambridge Health Authority, ex p. B* [1995] 2 All ER 129, 133 (CA). A refusal to refer the patient on financial grounds would have breached the NHS Executive's own guidelines. See note 32 above.

[40] Ibid. 138.

[41] Ibid. 137. The urgency of the case permitted almost no time for the decision to be prepared.

satisfaction will tend to be required. Indeed, few such cases will have realistic prospects of success. But the very fact that such clinical evidence were required would focus minds on ensuring that these unenviable decisions are reasonable and defensible, and would help to satisfy patients and the public that the question has been properly addressed. It was the failure to do so in *Collier* which makes that case so unsatisfactory. *Ex parte B* does not expressly require clinical evidence of this nature to be presented to the court as a general rule, though the decision itself relies upon it. However, if the case provides an example of the way in which these matters ought to proceed, it is reassuring for this reason.

An alternative way of exercising supervision under *Wednesbury* is for the courts to lay down principles which mark some of the boundaries of 'reasonableness', so that decision-makers have some indication of the categories of decisions that will fall on either side of the line. Consider a patient for whom treatment is available, but at very high cost, the effect of which is to use up resources which would otherwise be applied for the benefit of others. In *Airedale NHS Trust* v. *Bland* the House of Lords approved guidelines proposed by the British Medical Association on the *Treatment of Patients in Persistent Vegetative State*.[42] The guidelines recommend, amongst other things, that before life support facilities are discontinued to enable a patient to die, every effort should be made at rehabilitation for at least six months after the injury, and that the diagnosis of irreversible PVS should not be considered confirmed until at least twelve months after the injury, with the effect that any decision to withhold life-prolonging treatment will be delayed for that period.[43] Such a regime of treatment and care is expensive. There may be as many as 1,000 patients in this condition in the country, the total cost of treating whom has been

---

[42] '. . . the vegetative patient fails to regain any cognitive behaviour that would indicate function in the cerebral cortex—the grey matter responsible for consciousness, thinking, feeling, and responding in meaningful (as distinct from reflex) ways to stimuli from the surroundings. [However,] because the brain-stem and various other sub-cortical and more primitive parts of the brain are still functioning, the vegetative patient has a wide range of reflex activity, including breathing and, in some patients, a very limited capacity to swallow . . . [they] can continue to breath for years because the brain-stem is still functioning'. *Airedale NHS Trust* v. *Bland* [1993] 1 All ER 821 at 827.

[43] Ibid., 871 and 883.

estimated at £20 million.[44] A hospital manager, with targets to meet, might reasonably ponder whether such a use of money was prudent. Some might ask whether the period of twelve months could be reduced to, say, six months, or six weeks.[45] After all, the money can only be spent once. Sums of this magnitude could be used to provide treatment for whole categories of patient who might otherwise be denied care; for example, prosthetic hips for the elderly, kidney dialysis, infertility treatment, or intensive care units for premature babies. Is it within the reasonable discretion of a manager to issue guidelines based on economic considerations intended to divert resources from single expensive patients to groups of other less expensive patients? The question was not properly addressed in *Bland* because the hospital 'invited us to decide the case on the assumption that its resources were unlimited and we have done so.'[46] However, a number of observations were made in that case which bear on the issue. Lord Keith said: '. . . in general, it would not be lawful for a medical practitioner who assumed responsibility for the care of an unconscious patient simply to give up treatment where continuance of it would confer some benefit on the patient'.[47]

And Lord Browne-Wilkinson, recognizing the competition for scarce resources, posed the following question: 'the new technology raises practical problems. Given that there are limited resources available for medical care, is it right to devote money to sustaining the lives of those who are, and always will be, unaware of their own existence rather than treating those who, in a real sense, can be benefited, e.g. those deprived of dialysis for want of resources? He answered himself saying: '. . . it is not legitimate for

---

[44] J. Lawrence, 'Judgment affects 1,000 patients', *The Independent*, 5 Feb. 1993 3. With advances in medical technology, the number who are saved in this condition is likely to increase.

[45] In *Bland*, two of the consultants took only four months to reach 'the clear conclusion that there was absolutely no hope of any improvement . . . [and] felt it would be appropriate to cease further treatment' of the patient. See *supra* note 42, 825. In exceptional cases, however, patients have been reported as showing some degree of recovery after a year; see K. Andrews, 'Recovery of Patients after four months or more in the persistent vegetative state', 306 *British Medical Journal* 1597 (1993) and B. Jennet, 'Vegetative Survival: the Medical Facts and Ethical Dilemmas', 3(2) *Neurological Rehabilitation* 99 (1993).

[46] *Bland*, *supra* note 42, 857, *per* Hoffmann LJ.

[47] Ibid. 861.

a judge in reaching a view as to what is for the benefit of the one individual whose life is in issue to take into account the wider practical issues as to allocation of limited financial resources . . .'[48]

These observations suggest that the courts will not simply abstain from decisions that have to be made in circumstances of scarce resources. In laying down general guidelines, they indicate some of the boundaries of lawful conduct. Given the many differences of opinion as to how resources should be spent, there will be understandable reluctance to become actively involved in cases of this nature. Unarguably, however, it is essential to develop a better appreciation of the limitations of the health service and the expectations that patients can reasonably have of it. As the number of cases inevitably increases, a body of knowledge will accumulate which informs the public and serves to deter speculative litigation. The pronouncements of the courts are indispensable to individuals; they are also one of the most effective ways of promoting discussion and understanding of controversial issues. Both health service managers and the courts should be prepared to contribute to this process.

B. Claims under an Alternative Right

Access to resources may be available if the claim can be made under an alternative right. In *R* v. *Ealing DHA, ex parte F,*[49] the applicant was compulsorily detained in Broadmoor hospital under sections 37 and 41 of the Mental Health Act 1983. In 1991 a Mental Health Review Tribunal (MHRT) directed that he be conditionally discharged, such discharge to be deferred until proper psychiatric care could be provided in the community. The health authority, however, refused to make community care available and said that he should continue to be supervised in a regional secure unit. Its decision followed the refusal of a number

---

[48] Ibid. 879. Lord Mustill said of the same issue: 'In social terms it has great force, and it will have to be faced in the end. But this is not a task which the courts can possibly undertake. A social cost–benefit analysis of this kind, which would have to embrace "mercy-killing", to which exactly the same considerations apply, must be for Parliament alone'. Ibid. 893. Compare Hoffmann LJ who said 'in principle the allocation of resources between patients is a matter for the health authority and not for the courts'. Ibid., 857. Compare also the view of Balcombe LJ in *Re J*, note 29, *supra*.

[49] (1993) 11 BMLR 59.

of psychiatrists in the district to undertake responsibility for the case in the community. As a result, the patient was unable to leave Broadmoor hospital. The court put the question before it as follows: '[where] the MHRT is prepared to grant a conditional discharge but the relevant health authority is unable or unwilling to make available care in the community *for reasons other than lack of resources*, whether the patient is obliged to remain under maximum security.'[50]

The applicant relied on section 117(2)[51] of the Mental Health Act 1983 and section 3 of the National Health Service Act 1977. The former provides that it 'shall be the duty of the District Health Authority and of the local services authority to provide, in co-operation with the relevant voluntary agencies, after-care services for any person to whom this section applies until such time as the District Health Authority and the local social services authority are satisfied that the person concerned is no longer in need of such services.'

Otton J, applying this sub-section, said that he considered section 117(2) to be mandatory, in the sense that the duty is not only a general, but a specific duty owed to the applicant to provide him with after care services. However, he also said: 'If I am wrong in that interpretation, I am satisfied that such a duty can be spelled out from the general statutory framework, which requires DHAs to provide a comprehensive range of hospital and community psychiatric services, including appropriate services to meet the needs of mentally disordered offenders (see s. 3(1) of the National Health Service Act 1977).'[52]

Thus, he said

. . . if the DHA's doctors do not agree with the conditions imposed by the MHRT and are disinclined to make the necessary arrangements to supervise the applicant on his release, the DHA cannot let the matter rest there. The DHA is under a continuing obligation to make further endeavours to provide arrangements within its own resources, or to obtain them from other health authorities who provide such services, so as to put

---

[50] (1993) 11 BMLR 61, emphasis added.

[51] Section 117(1) provides: 'This section applies to persons who are detained under section 3 above, or admitted to a hospital in pursuance of a hospital order made under section 37 above, or transferred to a hospital in pursuance of a transfer direction made under section 47 or 48 above, and then cease to be detained and leave hospital.'   [52] Note 50, *supra*, 71.

in place practical arrangements for enabling the applicant to comply with the conditions imposed by the MHRT, or at the very least to make enquiry of other providers of such services.[53]

Two observations may be made about this case which restrict its application. First, the refusal to provide care in this case was not by reason of lack of resources. It concerned the suitability of the environment that could be provided for the patient. This, therefore, is a reason for considering *ex parte F* to be very different from the other cases in which resources have been central. Secondly, this is a case concerning the liberty of the individual. Since the issues involve compulsory detention, there is always an argument for constructing a statute in favour of individual freedom, even if greater resources are required to do so. Thus, in another case of detention under the Mental Health Act 1983, it was said:

There is . . . no canon of construction which presumes that Parliament intended that people should, against their will, be subjected to treatment which others, however professionally competent, perceive, however sincerely and however correctly, to be in their best interests. What there is is a canon of construction that Parliament is presumed not to enact legislation which interferes with the liberty of the subject without making it clear that this was its intention.

It goes without saying that, unless clear statutory authority exists, no one is to be detained in hospital or to undergo medical treatment or even to submit himself for medical examination without his consent. This is as true of a mentally disordered person as of anyone else.[54]

This is a persuasive way of interpreting section 117 of the 1983 Act; it suggests that there should be a predisposition in favour of the liberty of the subject. But it has no general impact on the rights of patients in general or the National Health Service Act 1977 as a whole, which give rise to many broader issues. If this is right, the judge's application of section 3 of the 1977 Act to the facts of *ex parte F* was unnecessary and may respectfully be doubted.

---

[53] Ibid. He continued 'If the arrangements still cannot be made then the DHA should not permit an impasses to continue but refer the matter to the Secretary of State so as to enable him to consider exercising his power to refer the case back to the MHRT under s 71(1)'.

[54] *R v. Hallstrom,* ex parte *W (No 2)* [1986] 2 All ER 306, 314, *per* McCulloch J.

C. Hospital Care and Community Care

The National Health Service does so much for us when we enter the world. Toward the end of our lives the story is rather different. We considered in Chapter 1 the additional demands we place on health service resources when we become elderly, and the fact that one health authority attempted to introduce measures to limit its responsibilities which were severely criticized by the Health Service Ombudsman. But the Ombudsman is not a judge and his decision does not provide a legal authority on which other cases can be based. What is the legal duty with respect to the long-term care of patients?

Very few cases have considered the matter, yet the distinction between health care and social services care is very significant. Health care provided by hospitals and in the community is free of charge. Social services care provided at home, or in nursing homes, may be subject to charges.[55] Clearly, the costs incurred by such care, perhaps over many years, is considerable and the distinction is extremely important. The issue arose recently in the case of *White* v. *Chief Adjudication Officer*[56] which concerned the long-term care of a group of elderly patients suffering mental illness. They had been cared for in hospital for many years but, in the opinion of a psychiatrist engaged by the health authority, hospital treatment was no longer necessary and they could be placed in a nursing home setting. The question arose as to the right of the residents to income support, so that the dispute was effectively between the Department of Social Security and the Mid Downs District Health Authority as to who was responsible for the cost incurred in providing care and accommodation to the residents. The Court of Appeal reasoned as follows. The nursing home was to be regarded as a 'hospital' within the definition in the National Health Services Act 1977, because it was an 'institution for the reception and treatment of persons suffering from mental

---

[55] See s. 44, National Health Service and Community Care Act 1990. Regulations for means-testing residents for residential or nursing home care are provided by the National Assistance (Assessment of Resources) Regs. 1992 (SI 1992, No. 2977, as amended). Unpaid costs may be recovered after their death by way of legal charge on their property. (See s. 22, Health and Social Services and Social Security Adjudications Act 1983.)

[56] 17 BMLR 68 (1994).

illness', namely 'mental disorder within the meaning of the Mental Health Act 1983'.[57] On that basis Ralph Gibson LJ said:

> I acknowledge that if the provision of nursing care by professionally trained nurses in an institution is minimal, as for example only rarely expected to be required, such an institution may not be a hospital. In this case, however, the fourteen applicants are mentally ill. They require appropriate nursing for and because of their illness. Forest Lodge [the nursing home] has, and has agreed to maintain, appropriate nurse staffing, including qualified mental nurses. Mr Day, who is in charge, is a mental nurse. All but one of the patients are on medication for their illness. Forest Lodge dispenses drugs on prescription. I would hold that Forest Lodge [is] a hospital.[58]

Thus, the residents were properly described as 'patients' suffering 'illness'. The nursing home provided care on behalf of the health authority, which was responsible for bearing the costs incurred. Does this decision provide a clear distinction for future cases? Age Concern says that the very use of the word 'illness' is being distorted because decisions to discharge elderly patients are not always based on medical considerations. Rather, the question of an individual's need for care may be determined on managerial and financial grounds.[59] In the result, there are as yet no general rules or standards in use throughout the country. In some areas provision for the elderly may be good, in others it may be appalling, unless funded privately. At this vulnerable time of life, and with the increasing numbers of us who will become dependent, such a haphazard system of responsibility is unacceptable. 'There is an urgent need to clarify the responsibilities of the NHS in providing and/or purchasing continuing care for elderly people. The current position is confused and inequitable. The care available appears to be largely a matter of chance.'[60]

Curiously, the Department of Health seems until recently to have treated the matter as if it were simply for the patient to

---

[57] See s. 128, National Health Service Act 1977, the definition section.

[58] *White* v. *Chief Adjudication Officer* 17 BMLR 68, 80 (1994).

[59] *Under Sentence: Continuing Care Units for Older People Within the NHS* (Age Concern, 1991). Concerns have also been expressed by the House of Commons Social Security Committee in *The Financing of Private Residential and Nursing Home Fees* (Fourth Report, 1990–1991 Session, HMSO).

[60] M. Henwood, *Through a Glass Darkly: Community Care and Elderly People* (King's Fund Institute, 1992) 39, and generally.

decide where he or she wished to stay. It advised that 'no NHS patient should be placed in a private nursing or residential care home against his/her wishes if it means that he/she or a relative will be personally responsible for the home's charges'.[61] And the minister for health confirmed that 'if the patient in an NHS bed does not feel willing to accept responsibility for private nursing home fees and is not in a condition to return to their home, they should remain under the care of the health authority'.[62] But this is simply to deny the financial pressures under which health authorities operate. In 1995 the Department of Health issued new guidance on *NHS Responsibilities for Meeting Continuing Health Care Needs*,[63] concerning the obligations of health and social services authorities to provide care to those with long-term needs. The guidance is more forthright. It states that: 'Where patients have been assessed as not requiring NHS continuing inpatient care, they do not have the right to occupy indefinitely an NHS bed . . . they do, however, have the right to refuse to be discharged from NHS care into a nursing home or residential care home.'[64]

How is the distinction to be drawn between those who require NHS care and those who do not, and what happens to those who are discharged from hospital against their will? The guidelines specify that the responsibility of the NHS to arrange and fund services includes:

specialist medical and nursing assessment; rehabilitation and recovery; palliative health care; continuing inpatient care under specialist supervision in hospital or in a nursing home; respite health care; specialist health care to support people in nursing homes or residential care homes or the community; community health services to people at home or in residential care homes, primary health care; [and] specialist transport services.[65]

---

[61] See *Discharge of Patients from Hospital* HC (89)5 (1989), para. 2, discussed in L. Marks, *Seamless Care or Patchwork Quilt: Discharging Patients from Acute Hospital Care* (King's Fund Institute, 1994), ch.3. The author notes the distressing circumstances in which patients are discharged alone from hospital in the absence of adequate liaison with GPs, local authorities, and other carers. Under s. 22 National Health Service Act 1977, an obligation is imposed on health authorities, FHSAs, and local authorities to 'co-operate with one another in order to secure and advance the health and welfare of the people of England and Wales'.

[62] Letter from Mrs. Virginia Bottomley to the Patient's Association, quoted in Age Concern, *Under Sentence, supra* note 59, 4.

[63] HSG(95)8 and LAC(95)5; (NHSE, 1995).   [64] Ibid., para. 27.

[65] Ibid., para. 10.

Responsibility for making these difficult decisions rests with the consultants and nurses responsible for the care of the individuals concerned, on the basis of a multi-disciplinary assessment of need, including where appropriate discussions with staff from social services and housing authorities.[66] This is primarily a matter for clinical discretion which is not effected by the availability of resources, except to this extent. The way in which funds are distributed between health and social services departments may differ from place to place. Some may have invested more heavily in the provision of health services in the community. In such an area discharge from hospital may be more appropriate because adequate health care is available from GPs and health visitors. By contrast, those areas which have less sophisticated facilities in the community may find that adequate care of the type required by the guidelines can only be provided in hospital. This suggests that closer co-operation between health and social services authorities will be required, with respect to both providing care in the present and its purchase for the future.

Those who are discharged from hospital against their wishes will continue to be entitled to receive primary care services from GPs in the same way as before, without the need to pay for them. This is the case whether the care is provided at home, or in a nursing or residential home. Included amongst these services will be specialist nursing advice such as continence and diabetic advice, stoma and catheter care, physiotherapy, speech therapy, and chiropody. However, it would not include meals on wheels or assistance with bathing, dressing, and mobility. They could be provided by the social services authority which may levy a charge for providing them.

To those who have funded the NHS since its inception, in the expectation that it would care for them when they were no longer able to care for themselves, these guidelines may seem a betrayal. There was talk in the late 1980s of the value of people's houses cascading down to younger generations and new wealth being available in society. Now, for many people, the value of their homes will not pass to their families. Instead, it will be used paying

---

[66] An informal review or appeal is available to those who disagree with the decision of the hospital to discharge them. The review is staffed by a panel including an independent chairman. See ibid., paras. 27–33.

for the cost of their care as residents in nursing homes. This is (to say the least) disappointing. However, a more positive view may be taken of the guidelines. The need to review NHS responsibilities for long-term patients was prompted by the case of the brain-damaged patient who was refused hospital care because his condition had stabilized and nothing more could be achieved for him in hospital. The matter was investigated by the Health Services Ombudsman. The chief executive of the health authority justified the policy on the ground that the authority 'could not meet every health need. Present policy was for shorter inpatient stays with continuing care being provided in the community. The authority did not provide for any long stay beds in hospital or have any contractual arrangements for such beds in private nursing homes.'[67]

As we saw in Chapter 1, the Health Service Ombudsman severely criticized the health authority and its policy for failing in its duty to the patient. The Ombudsman considered section 3(1)(e) of the 1977 Act, which imposes on the Secretary of State a duty to provide 'to such extent as he considers necessary to meet all reasonable requirements . . . such facilities for . . . the after-care of persons who have suffered from illness as he considers appropriate as part of the health service.' He said that the policy of the authority 'was unreasonable and constitutes a failure in the service provided by the authority'.[68] Arguably, the Court of Appeal would have agreed with the Ombudsman had it been asked to consider the matter. In *White* v. *Chief Adjudication Officer* the Court said that psycho-geriatric patients were 'ill' in the sense that they required constant nursing supervision by skilled nurses. The fact that their condititon had stabilized and that they no longer needed treatment in hospital did not prevent them from being patients within the responsibiity of the NHS. The two cases are broadly analogous.

The new guidelines on *Continuing Health Care Needs* adopt a similar view. They confirm that decisions about which categories of patient do, or do not, have a right to health care within the NHS are not to be determined by health service managers as a matter of

---

[67] *Health Service Commissioner, Second Report for Session 1993-94. Failure to provide long term NHS care for a brain-damaged patient* (HC 197, 1994), para. 18.
[68] Ibid., para. 22.

policy. Certainly, managers have their problems, but they do not include making decisions about patient care which are properly the responsibility of clinicians. The guidelines were passed as a response to the Ombudsman's adjudication and the Secretary of State has told the House of Commons' Health Committee that 'Health authorities who follow the new guidelines should not find themselves in a position of being rebuked by the Ombudsman'.[69] This confirmation of the responsibilities of the NHS to elderly patients is reassuring. Any claim to the contrary, intended to reduce their rights to care, has implications which concern the fundamental duty of the Secretary of State under the 1977 Act to provide 'a comprehensive health service'. A decision to restrict that duty would be for Parliament alone.

D. Would QALYs Provide a 'Comprehensive Health Service'?

The principle of the Quality Adjusted Life Year (QALY)[70] is intended to promote efficiency in the health service. It does so by suggesting that resources ought to be allocated in those ways which most improve the quality of people's lives over the longest period of time (but not necessarily to the largest number). A variation of such a principle has been proposed in Oregon, and it is clear that some categories of treatment under that system would simply not be offered to patients. In the UK the idea has attracted academic interest from health authorities but no one has yet suggested that it should be given prominence in practice. Would such a system be lawful under the National Health Service Act 1977? The Act does not talk in terms of priorities. It describes a broad range of services, some of which it is the duty of the Secretary of State to provide, others of which 'may' be provided in her discretion.

Take the example of the absolute duty to provide a comprehensive health service imposed by section 1 of the 1977 Act. We have seen that the courts have been reluctant to define this duty in a way which creates corresponding rights with respect to individual patients. On the other hand, under the principle of the QALY, entire areas of care might have to be excluded from health care

---

[69] *Priority Setting in the NHS: Purchasing* HC 134–II, Session 1994–95, 162. The legal status of guidelines is considered in ch. 5, section IV.

[70] QALYs and the Oregon experiment are discussed in Chapter 1.

provision, as is suggested by the State of Oregon. There would then be an issue as to whether such a system could be said to be 'comprehensive'. The complaint would be not that individuals were denied a right to treatment, but that the system had been set up in a way that was no longer comprehensive.

Health service economists will understandably reply that they propose only that we use our resources more effectively and in this sense the system is every bit as comprehensive under the QALY principle. Indeed, if it provides more efficient use of resources, it could be said to be more comprehensive. But the duty imposed on the Secretary of State is 'to secure improvement (a) in the physical and mental health of the people of [England and Wales], and (b) in the prevention, diagnosis and treatment of illness, and for that purpose to provide or secure the effective provision of services in accordance with this Act'. No allowance appears to be made for QALYs in this provision. Take the example of elderly patients. As we saw in Chapter 1, more and more of us are able to survive into old age and there has been a rapid expansion of those who survive beyond the age of seventy-five years. 'At the start of the NHS in 1948, their combined total numbered 1.7 million persons (or 3.4% of the total population); by 1990 they had more than doubled to around 4.0 millions (or 6.9% of the total population).'[71]

Obviously, our health needs are likely to increase as we grow older. The average cost to the NHS of caring for those over the age of seventy-five is about £1,570 each per year, whereas those between ages sixteen and sixty-five cost around £615.[72] Inevitably this tends to concentrate resources in one section of the community, so that those over the age of seventy-five, who account for about 7 per cent of the population, absorbed approximately 25 per cent of overall NHS expenditure in 1989/90.[73] Would the QALY principle discourage such a concentration of scarce resources on a relatively small proportion of people who, by definition, have a relatively short period of time in which to enjoy the improvement

[71] See *Compendium of Health Statistics* (Office of Health Economics, 8th edn.), section entitled 'Population and vital statistics'.

[72] See *The Government's Expenditure Plans 1989–90 to 1991–92* (Department of Health, Cm. 614, 1989), ch. 14.

[73] See *Compendium of Health Statistics*, *supra* note 71, section entitled 'Cost of the NHS'.

in health brought about by care? If it were said that their health needs ought not to be given the same recognition under the QALY approach a whole section of the community would be excluded from the care promised in *A National Health Service* to ensure that 'everybody in the country—irrespective of means, age, sex, or occupation—shall have equal opportunity to benefit from the best and most up-to-date medical and allied services available'.[74] It is difficult to see how such a system could be said to provide 'comprehensive health care' of the sort intended by the 1977 Act.

On the other hand, the Secretary of State's duty under the Act may be heavily qualified. Thus, he or she 'may' provide a range of other services, for example, 'invalid carriages for persons . . . suffering from severe physical defect or disability'[75] and 'a microbiological service . . . for the control of the spread of infectious diseases . . .'[76] and dental services 'to such extent as he considers necessary to meet all reasonable requirements.'[77] The effect of giving discretion to the Secretary of State may be to accommodate the introduction of principles of resource allocation similar to those suggested by QALYs. In the Netherlands there has been a proposal that dental care for adults should be removed from the package of services provided by its health service.[78] Arguably, similar discretion exists under the 1977 Act by virtue of the latitude given to the Secretary of State in respect of the provision of particular services, rather than health care in general.

II. THE GP'S TERMS OF SERVICE

Primary care is regulated by the FHSA by means of the GP's Terms of Service. The following examines (A) the relationship between GPs and FHSAs, (B) the obligations to 'a doctor's patients', (C) obligations to patients not on the doctor's list, and (D) the freedom to enter and leave the doctor–patient relationship.

---

[74] *A National Health Service* (Cmd. 6502, 1944) 47.
[75] See s. 5(2)(a), 1977 Act.
[76] See s. 5(2)(c) as amended by the Public Health Laboratories Act 1979, s. 1.
[77] See s. 3(1)(c) 1977 Act.
[78] See *Choices in Health Care* (Ministry of Welfare, Health and Cultural Affairs, 1992) 80.

A. Relationship between GP and FHSA

A specific duty is imposed on family health services authorities by the National Health Service Act 1977 to provide primary care. Thus:

(1) It is the duty of every Family Health Services Authority, in accordance with regulations, to arrange as respects their locality with medical practitioners to provide personal medical services for all persons in the area who wish to take advantage of the arrangements

(2) . . . the arrangements will be such that all persons availing themselves of those services will receive adequate personal care and attendance, and the regulations shall include provision-

(a) for the preparation and publication of lists of medical practitioners who undertake to provide general medical services;

T(b)for conferring a right on any person to choose, in accordance with the prescribed procedure, the medical practitioner by whom he is to be attended, subject to the consent of the practitioner and to any prescribed limit on the number of patients to be accepted by any practitioner;

(c) for the distribution among medical practitioners whose names are on the list of any persons who have indicated a wish to obtain general medical services but who have not made any choice of general practitioner or have been refused by the practitioner chosen.[79]

The 'personal medical services' which it is the duty of FHSAs to provide must include:

(a) all necessary and appropriate personal medical services of the type usually provided by general medical practitioners;

(b) child health services;

(c) contraceptive services, that is to say
  (i) the giving of advice to women on contraception,
  (ii) the medical examination of women seeking such advice,
  (iii) the contraceptive treatment of such women, and
  (iv) the supply to such women of contraceptive substances and appliances;

(d) maternity medical services; and

(e) minor surgery services.[80]

---

[79] S. 29, 1977 Act, as amended by the National Health Service and Community Care Act 1990, s. 2(1).

[80] See the National Health Service (General Medical Services) Regs. 1992 (SI 1992, No. 635), reg. 3.

GPs may apply to be included on the FHSA's Medical List[81] in order to provide general medical services to patients under an agreement with the FHSA known as the Terms of Service.[82] The Medical List contains, *inter alia*, the names of the doctors who have agreed to provide general medical services for the FHSA, the nature of the services they have agreed to provide, their practice address, and the times during which they will be available to see patients. In addition each FHSA must prepare and keep up to date a list of the patients for whom doctors on the Medical List are responsible.[83] Doctors may withdraw their names from the Medical List,[84] or have their names removed if they have died, ceased to be doctors, or had their names struck off or suspended from the Medical Register by the General Medical Council.[85]

Doctors make their services available as independent contractors, not employees. Their remuneration is provided by the FHSA and they may not receive fees from their patients.[86] However, the use of the common law of contract to describe this relationship between the parties has been doubted by the House of Lords. The matter was considered in a dispute concerning the remuneration due to a GP from his FHSA. The preliminary question arose of whether the dispute should be dealt with as if it were a matter of private law between private bodies, or as one of public law involving individuals and government departments. Lord Bridge dealt with the question as follows:

I do not think the issue in the appeal turns on whether the doctor provides services pursuant to a contract with the family practitioner committee [the precursor to the FHSA]. I doubt if he does and am content to assume that there is no contract. Nevertheless, the terms which govern the obligations of the doctor on the one hand, as to the services he is to provide, and of the family practitioner committee on the other hand, as to the payments

---

[81] Ibid., regs. 4–7. Doctors whose application to join the list is refused may appeal to the Secretary of State; ibid., reg. 17.   [82] Ibid., Sched. 2.

[83] Ibid., reg. 19.

[84] Ibid., reg. 6. Unless it is impracticable to do so, the doctor shall give the FHSA three months' notice of his intention to leave the Medical List and the FHSA shall make the necessary adjustment to it, see ibid., reg. 6(2) and (3).

[85] Ibid., reg. 7. The power of the General Medical Council to remove doctors from the Medical Register is contained in ss. 36 and 38 of the Medical Act 1983. Reg. 7 permits the doctor to appeal against such a removal to the Secretary of State.   [86] Ibid., Sched. 2, para. 38.

which it is required to make to the doctor, are all prescribed in the relevant legislation and it seems to me that the statutory terms are just as effective as they would be if they were contractual to confer upon the doctor an enforceable right in private law to receive the remuneration to which the terms entitle him.[87]

The same question arose in a case in which a doctor was unavailable to patients during a time in which he had agreed to be on duty. On the recommendation of the Family Practitioner Committee, the Secretary of State exercised his discretion to withhold £2,000 from the doctor's remuneration.[88] The doctor appealed on the ground that, since the nature of the relationship between him and the FPC was analogous to contract, the powers of the Secretary of State should be confined to a right to recover a proper sum of compensation for the loss caused by the breach. He should not, it was argued, be entitled to impose a penalty on the GP far in excess of the damage actually suffered. Having examined the Terms of Service and the provisions regulating the power to discipline GPs, Potts J said: 'the terms of the relevant statutes and regulations are such as to indicate unequivocally that the power to withhold money extends beyond, and is different from, any power to recover money as compensation for the lost value of services not performed. It forms part of a clear disciplinary scheme to ensure control of the service'.[89] Thus, he refused to interfere with the sanction. This suggests that the relationship between doctors and FHSAs must always be considered in its regulatory context and that the law of contract cannot be used as a framework for analysis.

B. Obligations to 'A Doctor's Patients'

'A doctor's patients' are those recorded by the FHSA as being on the doctor's list, or those whom the doctor has accepted onto his list, whether or not the FHSA has received notification that he has done so; but it also includes a number of other categories, in which

---

[87] *Roy* v. *Kensington and Chelsea FPC* [1992] 1 All ER 705, 709.

[88] See generally the powers provided in the National Health Service (Service Committees and Tribunal) Regs. 1992, (SI 1992, No.664), as amended by SI 1994, No. 634 discussed at p. 256 *et seq.*

[89] *R* v. *Secretary of Health,* ex p. *Hickey* 10 BMLR 12, 137 (1993).

there is no agreement between doctor and patient.[90] The duties owed by a doctor to his patients are described in paragraph 12 of the Terms of Service as follows:

(1) A doctor shall render to his patients all necessary and appropriate personal medical services of the type usually provided by general practitioners.

(2) The services which a doctor is required by paragraph (1) to render shall include the following[91]:

(a) giving advice, where appropriate, to a patient in connection with the patient's general health, and in particular about the significance of diet, exercise, the use of tobacco, the consumption of alcohol and the misuse of drugs;

(b) offering to patients consultations and, where appropriate, physical examinations for the purpose of identifying, or reducing the risk of, disease or injury;

(c) offering to patients, where appropriate, vaccination or immunisation against measles, mumps, rubella, pertussis, poliomyelitis, diphtheria and tetanus;

(d) arranging for the referral of patients, as appropriate, for the provision of any other services under this Act; and

(e) giving advice, as appropriate, to enable patients to avail themselves of services provided by a local social services authority.[92]

Also, under paragraph 43, a doctor shall order any drugs or appliances which are needed by the patient to whom he is providing treatment under these terms of service by issuing to that patient a prescription form.[93] The obligation to prescribe medicines

---

[90] See reg. 4(1)(a) and (b) of the National Health Service (General Medical Services) Regs. 1992, SI 1992, No. 635.

[91] Also note the special requirement that 'a doctor shall' invite newly registered patients (para. 14) and patients aged 75 years and over (para. 16) to participate in a consultation, either at the practice premises or, elsewhere. Patients not seen within 3 years should be provided with a consultation if they request it (para. 15, as amended by SI 1993, No. 540).

This 'preventive', rather than curative function, is described in great detail in the regulations. For example, for newly registered patients and those not seen within three years, the doctor is obliged to record in the patient's medical notes details of previous illnesses, immunizations, allergies, diseases, medication, offer a physical examination, record the findings, and offer appropriate advice.

[92] National Health Service (General Medical Services) Regs. 1992, *supra* note 90, Sched. 2, para. 12.

[93] Ibid., Sched. 2, para. 43. Note that the doctor 'shall provide' medicines which are immediately needed by a patient. See the National Health Service (Pharmaceutical Services) Regs. 1992 (SI 1992 No. 662), reg. 19(a). These obligations are

causes concern. Some are extremely expensive and impose a heavy burden on resources.[94] The problem of cost is considered in Chapter 5 in relation to the duty of FHSAs to impose 'indicated prescribing amounts' on GPs, which attempt to reduce spending on medicines.

In addition to these general duties, GPs may apply to the FHSA for inclusion on one of the lists of specialist practitioners. These list GPs who offer child health surveillance services, contraceptive services, maternity medical services and minor surgery services.[95] Only those practitioners who can show that they have suitable experience of the area, and where necessary suitable equipment, may be accepted by the FHSA onto the relevant list.[96]

The medical services will normally be rendered by a doctor 'at his practice premises.'[97] However, when 'in the doctor's reasonable opinion it would be inappropriate for the patient to attend the practice,' it may be necessary for the doctor to visit the patient at the patient's home, or at such other place as the doctor has informed the patient and the FHSA that he has agreed to visit the patient, or some other place within the doctor's practice area.[98] Doctors must be available to their patients twenty-four hours a day. The Terms of Service provide that 'a doctor is responsible for ensuring the provision for his patients of the services referred to in paragraph 12 throughout each day during which his name is included in the FHSAs medical list'.[99]

Not surprisingly, the obligation to undertake calls throughout the night is unpopular, largely because of the numbers of patients

subject to para. 44 of the General Medical Regs. which concerns the Limited List of drugs which may not be prescribed under the Terms of Service.

[94] See R. Gabriel, 'Picking up the Tab for Erythropoietin', 302 *British Medical Journal* 248 (1991).

[95] See National Health Service (General Medical Services) Regs. 1992 *supra* note 90, Part V.

[96] Ibid. Sched. 3, parts VIII–X. Detailed procedures are provided for FHSAs in considering such applications, and for appeals against their refusal to the Secretary of State (who may appoint a representative to hear the appeal); ibid., Part V.

[97] Ibid. Sched. 2, para. 13(a), as amended by National Health Service (General Medical Services) Amendment Regs. 1995 (SI 1995, No. 80), reg. 3.

[98] National Health Service (General Medical Services) Regs. 1992 *supra* note 90, Sched. 2, para. 13(b), as amended by National Health Service (General Medical Services) Amendment Regs. 1995 *supra* note 97, reg. 3(2).

[99] National Health Service (General Medical Services) Regs. 1992 *supra* note, Sched. 2, para. 18(1).

perceived as abusing the service. In one survey GPs said that fewer than half of their out-of-hours visits concerned genuine emergencies.[100] The difficulty, of course, is to know what should count as 'abuse'. Patients are not encouraged to make their own diagnoses of illness and, particularly for children, will naturally prefer to be safe than sorry when something unexpected occurs. It would clearly be undesirable if a policy designed to attack outright abuse had the effect of deterring those who need care. Specific regulations now provide for the provision of services to patients outside normal hours. Thus, if in the doctor's reasonable opinion a consultation is needed before the next time at which the patient could be seen during normal hours, he may render the relevant services at any of the places discussed above (including the practice premises). In addition, greater freedom has been given to doctors to use primary care centres outside normal hours. The services may be rendered 'at such other place as the FHSA has agreed . . . , and he has informed the patient, . . . is a place where he will treat patients outside normal hours'.[101]

Use of such centres requires the formal approval of the FHSA, which must be satisfied that the premises 'are likely to be reasonably convenient to the doctor's patients' and that they correspond with the general needs of the locality.[102] Practices may co-operate with one another on a rota basis which spreads the load of their out of hours obligations. (Doctors may agree to deputize for other doctors by undertaking responsibility for their patients.[103]) An invitation to patients to leave their homes and attend a health centre during the night may have the benefit of reducing needless out-of-hours visits, but it should not be used as a

[100] See P. Johnson, 'Doctor come now, my tortoise has gone', *The Doctor* 17 Feb. 1994, 32.

[101] National Health Service (General Medical Services) Regs. 1992 (SI 1992, No. 635), Sched. 2, para. 13, as amended by National Health Service (General Medical Services) Amendment Regs. 1995 (SI 1995, No.80), reg. 3(2).

[102] National Health Service (General Medical Services) Regs. 1992 (SI 1992, No.635), Sched. 2, para. 29A, added by National Health Service (General Medical Services) Amendment Regs. 1995 (SI 1995, No. 80), reg. 3(5).

[103] National Health Service (General Medical Services) Regs. 1992 (SI 1992, No. 635), Sched. 2, para. 25, as amended by National Health Service (General Medical Services) Amendment Regs. 1995 (SI 1995, No. 80), reg. 3(3). The use of deputies is discussed below.

blanket response to untimely calls. The law of negligence requires that patients who ought reasonably to have the benefit of a home visit actually receive one.

C. Obligations to Patients not on the Doctor's List

The following discusses the salient categories of responsibility to those not on the doctor's list, i.e. (a) emergency cases, (b) patients for whom the doctor is responsible as a deputy, and (c) violent patients who have been struck off the list, and assignees.

1. Emergencies

The Terms of Service require doctors to provide care at the site of an emergency in certain circumstances. Paragraph 4(1)(h) provides that a doctor's patients include:

persons to whom he may be requested to give treatment which is immediately required owing to an accident or other emergency at any place in his practice area provided that . . . he is available to provide such treatment . . . [and] provided there is no doctor who, at the time of the request, is under an obligation otherwise than under this head to give treatment to that person, or there is such a doctor but, after being requested to attend, he is unable to attend and give treatment immediately required.

The obligation is restricted to 'treatment which is immediately required' in the doctor's own practice area, or in the locality of the FHSA in which he is included, provided that no other doctor is obliged, or available, to provide care. The logic of the geographical restriction may be that visitors to an area will always be able to find help in a medical emergency by contacting a local doctor. Equally, a doctor should not be expected to be on duty throughout the country from wherever his or her practice happens to be.

It has been suggested that the obligation, limited in this geographical sense, is also an accurate statement of common law, so that doctors owe a duty of care in negligence to provide emergency care to patients who are not on their list. 'Emergency patients within his practice area . . . are a foreseeable class of person to whom, by accepting the position of GP within the health service, he has undertaken a duty, and a duty which should be

legal and not merely moral.'[104] Such a limited obligation has much
to recommend it. To the surprise of many European commentators, there is no obligation at common law to make any attempt
to assist a person who finds himself in a situation of danger. This is
so even if the rescue would be simple and involve no risk to the
rescuer. If this view of the duty of GPs is correct, however, the
common law obligation to give assistance to a stranger imposes on
them alone the duty to rescue. Arguably, there is nothing so
uniquely 'medical' in the principle of rescue which should require
doctors alone to be subject to such an obligation.

2. Responsibility of Deputies

As a general rule 'a doctor shall give treatment personally.'[105] It
would not be reasonable, however, to expect doctors to be
personally responsible for their patients every hour of every day.
For this reason, doctors have long made use of deputies, or
deputizing services, under which another doctor takes responsibility for a doctor's patients for a limited period of time. This
practice has received the approval of the General Medical
Council, which has said: 'in many branches of professional practice
doctors cannot at all times attend to all their patients' needs. It is
therefore both necessary and desirable that, when doctors are
absent from duty, arrangements should be made whereby their
professional responsibilities may be undertaken by suitably
qualified professional colleagues.'[106]

This approach is reflected in the Terms of Service, which
provide that the doctor:

shall be under no obligation to give treatment personally to a patient
provided that reasonable steps are taken to ensure continuity of the
patient's treatment, and in these circumstances treatment may be given
(a) by another doctor acting as a deputy, whether or not he is a partner
    or assistant of the patient's doctor; or
(b) in the case of treatment which it is clinically reasonable in the
    circumstances to delegate to someone other than a doctor, by a

---

[104] M. Brazier, *Medicine, Patients and the Law* (Penguin, 2nd edn., 1992) 362.
[105] National Health Service (General Medical Services) Regs. 1992 (SI 1992, No.
635), Sched. 2 para. 19(1)
[106] *Professional Conduct and Discipline: Fitness to Practise* (General Medical
Council, 1993), para. 40.

person whom the doctor has authorised and who he is satisfied is competent to carry out such treatment.[107]

What if something goes wrong during the time that the patient is being treated by, or awaiting treatment by, a doctor acting as a deputy? The Terms of Service distinguish between deputies whose names are on the medical list of an FHSA and those that are not. The patient's own doctor bears direct responsibility for the acts and omissions of deputies whose names are not on a medical list.[108] He is not responsible, however, for deputies who are on a medical list. Thus, under paragraph 21(2):

Where a doctor whose name is included in the medical list is acting as deputy to another doctor whose name is also included in the list, the deputy is responsible for
(a) his own acts and omissions in relation to the obligations under these terms of service of the doctor for whom he acts as deputy; and
(b) the acts and omissions of any person employed by him or acting on his behalf.

This distinction may often be sufficient to insulate a doctor from a complaint by the FHSA but it does not affect the position at common law. In negligence a doctor may be liable whether or not the deputy is on the medical list, if he or she has failed to take reasonable care of the patient. The obvious danger in using deputies, particularly from outside the practice, is that the deputy will probably not know the history of the patients he has been asked to attend and will be more likely to miss signs or symptoms that would have been recognized by the patient's own doctor. Also, deputizing services may not appreciate the urgency with which a patient requires a visit through ignorance of the patient's particular condition. In principle therefore '[a]ny deputizing arrangements should make provision for prompt and proper communication between the deputy and the doctor who has primary responsibility for the patients' care'.[109] There are unavoidable risks in using deputies, and reasonable care should be taken to minimize them.

---

[107] National Health Service (General Medical Services) Regs. 1992 (SI 1992, No. 635), Sched. 2, para. 19(2).
[108] Ibid., Sched. 2, para. 20(1), as amended by SI 1994, No. 633.
[109] *Professional Conduct and Discipline*, supra note 106, para. 41.

3. Violent Patients and 'Assignees'

Under the principle that primary care under the NHS should be available 'for all persons in the locality who wish to take advantage of the arrangements',[110] GPs' Terms of Service permits the FHSA to 'assign' unpopular patients to GPs with or without agreement. Thus, where a patient who is not on a doctor's list is refused acceptance by a doctor for inclusion on that list, he or she may apply in writing to the FHSA for assignment to a doctor. The application shall be considered by the FHSA,

which shall assign the patient to such doctor in its medical list as it thinks fit, having regard to
(a) the respective distance between the person's residence and the practice premises . . . ;
(b) whether within the previous six months the person has been removed from the list of any doctor in that part of the locality at the request of that doctor; and
(c) such other circumstances, including those concerning the doctors in that part of the locality and their practices, as the FHSA think relevant.[111]

The corresponding obligation of the doctor to accept FHSA 'assignees' is that such patients are included in the description of 'a doctor's patients' in the Terms of Service, to whom the GP is bound to make services available.[112] Obviously, there will be occasions when the duty to accept unpopular patients causes anxiety. In particular, in areas where the number of medical practices is small, doctors may find that a patient seems to be assigned to them with great regularity and that they share a patient with another practice on a 'three months on, three months off' basis. A doctor to whom a patient has been assigned may make representations to the FHSA against the assignment and require it to hear the patient's case against it.[113] Within seven days of the representation the FHSA must reconsider the decision in order to confirm or revise it,[114] pending which the doctor remains

---

[110] See s. 29 1977 Act.
[111] National Health Service (General Medical Services) Regs. 1992 (SI 1992, No. 635), reg. 21(2).
[112] Ibid., Sched. 2, para. 4(1)(d): '. . . a doctor's patients are . . . persons who have been assigned to him under regulation 21'.
[113] Ibid., Sched. 2, para. 21(5).   [114] Ibid., para. 21(6) and (9).

responsible for the patient.[115] No person who participated in making the initial assignment shall participate in the review.[116]

For the moment, the system works tolerably well and doctors have co-operated with the FHSA to ensure that services are always available to patients. There have, however, been problems involving violence.[117] What is the nature of the obligation in relation to patients who threaten or use violence towards a doctor or his or her staff? Is the duty to accept assignees absolute even in such extreme circumstances? Take the example of a patient who calls the doctor out to visit him in the middle of the night; perhaps he has a history of mental instability and aggressive behaviour. The patient attacks the doctor. Would it not be unreasonable for the FHSA to demand that a doctor should attend such a patient, at least without proper protection?

The problem was considered sufficiently serious to merit an amendment to the Terms of Service between doctors and FHSAs. Now, when a patient on a doctor's list has committed an act of violence against the doctor, or behaved in such a way that the doctor has feared for his or her safety, and the doctor has reported the matter to the police, 'the doctor may notify the FHSA that he wishes to have that person removed from his list with immediate effect.'[118] In these circumstances, although the patient will cease to be on the doctor's list from the time the doctor has notified the FHSA (by telephone or fax, provided the message is confirmed subsequently in writing[119]), the doctor may still not be able to terminate his obligations immediately because the patient remains one of the 'doctor's patients'.[120] Consequently, the doctor must continue to give the person any 'immediately necessary treatment until the expiry of fourteen days beginning with the date . . . when

---

[115] 1992 Regs. reg. 20(2), para. 21(10). [116] Ibid., para. 21(8).

[117] See V. Schnieden, 'How doctors can deal with violence in their workplace', *BMA News Review*, Feb. 1994 11, and J. Chadwick, 'Fighting Against the threat of brutality', *The Doctor*, 27 Jan. 1994 40.

[118] See the National Health Service (General Medical Services) Regs. 1992 (SI 1992. No. 635), para. 9A(1), as inserted by the National Health Service (General Medical Services) Amendment Regs. 1994 (SI 1994, No. 633), para. 8(4).

[119] National Health Service (General Medical Services) Amendment Regs. 1994 (SI 1994, No. 633), Sched. 2, para. 6.

[120] See para 4(1)(c) of the Terms of Service which specifically includes those to whom treatment must be given for fourteen days.

he requested the immediate removal of that person from his list, or until that person has been accepted by or assigned to another doctor, whichever occurs first'.[121]

When the doctor must continue to treat for a limited period, care should be taken to ensure that he or she is insulated from unreasonable risk. Notice that the treatment required is restricted to that which is 'immediately necessary', rather than that which is routine. Perhaps this more limited obligation could be fulfilled by referring the patient directly to the accident and emergency unit of a hospital, or by making home visits dependent on attendance by the police.[122] Where doctors are persistently threatened and attacked, the question arises whether the patient forfeits his right to treatment. No doctor is obliged to put him or herself at unreasonable risk by virtue of the FHSA's decision. In such a case, the doctor might be able to exclude such a patient from the practice premises by means of an injunction and insist that any future consultations take place in the presence of a police officer, or at a police station. Ultimately, however, if reasonable safety cannot be assured, it is suggested that the doctor would be entitled to refuse to accept the FHSA's assignment.

D. Freedom to Enter and Leave the Doctor–Patient Relationship

In principle, the parties are entirely free to enter or leave the doctor–patient relationship. The procedure for doing so is simple and neither is obliged to tolerate the other against his or her wishes. The mechanism for applying to a doctor to be accepted onto his or her list is straightforward. 'An application to a doctor for inclusion in his list for the provision of general medical services shall be made by delivering to the doctor a medical card or a form of application signed (in either case) by the applicant or a person authorised on his behalf.'[123]

---

[121] Ibid., the amendment is to para. 4(4) of the 1992 Regs. by para. 8(2) of the 1994 Regs. Under the new Regs. before an assignment is made the FHSA is obliged to consider the circumstances in which a patient has been removed from another doctor's list. See para. 21(11) of the 1992 Regs. as amended by para. 7 of the 1994 Regs.

[122] See *Violence Against GPs: Time for Resolute Action* (British Medical Association, 1994).

[123] 1992 Regs. reg. 20(1). For applications on behalf of others, see reg. 20(2).

Doctors, however, are in private practice. They are not employees of a health authority and are free to decide for themselves whether or not to accept an applicant to their list. Thus, a doctor may agree to accept a person on his list if the person is eligible to be accepted by him,[124] but (subject to the rules on assignment) is not obliged to do so. Equally, patients are not tied to any particular GP whose practice they have joined. They, too, are free to leave their current practitioner and apply to join another in the usual way. 'A person who is on a doctor's list of patients may apply to any other doctor providing general medical services for acceptance on that other doctor's list of patients.'[125]

Alternatively, a doctor wishing to sever his or her relationship with the patient is free to do so, subject only to giving the FHSA an opportunity to offer the patient another practice. 'A doctor may have any person removed from his list and shall notify the FHSA in writing that he wishes to have a person removed from his list and . . . the removal shall take effect (a) on the date on which the person is accepted by or assigned to another doctor; or (b) on the eighth day after the FHSA receives the notice, whichever is the sooner.'[126]

The reason for these freedoms is explained by the General Medical Council, and said to 'flow from the belief that a satisfactory relationship between patient and doctor will arise only where each is committed to it; consequently, if either party believes that the relationship has failed, they have a right to end it'.[127] Patients, therefore, retain absolute freedom to leave the list of a medical practitioner. Although the Terms of Service appear to permit the same freedom to doctors, the General Medical Council has expressed its view that doctors may not do so for illegitimate reasons. Thus doctors are advised that they may not remove a patient from their lists for economic reasons, for example because the patient needs expensive drug therapy, or refuses to participate in screening or immunization programmes. The Council expressed itself on the matter as follows:

---

[124] 1992 Regs. Sched. 2, para. 6.

[125] 1992 Regs. Sched. 2, para. 22(3). See also reg. 23(1).

[126] Ibid., Sched. 2, para. 9(1). See also *Removal of Patients from GP Lists* (GMSC, 1994).

[127] *Resource Constraints and Contracting: Professional Responsibilities in Relation to the Clinical Needs of Patients* (General Medical Council, 1992), para. 16.

. . . family doctors, as the professionals involved, have special responsibilities for making the relationship work. In particular, it is unacceptable to abuse the right to refuse to accept patients by applying criteria of access to the practice list which discriminate against groups on grounds of their age, sex, sexual orientation, race, colour, religious belief, perceived economic worth or the amount of work they are likely to generate by virtue of their clinical condition.[128]

These standards of conduct, required by a professional body, do not necessarily represent a good statement of law, although breach may expose the individual to the disciplinary proceedings of the General Medical Council. Given the independent status of GPs, such action may not be unlawful at common law. However, it ought to attract the attention of the FHSA. Its duty is to provide medical services 'for all persons in the area who wish to take advantage of the arrangements.'[129] The fulfillment of this duty could be seriously undermined if health authorities permitted doctors to act in this way. Accordingly, FHSAs ought actively to discourage it. Indeed, were such behaviour to be tolerated, it could give rise to an action in judicial review against the authority concerned for failing to fulfill its statutory duty.

[128] Ibid. Increasing numbers of GPs are refusing certain patients to their lists, e.g. 'troublemakers', those with mental illness, and elderly patients with chronic conditions. See *Association of Community Health Councils for England and Wales: Annual Report 1993–4* 4.

[129] S. 29, 1977 Act, as amended by the National Health Service and Community Care Act 1990, s. 2(1). See p. 146 *supra*.

5

The Rise of Health Service Managers

A feature of the new NHS is the increase in the number of people involved in its management, and their authority. In 1989/90 there were around 6,000 managers in the NHS. By 1992/93 the figure is said to have risen to around 24,000. Although part of the increase can be accounted for by the reclassification of some nursing staff, 'there was also a real growth in their number as direct result of government policies.'[1] This chapter considers the reasons for this change and the means by which managers exercise their authority in the health service.

I. RE-APPRAISING CLINICAL FREEDOM

One of the most profound effects of the reorganization of the NHS is the way in which it has moved its centre of gravity. Before the reforms, doctors exercised the most influential role in the management of health care. This section explains why their power has increasingly come under supervision while that of managers has tended to increase.

A. The 'Problem' of Medical Practice Variations

Assuming medical science to be in a continual state of development, differences of opinions between doctors are inevitable. The law of
. medical negligence permits a wide range of practice variations. So long as a doctor adheres to a practice which a responsible body of doctors would endorse, he will be insulated from criticism in negligence, even though a large majority may have taken a different clinical view of the case. Often, this is perfectly proper. The medical evidence on which a decision must be based may be

---

[1] C. Ham, *Management and Competition in the New NHS* (Radcliffe Medical Press, 1994) 50.

incomplete and inconsistent. In such a case, matters of diagnosis, prognosis, or surgical management unavoidably involve the exercise of judgment. Doctors may have been taught differently, or their own personal experience may be simply that some things work better than others. In this case, their own medical practice will tend to emphasize their particular expertise. Equally, a doctor who provides treatment which is unsuccessful may be less willing to resort to it in future.[2] This is an inevitable part of the evolution of medical science. To what extent, however, does this explain all practice variations?

Increasingly, health service managers have become critical of the professional latitude enjoyed by doctors, and less likely to accept without question the fact of medical practice variations.

Medicine is widely held to be a science, but many medical decisions do not rely on a strong scientific foundation, simply because a strong scientific foundation has yet to be explored. Hence, what often happens in the decision-making process is a complicated interaction of scientific evidence, patient desire, doctor preferences and all sorts of exogenous influences, some of which may be quite irrelevant.[3]

Medical research suggests that wide differences of practice exist which cannot be justified, even allowing for the gaps in the scientific evidence. A range of influences, which have little or nothing to do with medicine, may play a part. Medical 'fashion' may have a role[4] so that views may become 'accepted' without basic scientific evidence to support them. A fear of litigation may alter medical practice, in which one of the objectives of treatment is to anticipate what a plaintiff's lawyer will ask if the patient is dissatisfied with treatment and decides to litigate.[5] Diagnoses may be made more for the patient's peace of mind than for clinical

[2] T. Folmer Anderson and G. Mooney (eds.), *The Challenge of Medical Practice Variations* (Macmillan, 1990) 21. See also *Factors Influencing Clinical Decisions in General Practice* (Office of Health Economics, 1990).

[3] K. McPherson, 'Why do Variations Occur', in T. Folmer Anderson and G. Mooney, ibid., 17. See also J. Wennberg, 'Dealing with Medical Practice Variations', 3 *Health Affairs* 6 (1984).

[4] J. Burnham, 'Medical Practice à la mode: How Medical Fashion Determines Medical Care', 317 *New England Journal of Medicine* 1220 (1987).

[5] M. Ennis, A. Clark, J. Grudzinskas, 'Change in Obstetric Practice in response to fear of litigation in the British Isles' 338 *British Medical Journal* 616 (1991). Estimates of the huge sums of money wasted in this way in America are discussed in T. Brennan, 'Practice Guidelines and Malpractice Litigation: Collision or Cohesion', 16 *Journal of Health Politics, Policy and Law* 67, 72 (1991).

need.[6] 'Antibiotics, for instance, which account for over 10% of prescribed medicines, are often prescribed for colds, flu and sore throats caused by viral infections against which they are virtually ineffective.'[7] The method by which doctors are paid may also influence their willingness to recommend treatment. Those systems which remunerate doctors according to the numbers of patients treated (the 'fee for service' system, adopted in France and Germany) may be thought to encourage more medical interventions than systems which pay on the basis of the numbers of patients on their list, and which disregard whether or not they receive treatment (the capitation fee, used in the UK).[8]

Consider the following examples. In an age-standardized sample of hysterectomy operations, 700 hysterectomies were performed per 100,000 American women, 600 per 100,000 in Canada, 450 in Australia, 250 in the UK, and 110 in Norway.[9] Rates of Caesarian sections show similar variations between countries.[10] The number of cardiac operations in the UK is significantly lower than in other developed countries,[11] as is the number of those treated for kidney failure.[12] Patterns of prescribing show similar differences between European countries; the Germans are most concerned about their hearts, the French: their digestive systems, and the English: the state of their minds.[13] Each one of these interventions may have been successful, but variations on this scale suggest that some must have provided less benefit than others and it is at the margins that

[6] See C. Bradley, 'Uncomfortable Prescribing Decisions: a Critical Incident Study', 304 *British Medical Journal* 294 (1992) and A. Speight *et al.*, 'Underdiagnosis and Undertreatment of Asthma in Childhood', 286 *British Medical Journal* 1253 (1983).

[7] See *A Prescription for Improvement: Towards More Rational Prescribing in General Practice* (Audit Commission, 1994) at para. 22.

[8] S. Sandier, 'Health Service Utilisation Rates and Physician Income Trends', in *Health Care Systems In Transition, the Search for Efficiency* (OECD, 1990) who considers this influence on costs to be relatively weak.

[9] K. McPherson, *Variations in Hospitalization Rates: Why and How to Study Them* (King's Fund Institute, 1988).

[10] J. Lomas, 'Holding Back the Tide of Caesarians', 297 *British Medical Journal* 569 (1988);

[11] T. English and A. Bailey, 'The UK cardiac surgical register, 1977-82', 298 *British Medical Journal* 1205 (1984); R. Brooks, J. Koesecoff *et al.*, 'Diagnosis and Treatment of Coronary Disease: Comparison of Doctors' Attitudes in the USA and the UK', *The Lancet* (1988) i, 750.

[12] A. Wing, 'Why Don't the British Treat More Patients with Kidney Failure' 287 *British Medical Journal* 1157 (1983).

[13] B. O'Brien, *Patterns of European Diagnoses and Prescribing* (Office of Health Economics, 1984).

doubts have been expressed. If we wish to maximize the overall benefits of the health service, 'it is difficult to justify marginal operations when there are genuine unmet needs elsewhere.'[14] Equally, irrational treatment carries the risks of positively harming patients because medicine almost always presents an element of danger. The Audit Commission estimates that between 3 per cent and 5 per cent of all hospital beds in the UK may be occupied by people suffering wholly or largely from adverse drug reactions.[15]

With respect to differences of this nature, there is increasing interest in reappraising the value of medical discretion with a view to harmonizing practice and reducing waste. This means that the breadth of clinical freedom hitherto enjoyed by doctors is likely to be eroded.

B. Reappraising the Role of Managers

At the same time, there has also been an appraisal of the role of health service managers. Before the 1980s their role was compared to that of 'diplomats'. Their function tended to be passive: to reconcile conflicts between competing demands (from doctors, nurses, patients, and managers themselves) and 'to react to problems rather than to pursue objectives.'[16] Managers exercised only limited control because many of the activities of hospitals were determined centrally, or by senior clinicians acting in isolation. In addition, the absence of precise information on how and where money was spent in the service made the process of effecting change very difficult. In place of the general manager was a system of 'consensus management' of the NHS, in which the disparate elements of the NHS personnel—managers, doctors, nurses, midwives, health visitors etc.—were expected to produce generally held and acceptable local policies.[17] During this time

[14] K. McPherson, 'International Differences in Medical Care Practices', in *Health Care Systems in Transition: The Search for Efficiency* (OECD, 1990) 25.

[15] A Prescription for Improvement, *supra* note 7, para. 3; citing T. Emerson, 'Drug Related Hospital Admissions', 27 *Annals of Pharmacotherapy* 832 (1993); and C. Medawar, *Power and Dependence: Social Audit on the Safety of Medicines* (Social Audit, 1992). For this reason, the practice of 'defensive medicine' is unwise.

[16] See generally S. Harrison, D. Hunter, G. Marnoch and C. Pollitt, *Just Managing: Power and Culture in the National Health Service* (Macmillan, 1992) 26. This usefully considers much of the research conducted on the changing nature of the manager's role in the NHS.

[17] The idea of consensus management is described in P. Strong and J. Robinson, *The NHS Under New Management* (Open University Press, 1990), ch. 1.

managers engaged in 'problem-solving, organisation and maintenance and the facilitation of processes. [Managers accepted] the notion of "clinical freedom", that . . . restrictions on the doctor–patient relationship should be minimal, or at most confined to control over aggregate resources.'[18]

That system, even during the 1970s, was not without its critics. In 1979 the Royal Commission on the Health Service remarked that 'there is a risk that consensus management may sap individual responsibility by allowing it to be shared: it is important that managers should not be prevented from managing the services for which they are responsible.'[19] There was also concern that there were too many decisions taken by central government which displayed insensitivity to the needs of local communities.[20] Pressure for radical reform of the system developed during the 1980s and, at the invitation of the Prime Minister, a small group with a record of success in commerce was appointed to advise on ways in which the NHS should be managed. Its recommendations were contained in the Griffiths Report which stated: 'One of our most immediate observations from a business background is the lack of a clearly-defined management function throughout the NHS. By general management we mean the responsibility drawn together in one person, at different levels of the organisation, for planning implementation and control of performance.'[21]

It recommended that, despite the public nature of its activity, specific targets should be set and regularly assessed against performance. It said:

The NHS does not have the profit motive, but it is, of course, enormously concerned with control of expenditure. Surprisingly, however, it still lacks any real continuous evaluation of its performance

---

[18] S. Harrison, D. Hunter, G. Marnoch, C. Pollitt, *supra* note 16, 37. The same point is made by the Audit Commission in *Trusting in the Future: Towards an Audit Agenda for NHS Providers* (HMSO, 1994), para. 4.5.

[19] *Royal Commission on the National Health Service* (Cmnd. 7615, 1979), para. 20.15.   [20] Ibid., para. 6.9.

[21] *NHS Management Inquiry* ('The Griffiths Report', Department of Health and Social Security, 1983) 11. The contrary view is that 'a system which substitutes line management for consensus is no way to run a multi-disciplinary service, which depends on cooperation at all levels, and whose problems call for analysis . . . rather than rules promulgated from general managers ignorant alike of economics and of health.' See D. Black, *A Doctor Looks at Health Economics* (Office of Health Economics, 1994) 21.

against criteria. . . . Rarely are precise management objectives set; there
is little measurement of health output; clinical evaluation of particular
practices is by no means common and economic evaluation of those
practices is extremely rare. Nor can the NHS display a ready effectiveness
with which it is meeting the needs and expectations of the people it serves.
Businessmen have a keen sense of how well they are looking after their
customers. Whether the NHS is meeting the needs of the patient, and the
community, and can prove that it is doing so, is open to question.[22]

It recommended a management structure for the NHS in which
the creation of policy at national level would clearly be distinguished from the responsibility for its implementation and
operation; and that, at each level of operation, managers should
be set specific responsibilities and targets and be held accountable
for them:

the key division between general practice and the hospital sector was left
untouched. . . . What did change was their management. In each tier
[was] installed a single leader, a general manager. The NHS as a whole
was given a management board with a chief executive, every region now
had a regional general manager, every district a DGM, every unit a
UGM. There was, for the first time, a single line of command from the top
to the bottom of the service.
   The general managers, as their titles suggested, managed everyone.
Whereas the old district administrators simply chaired the meetings of the
management team, each general manager was a real boss, in charge of the
treasurers, the cleaners, the nurses, the doctors, the personnel department—the lot. Here, then, was a revolution. . . . In short, it was general
managers, not the clinical trades, who were now to decide . . . [23]

The Griffiths Report had significant impact and is now reflected
at every level of the NHS, both in structure and operation.[24]
Inevitably, the result of this change of emphasis in the health
service is to move organizational power toward managers. They
set performance targets, and because the managers are responsible
for those targets being met, will have to acquire greater authority

---

[22] *NHS Management Inquiry*, ibid., 10.
[23] *The NHS Under New Management, supra* note 17, 23.
[24] The new structure was introduced without the need for legislation, within the
broad framework established by the National Health Service Act 1977. See also
Implementation of the NHS Management Enquiry Report, HC(84)13 (Department
of Health, 1984).

eedom should
encouraged to
(A) clinical
, (C) medical

rt[30] hospitals
but priorities
o contribute
account for
The model
the clinical
sponsibility
s activity.

sources and
patients. . . .
strategy for
priorities for
n about the
comes the

take time
which the
parable.[32]
problems

Surgeons,
esponsible
uld have a
he should
idance for
MA, un-

leet', 296
e of each
ectorates
gers', 298
iculty of
hes', 308

For the present, the corporate
y of State is relatively distant
ntention of promoting local
or health.[26] Equally, effective
ear corporate objectives. Some
statement of the purpose of the
xpression of corporate purpose,
role of competition and the
market ought to be regulated, and
ntability between purchasers and
necessary. Without them, in-
ween regions and the 'national'
ll become fragmented and under-

S AS MANAGERS

diture is devoted to acute hospitals,
er cent of total NHS spending.[28]
directly responsible for the way in
It therefore makes sense to involve
hich spending priorities are decided.
lopment. Traditionally, managers and
ought to posses entirely different and
rations.

ndividual interests are subordinated to the
s an essentially collectivist one, emphasising
ng the corporate mission and goals of the
, medicine's values stress the individual, the
ctor will work on behalf of the best interests

ard, 'Performance Indicators', in R. Maxwell (ed.),
Service (Policy Journals, 1988).
he annual *Priorities and Planning Guidance for the*
(93)54, and EL(94)55.
l and C. Spry, *Towards an Effective NHS* (Office of
. See also the assessment of the impact of managers in

NHSME, undated), para. 29.
s managers: poachers turned gamekeepers', 35 *Social*
t 562 (1992).

Thus, doctors balk at the idea that their clinical fr
be compromised. Nevertheless, doctors have been
join the process of management by means of
directorates, (B) the resource management initiative
audit, and (D) clinical practice guidelines.

A. Clinical Directorates

Following the recommendations of the Griffiths Repo
have created units responsible for taking decisions ab
and resources. Doctors therefore have been invited t
solutions to managerial problems, and are expected to
their spending to the hospital general manager.
adopted for turning doctors into managers is that of
directorate, in which doctors, as directors, assume re
for the performance of a particular part of a hospital'.

> Clinicians must participate effectively in the utilisation of r
> help to generate further resources for the hospital to care for
> The main tasks of a clinical director include the definition of a
> developing and improving services for patients, the setting of
> the budget and the provision of timely and accurate informatio
> performance of services. With responsibility for these tasks
> accountability of the clinical director to the hospital.[31]

No doubt the effectiveness of clinical directorates will
to assess and there may be doubt about the extent to
concept 'performance' in hospitals is measurable or comp
Some say that clinical directorates will not ease the

---

[30] *Report of the NHS Management Inquiry, supra* note 21, 6.

[31] *Clinical Directorates—A Guide for Surgeons* (Royal College of
Edinburgh, 1993) 2. The guidance continues: 'Each clinical director is r
for producing a business plan for his, or her, directorate . . . He sho
vision of what the directorate should be providing in five years' time and
introduce the necessary steps to achieve that end.' Ibid. 6. See also *Gu
Clinical Directors* (Central Consultants and Specialists Committee, E
dated).

[32] See E. Scrivens, 'Doctors as Managers: Never the Twain Shall M
British Medical Journal 1754 (1988), who considers that the inexperienc
party of the culture and aspirations of the other suggests that clinical dir
are unlikely to succeed. But compare R. Smith, 'Doctors Becoming Mana
British Medical Journal 311 (1989) for a more positive view. On the dif
measuring performance see C. Orchard, 'Comparing Healthcare Outcor
British Medical Journal 1493 (1994).

posed by limited resources. Trusts, for example, which invest in doctors for their prestige may positively increase the difficulties faced by managers intent on distributing their resources more rationally.[33] Recent research suggests that clinicians have not taken easily to becoming managers. The role of the 'clinical' manager responsible for setting levels of performance and expenditure in a particular unit or section of a hospital is often unclear. There is a shortage of individuals willing and able to act as managers with authority over those with whom they have always considered themselves equal. And there may have been reluctance to accept the imposition of such authority. Nor is there a successful model on which pilot projects could be based.[34] For the present at least, many clinical directors are not part of the formal team responsible for negotiating and entering contracts with health authorities and GP fund-holders, though most considered that they ought to have a greater say and that insufficient weight was being given to clinical issues by those responsible for the process.[35]

B. Resource Management Initiative

A necessary component of clinical directorates is resource management initiative, which evaluates the success with which clinicians have carried out their responsibilities and measures the various elements of cost involved in medical decision making.[36] For example:

clinicians could be provided monthly or quarterly with computerised data specifying the number of patients they had seen and the type, cost and result of the investigative tests they had requested, broken down by clinical condition and individual patient. These could be compared with the data of previous quarters. . . . As a result they may wish to alter clinical practices and/or negotiate a change in future budget or service priorities with unit managers.[37]

---

[33] D. Hunter, 'Doctors as managers' *supra* note 29, 562 (1992).

[34] These observations are made by the Audit Commission in *Trusting in the Future: Towards an Audit Agenda for NHS Providers* (HMSO, 1994), para. 35.

[35] See *Connecting Clinical Directors* (McClean, Jones, McCarthy Ltd (consultants), Manchester, 1994).

[36] See T. Packwood, J. Keen and M. Buxton, *Hospitals In Transition—The Resource Management Experiment* (Open University Press, 1991).

[37] T. Packwood, M. Buxton, and J. Keen, 'Resource Management in the National Health Service: a first case history', 18 *Policy and Politics* 245, 248 (1990).

The idea is to encourage hospital managers and clinicians to agree on objectives and priorities and to devolve responsibility for their accomplishment to tiers of authority further down the hierarchy. No specific formula has been set down, no generally accepted means of measuring whether improvements in patient care have been achieved, and there are no objective standards by which goals can be put in order of priority. The idea behind the system is to improve patient care by giving doctors and nurses a greater role in the management of resources and devolving responsibility for budgets to clinical teams within hospitals, enabling managers to negotiate workload agreements with these clinical teams, and improving information systems to provide staff with better data about their services. However:

the costs of implementing resource management were underestimated and . . . the process of involving doctors is more complex and time consuming than had been assumed. Research also suggests that there are few tangible benefits yet to emerge in terms of better services for patients and improved value for money. . . . Even after five years of experimentation . . . no hospital is yet able to claim to have a fully developed resource management process in place in which doctors and other staff are involved in the way envisaged in the Griffiths Report.[38]

There is obvious merit in including doctors in the management of health care resources, but this involvement significantly affects the traditional concept of the doctor–patient relationship. Clinicians now have managerial obligations to hospital managers as well as to patients, so that the director's own clinical practices, and those of the colleagues for whom he is responsible, may be modified. Some will ask: how far can considerations of management interfere with relations between doctor and patient? This is surely a matter driven solely by clinical considerations which provide the basis of the relationship of trust between doctor and patient. Medical audit and clinical practice guidelines have provided a means of encouraging doctors to re-appraise their own practices and priorities.

As the authors note, 'the extent to which Resource Management has so far enhanced clinical review depends on the availability of case-mix information and . . . sufficient data to enable the study and comparison of case histories [sic]. As yet the systems are new-born and have limited cover.' Ibid. 252.

[38]C. Ham, *Health Policy in Britain* (Macmillan, 1993, 3rd edn.) 179–80.

C. Medical Audit

'Medical audit can be defined as the systematic, critical analysis of the quality of medical care, including the procedures used for diagnosis and treatment, the use of resources, and the resulting outcome and quality of life for the patient.'[39] The logic of medical audit is to encourage doctors to adopt a critical and evaluative attitude to medical decision making. If, as some research suggests, patients are sometimes treated more from habit than positive choice about clinical benefit, then the process ought to enable the light of experience to shine on those practices which are ineffective or inappropriate compared to others. Audit is a voluntary system of assessment which may be applied to the whole range of medical services, from the treatment offered to individuals to the large-scale assessment of medical technologies. For example, the extensive research conducted into treatment regimes has demonstrated the value of low doses of aspirin to those at risk of heart attack,[40] that amniocentesis carrries a risk of miscarriage and may cause breathing difficulties,[41] and that an extension of day-case services provides good quality services to patients and excellent value for money.[42] In future, hospitals will increasingly be expected to show what proportion of patients survived surgery so that comparisons between hospitals, and between surgeons, can be made. The principle of medical audit appears to be extremely valuable. How effective has it been in practice?

Although the large-scale studies carry persuasive authority, the value of audit when applied to individual doctors is more difficult to assess. Some regard the whole process with suspicion and consider it a waste of time and effort.[43] The extent to which doctors and other medical staff have become involved varies from place to place, as do the ways in which audit has been

---

[39] *Working for Patients: Medical Audit (Working Paper 6)* (HMSO, 1989) 3.

[40] ISIS-2, 'A Randomised Trial of Intravenous Streptokinase, Oral Aspirin, both, or neither among 17,187 cases of suspected Acute Myocardial Infarction', [1988] ii *The Lancet* 753.

[41] A. Tabor, M. Masden *et al.*, 'Randomised Controlled Trial of Genetid Amniocentesis in 4,606 low risk women', [1986] i *The Lancet* 1287.

[42] *A Short Cut to Better Services. Day Services in England and Wales* (Audit Commission, 1990).

[43] N. Black and E. Thompson, 'Obstacles to Medical Audit: British Doctors Speak', 36 *Social Science and Medicine* 849 (1993).

introduced.[44] A survey of audit procedures adopted in hospitals revealed that there is no consistency as to the composition of the audit team, except that consultants are generally included and patients are almost always excluded.[45] Nor is there a common practice concerning the medical evidence on which the audit is conducted. Case note review is the most common, mortality and morbidity review less so, and patient surveys are used only rarely.[46]

One of the difficulties in comparing the results of audits from different hospitals or practices is that there are no uniform standards on which comparisons can be based. Proper measurement of the success rates of a particular hospital or surgeon requires knowledge of the health of patients before admission. Patients admitted to hospital in very poor health are less likely to do well, no matter who is responsible for their care. And hospitals in areas of relative affluence will generally expect better results than those situated in areas of poverty. But accurate measurement of 'inputs' is extremely difficult. For this reason 'objective' standards are unlikely to be achieved in the process of medical audit. Inevitably, in the absence of persuasive research findings, doctors will continue to disagree about the significance of particular clinical results, about the risks and benefits of a treatment, and the relative value to be attached to different findings by the audit. Some will say that, notwithstanding the evidence of the medical audit, their experience of a particular clinical practice is good and that they will not abandon it on the basis of the findings of a limited medical audit.[47]

For the moment, therefore, medical audit may be an important part of the consultant's clinical authority over junior staff. It is less effective in the management of consultants, who tend to accept differences between themselves as a necessary part of clinical freedom.[48] Traditionally, consultants have not been asked to

---

[44] See generally S. Kerrison, T. Packwood, M. Buxton, 'Monitoring Medical Audit', in R. Robinson and J. Le Grand (eds.), *Evaluating the NHS Reforms* (King's Fund Institute, 1994).

[45] *Evaluating Audit: The Development of Audit* (CASPE Research, London, 1994) 38. [46] Ibid., 82.

[47] See the differences expressed by consultants with respect to the propriety of spinal surgery in *Defreitas* v. *O'Brien* [1993] 4 Med LR 281 discussed at p. 92 *supra*.

[48] 'Monitoring Medical Audit', *supra* note 44, 167–171.

account for their clinical decisions. Medical audit, however, introduces the possibility of their being required to do so, not to other consultants but to non-clinical managers. This raises a more sensitive question. Given the need of hospital managers to demonstrate the clinical effectiveness of their units, pressure will be brought to bear on those who insist on adhering to standards which have been undermined by medical audit. Conflict between them is inevitable and may ultimately have to be resolved by votes of confidence, for example by the board of an NHS Trust in its managers and consultants. In the few cases when such votes have been taken, the consultants seem to have prevailed over the managers.[49]

Two further points arise here. First, as the science of making comparisons between different institutions develops, so it seems natural to say that minimum standards as assessed by a team of accreditors should be achieved by all.[50] In America, for example, the Joint Commission on the Accreditation of Healthcare Organisations exists to monitor, compare,and make public its findings with respect to hospital performance. Hospital funding depends on an inspection and approval by the accreditors. For the moment, medical audit in the UK does not seek to achieve the same objectives. The procedure is essentially voluntary and may seek simply to promote efficiency at an internal level, in which case there is no need for the results to be made public. Alternatively, it may be used for the benefit of purchasers, to enable useful comparisons to be made with respect to the quality and price offered by providers of health care. Equally, this means of measuring performance may tempt a minister to introduce a system of national accreditation. The form which such accreditation would take, and the significance attached to it, would depend on the purpose which it was intended to achieve.

The second point concerns the significance of clinical practice guidelines.

---

[49] See e.g. 'Consultants force NHS Trust head to resign', *The Independent* 26 Nov. 1994 5 and 'Third NHS Trust Chief Comes Under Fire', *The Independent* 6 Dec. 1994 2.

[50] See R. Klein and E. Scrivers, 'The Bottom Line', *Health Services Journal*, 25 Nov. 1993 25.

D. Clinical Practice Guidelines

One of the effects of medical audit has been to reveal the extent of practice variations between doctors. The habitual, rather than rational, way in which some operate, and the difficulty in justifying both the outcomes of their treatments and the differences in their costs, have significantly promoted the idea of clinical practice guidelines.[51] They have concerned matters of clinical practice and hospital management, and have been formulated on the basis of both local experience and the recommendations of national professional bodies. As the experience of audit accumulates, their number is likely to increase.

The development of guidelines is part of a significant cultural shift, a move away from unexamined reliance on professional judgment toward more structured support for, and accountability of, such judgment. The explosion of medical information and the increased complexity in today's health care system has made this support necessary. . . . Moreover, the need for standards in terms of administrative accountability to the payers—private insurers, corporations and government—has spurred the development of guidelines.[52]

Guidelines and protocols undoubtedly affect clinical freedom. For example, unless a doctor has very good reason for doing so, it would not be prudent for him to expose a patient to risks which had been contra-indicated by this form of peer review. If treatment were unsuccessful and the patient were injured, the guidelines or protocols would inevitably be used to support the patient's claim. In this way, despite the mixed reception they have received from the medical profession and the differing methods by which they have been introduced, they have already had an impact on attitudes. Guidelines are intended to achieve a number of objectives: to reduce the incidence of variations in practice, to promote the best medical outcomes, and to maximize the efficient use of resources. This development poses a number of questions. Exactly what are clinical practice guidelines, are they likely to effect changes in medical practice, what legal status do they

---

[51] *Evaluating Audit: The Development of Audit, supra* note 45, 94 and app. C.

[52] D. Garnick, A. Hendricks, T. Brennan, 'Can Practice Guidelines Reduce the Number and Costs of Malpractice Claims?', 266 *Journal of the American Medical Association* 2856, 2857 (1991)

possess, and are they likely to increase, or reduce, the incidence of medical malpractice litigation? Lastly, what additional authority will guidelines bestow on health service managers?

Clinical practice guidelines are difficult to define because they come in a variety of forms, from general background information of the sort found in textbooks, or the ethical standards of the General Medical Council,[53] to specific recommendations tailored to particular conditions and patients. In this latter category, some may intend to introduce procedural changes,[54] others may be expected to have more impact on practice.[55] Exceptionally, some are not actually 'guidelines' at all, but have the force of law.[56] For the present, however, there is doubt as to whether the guidelines are capable of bringing about dramatic change in clinical practice, although they could introduce a trend toward greater uniformity which could become more pronounced in the future. Why is this?

First, the very persistence of variations in clinical practice is evidence that doctors continue to have widely differing opinions about the efficacy and value of the treatments available to them. In many cases, therefore, there will be disagreement as to the propriety of a guideline, because: 'the science of developing practice guidelines is at an early stage and few currently available practice guidelines have the . . . attributes of good practice . . . ([namely]: validity, reliability, clinical applicability, clinical flexibility [sic], multi-disciplinary process of development, scheduled review to determine whether revisions are necessary, and documentation).'[57]

Guidelines accepted today may be undermined by medical research tomorrow. Uncertainty is endemic to the science (or art)

[53] See *Professional Conduct and Discipline: Fitness to Practise* (General Medical Council, 1993).

[54] Particularly with respect to protocols concerning the testing of medicines on volunteers. See e.g. *The Ethical Conduct of Research on the Mentally Incapacitated* (Medical Research Council, 1991) and *Guidelines on the Practice of Ethics Committees in Medical Research Involving Human Subjects* (Medical Research Council, 1991).

[55] For an example of an influential set of guidelines, see C. Roberts *et al.*, 'Influence of the Royal College of Radiologists guidelines on hospital practice: a multicentre study', 304 *British Medical Journal* 740 (1992).

[56] See Part IV of the Mental Health Act 1983, dealing with the treatment of patients without consent, and the *Mental Health Act Code of Practice* (Mental Health Act Commission).

[57] 'Can Practice Guidelines Reduce the Number and Costs of Malpractice Claims?', *supra* note 52, 2858–89 (1991).

of medicine.[58] Disagreement between doctors may arise both as to the conclusions which should be drawn from agreed evidence, and as to the veracity of the evidence itself. How extensive was the study, over what period was it conducted, how convincing was its methodology, and how representative was the sample on which it was based? These are all matters about which reasonable people may have differing opinions, which are likely to change with developments in clinical evidence. Even if guidelines were accepted, therefore, they would have to be reviewed regularly to ensure that they continued to reflect the mainstream of modern medical opinion.

Secondly, though a general guideline may be accepted by a medical discipline, it may not significantly affect day-to-day clinical practice in which variations are widespread. 'There are wide differences in the nature of clinical problems that need to be assessed. Some . . . may be amenable to a limited set of guidelines that can be applied during the treatment of a wide spectrum of patients. . . . Other clinical problems may require a more sophisticated set of guidelines with numerous options for patients with different characteristics.'[59]

Variations between patients are inevitable, caused, for example by the varying severity of their condition, age and physical characteristics, and whether the complaint is complicated by other problems. Therefore, variations in the regime of treatment recommended will also be unavoidable. Thus, responsible guidelines cannot be adhered to as if they were recipes in a cookery book and alternative options and exceptional cases may also have to be considered. Naturally, many doctors resist the use of standards, particularly those which restrict their clinical freedom. 'Consultants would argue that they wanted "guidelines" not "tramlines".'[60] They will always have to be flexibly expressed and include a reminder that they cannot be applied blindly to patients and that each case remains the clinical responsibility of the doctor concerned. Bear in mind too that practice guidelines are favoured

[58] See D. Eddy, 'Variations in Clinical Practice: The Role of Uncertainty', 3 *Health Affairs* 74 (1984).
[59] E. Hirschfeld, 'Should Practice Parameters Be the Standard of Care in Malpractice Litigation', 266 *Journal of the American Medical Association* 2886, 2887 (1991).
[60] 'Monitoring Medical Audit', *supra* note 44, 163.

by governments and insurers eager to improve efficiency in health care. The Clinton administration in America committed itself to the development of practice guidelines,[61] as has a government committee of The Netherlands.[62] The UK is moving in the same direction. Cynics will suspect that economic issues, rather than clinical outcomes, provide the major pressure for their introduction.[63] In truth, the efficient use of resources and good clinical outcomes may often have much in common. Equally, however, exceptional cases may require exceptional treatment which fall outside recommended procedures.

What impact will the growth of guidelines have on malpractice litigation? Inevitably, they will feature largely in the cases presented by both plaintiff and defendant. Since they will often have been prepared and approved by prestigious medical authorities, they will possess considerable persuasive weight in evidence. It is impossible to say who stands to gain most from guidelines.[64] In principle, as the traditional test of medical negligence confirms, so long as a responsible minority of practitioners can be found to support a variation in clinical practice, common law will endorse their action.[65] This will have a conservative effect and tend to benefit doctors. On the other hand, an extensive American survey[66] has suggested that the proportion of patients who litigate as a result of suffering damage from treatment is extremely small, perhaps as low as 2 per cent. By contrast, very large numbers of claims are made where there is

---

[61] See its Health Security Plan which 'expands research related to the research of medical treatments, fosters the development of practice guidelines and provides other information to help doctors, nurses and other professional deliver more effective care.' *Health Security: Preliminary Plan Summary* (US Government Printing Office, 1993) 15. See also *The Future of Healthcare: Physician and Hospital Relationships* (American College of Health Executives, 1993).

[62] 'Scientific associations, professional organisations, and health facilities must themselves take the initiative in setting up protocols, guidelines and essential lists for appropriate care.' *Choices in Health Care* (Committee on Choices in Health Care, Netherlands Ministry of Welfare, Health and Cultural Affairs, 1992) 25.

[63] See J. Ayres, 'The Use and Abuse of Medical Practice Guidelines', 15 *Journal of Legal Medicine* 421, 436 (1994).

[64] See T. Brennan, 'Practice Guidelines and Malpractice Litigation, *supra* note 5, 67 (1991).

[65] See *Lowry* v. *Henry Mayo Newhall Memorial Hospital* 229 Cal Rptr 620 (Cal App 2d, 1986) in which there was a legitimate departure from guidelines issued by the American Heart Association on cardiopulmonary resuscitation.

[66] See P. Weiler, H. Hiatt, J. Newhouse *et al.*, *A Measure of Malpractice* (Harvard University Press, 1993).

evidence neither of negligence, nor iatrogenic (doctor-induced) injury. If correct, this suggests that lack of information as to suitable and appropriate standards is responsible for both under-representation of legitimate claims and over-representation of illegitimate ones. Clearly, if the existence of guidelines tended to redress that imbalance, by enabling plaintiffs more easily to prove that they had received improper care, the proportion of successful claims would increase. Conversely, resources spent on defending hopeless claims might be saved.

Could those responsible for drafting, approving, and promoting guidelines be in any way liable to patients? It is almost in-conceivable for a number of reasons. First, as a matter of clinical practice, guidelines should never be relied on uncritically. Doctors must always be prepared to modify or depart from them as the patient's needs require. It would also be most unlikely that a guideline would be expressed in a way which exposed its originator to liability. Secondly, the courts have been very reluctant to make one party liable for the negligent act of another person. It would be exceptional for the failure of a doctor to administer proper care to be made the responsibility of those who promoted the guideline.[67]

III. NON-CLINICAL REGULATION

The managerial techniques discussed above remain within the control of doctors themselves. By contrast, the following are imposed on doctors by managers.

A. Choice of Medicine

The cost of medicines to the NHS increases relentlessly and there is concern that not all of it is justified. 'Although much of the variation between prescribers can be explained by factors such as age, there remain wide unexplained differences.'[68] In its report on

---

[67] See *Murphy* v. *Brentwood DC* [1991] 1 AC 378, *Smith* v. *Littlewoods Organisation* [1988] AC 241.

[68] See *A Prescription for Improvement*, supra note 7, 1. 'Demography alone would explain only a 5% rise in expenditure over the last decade . . . [but elderly patients] now receive 43% of all prescribed medicines compared to 36% in 1982.' Ibid. para. 9.

Repeat Prescribing by General Practitioners in England[69] the National Audit Office estimated that, of a total of £2.6 billion paid by the Department of Health for prescriptions, perhaps two-thirds were prescribed on a repeat basis. No doubt, as the report acknowledges, there are many advantages for both doctor and patient in avoiding the need for frequent consultations during long-term therapy. Equally there are disadvantages, both clinical and financial, if the patient's compliance with the therapy, or benefit (or harm) from it, are not regularly monitored. Without more research, there is no more than a suspicion that unregulated repeat prescribing ought to be discouraged, and that closer supervision over the practice could achieve savings.

On the other hand, medicines are often extremely cost-effective. They may obviate the need for admission to hospital or surgery. A crucial question that is yet to be resolved concerns the relative costs and benefits of medicines. If medicines are not properly prescribed, overall morbidity will tend to increase, more of us will require surgery and some of us will be unable to return to work.[70] This would be bad for patients and particularly when we take up valuable hospital beds, extremely poor value for money. Other factors also explain the upward trend in GP prescribing. GPs are required under their Terms of Service to undertake more 'preventive' medicine by encouraging healthy patients to submit themselves for periodic check-ups.[71] Inevitably a proportion will be found to require medication who, in the past, would have received none. In addition, clinical and pharmaceutical advances have enabled more people to be treated in the community, under the supervision of GPs, and the cost of effective modern medicines is high. Lastly, patients are becoming more informed about the medicines available to treat their conditions and less deferential to

---

[69] *Repeat Prescribing by General Practitioners in England* (National Audit Office, HMSO, 1993).

[70] See J. Griffin, *Cheap Prescribing—Can We Afford It?* (Association of the British Pharmaceutical Industry, 1994). The issue of assessing the economic costs and benefits of medicines is addressed in *Guidance on Good Practice in the Conduct of Economic Evaluations of Medicines* (Department of Health and Association of the British Pharmaceutical Industry, 1994).

[71] In particular: newly registered patients, patients not seen within three years, and those over seventy-five years old. See the National Health Service (General Medical Services) Regs. 1992 (SI 1992, No. 635), Sched. 2, paras. 14–16.

doctors. Consequently, they are more inclined to request a particular medicine from their doctor. Each of these considerations has implications for the costs to the NHS of medicines.

1. Indicative Prescribing Amounts

Concern about the irrational use of medicines has led the Government to introduce a scheme designed to put downward pressure on prescribing. GP spending on pharmaceuticals is now subject to regulation by indicative amounts,[72] or 'target budgets'.[73] The scheme, which does not apply to GP fund-holders,[74] requires FHSAs to impose a notional amount on GP drug spending. The corresponding duty of GPs is contained in section 18 of the 1990 Act: 'The members of a practice shall seek to secure that, except with the consent of the relevant Family Health Services Authority or for good cause, the orders for drugs, medicines and listed appliances given by them . . . in any financial year [do] not exceed the indicative amount notified for the practice.'

The stated object of the scheme is not to inhibit clinical discretion. Indeed, it is incapable of doing so because GPs have an existing obligation to FHSAs under their Terms of Service to 'order any medicines or appliances which are needed' by their patients.[75] In proper circumstances GPs will be entitled, indeed expected, to exceed the amount prescribed by the FHSA. One of the salient principles underlying the scheme is of the 'patient's entitlement to receive all the medicines they [sic] require'.[76] An influx of new patients to the list, or unexpectedly expensive requirements from particular patients, would justify exceeding the recommended amount.[77] However, the ultimate sanction against

---

[72] See section 18, National Health Service and Community Care Act 1991 and National Health Service (Indicative Amounts) Regs. SI 1991 no. 556.

[73] The phrase is informally introduced in *Prescribing Expenditure: guidance on allocations and budget setting 1994/95* (EL(94)2, NHSME, 1994), which discusses the principles on which the amounts shall be assessed.

[74] See the National Health Service and Community Care Act 1990, s. 18(2). Fund-holders are responsible for their own budgets.

[75] National Health Service (General Medical Services) Regs. 1992, SI 1992. No. 635, Sched. 2, para. 43.

[76] *Prescribing Expenditure*, *supra* note 73, para. 2.

[77] See selection of ministerial statements gathered by J. Jacob in his annotations to section 18 of the 1990 Act in *Current Law Statutes Annotated*, 1990, vol. 2.

overspending is for a deduction to be made from a GP's remuneration when: 'the cost of any drug or appliance ordered by a doctor on a prescription form in relation to any patient is, by reason of the character of the drug or appliance in question or the quantity in which it was so ordered, in excess of that which was reasonably necessary for the proper treatment of that patient.'[78]

One would expect discussions between GPs and FHSAs to avoid the need for invoking this procedure, so that it will be used very rarely. In serious cases, however, the amount of money to be deducted from a doctor's remuneration should relate to the costs incurred by the excessive prescribing.[79] What counts as 'excessive'? Guidance from the NHSME suggests that:

there are several types of prescribing which may give rise to a perception on the FHSA's part that there may have been excessive prescribing . . . [e.g.] where it appears that far too much of a drug is prescribed for the condition under treatment . . . ; where two drugs with the same apparent mode of action are prescribed when beneficial synergy is not expected . . . ; where too many drugs appear to have been prescribed for a single condition. This may be where treatment is begun or drugs are added without deletion of previous treatment . . . ; [or] where additional drugs are routinely prescribed prohylatically to meet infrequent side effects.[80]

This suggests that the scheme is designed to cut out waste. It is not intended to inhibit the GPs reasonable clinical discretion. Doctors who prescribe drugs in a manner which meets with the disapproval of their peers, or at prices generally regarded as unreasonably extravagant, ought to be criticized for wasting public funds. More usually, of course, cases will not fall into this description. Clinical discretion is a flexible concept which cannot be applied in black and white terms. Doctors obviously have widely differing opinions about what is reasonable and justifiable. What is the position, therefore, of a doctor who is criticized by the

---

[78] See the National Health Service (Service Committees and Tribunal) Regs. 1992, SI no. 664, reg. 15(1) and paras.15 and 16. Appeal against such a decision, either as to the decision to make a deduction, or the amount, is available to the Secretary of State. See para. 15(19)–(31).

[79] Ibid., para. 13. The principle is flexible. Such a sum may be reduced in cases concerning very expensive drugs, or increased in cases of very inexpensive drugs or persistent excessive prescribing. See para. 14.

[80] *Excessive prescribing by GPs: referral to a Professional Committee* EL(92)90 (NHSME, 1992), annex B, para. 8.

FHSA but who has support from colleagues for his or her prescribing practices? Who is the judge of 'waste'?

Both common law and statute[81] respect the doctor's clinical discretion provided that a reasonable body of medical opinion is prepared to defend, though not necessarily agree with, the action of the doctor concerned. Negligence takes no account of the fact that a judge happens to prefer the view of one responsible body of medical experts to another.[82] Thus, any overspending which could be defended by a reasonable body of medical opinion ought to be immune from criticism by the FHSA. The words 'good cause' in section 18, and 'reasonably necessary' and 'proper treatment' in the regulations, must be understood in this light. Any interpretation which encroached on GPs' clinical discretion would expose them to conflicting obligations to the patient and the administrator. There would be a risk of the doctor suffering a deduction of remunera-tion for adhering to standards which the common law has respected for decades. Conversely, he would be open to an action in negligence for giving inadequate care to his patient.[83] Any such rule would seriously undermine the confidence which is the bedrock of the doctor–patient relationship. Support for this view is available from the Audit Commission which has said that:

> GPs must not be required to make decisions on non-clinical grounds about whether or not high cost treatments such as growth hormone and fertility drugs should be provided on the NHS. . . . the needs and characteristics of the individual patient must be paramount . . . it is essential to pursue economies in the annual drugs budget without detriment to care.[84]

Precisely this view has been adopted by the Department of Health. 'The Government fully recognises that effective patient care may sometimes require the prescribing of relatively costly

---

[81] The National Health Service (General Medical Services) Regs. 1992, SI 1992 no. 635, Sched. 2, paras. 12 and 43 discussed on pp. 146–50, *supra*.

[82] *Maynard* v. *West Midlands Health Authority* [1985] 1 WLR 634.

[83] 2,000 people die each year from asthma, of which 80% are said to be avoidable by increased use of inhaled corticosteroids. See *A Prescription for Improvement*, *supra* note 7, para. 34.

[84] Ibid., paras. 27, 79. It recommends increased use of generic prescribing subject to the caveat that 'increased generic prescribing must never be regarded as an end in itself; consideration must always be given to whether a particular drug is appropriate for treating a patient's condition.' See para. 50.

drugs. It remains committed to ensuring that patients get the drugs that their doctors judge appropriate to their clinical needs.'[85] Arguably, therefore, any attempt to discipline a doctor for exercising his proper discretion in these circumstances would be unlawful. The appropriate remedy for the doctor is either judicial review,[86] or an action for breach of the Terms of Service between the doctor and the FHSA.

No doubt, this presents a problem for FHSAs. They must manage a budget allocated by the Regional Health Authority and are obliged to remain within the limits of its allocation.[87] How can they protect the interests of patients, by seeing that they receive the medicines they require, and yet remain within budget? Children with growing disorders need growth hormone treatment which may cost around £7,000 for a six-month course of treatment.[88] Essential treatment of renal failure may cost £12,000 per year.[89] The introduction of genetically modified medicines will make the problem worse. One product which reduces mortality in patients with gram negative septicaemia costs £2,200 for a single dose.[90] Would an FHSA be justified in penalizing doctors who refused to prescribe cheaper or less convenient tablets and insisted

[85] *Priority Setting in the NHS: The NHS Drug Budget. Government Response to the Second Report from the Health Committee Session 1993–94* (Cm. 2686, 1994) 11.

[86] A similar form of argument succeeded in *Secretary of State for Education and Science* v. *Tameside MBC* [1977] AC 1014, on the construction of s. 68 of the Education Act 1944. Lord Salmon said (at 1070) '. . . before the Secretary of State can lawfully issue directions under it he must satisfy himself not only that he does not agree with the way the authority have acted or are proposing to act nor even that the authority is mistaken or wrong. The question he must ask himself is: "Could any reasonable local authority act in the way in which this authority has acted or is proposing to act". If, but only if, he is satisfied on any material capable of satisfying a reasonable man that the answer to the crucial question is "No," he may lawfully issue directions under section 68.'

[87] See the National Health Service Act 1977, s. 97B(1) as amended by s. 5, Sched. 3, para. 10 of the Health and Social Security Act 1984.

[88] 'Unlicensed Uses for Growth Hormone', (anon.) 32 *Drugs and Therapeutics Bulletin* 53 (1994).

[89] R. Gabriel, 'Picking up the Tab for Erythropoietin' 302 *British Medical Journal* 248 (1991). And see the subsequent correspondence at 407 and 592. Some hospitals attempt to down-load these costs by retaining responsibility for treatment, but asking doctors to write the prescriptions for the medicines. See '£120m. cost is dumped on to GPs', *General Practitioner* 24 June 1994 18. GPs who prescribe medicines without retaining adequate supervision of patients expose themselves to risk of negligence if the treatment goes wrong.

[90] M. Orme, 'How to Pay for Expensive Drugs', 303 *British Medical Journal* 593 (1991). See also R. Williams, 'Can we Afford Medical Advances?', 27 *Journal of the Royal College of Physicians* 70 (1993).

on the more expensive ones? These remain clinical questions. It would be unreasonable for an FHSA to instruct a responsible doctor as to the treatment a particular patient ought to receive. Of course, FHSAs are perfectly entitled to encourage GPs to reduce their spending on medicines (say) by issuing general guidelines which recommend certain regimes of treatment over others, or incentive schemes which reward practices which achieve savings on their indicated prescribing amount.[90a] Ultimately, however, GPs retain responsibility for the proper treatment of their patients and may not hide behind the pressures imposed on them by health managers if things go wrong.

Clearly, drug costs present a challenge to the NHS which has not been properly addressed. If restrictions are to be imposed on GPs, the matter cannot be made the responsibility of FHSAs. Their duty is to ensure that GPs adhere to the Terms of Service by prescribing the medicines which patients need. Any other duty designed to curb responsible clinical freedom exposes them to an unacceptable conflict of interest. If particular treatments are to be restricted, the matter ought to be considered at national level under the supervision of the Secretary of State. Such a discussion will have far-reaching implications for the doctor–patient relationship, as well as for the basic obligation of the Secretary of State to provide a 'comprehensive health service' under the National Health Service Act 1977. For the present, a limited attempt to consider the problem has been made in relation to the use of local formularies and selected lists of medicines.

2. Local Formularies and Selected Lists

One method of containing costs is to limit the variety of drugs which doctors may prescribe to patients. Such a restriction already operates in the form of a 'black-list' of drugs for which GPs may not issue an NHS prescription.[91] The list was introduced in 1986 and was intended to save money by discouraging use of 'drugs

---

[90a] See the National Health Service (Functions of Family Health Service Authorities) (Prescribing Incentive Schemes) Regulations 1995 (SI 1995, No. 692).

[91] The list of 'Drugs and other substances not to be prescribed for supply under pharmaceutical services' is contained in the National Health Service (General Medical Services) Regs. (SI 1992, No. 635), Sched. 10. It extends to around 2,000 products.

for handling ECRs should be simple, quick and n
d designed in discussion with local GPs and ot

or handling ECRs should complement, and not dist
ctice in deciding to admit or make appointments to s

ssible patients should not be aware of the administrati
ging ECRs;

alth information is confidential, and access to it should
now' basis. Patient name should not routinely be include
tion of ECRs.[100]

s on which an ECR could be refused by a DHA ar
ery limited. Purchasers should respect the clinica
GPs and other clinicians who decide on individua
that it will be rare for a clinician's choice of consultant
unwarranted. In particular 'it is not acceptable for a
refuse authorisation solely on the grounds of the
ost of the treatment in relation to the contracted
he only grounds on which refusal may be acceptable
ws:

ent is not the purchaser's responsibility, i.e. the patient is not
ct resident or the patient is, for the treatment planned, a
ibility of a GPFII;

prior authorisation for the ECR was not sought where it was
lly reasonable to expect the provider to have done so;[101]
ferral is not justified on clinical grounds. In making such
ents the DHA would be expected to ensure that it takes
priate clinical advice. This would include instances where such
l advice has led to the development and agreement of clear
al protocols and the threshold has not been met;
ternative referral would be equally efficacious for the patient,
g account of the patient's wishes.[102]

e funding for a particular ECR is refused, it is the
ibility of the purchaser to inform both patient and provider
decision. Reasons for the refusal should be made clear.

idance on Extra Contractual Referrals (NHSME, 1993) para.6.
though 'GPs should be encouraged to discuss any referrals outside
s with a named contact point in the DHA before referral . . . though
rs should not insist on such discussions prior to the referral.' Ibid., para. 4.
id. paras. 49–52.

which were considered to be unsafe, obsolete, or of marginal therapeutic value.'[92] There are new proposals to extend the black-list to cover drugs which have *greater* therapeutic value, including contraceptives and drugs acting on the skin; this raises further important issues about clinical freedom.

Before a medicine can be made available to the public, it must have been granted a product licence by the Department of Health which acts as the licensing authority. In considering whether to grant such a licence, it must give particular consideration to the safety, efficacy, and quality of the product,[93] but it may not take into account the superior efficacy of another product,[94] or refuse to grant a licence on any grounds relating to price.[95] Thus, a medicine may receive a licence even though it is less efficacious and more expensive than its competitors. The system of licensing is entirely separate from the NHS and is solely concerned with protecting the public by monitoring the overall standards achieved by drug manufacturers. Arguably, therefore, medicines ought to satisfy an additional test before they are made available under the NHS i.e. that they represent good value for money. This is the argument for the limited list.

A more positive approach has been suggested: that we should be more specific about preferred medicines by introducing a 'white-list' of medicines, or a Selected List, which covers the cross-section of patients' needs and from which doctors should always prescribe. The House of Commons Health Committee has recommended a logical extension of this argument: that there should be a National Prescribing List for the entire service.[96] The Committee suggest that all new drugs should be granted a product licence in the normal way, but that the medicine should be evaluated over a five-year period during which time its therapeutic value would be assessed by clinical trials. Those which were found to be ineffective, or more expensive without additional therapeutic value, could be excluded from the National List. In this way a

[92] See *Priority Setting in the NHS: The NHS Drug Budget* (Health Committee, Second Report, HC-I, Session 1993–94, HMSO), para. 101. The list covers mild to moderate pain-killers, indigestion remedies, laxatives, cough and cold remedies, vitamins, tonics and benzodiazepine sedatives and tranquillizers. See ibid., para. 98.   [93] See the Medicines Act 1968, s. 19.

[94] Ibid.   [95] Ibid., s. 20(2).

[96] *Priority Setting in the NHS: The NHS Drug Budget, supra* note 92, para. 132.

national formulary could be created. These proposals are currently under review by the Government.[97]

What of the exceptional case of the product which has been excluded from the List, but which is of proven value to a particular patient with idiosyncratic characteristics? (Patients with skin conditions, such as eczema, appear to react in diverse ways to different treatments.) The Health Committee say:

In these circumstances the primary concern should always be the patient's welfare, and it is imperative that when a drug which is not on the List is required, it should be made available. In no circumstances should a patient be denied a medicine for which there is evidence of genuine need. In exceptional circumstances the doctor should be permitted to prescribe the medicine on the NHS, *provided that he or she has secured the prior agreement of the local FHSA pharmaceutical adviser.*[98]

Presumably, the agreement of the FHSA would be withheld only in the most exceptional case and never on financial grounds alone. It may no longer be sufficient simply to say that prescribing habits are matters of personal preference. This makes the point, however, that GPs must retain ultimate responsibility for patients. It would be no defence for a doctor to say that proper treatment was denied because of the pressures imposed by FHSA administrators.

B. Choice of Consultant: Extra Contractual Referrals

In the past, the recommendation of the British Medical Association has been that 'general practitioners should always acquiesce in any reasonable request by a patient for a second opinion'[99] with the presumption that the choice of consultant was a matter for the referring doctor to decide. What freedom do GPs retain in the choice of consultant?

NHS contracts under the National Health Service and Community Care Act 1990 require District Health Authorities to make agreements with hospitals with respect to the services required by its residents. In doing so, they will seek to make provision for those most often in need of care and the most common conditions

[97] See *Priority Setting in the NHS: The NHS Drug Budget. Government Response to the Second Report from the Health Committee Session 1993–94, supra* note 85, 10.   [98] Ibid., at para. 137, emphasis in original.
[99] *Rights and Responsibilities of Doctors* (British Medical Association, 1988) 85.

Thus, referrals should be made when clinically required. This will reassure those with uncommon conditions for which their DHA has not arranged a block contract, and those whose conditions become so serious as to require specialist facilities as tertiary referrals. Arguably, the requirement of a 'comprehensive' health service obliges the DHA to take reasonable steps to provide treatment for all its residents taking account of national resources. Of course, demand for a particular treatment may be so low, or its cost so high, or its efficacy so unproved, that facilities are not available from any hospital.[103] In this case the treatment will not be provided. But if it is available, it ought never to be denied simply on the ground that no contract has been arranged under which it may be treated. A comprehensive *national* health service requires more than a patchwork of uncoordinated local facilities. The system of health service resources ought to be examined from a national rather than a local perspective, and reasonable reserves ought to be set aside to allow deserving cases to receive extra contractual treatment.[104]

Some money, therefore, must be allocated by DHAs to cover the costs of ECRs.[105] Health authorities have records of previous referral patterns and are obliged to make reasonable provision based on their past experience. A failure to cater for a known demand, either by contractual or extra contractual means, would require explanation. Equally, one must concede that money has always been short in the NHS and that there is nothing new about waiting lists. For this reason, it would be difficult to criticize an authority which put sufficient funds aside to deal with emergency and urgent cases on an extra contractual basis, but which consigned to a waiting list those patients whose conditions could *reasonably* be considered to be of secondary priority. These patients would await funding from the following year's budget.

---

[103] Kidney dialysis is often in short supply, see D. Gill, S. Ingman, and J. Campbell, 'Health care provision and distributive justice: end stage renal disease and the elderly in Britain and America', 32 *Social Science and Medicine* 565 (1991).

[104] See J. D. Williamson, 'Dealing with extra contractual referrals', 303 *British Medical Journal* 499 (1991), which suggests nine criteria for deciding whether to approve an ECR.

[105] For the system of payment for extra contractual referrals, see 'Tariffs for Extra Contractual Referrals' FDL(91)34 (NHSME) and 'Information to Support Invoicing for Extra Contractual Referrals' FDL(91)37 (NHSME).

IV. THE TOOLS OF MANAGEMENT: GUIDELINES AND CIRCULARS

Regulations within the NHS come in a number of forms. We have considered the major common law and statutory means by which the system is supervised. In addition, reference has been made to the many statutory instruments made under the direct authority of an Act of Parliament. These we can refer to as 'laws'. Quite apart from the law, however, are the numerous health service guidelines (HSGs) and executive letters (ELs) distributed from the NHS Executive (the new name for NHS Management Executive).

Health Service Guidelines are the main way of communicating with the NHS . . . The purpose of HSGs is to convey standing guidance to NHS authorities of policy and operational matters. . . . ELs are meant to give guidance about policy or legislative changes, which need action, and/or which involve allocation of funds, and/or which is urgent and will be followed up with more substantive material later. They are important, probably urgent and necessarily short-lived.[106]

Clearly, at a day-to-day level, these exercise very considerable influence over the ways in which the system evolves and the solutions adopted to the problems it faces. They are essential to a proper understanding of the National Health Service, both as to regulation and accountability. They are more flexible than statutory instruments because the time and formality involved in their introduction and cancellation is reduced and they may be expressed in less technical language amenable to a lay readership. Some may seek only to influence the distribution of responsibilities within the system and have effects which are contained within the system of management. In such a large organization, it is prudent that internal regulations are communicated effectively. Others, however, may have consequences which concern the way in which patients are treated, or who has access to care. These raise much greater difficulty. What is their status in law? Two matters need to be addressed: first their legitimacy, and secondly the extent to which they create rights.

As to their legitimacy, these guidelines and circulars often do not emanate directly from the Secretary of State for Health through the Department of Health. Nor are they widely published,

---

[106] The NHS Communications Guide (NHSME, 1991), para. 4.

although they are ususally made available on request. They
emanate from the NHS Executive. The NHSE has no statutory
identity, nor is it an elected body. It is the management arm of the
NHS, accountable to the Secretary of State, who in turn is
accountable to Parliament. Exceptionally, Parliament may give
NHS guidelines and circulars the same legal effect as statutory
instruments, in which case they must be considered to be laws.[107]
More commonly, however, they cannot be so desribed because
their authority does not come from Parliament. Under the
Wednesbury principle of managerial reasonableness,[108] the
Secretary of State is entitled to use a range of measures which
assist the functioning of the system, provided they are lawful, i.e.
permitted by the National Health Service Acts or the common
law. The same analysis applies to the numerous statutory
regulations under which the Acts of 1977 and 1990 are given effect.
This order of analysis is important because guidelines and circulars
which contradict them are unlawful.[109]

This explanation is satisfactory in theory, but the position may
be more difficult in practice. The difficulty was raised by Lord
Bridge in *Gillick* v. *West Norfolk AHA*.[110] The case involved a
circular advising health authorities that GPs who prescribed
contraceptive pills to children under the age of sixteen without
their parents' consent would be acting lawfully. His Lordship
conceded that a guideline or circular which was contrary to law
could have no legal effect and should be corrected by means of a
declaration.[111] In this case, however, His Lordship observed that
the circular was not issued in the exercise of statutory powers or
the performance of any statutory function. It was purely advisory,
and GPs were in no way bound by it. In these circumstances, he
reasoned that a *Wednesbury* review on grounds of an unreasonable
exercise of statutory discretion was not possible. He said:

[107] See e.g. National Health Service and Community Care Act 1990, Sched. 2,
para. 6(2)(e) by which an NHS Trust shall comply with 'guidance or directions (by
circular or otherwise)' issued by the Secretary of State. The provision is discussed in
Chapter 6 below.

[108] Discussed in Chapter 4 above.

[109] This means of analysis was used by the Court of Appeal to invalidate
guidelines concerning the giving of contraceptive services to children under sixteen.
See *Gillick* v. *West Norfolk and Wisbech AHA* [1985] 1 All ER 533, 538. The
guidelines were subsequently reinstated by the House of Lords, [1985] 3 All ER
402. See Lord Scarman, 415.   [110] [1985] 3 All ER 402.

[111] Ibid. 427.

Such a review must always begin by examining the nature of the statutory power which the adminsitrative authority . . . has purported to exercise, and asking, in the light of that examination, what were, and what were not, relevant considerations for the authority to take into account in deciding to exercise its power. It is only against such a specific statutory background that the question whether the authority has acted unreasonably, in the *Wednesbury* sense, can properly be asked and answered. Here there is no specific statutory background reference to which the appropriate *Wednesbury* questions could be formulated.[112]

He declared the circular to be valid at common law, and therefore a lawful exercise of adminsitrative authority. Notice, however, that since it was advisory and not binding it did not deny rights to patients—indeed, it confirmed the existence of such rights. The same must also be the case as regards guidance on matters of internal management.

However, a different issue arises when the guideline or circular is expressed in mandatory terms and raises questions concerning access to care or affects other common law rights. Two examples make the point. We considered in Chapter 3 the obligation to provide long-term care for patients whose condition has stabilized. An executive letter advises that such patients may have to be discharged from hospital. In Chapter 8 we consider an example of health service guidance on the duty of confidentiality owed by doctors to patients when health service managers need access to patient records as part of their obligation to maintain quality. In each case, their lawfulness depends on the preliminary determination that they have remained within (respectively) section 3 of the National Health Service Act 1977 and the common law on confidentiality.

The second matter concerns their legal consequences for patients. As a general principle, clear and unambiguous promises made in statements and representations by public authorities ought to be adhered to until they are revoked; this is a matter of good administration.[113] It would be inconsistent and unfair to do otherwise. Thus, they are capable of conferring rights on individuals if they have created a 'legitimate expectation' that a certain

---

[112] [1985] 3 All ER 426.
[113] See *A-G of Hong Kong* v. *Ng Yuen Shiu* [1983] 2 AC 629, 637 *per* Lord Fraser.

procedure or policy will be followed. Legitimate expectations have been created for prisoners under the Prison Rules[114] and immigrants under the Immigration Rules.[115] They have been described as follows:

If a public body has made a representation to a specific individual or group of individuals that a particular policy will be followed, or that they will be informed before such change of policy takes place, then the individual will be entitled to insist that the policy is pursued in relation to the instant case, provided the implementation of the policy does not conflict with the authority's statutory duty.[116]

Legitimate expectations created by guidelines and circulars may concern substantive rights, or a procedural right to be heard before a decision is made. Indeed, plain and simple principles of good administration may be sufficient to create such an expectation in the absence of any express policy. For example, a recent case has confirmed the right of elderly residents in a nursing home to be consulted about plans to close the home, or to move individual residents to accommodation elsewhere. They had been 'enjoying some benefit or advantage of which the county council now propose[d] to deprive them.'[117] That was sufficient to confer a right to be consulted and to have their views heard, since their expectation was that they would be able to stay. Clearly, some health service guidelines and the *Patient's Charter* would be capable of creating legitimate expectations, although executive letters might not do so since they are addressed to particular health service managers only and are intended for short-term reference. It is impossible to generalize, and each case must be examined to see how and when the representation has been expressed, its effects, and any caveats which qualify it.

---

[114] See *O'Reilly* v. *Mackman* [1983] 2 AC 237.

[115] See *R* v. *Secretary of State for the Home Department* ex p *Khan* [1985] 1 All ER 40.

[116] P. Craig, *Administrative Law* (Sweet & Maxwell, 3rd edn., 1994) 395. See also *Council of Civil Service Unions* v. *Minister for the Civil Service* [1985] 1 AC 374 408, *per* Lord Diplock.

[117] *R* v. *Devon County Council*, ex p *Barker* [1995] 1 All ER 73, 91 *per* Simon Brown LJ.

6

Accountability in the Health Service

We have already dealt with a number of issues concerning accountability,[1] indeed, it is one of the themes that runs throughout the book. Common law standards of care and the patient's right to damages were considered in Chapter 3. Chapter 4 examined the salient statutory duties imposed on the Secretary of State under the National Health Service Act 1977 and the rights and duties which exist between GPs and FHSAs. Medical audit was examined in Chapter 5, and in Chapter 7 we shall deal with complaints and matters of professional discipline. All touch on the general question of accountability. This chapter considers the variety of ways in which managers and doctors may be held accountable for their decisions when negligence, or other complaints, are not the salient issues. It describes the framework in which health authorities, NHS Trusts, and GP fund-holders may be monitored and assessed. The matter has become more important with the introduction of the internal market for health and the devolution of power to local providers. Before doing so, however, we discuss some of the general concerns surrounding the idea of accountability.

I. PRINCIPLES OF ACCOUNTABILITY

When so much money is invested in the National Health Service, and when the consequences of mismanagement can be so serious, the question of accountability is central. 'Accountability', however, is an imprecise word. Clearly, it concerns holding individuals, or bodies, responsible for their decisions, which assumes that they

---

[1] See generally D. Longley, *Public Law and Health Service Accountability* (Open University Press, 1993).

have been given objectives which can be assessed against broadly measurable criteria. But there are many layers of authority in the NHS, and many different ways in which one party may be held answerable to another. There is also the broader question of accountability to the public.[2] In this section we examine issues of management, probity, and democracy; and the problems posed when private contractors are engaged to carry out functions on behalf of the NHS.

A. Management, Probity, and Democracy

1. Management

One way of describing accountability is to detail the management structure of the NHS by asking who reports to whom. For example, the Secretary of State is subject to the scrutiny of Parliament by means of Select Committees and Parliamentary Questions. On matters of policy she is advised by the NHS Policy Board which helps formulate strategy and overall objectives. By contrast, operational matters of day-to-day management are the responsibility of the NHS Executive (NHSE) which is accountable to the Policy Board. The Executive is in a curious position. Like the Policy Board, it has no statutory role but its interests are considered to be inseparable from those of the Government. Thus, the Department of Health has said that the Executive is 'unequivocally part of the Government, responsible for implementing the Government's policies for the NHS, holding health authorities to account on behalf of Ministers, and supporting and advising Ministers on health service matters.'[3]

Once objectives and targets have been agreed centrally, they become the responsibility of regional health authorities (which the Government proposes to abolish in 1996 by absorbing their functions into the Department of Health as regional 'offices') and district health authorities. In principle, DHAs enter corporate

---

[2] Many of the responsibilities within the NHS are considered in *Managing the New NHS—Functions and Responsibilities in the New NHS* (NHSE, 1994) and *Public Health in England: Roles and Responsibilities of the Department of Health and the NHS* (NHSE, 1994).

[3] *Review of the Wider Department of Health* (The 'Banks Report', Department of Health, 1994), para. 2.6.

contracts with regions, who in turn enter into similar arrangements with the NHSE. This devolution of responsibility to the various organs of the NHS does not deprive the Secretary of State for Health of power to manage the system. She retains the discretion to issue mandatory directions to health authorities, who are bound to comply.[4] The way in which these bodies interact, and many of the tensions which arise between them, doctors, and patients are dealt with in other chapters.

But a simple description of the management structure of the NHS is a very limited way of analysing accountability. After all, the NHS is financed from general taxation and provides a public service. It ought also to be sensitive to matters which concern those whom it serves and who pay for it. One such concern is about proper standards of public life.

2. Probity

Managers have acquired more influence and responsibility in the reformed NHS and their authority is likely to increase. This shift of power away from clinicians has caused unease. With the introduction of market principles concern has been expressed about a change of 'culture' in the National Health Service,[5] that 'people [who] come from outside . . . perhaps do not have the disciplines of dealing with public money that are present in the Civil Service as a whole'.[6] A similar observation was made in a report to the Chief Executive of the NHS that there is 'a perception, both within the NHS and amongst the public, that public service values have suffered in the development of the NHS market and a more business like approach to management of the NHS.'[7]

What is the substance of these misgivings? When managers in

---

[4] See s. 13, National Health Service Act 1977, as amended by sched.1, para.33, Health Services Act 1980, and sched. 10, National Health Service and Community Care Act 1990. Such a power may be threatened, but is very rarely used.

[5] See M. West and R. Sheaff, 'Back to Basics', *Health Service Journal*, 24 February 1994, 26.

[6] See the Public Accounts Committee's report on *West Midlands Regional Health Authority: Regional Managed Services Organisation* (HC 485, 1993), para. 322.

[7] *Public Enterprise Governance in the NHS* (Report of the Corporate Governance Task Force to Sir Duncan Nichol, NHSME, 1994) para. 17.

the public services are paid according to salaries which are perform-ance related there may be a disincentive to keep the interests of patients uppermost in mind. And when targets have to be achieved, short-term goals may become more important than overall improvements in health care. The issue was raised following a House of Commons Committee report on the West Midland Regional Health Authority which was alleged to have wasted at least £20 million on a computer system which was rapidly abandoned; to have permitted a defective contracting process to favour one bidder for the computer systems over others; to have failed to prevent conflicts of interest arising through the appoint-ment of managers with continuing commercial interests in contractor business; and generally to have failed to secure accountability in the region.[8] The matter prompted the Chief Executive of the NHS to appoint a task force to examine the complaint and make recommendations. It reported in forthright terms as follows:

The events in West Midlands and Wessex Regional Health Authorities have underlined the need for a reformulation of the principles of organisational behaviour and personal conduct in undertaking NHS business. It seems to us that there is a need to reassert an absolute standard of honesty in conducting public business involving the assets of the NHS and secondly there needs to be a much greater recognition that personal integrity in the day to day behaviour of all NHS personnel—as important for chairmen and members of boards as for employees, needs urgent reinforcement in all NHS authorities and trusts. Probity in conducting NHS business must be matched by integrity in personal conduct.[9]

The report recommended the establishment of a clear code of conduct for those responsible for managing the NHS as a result of which the Secretary of State introduced *A Code of Conduct and Accountability*[10] in which she says with respect to the use of public funds: 'Public service values matter in the NHS and those who work in it have a duty to conduct NHS business with probity. They

---

[8] Public Accounts Committee's report, *supra* note 6. Similar misgivings have been expressed with respect to other public bodies. See *The Proper Conduct of Public Business* (HC 154, Public Accounts Committee, 8th Report, Session 1993–94).

[9] *Public Enterprise Governance in the NHS*, *supra* note 7, para. 11.

[10] See *Code of Conduct and Accountability* (Department of Health, 1994). See also *Codes of Conduct and Accountability* (NHSE, EL(94)40).

have a responsibility to respond to staff, patients and suppliers impartially, to achieve value for money from the public funds with which they are entrusted and to demonstrate high standards of ethical conduct.'[11]

The Code sets down a framework for good management. It obliges those who serve on NHS Boards to declare any interests which they have in NHS contracts and to establish audit and remuneration committees. So much for the *conduct* of appointees to public bodies. Concern has also been expressed about the system of their *appointment*. Given the large numbers of directors required to serve on the boards of NHS Trusts, considerable influence is vested in the Secretary of State and the Trusts themselves in choosing who to appoint.[12] What skills ought the directors of hospitals to possess? Ought they to represent a balanced cross-section of political interests? Should business or clinical concerns predominate? To what extent is it reasonable for the Secretary of State herself to wield so much influence, and how may she be made accountable so that the public are reassured there has been no abuse of patronage? No statutory procedures are available to provide scrutiny of this nature. Would it be going too far to say that we need a QUANGO to monitor the QUANGOs? In 1994, the Prime Minister, John Major, set up the *Committee into Standards in Public Life*[11a] to consider, *inter alia*, appointments to NHS boards. It recommended that this responsibility ought to remain the Minister's, but that existing safeguards were insufficiently robust to prevent abuse. It advised, therefore, that (i) appointments should be subject to clear principles of selection, i.e.: of appointment on merit and competence, and that boards should contain a balance of political skills and backgrounds, including an independent member; and (ii) the process should be monitored and scrutinized by an open, independent Commissioner for Public Appointments, backed up by a clear code of conduct for board members.

---

[11] Ibid. 2.

[11a] *Standards in Public Life* (Cm. 2850, 1995, 'The Nolan Report'). The report also examined the conduct of members of Parliament and appointments to the executive.

[12] See National Health Service Trusts (Membership and Procedure) Regs. 1990 (SI, 1990, No. 2024). Under reg. 3 the Secretary may appoint a number of non-executive directors to NHS Boards. They are responsible for appointing the executive directors; see regs. 17 and 18.

3. Democracy

In a political climate in which 'open government' is encouraged,[13] the process of accountability has to embrace patients. The *Code of Conduct* recommends that 'there should be a willingness to be open with the public, patients and staff'.[14] However, openness is of limited value unless it is also sensitive and responsive. Openness should enable people to exercise some influence over the services provided. Once that proposition has been accepted why not proceed to the next logical step? Why not introduce a greater degree of democracy in the planning and provision of health services by subjecting the responsible officers to local elections?

Precisely this proposal has been made by the Association of Metropolitan Authorities (AMA).[15] It observes that DHAs, NHS Trusts, and GPs are responsible for managing large sums of money on behalf of the NHS but are not democratically accountable to local people. Instead, they are driven by the pressures introduced by the internal market in which, it suspects, short-term financial concerns dominate the proper planning of health care in local communities. In addition, it observes that social services and community care are presently provided by local authorities. To extend their responsibility for these to health services would end the phenomenon of 'cost-shunting' whereby health authorities are inclined to discharge long-term patients into the community, where they become a charge on local authorities. It would also tend to integrate the provision of social, community, and health services. The AMA recommends therefore that DHAs and FHSAs should be abolished and their purchasing roles absorbed by local authorities. A local Health Commissioner would have responsibility for implementing the function, under the supervision of a designated committee, but within a financial and strategic framework established by the Secretary of State. It acknowledges that such a system would give extensive power to local officials but says that 'its openness and the experience that

---

[13] See *Open Government* (Cm. 2290, 1993).

[14] *Code of Conduct and Accountability* (Department of Health), *supra* note 10, 3.

[15] *Local Authorities and Health Services* (Association of Metropolitan Authorities, 1994). See also D. Hunter 'The case for cooperation between local authorities and the NHS.' 310 *British Medical Journal* 1587 (1955).

most authorities have in making committees effective decision-making bodies strongly suggests that the health commissioning function should be undertaken by a committee of elected members'.[16]

For its part, the British Medical Association (BMA) doubts whether such a system could work effectively.[17] It observes that participation by local electors in the democratic process is notoriously small and that the real increase in democratic control might be very limited. We have already noted the relative paucity of information surrounding the provision of health services and the difficulties faced by patients in making informed choices. Obviously, much more education would be needed to enable electors to make reasoned decisions about the allocation of scarce resources. In addition, the BMA is concerned that in a *National Health Service* some fundamental principles must be preserved, primarily that the service be universally available on an equitable basis. To delegate responsibility for health services to local electors could undermine those principles by exposing the process to local political interests. This suggests that, despite increasing interest in extending accountability in the health service there are profound difficulties associated with the idea of opening up the management of health to local electorates.

B. Contracting-Out and Market Testing

In Chapter 3 we considered the liability of health authorities which contract out services to independent providers who are negligent. Leaving negligence aside, by what other means may the provision of such services be monitored and who ought to be held accountable for them? Before considering this question it is necessary to address the idea of market testing. The principle was formally introduced in *Competing for Quality*[18] which set out the Government's intention to encourage and extend the practice of inviting private contractors to compete with the in-house services offered by hospitals and other public bodies. Contracting out began with catering, domestic, and laundry services but may now extend to the whole range of services required by in the NHS;

---

[16] Ibid. para. 4.4.
[17] *Accountability in the NHS* (British Medical Association, 1994).
[18] Cm. 1730 (1991).

for example: car parking, maintenance of clinical records, legal services, blood testing, and estates management. Of course, there are both advantages and disadvantages in such a policy. Competition should encourage providers to improve the quality of their services while maintaining attractive prices. On the other hand, the possibility is introduced that services will be interrupted from time to time by being offered to different contractors and so become more fragmented and difficult to supervise. It also makes the employment of NHS staff less secure.

If something goes wrong with a service which has been contracted-out to a private provider, who is responsible? This brings us back to the problem of 'accountability'. Parties to contracts are accountable to one another in the common law of contract and it is no different with contracting-out. Health authorities will agree specific terms of contract with private contractors. Targets can be set and insisted upon, and competing offers of potential contractors can be compared. If the service provided by one contractor is unsatisfactory, either in terms of quality or price, other contractors may be approached.[19] In this sense, accountability is improved. As between the contracting parties this may be advantageous. But what about the obligations owed to the public? Say there is a failure to provide a required standard of service. Who is responsible if something goes wrong: the health authority or the private contractor?

The matter is now governed by the Deregulation and Contracting Out Act 1994. During its passage through Parliament, the Government was clear that responsibility would rest with the public authority. A spokesman said of the relevant provision of the Bill:

Much has been made . . . of the need for Ministers, office holders and local authorities to remain accountable for the actions of contractors who carry out statutory functions. . . . The purpose of the clause is to ensure that responsibility remains with the public authority even though the service may not be provided by the public-sector provider. . . .

I accept that those whose statutory duties are contracted out under the power must continue to be accountable for those functions as they are at present. Our policy is that the public interest in general, and the interest of the third party in particular, should not be disadvantaged by virtue of a

---

[19] See I. Harden, *The Contracting State* (Open University Press), 1992.

function being carried out by a contractor, rather than a civil servant. Lines of accountability and means of redress must not be diminished.[20]

Thus, a statutory function may be contracted out to a private contractor, an 'authorised person'. However, the public authority retains responsibility for the failures of such a person. Section 72(2) of the 1994 Act provides that:

Subject to subsection (3) below, anything done or omitted to be done by or in relation to the authorised person (or an employee of his) in, or in connection with, the exercise or purported exercise of the function shall be treated for all purposes as done or omitted to be done . . . in the case of a function of a Minister or office-holder, by or in relation to the Minister or office-holder in his capacity as such . . .

In Parliament, this provision was said to mean that the Minister, or public authority: 'will remain accountable . . . and will be legally liable for the acts and omissions of contractors. . . . That means that Ministers ultimately remain accountable to Parliament, in the same way as at present, for the provision of public services required by statute. No change will be brought about in that by means of this Bill.'[21]

This appears to be absolutely clear. Public authorities remain liable for all the failings of the private contractors to whom services have been contracted out and the position of patients is unchanged. However, the matter is confused by section 72(3) which provides that: 'Subsection (2) above shall not apply for the purposes of so much of any contract made between the authorised person and the Minister, office holder or local authority as relates to the exercise of the function'.

Although this appears to nullify the effect of the general rule in section 72(2), that is not its intention. The general rule is intended to preserve the rights of third parties, such as patients, against the public authority. It does so by merging the legal identity of the public authority with that of the private provider. This prevents a minister from hiding behind a private contractor who fails to perform a statutory function imposed, for example, by the National Health Service Act 1977. The Minister is not entitled to say, therefore, 'it was not my fault.'

---

[20] *Deregulation and Contracting Out Bill* (House of Commons Official Report, Standing Committee F, 21 Apr. 1994), cols. 1081, 1082.
[21] Ibid. col. 1082.

Section 72(3) separates their legal identity only with respect to 'the exercise of the function' specified in the contract between them, and thus retains their right to sue one another for non-performance. It does not, and cannot, shift the responsibility for fulfilling the function itself. The subsection is concerned with the standards of performance agreed by the parties, and preserves a right to sue for damages for any breach by the private contractor. Thus, under Section 72(3) some such breaches may constitute breaches of a statutory function, in which case the public authority remains responsible under the relevant statute (and may recover any losses caused thereby). Other such breaches may be of technical concern only which do not constitute failure to fulfil a statutory function. Here, too, the public authority retains its rights to damages.[22]

II ACCOUNTABILITY OF NHS TRUSTS

Hospitals and other facilities previously managed or provided by health authorities may become NHS Trusts.[23] Before doing so the RHA is obliged to consult community health councils of the relevant area and other persons or bodies as they consider appropriate. In deciding whether to grant Trust status to an applicant the Secretary of State is particularly concerned that proposals meet four main criteria, namely:

[1] that the establishment of a Trust will give clear benefits and improve [the] quality of services to patients; [2] that management has the skills and capacity—including strong, effective leadership, sufficient financial and personnel management expertise, and adequate information systems—to run the unit effectively; [3] that senior professional staff, especially consultants, are involved in the management of the unit; and [4] that the Trust will be financially viable.[24]

A. Powers of NHS Trusts

Trusts earn revenue from contracts with both NHS purchasers and others, and have operational independence. As the Department of

[22] Note that any criminal liability incurred by those to whom services had been contracted out would not be considered 'as done, or omitted to be done', by the public authority. See s. 72(3)(b) of the 1994 Act.
[23] National Health Service and Community Care Act 1990, section 5.
[24] *Working for Patients. NHS Trusts: A Working Guide* (NHSME, 1990) 28.

Health put it: 'Trusts have the power to make their own decisions
—right or wrong!—without being subject to bureaucratic
procedures, processes or pressure from higher tiers of management.' They are encouraged to use this new freedom to achieve
better, faster decision making for the benefit of their patients,
community, and staff.[25] How broad is their discretion?[26] Regulations concerning their financial rights and duties are relatively
clear. Trusts have a statutory obligation to balance their books at
the end of each financial year[27] and, subject to specific financial
provisions,[28] have power to do anything which appears necessary
or expedient for the purposes of or in connection with the
discharge of their functions, including in particular power

(a) to acquire and dispose of land or other property;
(b) to enter into such contracts as seem to the Trust to be appropriate;
(c) to accept gifts of money, land or other property, including money,
    land or other property to be held on trust, either in general or any
    specific purposes of the NHS Trust or for all or any purposes relating
    to the health service; and
(d) to employ staff on such terms as the trust think fit.[29]

Strikingly, the precision of their financial position is not matched
with respect to their duties to patients. In pursuit of its financial
objectives could a Trust simply cease admitting patients over a
certain age, or close the units it considered too expensive, or offer
care to private fee-paying patients only? Could it allow the hospital
to be used entirely by a company specializing in the provision of
private health care, which would be likely to exclude those
suffering from chronic illness and focus resources on acute care
only?[30] Could it cease the business of health care altogether and
lease its premises to a shopping complex?

[25] Ibid. 2.
[26] See R. Long and B. Salter, 'Confusion and Control', *Health Services Journal*,
5 May 1994 18.   [27] See section 10 of the 1990 Act.
[28] Detailed in Sched. 3 of the National Health Service and Community Care Act
1990. Note that those acting on behalf of health authorities may not be proceeded
against personally in relation to disputes arising through matters of this nature,
unless they concern matters arising under the health and safety legislation. See the
National Health Service Act 1977, section 125.
[29] Ibid., Sched. 2, para. 16(1).
[30] Ibid. Sched. 2, para. 13: 'An NHS Trust may enter into arrangements for the
carrying out, on such terms as seem to the trust appropriate, of any of its functions
jointly with any Regional, District or Special Health Authority, with another NHS
Trust or with any other body or individual.'

The powers and responsibilities of NHS Trusts arise exclusively from the statute under which they are created. Their rights and obligations are confined within this statutory limit and any action taken beyond it will be *ultra vires* and unlawful. 'What you have to do is find out what this statutory creature is and what it is meant to do; and to find out what this statutory creature is you must look at the statute only, because there and there alone is found the definition of this new creature.'[31] Not all of the proper functions and responsibilities of NHS Trusts can be specified expressly and it is perfectly proper for such statutory bodies to undertake activities which are 'incidental to, or consequential upon those things which the Legislature has authorised.'[32] Thus, the express powers of NHS Trusts have to be interpreted in the light of a number of other obligations.

B. Responsibilities of NHS Trusts

Section 5(1)(a) of the National Health Service and Community Care Act 1990 provides that the Secretary of State may by order establish NHS Trusts 'to assume responsibility, in accordance with this Act, for the ownership and management of hospitals or other establishments or facilities which were previously managed or provided by Regional, District or Special Health Authorities.' Such an order shall be made by statutory instrument[33] so that the nature and function of each NHS Trust hospital is set down in the regulation by which it is created and the NHS Trust must carry out 'effectively, efficiently and economically the functions for the time being conferred on it by [such] an order'.[34] The regulations by which NHS Trust hospitals have been created read in every case as follows:

(1) The trust is established for the purposes specified in section 5(1)(a) of the [1990] Act.
(2) The trusts's functions (which include the functions which the

---

[31] *Hazell* v. *Hammersmith and Fulham LBC* [1990] 3 All ER 33, 46 *per* Woolf LJ.
[32] *A-G* v. *Great Eastern Railway Co* (1880) 5 App Cas 473, 478 *per* Lord Selborne LC. See also *Baroness Wenlock* .v *River Dee Co* (1885) 10 App Cas 354. For an example of *ultra vires* activity see eg *A-G* v. *London CC* [1990] 1 Ch 781.
[33] The requirements of such an order are specified in the National Health Service and Community Care Act 1990, Sched. 2, Part I.
[34] Ibid. Sched. 2, para. 6(1).

Secretary of State considers appropriate in relation to the provision of services by the trust for one or more health authorities) shall be

(a) to own and manage hospital accommodation and services provided at [name and address];

(b) to manage community health services provided from [name and address].[35]

Thus, the responsibility to own and manage 'hospital accommodation and services' defines the nature of the duty imposed and precludes any other activity. It does not, however, indicate how, and for whom, these responsibilities should be discharged. What about the temptation to introduce policies which exclude 'expensive' patients from care? Arguably, a Trust's duty is not identical to that imposed on the Secretary of State to provide 'a comprehensive health service' under section 3 of the National Health Service Act 1977, because 'an NHS Trust shall not be regarded as the servant or agent of the Crown'.[36] On the contrary, the point of an internal market for health is to enable hospitals to discover for themselves how best to manage their resources, if necessary by limiting their services to certain categories of patient only.

But this is an unattractive interpretation of the duties of NHS Trusts. An alternative view is that the Secretary of State's power to confer rights and duties under the regulations must be interpreted subject to a crucial implication. The only powers available to the Secretary of State are those provided by the National Health Service Acts themselves. The 1977 Act imposes a specific duty to continue the promotion of a comprehensive health service.[37] It is inconceivable that Parliament could have intended that the Minister for Health be able to undermine the duties imposed on her by the 1977 Act by conferring less extensive obligations on NHS Trusts. By implica-tion, therefore, NHS Trusts must be obliged to promote the same objectives as the

[35] This example is taken from the Harrow and Hillingdon Healthcare National Health Service Trust (Establishment) Order 1994, SI 1994, No. 848. Ambulance services have been created with similar appropriate wording.

[36] National Health Service and Community Care Act 1990, Sched. 2, para. 18. Note too that the obligation of regional and district health authorities to 'exercise the specific health service functions' detailed in the National Health Service Functions (Directions to Authorities and Administrative Arrangements) Regs. 1991, SI 1991, No. 554, does not extend to NHS Trusts.

[37] Sections 1 and 3 of the 1977 Act.

Secretary of State. This is the more persuasive interpretation of the regulations, particularly since the 1990 Act expressly grants to the Secretary of State powers to supervise Trusts. Thus, an NHS Trust 'shall comply' with any directions given to it by the Secretary of State with respect to:

prohibiting or restricting the disposal of, or any interest in, any asset . . . in respect of which the Secretary of State considers that the interests of the National Health Service require that the asset should not be disposed of; [and] compliance with guidance or directions given (by circular or otherwise) to health authorities, or particular descriptions of health authorities.[38]

Accountability to the Secretary of State arises in four ways. [1] For each accounting year an NHS Trust shall prepare and send to the Secretary of State an annual report in such form as may be determined by the Secretary of State.[39] [2] An NHS Trust shall furnish to the Secretary of State such reports, returns and other information, including information as to its forward planning as, and in such form, as he or she may require.[40] [3] At such time or times as may be prescribed, an NHS Trust shall hold a public meeting at which its audited accounts and annual report and any report on the accounts made pursuant to subsection (3) of section 15 of the Local Government Finance Act 1982 shall be presented.[41] [4] In such circumstances and at such time or times as may be prescribed, an NHS Trust shall hold a public meeting at which such documents as may be prescribed may be presented.[42]

Doubt remains, however, as to the adequacy of this supervision. The idea has been to give Trusts the power to determine for themselves the directions to be taken, but the relatively light degree of control exercised over them has concerned the House of Commons Health Committee. It said:

Trusts are not legally required to be accountable to the public and it is for each Trust to determine whether it wishes to open its routine meetings to the public or Community Health Council representatives. The financial accountability of Trusts lies in the presentation of their business plans to the NHSME and their operational accountability is to be achieved via contracts with purchasers. It remains to be seen whether these consulta-

---

[38] Sched. 2, para. 6(2)(d) and (e) of the 1990 Act.
[39] Ibid. Sched. 2, para. 7(1).   [40] Ibid. para. 8.
[41] Ibid. para. 7(2).   [42] Ibid. para. 7(3).

tion mechanisms are sufficient to achieve an effective level of account-ability to patients and the wider public.[43]

The position of Trusts, like that of GP fund-holders, precisely demonstrates the tension between the benefits of the internal market and the need to retain proper supervision and account-ability. Innovation and freedom may certainly produce significant benefits for patients. On the other hand, unlike the position with private companies, if the directors take irresponsible risks it is not they who will lose their investments but the service as a whole. They could probably not be held personally responsible for any losses incurred by a Trust.[44] Given the vast sums of public money involved, in future there is likely to be greater emphasis in providing a more certain framework for the operation of the Trusts.

C. Accountability to Patients

Patients and managers do not always share the same priorities. Managers have a 'duty to make choices'[45] between patients, treatments, staffing, and the use of resources generally. They are concerned to see that hospital beds generate revenue. It may make good financial sense, for example, to reduce the need for nursing staff over weekends by closing wards and moving patients into temporary beds until the start of the following week. Arrange-ments of this nature were used in relation to a patient suffering the terminal stages of cancer. Over a period of ten weeks, she was moved from one ward which she occupied during the week to a variety of others for weekends. She suffered claustrophobia, but was sometimes given a 'small side room' for the weekend. In addition, she was not given the care necessary to prevent the occurrence of pressure sores, nor were her drainage bags regularly changed. She died three days after her transfer to a hospice, after

---

[43] *NHS Trusts: Interim Conclusions and Proposals for Future Inquiries* (House of Commons, Health Committee Report, HC 321, Session 1992–93), para. 73.

[44] See *Tamlin* v. *Hanniford* [1949] 1 KB 18, 23 *per* Denning LJ. Speaking of the British Transport Commission, he said: 'If it should make losses and be unable to pay its debts, its property is liable to execution but it is not liable to be wound up at the suit of any creditor. The taxpayer would, no doubt, be expected to come to its rescue. . . . Indeed, the taxpayer is the universal guarantor of the corporation.' See also s. 125, 1977 Act.

[45] See Lord Donaldson MR in *Re J* (a minor) 4 All ER 614, 623.

which her husband complained to the Health Service Ombudsman. The Commissioner regarded these arrangements as 'totally unsatisfactory'. He said: 'Never before have I encountered such a lack of regard for the welfare of a vulnerable patient as in [this] case where a financial decision produced a level of service so bereft of compassion that it ought never to be tolerated.'[46]

Considering the Commissioner's report, the House of Commons Select Committee on the Ombudsman said:

labels and nursing plans obscured an essential fact, which should have been obvious to any sensitive manager. The patient was so seriously ill that a five-day ward was wholly inadequate, if not cruel. We understand the financial pressures under which hospital managers often have to work and that a five day ward was established to ensure a continuation of care for as many patients as possible. It was introduced, however, without any consultation with nurses. . . . The five-day ward was instituted without due regard to the changes in practice necessary to protect standards of care. The mere provision of a bed is not enough.[47]

This form of accountability via the Ombudsman is important because it often brings about practical changes in systems of organization.[48] More difficult is the question of damages. Sums paid to patients by way of compensation are accounted for by the hospital responsible for the accident in question. Since the payment of compensation produces an immediate reduction in its spending capacity, there is a profound incentive to discourage patients from litigating.[49] After all, the payment of a six-figure sum of damages may jeopardize the operation of a hospital unit, or the purchase of a CAT scanner, which in turn will reduce capacity to serve other patients and earn revenue. Bearing in mind the public duty of the NHS, ought requests for information in relation to a claim for compensation to be discouraged? What significance

---

[46] *Report of the Health Service Commissioner for 1991–92* (HC, 388, 1993) 7.
[47] Ibid. ix.
[48] The hospital concerned subsequently introduced two seven-day wards, providing 62 beds, for patients requiring terminal care, ibid.
[49] See *A Health Standards Inspectorate* (Association of Community Health Councils for England and Wales and Action for Victims of Medical Accidents, 1993) 2: 'many victims [of medical mishap] feel they do not get [impartiality] within the self-regulatory system which operates in the Health Service. . . . Evidence for this . . . is afforded by the number of Health Authorities who have steadfastly denied liability, only to settle out of court, often within hours of the case being called. Such an approach is distasteful, unacceptable and demeaning.'

ought to be given to the interests of patients in decisions of this nature?[50] In one case, a hospital had reason to be concerned about the clinical performance of one of its consultants. It appointed two well respected clinical assessors to advise it on the standard of care achieved by the consultant. They reported: 'Enquiries into the patients being operated upon has given us considerable concern that there is an inappropriate selection of patients for surgery [by the consultant] as well as their management in the post-operative period which is not always ideal, leading to a high mortality and morbidity.'[51]

In another case a woman had a benign tumour in her breast. The lump could and should have been subjected to microscopic examination before a decision was taken on whether or not radical mastectomy was necessary. The doctor removed the entire breast without awaiting the results. The patient was later told that the lump had been benign but when she asked why the entire breast had been removed the hospital was not candid with her. On the contrary, 'she was led to believe that the practice followed had been usual and proper, and indeed that she had, in the circumstances, every reason to count herself fortunate.'[52]

In such cases, should hospitals be under any duty to disclose their misgivings about a patient's treatment, even if this might assist an action for damages against the hospital or health authority? Bearing in mind the public duty of the NHS, should requests for information in relation to a claim for compensation be discouraged? In a public service which claims to put the interests of patients first, there ought to be a willingness to help patients when things have gone wrong. In principle, the Department of Health recognizes the patient's right to an explanation when things go wrong. It says:

patients (or their family) have the right to expect a full and sensitive explanation of what has gone wrong, a frank assessment of the likely

---

[50] Concern about proper standards of conduct after the 'privatization' of elements of a large range of public services was expressed by the Public Accounts Committee of the House of Commons in *The Proper Conduct of Public Business* (HC 154, 1994, HMSO).

[51] *Lyndon* v. *Yorkshire RHA* 10 BMLR 49, 52 (1993). The case concerned the suspension of the consultant and not the truth of the allegations against him.

[52] *Dobbie* v. *Medway Health Authority* 5 Med LR 160, 165 (1994). Surprisingly, her subsequent action for damages was barred under the Limitation Act 1980.

consequences, and—as far as this is possible—the offer of further treatment or care to mitigate any lasting ill-effects. *In addition*, if there are grounds for believing that clinical negligence . . . has contributed to the accident, it is open to patients or their relatives to seek redress through the courts.[53]

For patients this is precisely the time when candour is most important. Ethics demand that the self-interest of the hospital ought not to be used to hinder good claims. This is an important statement of policy which, in certain circumstances, may have the support of the common law. The question of the patients's legal right to such information is considered in Section V below.

III. ACCOUNTABILITY OF GP FUND-HOLDERS

For some time GPs have been considered to be the 'gate-keepers' of the National Health Service. In this role, which has never been formally described, they filter access to the system so that needy patients receive treatment and resources are not wasted. To some extent therefore, GPs have long been perceived as having some managerial responsibility. At the same time, however, there is concern that doctors do not always perform this function very efficiently. Wide variations of practice between doctors have been noticed, in both the prescription of medicines and the referral of patients to hospital, which cannot be explained simply by legitimate differences of clinical opinion.

The response was to offer GPs greater incentive to use NHS finances sparingly. The mechanism by which competition has been introduced into health care encourages GPs to be more cautious about the way in which the money is spent. By the introduction of fund-holding status, GPs are given a sum of money to spend in the ways they consider most suitable for their patients. The significant encouragement to reconsider the way in which money is spent on patients is that fund-holding practices are entitled to retain any moneys saved in the financial year and to

---

[53] *Clinical Negligence: Proposed Creation of a Central Fund in England* (NHSME, 1994) 1 (emphasis added). Do not forget that in legally aided claims in which the plaintiff is unsuccessful, the authority has to bear the costs of the action it has won. Even costs alone may be difficult for NHS Trust Hospitals to manage.

plough it back into the practice for the benefit of patients. The Government presented its proposal to introduce fund-holding practices as follows:

> The scheme will give GPs the chance to make decisions about how NHS money can best be used. . . . Fund holding GPs will be able to choose the hospital to which they send their patients and pay those hospitals directly for certain services provided for their patients . . . Fund holding practices will be making a major contribution to the overall aim of generating efficiency in the hospital system in the interests of their patients. . . . General Practice Funds are a practical acknowledgement of the often-repeated statement that GPs are the 'gatekeepers' of the NHS.[54]

By April 1994 around a third of both GPs and general practices were fund-holders. There were 1,673 funds in the scheme, with total budgets of over £2,800 million, or about 9 per cent of NHS resources.[55] What new responsibilities have fund-holders acquired and what conflicts of interest may arise within the system?

A. The Fund-holders 'Allotted Sum'

Practices may apply for fund-holding status to the RHA. The application shall be approved if it satisfies certain conditions: namely that there are at least 5,000 patients on the practice list that the application is made by all the members of the partnership, and that the practice is capable of managing an allotted sum effectively and efficiently and possesses the equipment and expertise necessary to do so.[56] Successful applicants shall be paid an 'allotted sum' by the FHSA which shall be 'determined in such manner and by reference to such factors as the Secretary of State may direct'.[57]

---

[54] *Working for Patients: Funding General Practice* (DH, 1989), section 1.

[55] See *General Practitioner Fundholding in England* (HC 51, Session 1994–95, National Audit Office).

[56] See section 14 of the 1990 Act and the National Health Service (Fund-holding Practices) Regulations 1993, SI 1993, No.567, Part II and sched. 1, as amended by 1995 Regulations (SI, 1995, No 693) which also introduce a more limited form of 'community fund-holding' available to practices with 3,000 or more patients.

[57] Section 15(1) of the National Health Service and Community Care Act 1990, as amended by the National Health Service (Fund-holding Practices) Regs. 1993, *supra* note 56, under the powers made available in section 17 of the 1990 Act.

The uses to which the fund may be put are closely restricted.[58] Fund-holders remain bound by their Terms of Service to the FHSA and, except in limited circumstances, may not use the sum as a means of remunerating themselves.[59] Since fund-holding GPs are already bound by their Terms of Service to provide 'general medical services' to patients, it would make no sense to provide the allotted sum to pay for the same services.[60] Thus the regulations provide that:

the members of a fund-holding practice shall apply the allotted sum so as to secure the purchase of such goods and services, *other than general medical services* . . . as are necessary for the proper treatment of individuals on the lists of patients of the members of the practice and are appropriate in all the circumstances having regard, in particular, to the needs of all those individuals.[61]

Therefore, the sum may be spent on additional services approved by the Secretary of State,[62] provided by the doctors themselves, by consultants, or employees, and to pay those who provide such services[63] to the practice's patients.[64] The precise arrangements under which fund-holders are regulated differ from region to region, and may take the form of a bilateral NHS

---

[58] See section 15(6) of the National Health Service and Community Care Act 1990. A small number of fund-holders have been selected to test the feasibility of 'total fund-holding' in which the practice is responsible for the purchase of all hospital and community care. See *Developing NHS Purchasing and Fundholding*, HSG (95)4 (NHSE, 1995).

[59] See the National Health Service (General Medical Services) Regs. 1992, SI 1992, No. 635, para. 38. A doctor 'shall not, otherwise than by virtue of these Regulations, demand or accept a fee or other remuneration for any treatment . . . whether under these terms of service or not, which he gives to a person for whose treatment he is responsible under paragraph 4' (which describes 'a doctor's patients').

[60] Thus, the costs incurred in prescribing drugs, medicines, and listed appliances may be recovered by the regional health authority from the allotted sum, see section 15(7)(a) of the National Health Service and Community Care Act 1990.

[61] National Health Service (Fund-holding Practices) Regulations 1993, *supra* note 56, reg. 20(1). See also Sched. 2, para. 12 (emphasis added).

[62] Ibid. reg. 20(2). The list is published in a letter from the NHS Executive, see *List of Goods and Services Covered by the GP Fundholding Scheme* (NHSME, 25 Mar. 1993).

[63] The allotted sum may be used to pay the salaries of those who provide additional services to patients, as well as in connection with the management or administration of the practice. Ibid. reg. 22(1).

[64] Ibid. reg 20(2): 'to persons for providing, on the practice premises, services which are necessary for the proper treatment of individuals who are on the lists of patients who are members of the practice.'

contract between fund-holders and regions, under which both sides have rights and duties.

Under previous regulations it was possible for fund-holders to create private health companies, from which they could take remuneration as directors. New regulations disallow this practice. The circumstances in which fund-holders may derive income from their fund are limited and such payments require the approval of the relevant health authority who must be satisfied that it is being paid for specified services only.[65] Any such payments must 'be made directly to the medical practitioner who provides the services or to the partnership of which he is a member and not to any third party.'[66] In this way, private companies cannot flourish by means of payments from the allotted sum.

B. Savings from the 'Allotted Sum'

The determination of an appropriate allotment is not an exact science. It depends on a wide variety of factors and requires the exercise of judgment about the relative needs of patients and populations about which available information is inaccurate and incomplete. The Department of Health has said that it:

encountered significant difficulties in developing a capitation based methodology for setting the [Hospital and Community Health Services] element of the scheme. These arose both from the inadequacies of the available data and from the technical problems associated with under-taking analyses with applications at the individual practice level . . . the data available on outpatients and diagnostic tests were not of sufficient quality at national level to support analysis.[67]

In addition to these uncertainties, the sums allotted to different fund-holders are extremely difficult to compare because the tools for doing so are relatively undeveloped. Nevertheless, many fund-holders have been able to achieve savings from their allotted sums, which suggests that they have not been treated with undue

---

[65] The list of approved services is included in the National Health Service (Fund-holding Practices) Regulations 1993, *supra* note 56, Sched. 3 and *GP fund-holding practices: the provision of secondary care* (HSG(93)14, NHSME, 1993), Annex B.

[66] See National Health Service (Fund-holding Practices) Regulations 1993, reg. 23 and *GP fund-holding practices: the provision of secondary care*, ibid.

[67] *General Practice Fundholding: Guidance on setting budgets for 1993/4*, EL(92)83, annex C, para. 5.

parsimony.[68] In 1992–3 £28.3 million was saved from the sums allotted, some 3.5 per cent of the total allocations, 'of which thirty-two per cent [of practices] had used the savings to improve the practice premises'.[69] One of the incentives of becoming a fund-holder is to achieve financial independence, and to save money in order to plough it back into the practice. Thus, in respect of any financial year, after the practice accounts have been audited by the Audit Commission, a fund-holding practice has four years in which to accumulate savings. Such monies may continue to be spent on the provision of additional medical goods and services for its patients, and on the payment of remuneration to employees and consultants. In addition, however, savings may be applied for any one or more of the following purposes:

(a) the purchase of material or equipment which:
     (i) can be used for the treatment of patients of the members of the practice;
     (ii) enhances the comfort or convenience of patients of the members of the practice;
     (iii) enables the practice to be managed more effectively and efficiently; or
(b) the purchase of material or equipment relating to health education; or
(c) the improvement of any premises from which the members of the practice carry on their practice whether by improving the structure of the premises or the purchase of furniture and furnishings for the premises.[70]

Overall supervision of the uses to which the allotted sum is put is vested in the regional health authority. It may recover any parts of the sum which appear to have been misapplied by the practice[71] by an action in civil debt against the practice or its members, jointly or severally.[72] It remains to be seen how strict the interpretation of these regulations will be. Presumably a practice will be permitted

---

[68] See *GP Fundholding: Market Effects and Allocation Issues* (Health Care Management Association and Chartered Institute of Public Finance and Accountancy, 1994). In the West Midlands 'GP fundholding hospital services underspent by £1.7 million (10%) in 1991/92 and c.£3 million (6%) in 1992/93', para. 1.2.

[69] See *General Practitioner Fundholding in England* (HC 51, Session 1994–95, National Audit Office), para. 4.11.

[70] National Health Service (Fund-holding Practices) Regs. 1993, *supra* note 56, reg. 24(2).   [71] Ibid. reg. 25(1).   [72] Ibid. reg. 25(8).

to effect essential repairs to its premises by using its savings. But would it be allowed to purchase practice (or 'company') cars for the partners?

More importantly still, what priority should patients receive in decisions about savings? Ought patients on waiting lists to be dealt with before money is spent on interior redecoration? Say a local hospital is unable to treat a patient immediately and has him on its waiting list. At the same time, the practice would like to refurbish its premises. Should the practice ensure that the patient is dealt with first, if necessary by paying for him to be treated elsewhere? Perhaps, if the need for refurbishment is urgent and those on waiting lists will be seen very soon and are not suffering inconvenience, it may be justifiable to put the premises before the patient. In other cases, however, it is arguable that the obligations imposed by the GP's Terms of Service to render 'all necessary and appropriate personal medical services of the type usually provided by general practitioners'[73] require as a general rule that patients should come first. If this is right then, before spending money on improvements, fund-holders should always examine their waiting lists to see if contracts can be arranged with other hospitals, including private hospitals, which are able to provide treatment more quickly.

Will the incentive toward savings disincline GPs to provide the standard of care which patients are entitled to expect? Will expensive drugs be prescribed properly and complicated conditions of illness be referred to hospital as quickly as before? Or will there instead be a tendency to wait and refer patients for hospital treatment as emergency cases, since the practice does not bear the expense of accident and emergency care.[74] 'The London Ambulance Service has told us that there is a tendency in London for some GPs to tell their patients to dial 999 if the condition worsens. This does not represent adequate primary care.'[75] And, with respect to hospital doctors, will they be encouraged to over-treat cost per case contracts, on the ground that it will be easier to

---

[73] See the National Health Service (General Medical Services) Regs. 1992, SI 1992, No. 635, Sched. 2, para. 12(1).

[74] See section 3(5) of the National Health Service and Community Care Act 1990.

[75] *Report of the Inquiry into London's Health Service, Medical Education and Research* (The 'Tomlinson' Report, HMSO, 1992) 13.

run up larger bills for patients subject to individual agreements, than for those covered by block contracts?[76]

Like all GPs in private practice, fund-holders are engaged by the FHSA as independent contractors and not as employees. Their scales of remuneration are set down in the Terms of Service[77] and are based on the number of patients on the doctor's list and its composition. Remuneration is enhanced for doctors who would expect to be called upon more often by virtue of the age of their patients. To this extent, the incentive to refuse, or attract, demanding patients applies equally to non-fundholders. Also, the limit of financial responsibility to each individual patient of fund-holders is £5,000 in any one financial year, after which the district health authority becomes responsible for paying for the cost of the treatment.[78] Some of us will always be regarded as 'heart-sink' patients, but the system does not appear to discourage fund-holders any more than ordinary GPs from accepting us as patients.

C. Exceeding the 'Allotted Sum'

What happens if a fund-holding practice is unable to remain within the sum allotted to it? In 1992–3, overspending totalled £9.8 million.[79] Good reasons may well exist to explain this. Additional patients may have been accepted onto the doctor's list, there may have been an increased demand for prolonged care amongst a group of patients, or the original assessment may simply have been wrong. Regional health authorities are expected to hold in reserve sufficient funds to deal with this contingency. The amount allotted to a practice may be varied in the light of changed circumstances and as there may be 'payments on account of the allotted sum at such times and in such manner as the Secretary of State may direct',[80] the adjustment may be made as and when required.

---

[76] See generally H. Glennerster, M. Matsanganis *et al.*, 'GP Fundholding: Wild Card or Winning Hand?', in R. Robinson and J. Le Grand, *Evaluating the Health Service Reforms* (King's Fund Institute, 1994) 74.

[77] See the National Health Service (General Medical Services) Regulations 1992, *supra* note 73, Part VI.

[78] National Health Service (Fund-holding) Regulations 1993, *supra* note 56, reg. 21.

[79] *General Practitioner Fundholding in England*, *supra* note 69, para. 4.18.

[80] See section 15(3)(a) of the National Health Service and Community Care Act 1990.

If the overspending cannot be justified then fund-holding status may be withdrawn from the practice,[81] either with effect from the start of the next financial year or immediately.[82] In this case the rights and liabilities of the fund-holding practice are transferred to the regional health authority.[83] What of a less extreme example? A fund-holding practice fears that it may have spent its money imprudently at the start of the financial year. Can it attempt to retrieve the situation towards the end of the year by not prescribing medicines, or by referring patients for emergency treatment, in order to reduce demand on its fund? Here, it may be possible to draw a contrast with the way in which health authorities have been held accountable in the past. Recall the case of *Collier*, in which the court simply accepted the health authority's say-so that an urgent operation in hospital could not be performed because the necessary resources could not be made available. The case suggests that, with respect to secondary care, it is very difficult to use the law to oblige a hospital to provide treatment. Fund-holders, however, arc obliged to account to the FHSA for their use of the fund on a monthly basis[84] and it would be possible to scrutinize the accounts to identify how the problem had arisen. They also remain bound by their Terms of Service to provide care for their patients. It would not be proper for a practice to attempt to remedy its own errors and shortcomings by failing to provide patients with the proper standard of care. Arguably, were a doctor to do so, he would breach his Terms of Service with the FHSA. In addition, if the patient could show that the failure to treat had caused damage, the doctor could be subject to an action in negligence for failing to take reasonable care.

But there may arise a still more difficult problem in the future. The Government's policy is to encourage as many practices as

[81] See 'Operations put on hold as fund-holder goes over budget', *Health Service Journal*, 4 Nov. 1993 4. One practice 'overspent on its hospital budget of £550,000 by £66,000. As a result it had to contact the providers it had contracts with to instruct them not to carry out any more non-urgent operations until the situation can be reviewed after Christmas.' See 'Fools' Gold' *Health Service Journal* 11 Nov. 1993 11.

[82] National Health Service (Fund-holding Practices) Regulations 1993, *supra* note 70, Part IV. Such a procedure is uncommon, but see 'GP surgery first to be stripped of fundholding', *The Independent*, 10 Mar. 1993 2.

[83] National Health Service (Fund-holding Practices) Regs. 1993, ibid. reg. 18(1).

[84] Ibid. Sched. 2, para. 10.

possible to become fund-holders in order to emphasize their 'gate-keeping' role. What would be the position if the majority of practices had become fund-holders and that, without error or waste on the part of doctors, the funds allotted were systematically exhausted by doctors before the end of the year simply because they were inadequate? Of course, health authorities will be expected to retain some funds to meet this problem, but they too will be subject to the shortages, (say) because the Department of Health is unable to make sufficient money available to provide a standard of care consistent with previous years. Unlike the situation in which the practice is guilty of overspending, the cause of the problem is not error or waste, but insufficient funding from the central authorities. Are we simply moving the problem of funding from the secondary to the primary care sector? As we saw in *Collier*, the courts have resisted the temptation to order that urgent patients should receive treatment. Should we expect a different response if the same problem arose not in hospital but in the GP's surgery? There is a clear tension between a doctor's duty under the Terms of Service to provide 'any drugs or appliances which are needed' by the patient,[85] and the realities of Government funding. This matter is discussed in Chapter 5 in connection with indicative prescribing amounts.

D. Fund-holding Consortia

Fund-holders have combined to form consortia as a means of improving their bargaining strength with hospital providers and others such as suppliers of computer equipment. Clearly, if half a dozen practices, each with around 10,000 patients, form a consortium, hospitals and others will be keen to attract business of that magnitude and may be prepared to modify their prices, or general conditions, accordingly. The logic of the market is to encourage developments of this nature, but these advantages carry their own costs. First, one of the curious features of large combinations of purchasers, who pool their resources and bargain through a central negotiator, is that the consortium may become indistinguishable from a DHA. Skilled negotiators may be

---

[85] See National Health Service (General Medical) Regs. 1992, *supra* note 73, Sched. 2, para. 43.

engaged to act on behalf of the consortium. But the personal involvement of GPs is lost if they cease to be individually responsible for their patients and if contracts for entire groups are arranged on a block basis, as is the case with DHAs.

In addition, such a large organization incurs transaction costs which duplicate those already incurred by DHAs. Unlike health authorities, however, fund-holders are not directly supervised by the Secretary of State for Health. They may decide to purchase from different hospitals in successive years. This may put downward pressure on prices, but it also makes long-term planning for hospitals extremely difficult. How would national strategy operate in a district in which a 'super-fund' had a larger proportion of central funds than the DHA? Could hospital care be guaranteed to the patients of non-fundholding GPs?

As the Department of Health acknowledges, it is important to ensure that the benefits of consortia are realised without their costs. It has stressed, therefore, that fund-holders within a consortium remain individually responsible for their own budgets and that 'each fundholder remains separately accountable for meeting national and local objectives and for the quality of services provided and purchased'.[86] The Department has also addressed the possibility of a powerful consortia pursuing objectives which contradict those established at national or local level. When such large sums of money, and the care of so many patients, are involved this feature of the internal market invites regulation. There is general agreement that fund-holders should co-operate with the purchasing plans of health authorities. The Government says that fund-holders should:

set out how the practice intends to use its funds and management allowances over the coming year and demonstrate the practice's contribution to national targets and priorities as well as locally agreed objectives;

[and] submit [an annual practice plan] to the health authority. It will be the health authority's responsibility to confirm that fund-holders' plans are consistent with national targets and, in aggregate, meet national targets and objectives.[87]

---

[86] *GP Fundholding Consortia* (EL(92)92, NHSME, 1992), para. 5(iii).

[87] *An Accountability Framework for GP Fund-holding—Toward a Primary Care-led NHS* (NHSE, 1994), para. 5.1. See also *Their Health, Your Business: The Role of the District Health Authority* (Audit Commission, 1993), para. 17.

Co-operation of this nature is clearly desirable, but is it obligatory? The current means of making fund-holders account-able for their decisions are directed to financial efficiency and stability within the practice.[88] The regulations do not provide sanctions against fund-holders who fail to co-operate in this way. For the moment, therefore, co-operation between health authorities and fund-holders must depend on goodwill between the parties.

An alternative system of retaining the benefits of the market place, whilst dispensing with its tendency to work in competition with national strategy, is to introduce a system in which GPs exercise more influence over the decisions of hospitals and the DHA. The Audit Commission has speculated about the possibility of involving GPs in the commissioning of health care not in individual practices, but in groups. In this scheme, the group would negotiate with local commissioning authorities (FHSAs or DHAs) as a means of promoting the health of an entire community, rather than the patients of a single practice in competition with others; and whether a practice was fund-holding or not would be irrelevant. Under this arrangement: 'local agreements between commissioning authorities and GPs could start to blur the distinction between fund-holding and non-fundholding status, while ensuring that the activities of GPs are consistent with overall policy, and that commissioning authorities are providing what GPs need.'[89]

In principle, this arrangement could be effective, but one wonders what incentive overworked GPs can be offered to undertake more work as commissioners of health care, not for their own patients but on behalf of the entire community. If the attractions of fund-holding are not replaced, few doctors are likely to undertake additional obligations of this nature. In this case the job would tend to be done by health service administrators, and we would effectively return to the position before fund-holding

---

[88] See the National Health Service (Fund-holding Practices) Regulations 1993, *supra* note 70, Sched. 2.

[89] *Practices Make Perfect: The Role of the Family Health Services Authority* (Audit Commission, 1993), para. 165. See also J. Graffy and J. Williams, 'Purchasing for All: An Alternative to Fundholding', 308 *British Medical Journal* 391 (1994).

was introduced. This may be the preferable solution, but it would be wrong to call it a new reform.

IV. ACCOUNTABILITY TO STATUTORY BODIES

A number of statutory bodies have been created with responsibility for monitoring standards in the National Health Service.

A. Community Health Councils

Community health councils (CHCs) form the link between those who administer the NHS and the people who use it. They deal both with the larger policy issues of resource allocation and advising individuals about problems, or the availability of services. The Secretary of State is under a duty to create a community health council for each District Health Authority[90] so that it may 'represent the interests in the health service of the public in its district'[91] and 'keep under review the operation of the health service in its district and make recommendations for the improvement of that service', and generally to advise DHAs on matters concerning the operation of the health service as it thinks fit.[92] To enable these broadly worded functions to be performed, corresponding obligations are imposed on DHAs and FHSAs to co-operate with CHCs. Thus, DHAs and FHSAs have a duty to consult the relevant CHC whenever they are considering any substantial development or variation of the health service in the district. If there is insufficient time for such consultation the decision of the authority may be put into effect and it shall notify the CHC immediately of the decision taken and the reason why no consultation has taken place.[93] Also, the DHA or FHSA is obliged

---

[90] National Health Service Act 1977, s. 20. The boundaries of each need not be identical but the duty shall not be discharged unless 'there is no part of the district of a District Health Authority which is not included in some Community Health Council's district'. See s. 20(1)(b). [91] Ibid. Sched. 7, para. 1(a).

[92] The Community Health Councils Regs. 1985, SI 1985, No. 304, at reg. 18.

[93] Ibid., regs. 19(1) and (2). The duty of DHAs to consult does not extend to decisions to create NHS Trusts in a district. See the Community Health Councils (Amendment) Regs. 1990, SI 1990, No.1375, reg. 2(7). It is imposed on the Secretary of State instead, by s. 5, National Health Service and Community Care Act 1990.

to provide such information about the planning and operation of health services in the district as the CHC reasonably requires to carry out its duties,[94] and to afford CHCs a right of access to their premises.

CHCs have intervened to effect developments in local services, for example, to press for the provision of a hospice in a district which lacked such a facility, or to persuade the Secretary of State that the planned closure of a GPs' maternity hospital was wrong.[95] In *R* v. *North West Thames RHA,* ex p *Daniels*[96], the RHA failed to consult the relevant CHC in respect of a decision to close a particular hospital unit and relocate its functions to another hospital. The closure meant that a boy of two could not be treated in that unit for a rare bone marrow disease, despite the fact that its ethical committee had approved the operation and a suitable bone-marrow donor had been found. His father challenged the decision to move the unit on the grounds of the failure to consult the CHC. The Divisional Court held that such a decision amounted to 'a substantial variation' of the service and that the failure to consult was therefore unlawful. However, there was absolutely nothing that could be done about it. The unit had moved and the treatment would, if possible, be provided in the new location. The court declined to take any action, even to issue a formal declaration of the unlawfulness of the decision, because it would have been of no benefit. There was no point in quashing a decision to close a unit in a hospital which no longer existed. What pressure, therefore, can CHCs be expected to exercise over DHAs in these circumstances?

One cannot generalize from a single case, but it does suggest the need for a fundamental expansion of the role of CHCs. The Secretary of State has called for greater willingness on the part of NHS managers to be open with the public, patients, and staff. Reasons should be given when changes are proposed and information should be made available before decisions are reached. Her code of accountability recommends that: 'NHS Trusts and authorities should forge an open relationship with the

---

[94] The Community Health Council Regs. 1985, at reg. 20.
[95] See *Working for a Better Health Service* (Association of Community Health Councils for England and Wales (leaflet, undated).
[96] 19 BMLR 67 (1994).

local community and should conduct a dialogue about the service provided. NHS organisations should demonstrate to the public that they are concerned with the wider health of the population'.[97]

Yet, for the moment, the duty to consult seems not to extend to NHS Trusts and is still restricted to DHAs.[98] In the past, when many of the major decisions about hospital resources were taken by DHAs, it was sensible for them to have a duty to consult with CHCs. Now, however, DHAs are primarily concerned with commissioning health care. Responsibility for running hospitals belongs to NHS Trusts, who decide for themselves how best to respond to the demands made of them. Why not extend the duty to consult to NHS Trusts? CHCs provide a forum in which there is considerable experience and expertise and a natural avenue through which 'an open relationship with the local community' could be established. There is a strong case, there-fore, for bringing NHS Trusts within the review of CHCs. For such a role to be performed effectively additional resources are likely to be needed. 'Most CHCs still have only two staff. This is not adequate for the current workload. It also represents serious practical difficulties, in that with only two staff, either of whom may be out of the office frequently, it is hard to keep the office open to the public at regular times.'[99]

Who should be responsible for establishing CHCs and appointing their members? At present this responsibility belongs to RHAs.[100] Given the proposals to abolish RHAs in 1996[101] new regulations will be required for CHCs to be retained. To maintain their independence DHAs should not assume that responsibility. There may be differences of opinion as to the manner in which purchasing authorities should allocate resources. It would not be right for DHAs to be responsible for establishing and appointing members to a body with which it could have such differences. It would also be difficult for CHCs to retain real credibility in such a

[97] See *Code of Conduct and Accountability, supra* note 10, 3.

[98] See regs. 20 and 21, Community Health Councils Regs. 1985, *supra* note 92. By contrast, NHS Trusts Hospitals must afford access to premises to CHCs. See Community Health Council (Amendment) Regs. 1990, *supra* note 93, reg. 2(12).

[99] *Ensuring Effective CHCs in the New Structure* (Association of Community Health Councils for England and Wales, 1994) para. 12.

[100] See the Community Health Councils Regs. 1985, SI 1985, No. 304 at reg. 2.

[101] See *Managing the New NHS, supra* note 2.

relationship. Similar observations could be made in respect of the Department of Health. The Association of Community Councils has recommended the creation of an independent special health authority to fulfill this function.[102]

B. The Audit Commission and National Audit Office

The reports of the Audit Commission and National Audit Office have provided many valuable insights into the working of the NHS. The reports have been referred to throughout this book and will not be discussed again here. A brief description of the two bodies, however, is required. The more specialist of the two is the Audit Commission.[103] It is a relatively small body of between fifteen and twenty people whose duty it is to audit the accounts of local authorities, health authorities, and GP fund-holding practices.[104] The principle on which it functions is to ensure that each has adhered to statutory regulations and has made 'proper arrangements for securing economy, efficiency, and effectiveness in its use of resources.'[105] In addition, it undertakes comparative and other studies to enable it to make recommendations for improving economy, efficiency, and effectiveness of services and improving the financial and other management of such bodies.[106] The National Audit Office has broader responsibility for auditing the activities of all public authorities. It has about 850 staff, half of whom are accountants. It 'may carry out examinations into economy, efficiency and effectiveness with which any department, authority or other body . . . has used its resources in discharging its functions'.[107]

Both have broad powers which have been restricted in one important respect. Neither the Audit Commission nor the National Audit Office is entitled 'to question the merits of the policy objectives' of the Secretary of State, department, authority, or

---

[102] *Ensuring Effective CHCs in the New Structure, supra* note 99, para. 31.

[103] Its full title is the Audit Commission for Local Authorities and the National Health Service, see s. 11, Local Government Finance Act 1982, as amended by Sched. 4, para. 1, National Health Service and Community Care Act 1990.

[104] 1982 Act, ss. 12(ea) and (3A).

[105] 1982 Act, ss. 15(1)(a) and (c).

[106] 1982 Act, s. 26(1).

[107] National Audit Act 1983, s. 6.

body under examination.[108] They may, however, consider the way in which such policies have been implemented.[109] Thus the wisdom of the introduction of an internal market is beyond their jurisdiction, but they may make recommendations on the way on which the market ought to function. Equally, the distinction between matters of 'policy' and matters of 'operation' is often unclear and there may be differences of opinion as to where the line should be drawn.

C. Clinical Standards Advisory Group

The Clinical Standards Advisory Group (CSAG) has been created by the National Health Service and Community Care Act 1990 to 'provide advice on the standards of clinical care for, and access to and availability of services to, national health service patients'.[110] It may carry out investigations and give advice at the request of Health Ministers and health service bodies, including NHS Trusts. Its reports have been discussed in previous chapters. Unlike the Audit Commission, its research is not expressly confined to matters within the policy objectives of the Secretary of State. In *Cystic Fibrosis*[111] and *Neonatal Intensive Care*[112] it questions the benefits to be achieved from competition for those with un-common problems. The internal market is less helpful in these cases because the demand may vary from year to year and the quality of care provided may differ from hospital to hospital (bearing in mind the open-ended nature of the treatment) depending on whether it has invested in developing a specialist unit or not. Rather than making districts responsible for purchasing care for relatively few people, it recommends that the respons-ibility be accepted at regional level, where the demand is more constant and clinical standards can be set and monitored more usefully.

---

[108] The same words are used in s. 27(1), Local Government Finance Act 1982 as amended by Sched. 4, para. 19(1), National Health Service and Community Care Act 1990; and s. 6(2), National Audit Act 1983.

[109] 1982 Act, ss. 27(6) as amended by Sched. 4, para. 19(2), National Health Service and Community Care Act 1990.

[110] 1990 Act, s. 62(1). 'Clinical Care' means 'any action which is taken in connection with the diagnosis of illness or the care or treatment of a patient, and which is taken solely in consequence of the exercise of clinical discretion.' See s. 62(7), 1990 Act.

[111] CSAG, HMSO, 1993. See also pp. 53–54, *supra*. [112] Ibid.

The Government has responded to these observations in a positive way by suggesting that specialist services be provided on a co-ordinated basis, so that individual units can develop the expertise necessary to perform effectively, rather than acting in competition in a way which dilutes the quality of care available.[113] To this extent, therefore, competition between hospitals is discouraged and districts should seek to cater for conditions where demand is limited by pooling their resources, perhaps by making one district responsible for acting on behalf of a number of others. The Department of Health's responses suggest that CSAG will play an important role in ensuring that managerial strategies do not obstruct the quality of care available to patients.

D. A Future for Accreditation?

Accreditation seeks to measure the performance of hospitals against external criteria, but both aspects of this description leave room for disagreement. Hospitals do not yet need accreditation, nor is their funding dependent upon it. Some will argue that the statutory bodies mentioned above, together with the internal market and medical audit, are effective to discourage poor performance and that formal accreditation is unnecessary. Also, the experience of accreditation in America suggests that it is insufficiently refined to measure accurately the quality of health care provided because the science of measuring hospital outcomes is still in its infancy. Thus, the Joint Commission on the Accreditation of Healthcare Organizations may assess the care with which hospitals store confidential information, control the spread of infection, review the palliative care given to dementia patients in nursing homes, or the standards relating to the use of advance directives.[114] But it is more difficult to compare the performance of hospitals of different regions dealing with different socio-economic groups of patients.

So much for the present. For the future, governments on both sides of the Atlantic have shown interest in developing measures

---

[113] See *Government Response to the Reports of the Clinical Standards Advisory Group* (HMSO, 1993) and *Contracting for Specialist Services* (NHSME, 1993).

[114] See *Background on Health Care Quality* (Joint Commission on Accreditation of Healthcare Organisations, 1994).

which would enable comparisons of this nature to be made. The CSAG has recommended that certain areas of medical practice should be subject to national targets because standards of care may vary and there may be difficulty in planning services,[115] to which the Government has responded: 'we welcome the suggestion of developing, in discussion with managers and the profession, national guidelines concerned with service specifications and quality standards.'[116] Once we begin to speak of national standards and targets it is easy to consider the advantages which accreditation could bring to patients and purchasers of health care, provided it is accurate and reliable.

V. ACCESS TO MEDICAL RECORDS

An effective system by which bodies may be held accountable for their actions depends on information. The following discusses the individual's right of access to their medical records.

A. Common Law Rights of Access

Canadian authority holds the nature of the doctor–patient relationship to be such that patients have a right of access to information kept about them which relates to their medical condition. The Canadian Supreme Court reasoned that:

The fiduciary duty to provide access to medical records is ultimately grounded in the nature of the patient's interest in his or her records . . . information about oneself revealed to a doctor acting in a professional capacity remains, in a fundamental sense, one's own. The doctor's position is one of trust and confidence. The information conveyed is held in a fashion somewhat akin to a trust. While the doctor is the owner of the actual record, the information is to be used by the physician for the benefit of the patient. The confiding of the information to the physician

---

[115] See eg *Coronary Artery Bypass Grafting and Coronary Angioplasty* (CSAG, HMSO, 1993), para. 8.1; *Cystic Fibrosis* (CSAG, HMSO, 1993), para. 8.37; *Neonatal Intensive Care*, ibid. para. 9.7.

[116] *Government Response to the Reports of the Clinical Standards Advisory Group*, *supra* note 113, 7.

for medical purposes gives rise to an expectation that the patient's interest in and control of the information will continue.[117]

In England, the Court of Appeal speculated about a similar right of access to medical records arising from the fact that, since patients have a right to have their questions answered before treatment is given 'as truthfully and as fully as the questioner requires',[118] the duty to respond to questioning after treatment ought to be equally strict. Lord Donaldson said: 'a doctor is under a duty to answer his patient's questions as to the treatment proposed. We see no reason why there should not be a similar duty on hospital staff. . . . Why . . . is the position any different if the patient asks what treatment he has in fact had?'[119]

When the matter arose for consideration in the case of *ex p Martin*, the existence of a common law right of access to medical records was accepted by the Court of Appeal, subject always to the overriding right of the doctor to conceal from the patient such aspects of his history as might damage his best interests, for example because it would be detrimental to his health. Evans LJ said that 'there is no good reason for doubting either that a right of access does exist or that it is qualified to that extent at least'.[120] That is to say: the right is subject to the patient's best interests. However, the precise extent of the right was not examined because the Court found that the records should not have been disclosed in that case since they were likely to have caused harm to the applicant. No doubt subsequent cases will test the precise nature and extent of the doctor's discretion to withhold records on the basis of psychiatric risk and address the question why, if patients are entitled to expose themselves to risks by refusing medical treatment under the law of consent, they should not also be permitted to expose themselves to a risk of damage by deciding to see medical records which are kept about them.

---

[117] *McInerney* v. *MacDonald* 93 DLR (2d) 415, 424 (1992). The right of access was made subject to the patient's health not being put at unreasonable risk by the disclosure.

[118] See Lord Bridge in *Sidaway* v. *Royal Bethlem Hospital Governors* [1985] AC 871, 898. See also Lord Diplock, 895.

[119] *Lee* v. *South West Thames Regional Health Authority* [1985] 2 All ER 385, 389. See also *Naylor* v. *Preston AHA* [1987] 2 All ER 353, 360, *per* Lord Donaldson MR.

[120] *R* v. *Mid Glamorgan FHSA ex p Martin* [1994] 5 Med LR 383, 398.

This analysis of a patient's *right* of access to medical records may be extended to a doctor's *duty* to disclose them. In *Stamos* v. *Davies*[121] the defendant doctor intended to take a biopsy from the plaintiff's lung. By mistake he punctured his spleen which subsequently caused the patient persistent pain. The defendant told the patient nothing about the mistake. Some time later the plaintiff required treatment in an accident and emergency unit. The surgeon discovered a large collection of blood in the plaintiff's abdomen and removed the damaged spleen. The plaintiff sued the defendant for his failure to disclose the fact that the biopsy had caused unintended damage. The High Court of Ontario upheld the claim. Given the pain suffered by the plaintiff and the need for corrective surgery, it said: 'there was a duty on the defendant to inform the plaintiff that he had entered his spleen. The plaintiff asked the defendant what he had obtained at the biopsy. The defendant's failure to be candid with the plaintiff was a breach of duty.'[122]

Both *ex p Martin* and *Stamos* present plaintiffs with a problem, however. Under well established principles of the law of negligence, it is not sufficient for a plaintiff to prove only that he was the victim of a breach of the duty of care. He must go on to prove that the breach caused him damage. Commonly, no damage is caused by a non-disclosure of information. Certainly the patient is left in ignorance, but he is not damaged thereby. So, in the absence of any right to claim damages for the non-disclosure, the 'duty' to disclose seems to be something of a misnomer. But this is not always the case.

Where the clinical error is such as to expose the patient, or others, to risk of further harm, the doctor may be under a duty to disclose the danger to the patient in order for suitable remedial treatment to be offered.[123] Failure to do so, which causes avoidable damage, or pain and discomfort, (as in *Stamos*), would merit compensation. This principle is analogous to the duty imposed on manufacturers to recall defective products once the

---

[121] 21 DLR (4th) 507 (1985).

[122] Ibid 523. See also *Gerber* v. *Pines* (1934) 79 *Sol Jo* 13 (tip of hyperdermic needle broke off and lodged in the plaintiff's body.)

[123] See G. Robertson, 'Fraudulent Concealment and the Duty to Disclose Medical Mistakes', (1987) 25 *Alberta LR* 215.

defects have come to light.[124] Such an approach was applied in
Pittman v. *Bain*.[125] The plaintiff was transfused with blood
infected with HIV in 1984, before the virus was capable of being
detected. The following year a test for identifying infected blood
was developed and it became possible to trace the recipients of the
infected transfusions. However, it was only in 1989 that the
plaintiff's doctor was notified that his patient was at serious risk of
having been contaminated, by which time his wife had also
become HIV positive. The court was satisfied, by analogy with the
product liability cases, that a blood bank has a proximate
relationship with the person to whom blood is transfused. Where,
after the transfusion, the blood bank learns that its product may
have been contaminated, it is under an obligation to advise the
recipient, and to do so expeditiously.[126]

Similarly, once the hospital had been informed of the danger
presented by its blood transfusions, it had a duty to examine its
own records to determine which of its previous patients were at
risk, and to inform them or their GPs accordingly. On the facts of
the case, the Canadian Red Cross Society and the hospital were
held to have failed in their duty to set up effective systems by
which such records could be examined, and of failing to act with
proper haste once the systems had been put in place. The claims in
negligence of both the plaintiff and his wife were successful.[127]

This is sensible and logical when applied to the risk of physical
or psychological harm. Could it be extended to economic harm? Is
a patient 'harmed' by not being informed that he has been the
victim of medical negligence and has a right to recover a large sum
of damages? Arguably, such a denial of a right deprives the patient
of a financial benefit, but it does not cause him harm. If this
interpretation is correct, no right to damages arises from a failure
to inform the patient of his right to damages.

---

[124] See e.g. *Walton and Walton* v. *British Leyland UK Ltd* (1978, unreported,
QBD, reproduced in C. Miller and B. Bailey, *Consumer and Trading Law Cases
and Materials* (Butterworths, 1985) 59), (cars with defective breaks). See also
Wright v. *Dunlop Rubber Co* (1972) 13 KIR 255, 272 (carcinogenic chemicals in the
workplace) and *Braniff Airways Inc* v. *Curtiss Wright Corp* 411 F.2d 451 (2nd Cir,
1969), (defective aeroplane).   [125] 112 DLR (4th) 257 (1994).
[126] Ibid. 372.
[127] The doctor shared liability for failing to notify the plaintiff. The defendants
were responsible for the wife's infection, which could have been avoided. The
husband's claim for damages was based on the years of lost life which might have
been saved had suitable treatment been made available expeditiously.

B. Pre-action Discovery of Documents

The policy of the law is to ensure that parties enter court with their cards on the table so that cases are not lost as a result of an unexpected legal ambush. The process by which parties exchange documents to facilitate this objective is known as discovery. Thus, a person who appears likely to have a claim in respect of personal injuries or death may request discovery of documents against 'a person who appears to the court likely to be a party to the proceedings and to be likely to have or to have had in his possession, custody or power any documents which are relevant to an issue arising, or likely to arise, out of that claim'.[128] Indeed, those who will *not* be parties to the action can also be ordered to disclose relevant documents.[129] The power cannot be used to mount a 'fishing expedition' because the court must be satisfied of the likelihood of a claim.[130] Obviously, actions in medical negligence make frequent use of this power which enables a potential litigant to see documents held, for example, by a hospital, in order to assess whether or not to pursue an action. It is immaterial that the likelihood of the claim being made is dependent on the outcome of the information disclosed.[131]

The documents need not be disclosed to the plaintiff personally. The court may order that discovery be made either to the applicant, or his legal advisors, or his legal and medical advisors, or other professional advisors, or (if he has no legal advice) his medical or other professional advisor.[132] Also, the applicant will not be entitled to see any documents protected by legal professional privilege, i.e. documents passing between a lawyer and client and made in connection with the request for, or giving of, legal advice concerning a claim or potential claim. The rule would appear, however, not to cover an enquiry into an accident undertaken for the *dual* purpose of investigating its causes in order to improve safety and as the basis of a report to be submitted to legal advisors. For the privilege to attach, submission to lawyers

---

[128] Supreme Court Act 1981, s. 33(2).
[129] Supreme Court Act 1981, s. 34.   [130] Ibid.
[131] See *Dunning* v. *United Liverpool Hospitals Board of Governors* [1973] 1 WLR 586 and *Shaw* v. *Vauxhall Motors Ltd.* [1974] 1 WLR 1035.
[132] See Supreme Court Act 1981, ss. 33(2) and 34.

for use in litigation must be the *dominant* purpose for which the document was prepared.[133] Routine investigations into mishaps which are intended to improve standards of safety, therefore, appear not to be protected by the rule. But those undertaken with litigation uppermost in mind will be excluded from discovery, even if this deprives the plaintiff of the only evidence on which his or her cause of action could be based and, thus, their right to claim damages. Precisely this occurred in the case of *Lee* v. *South West Thames RHA*,[134] in which the plaintiff, a young boy, suffered severe scalding at home. He was taken to one hospital and soon after transferred to another and so was treated by two health authorities. During the time spent with one of them, he suffered brain damage in circumstances which suggested negligence. An investigation into the accident was undertaken and a report produced by one of the authorities which refused to disclose it to him. He applied to the court for access to it as the best evidence on which to prove his claim for damages. His application was denied on the ground that it was a privileged document.

No doubt, *Lee* is consistent with legal authority, but it leaves an extremely nasty taste in the mouth when it is used by health authorities to frustrate legitimate claims against them by patients for whose injuries they may have been responsible. The case exposes the tenuous nature of the supposition that health authorities ought always to promote patients' best interests.

C. Data Protection Act 1984

A general right of access to computerized data is provided by the Data Protection Act 1984. Thus, an individual shall be entitled '(a) to be informed by any data user whether the data held include personal data of which that individual is the data subject; and (b) to be supplied by any data user with a copy of the information constituting any such personal data held by him.'[135]

As regards the physical or mental health of data subjects, however, this general right is subject to a separate regime,[136]

---

[133] See *Waugh* v. *British Railways Board* [1979] 3 WLR 530.
[134] *Supra* note 119.
[135] Data Protection Act 1984, s. 21.
[136] The exception is provided by section 29(1) of the 1984 Act and introduced by the Data Protection (Subject Access Modification)(Health) Order 1987 (SI 1987, No. 903).

which applies if the data are held by a health professional; or if the data are held by a person other than a health professional but the information constituting it was first recorded by or on behalf of a health professional.[137] In this case the general right of access is modified so that data shall not be disclosed if it:

(a) would be likely to cause serious harm to the physical or mental health of the data subject; or

(b) would be likely to disclose to the data subject the identity of another individual (who has not consented to the disclosure of the information) either as a person to whom the information or part of it relates or as the source of the information or enable that identity to be deduced by the data subject either from the information itself or from a combination of that information and other information which the data subject has or is likely to have.[138]

Those who believe that they have wrongly been denied access to information may apply to the court which may order disclosure if it is satisfied that there has been a contravention of the regulations.[139] What evidence would be needed? Unlike the Access to Health Records Act 1990,[140] the Data Protection Act 1984 gives the court no right of access to the records to determine for itself whether the refusal to disclose is proper (though litigants may agree to such a course of action) and it is difficult to see how the majority of those with misgivings of this nature could be expected to persuade a court that access had been denied wrongly.

Children have the same rights as adults provided that they are competent to make the application. Presumably, a six-year old applicant could not be said to intend to make any application at all since he would usually not understand what it was, or why it was being made. However, a 'Gillick' competent[141] child has the same rights of access as an adult. Parents may make applications on behalf of their children.[142] The Act enables the data subject to

---

[137] Ibid. reg. 3(2).
[138] Ibid. reg. 4(2). Para. (b) does not protect the identity of health professionals who have been involved in the care of the patient, or when the identity of others can be omitted or deleted. See reg. 4(3).
[139] 1984 Act, s. 21(8).
[140] Discussed *infra*.
[141] See *Gillick* v. *West Norfolk and Wisbech AHA* [1985] 3 All ER 402.
[142] 1984 Act, s. 34(6)(a).

have errors in the data corrected or erased[143] and provides for compensation for any damage caused by inaccurate data, loss, or unauthorized disclosure.[144]

D. Access to Health Records Act 1990

The Access to Health Records Act 1990 gives a right to written health records made after the commencement of the Act,[145] in the same way as the Data Protection Act 1984 for electronically stored records. A 'health record' means a record which consists of (a) information relating to the physical or mental health of an individual who can be identified from that information, or from that and other information in the possession of the holder of the record; and (b) has been made by or on behalf of a health professional in connection with the care of that individual; but it excludes access to personal data under the Data Protection Act 1984.[146] What is information 'relating to' an individual made 'in connection with' his care? It must include correspondence between GPs and hospital consultants, nursing records and X-rays, which must be shown to the applicant and copied for him if required.[147] The Act applies to the records of private doctors and hospitals as it does to the NHS.

What is 'in connection with' a patient's care? Take the example of the patient who has made a clinical complaint under the Independent Professional Review procedure,[148] in which two independent consultants prepare a report which is disclosed to the health authority but not to the patient. Does the report fulfil the criteria set down in the 1990 Act? The Department of Health has said that such a report is not made 'in connection with' the care of that individual.[149] True, the consultants' report does not arise

---

[143] 1990 Act, s. 24.   [144] 1990 Act, ss. 22 and 23.
[145] 1990 Act, s. 5(1)(b). The Act came into force on 1 Nov. 1991.
[146] 1990 Act, s. 1(1). Where records contain terms which are not intelligible without explanation, an explanation of those terms shall be provided with the record, see s. 3(3).
[147] 1990 Act, s. 3(2). Access shall be given within 21 days of the application in respect of records made within 40 days of the application, or, in any other case 40 days of the application. See s. 3(5). Reasonable copying charges may be made.
[148] Discussed in Chapter 7.
[149] In response to correspondence with the ACHCEW. See *Access to Health Records Act 1990—The Concerns of Community Health Councils* (Association of Community Health Councils for England and Wales, 1994) 4.

directly out of the patient's treatment, but it is certainly connected with it. That, after all, is precisely the reason for the patient's complaint and the consultants' report. If the policy of the Act is to widen access to 'health records' there is no reason to interpret the phrase narrowly or for responsible consultants to object to their reports being made available to patients.

'Health professional' means any of the following: (a) a registered medical practitioner; (b) a registered dentist; (c) a registered optician; (d) a registered pharmaceutical chemist; (e) a registered nurse, midwife, or health visitor; (f) a registered chiropodist, dietician, occupational therapist, orthoptist, or physiotherapist; (g) a clinical psychologist, child psychotherapist or speech therapist; (h) an art or music therapist employed by a health service body; and (i) a scientist employed by such a body as head of a department.[150]

The 1990 Act gives access to health records to the following categories of person:

(a) the patient;
(b) a person authorized in writing to make the application on the patient's behalf;
(c) where the record is held in England and Wales and the patient is a child, a person having parental responsibility for the patient;
(d) where the record is held in Scotland and the patient is a pupil, a parent or guardian of the patient;
(e) where the patient is incapable of managing his own affairs, any person appointed by a court to manage those affairs; and
(f) where the patient has died, the patient's personal representatives and any person who may have a claim arising out of the patient's death.[151]

However, access to the health records shall not be given under (a) and (b) 'unless the holder of the record is satisfied that the patient is capable of understanding the nature of the application.'[152] Children may apply for their own records, but if an application is made on their behalf under (c) and (d) access shall not be given unless the holder is satisfied either that the patient has consented to the making of the application or, if the patient is

---

[150] 1990 Act, s. 2(1).   [151] 1990 Act, s. 3(1).
[152] 1990 Act, s. 4(1).

incapable of consenting, that access would serve his or her best interests.[153] Thus, children have the right to prevent parents having access to their records. Nor shall access be given under (c), (d), (e) or (f) of any records obtained 'in the expectation that they would not be disclosed.'[154] The record holder will be the patient's GP, or the FHSA (with respect to primary care) and the NHS Trust or DHA (in the case of secondary care).

The holder of the record is given considerable discretion in deciding whether and how much to disclose. Access shall not be given to any part of a health record which in the opinion of the holder of the record, would disclose:

(i) information likely to cause serious harm to the physical or mental health of the patient or of any other individual; or
(ii) information relating to or provided by an individual, other than the patient [or a health professional who has been involved in the care of the patient[155]], who could be identified from that information.[156]

When the holder of the health record is a health service body (an NHS Trust hospital, DHA, or FHSA) it must take advice from the appropriate health service professional before deciding whether the record ought to be disclosed.[157] This is clearly a delicate matter for doctors. Patients may suffer 'serious harm' if medical information is disclosed without sensitivity.[158] On the other hand 'the fact that information has been withheld could be as harmful to patients as the information itself.'[159] Clearly, this exclusion is intended to keep records from patients only in the most extreme cases. Doctors may not use it simply on the ground that the patient's feelings might be hurt, or that disclosure might provoke litigation against a fellow doctor.

---

[153] 1990 Act, s. 4(2).   [154] 1990 Act, s. 5(3).
[155] 1990 Act, s. 5(2)(b).
[156] 1990 Act, s. 5(1). The Act does not impose a duty to say that part of the record has been withheld. The Department of Health suggests that 'the holder may not wish to volunteer the fact that information has been withheld. If confronted with a direct request as to whether access has been given to the whole of the record a holder is entitled to respond that the requirements under the Act as to access have been fully complied with.' See *Access to Health Records Act 1990—A Guide for the NHS* (1991) 21. This seems intended to deceive.
[157] 1990 Act, s. 7.
[158] See C. Hewlitt, 'Killed by a Word', 344 *The Lancet* 695 (1994), discussing the case of a patient whose health deteriorated and who died after he mistakenly believed he had a terminal form of leukaemia.
[159] *Access to Health Records Act 1990—A Guide for the NHS*, supra note 152.

A patient who is not satisfied that his records have been properly disclosed may apply to the High Court or County Court for disclosure.[160] The court has power to see for itself the content of the record 'for the purpose of determining any question whether an applicant is entitled to be given access' to the record.[161] This appears to impose on the court a duty to determine for itself whether the refusal to disclose the records is justifiable, rather than obliging it to defer to the views of doctors. For example, although the power to withhold information is exercisable 'in the opinion' of the record holder, a court might wish to be satisfied that the disclosure is 'likely' to cause 'harm', and to see that it is 'serious' and not trivial. However, the Court of Appeal seems to have taken a less strict view of the test. Nourse LJ said: 'A doctor, likewise a health authority, as the owner of a patient's medical records, might deny him access to them if it was in the patient's best interests to do so, for example if disclosure would be detrimental to his health. . . . [T]hat [would be] a complete answer [to the application].'[162]

With respect, broadly phrased tests of 'best interests' and 'detriment to health' are precisely not what were intended by the 1990 Act, which requires more specific and compelling evidence of harm before access may be denied.

E. Access to Medical Reports Act 1988

Under the Access to Medical Reports Act 1988 individuals have the right of access to medical reports written by doctors for employers or insurance companies.[163] The Act applies only to doctors who are or have been responsible for the clinical care of the individual[164] and not to doctors engaged only for the purpose of writing the report who have no clinical responsibility to the individual. In the case of doctors who have, or have had, such responsibility, the request for a medical report must be made with the consent of the patient[165] and 'An individual who gives his

---

[160] Prior use of the Hospital Complaints Procedure Act 1985 would also be possible (see Chapter 7). [161] 1990 Act, s. 8(4).
[162] *R* v. *Mid Glamorganshire FHSA and another,* ex p *Martin, supra* note 120, 396.
[163] Access to Medical Reports Act 1988, s. 1.
[164] 1990 Act, s. 2(1). [165] Ibid. s. 3(1).

consent . . . to the making of an application shall be entitled, when giving his consent, to state that he wishes to have access to the report to be supplied in response to the application before it is supplied'.[166]

It follows from this that if the individual chooses to see the report, the person applying for it shall notify the individual and the practitioner of the fact at the time the request is made and the practitioner shall not supply the report unless he has given the individual access to it, or unless twenty-one days have passed since the date of the application.[167] Alternatively, the individual may notify the practitioner that he or she wishes to see the report.[168] A right of access remains for up to six months after the date on which it was supplied.[169]

Access to a report may be denied, in whole or part, if it would 'in the opinion of the practitioner be likely to cause serious harm to the physical or mental health of the individual or others'[170] or would 'indicate the intentions of the practitioner in respect of the individual'.[171] Nor is disclosure required when it would be 'likely' to reveal information about another person, or reveal the identity of another person who has supplied information to the practitioner, unless that person has consented, or he is a health professional who has been involved in the care of the individual and the information relates to or has been provided in that capacity.

---

[166] 1990 Act, s. 4(1).   [167] 1990 Act, s. 4(2).
[168] 1990 Act, s. 4(3).   [169] 1990 Act, s. 6(3).
[170] The words 'or others' are not included in the analogous provisions of the Data Protection Act 1984 or the Access to Health Records Act 1990.
[171] 1990 Act, s. 7.

7

Complaints and Professional Discipline

By what means may patients and health service employees make complaints about the health service? And how are matters of professional discipline involving doctors dealt with by FHSAs, the General Medical Council, NHS Trusts, and Health Authorities?

I. COMPLAINTS

Franz Kafka might have written a novel about NHS complaints. 'An aggrieved patient wishing to pursue a complaint faces a procedural maze of considerable complexity: first, in the varied institutional structure of the NHS itself, covering general practice and community health as well as hospitals; second, in the distinction which has to be made between clinical and non-clinical complaints'.[1]

The complaints system is widely considered to be unsatisfactory and will be reformed to make it more effective, more uniform, and more accessible to patients, no matter where in the system the complaint happens to arise.[2] The following, however, describes the present system of complaints.

A. Hospital Complaints

The system for investigating hospital complaints depends on whether the complaint concerns (1) non-clinical management or (2) clinical judgment.

---

[1] *Review of the Parliamentary Commissioner and Health Service Commissioner Schemes* (Reading Centre for Ombudsman Studies, Evidence to the Select Committee on the Parliamentary Commissioner for Administration, 1993), para. 14.

[2] See *Being Heard—A Report of a Review Committee on NHS Complaints Procedures* (The 'Wilson Report', Department of Health, 1994)

1. Non-clinical Complaints

Twenty-five per cent of all the grievances upheld by the Health
Service Ombudsman in 1991–2 concerned the handling of
complaints.[3] This is a poor reflection on a system introduced by
the Hospital Complaints Procedures Act 1985 which imposes on
the Secretary of State a 'duty' to issue directions to health
authorities to secure the introduction of arrangements: '(a) for
dealing with complaints made by or on behalf of persons who are
or who have been patients of [a] hospital and (b) . . . [that] steps
are taken for publicising the arrangements so made, as (in each
case) are specified or described in the regulations.'[4]

Those directions were duly issued in Department of Health's
circular, *Health Service Management Hospital Complaints
Procedure Act 1985*, which requires all NHS hospitals[5] to appoint a
'designated officer' with specific responsibility for dealing with
complaints. He or she ought to occupy a senior position within the
hospital in order to deal effectively with investigations and may be
the chief executive. 'The duties of a designated officer must
include responsibility for receiving, and seeing that action is taken
upon, any formal complaint made at the hospital or hospitals for
which he is given responsibility, and where the complainant had
indicated a wish for him to do so, assisting in dealing with a
complaint that is likely to be able to be dealt with informally.'[6]

Formal complaints should normally be made in writing within
three months of the matter complained of, subject to a discretion
to extend that time for good cause. Both parties should be given
the opportunity to make observations and comments to the
designated officer who should investigate the complaint
'promptly'.[7] Health authorities should seek to learn from their
mistakes by monitoring progress, considering trends in complaints,
and taking remedial action as required.[8] This responsibility has not

---

[3] *Select Committee on the Parliamentary Commissioner for Administration.
Report of the Health Service Commissioner for 1991–92* (HC 388, Session 1992–93)
para. 53.

[4] Hospital Complaints Procedures Act 1985, s. 1. The directions acquire their
authority from s. 17, National Health Services Act 1977.

[5] HC(88)37. NHS Trust hospitals are included by the National Health Service
and Community Care Act 1990, Sched. 9, para. 29.

[6] Ibid. Annex A, para. 2(2).　　　　　　　　　　　　　[7] Ibid. para. 4.

[8] Ibid. para. 5.

been duplicated at national level. Oddly, when the policy of the health service reforms is to enable doctors and patients to select the best performers in the NHS, 'there is no centrally agreed categorisation of complaints in the National Health Service in England and Wales, nor standard reporting of outcomes. This deprives both the NHS and the public at large of important information on the performance of the Health Service. Too much has been left to local discretion in this regard.'[9] This shortcoming requires attention.

This may become more important if patients are referred to private hospitals for treatment. Private hospitals are entirely independent of the Hospital Complaints Procedures Act 1985. On what basis, therefore, will doctors and their patients be able to select treatment from the private sector? Some attempt has been made to encourage the disclosure of information of this nature from private hospitals in the *Patient's Charter*, which provides for the 'right to have any complaint about NHS services—whoever provides them—investigated and to receive a full and prompt written reply from the chief executive or general manager.'[10] Guidance on the *Patient's Charter* provides that when DHAs or GP fund-holders purchase services from hospitals in the independent sector:

they must stipulate in their contracts that any complaints about services by or on behalf of patients will be dealt with in accordance with procedures similar to those prescribed in directions made in reference to the Hospital Complaints Procedures Act 1985.[11]

But it is difficult to know how private hospitals could be forced to comply, either to implement the procedures or to monitor and remedy undesirable trends. After all, the contract will be between the hospital and the health authority or GP fund-holder. The patient will not be a party to it so will have no action for breach of contract. One suspects that that NHS purchasers will have limited time and energy to pursue complaints on the patients' behalf. Arguably, private hospitals which wish to contribute services to

---

[9] *Select Committee on the Parliamentary Commissioner for Administration. Report of the Health Service Commissioner for 1991–92, supra* note 3, para. 55.
[10] *The Patient's Charter* (Department of Health, 1991) 11.
[11] *Implementing the Patient's Charter* (HSG(92)4, NHSME, 1992) annex 3. See also Circular HC(88)37.

the NHS should enter into a contract with the Secretary of State for Health and be subject to the same law as NHS hospitals. If they wish to take the benefits of providing services on behalf of the NHS, they should be subject to equally strict obligations concerning patients with complaints.

2. Clinical Complaints Excluded

Both the Health Service Ombudsman and the procedures under HC(88)37[12] are excluded from investigating complaints concerning the exercise of clinical judgment. The present system for dealing with clinical complaints was introduced in 1981 by Circular HC(81)5, *Memorandum of an Agreement for Dealing with Complaints Relating to the Exercise of Clinical Judgment by Hospital Medical and Dental Staff.* This procedure has been criticized because 'the current complaints system in the National Health Service seems designed for the convenience of providers of the service rather than of complainants'.[13]

Complaints about clinical judgment are subject to a three-stage procedure. Stage One requires the consultant in charge of the patient to deal with the complaint directly, either in person or in writing, and to attempt to resolve the matter 'within a few days'.[14] If other doctors are involved in the case the consultant should discuss it with them and any reasons for delay ought to be explained to the complainant. Thereafter the matter usually rests with the district administrator to reply to the complainant in terms which have been agreed by the consultant concerned, unless the consultant wishes to reply him or herself.

Should the complainant be dissatisfied with the reply, the complaint may enter Stage Two of the procedure. This time, the complaint must be addressed in writing to the district health authority, one of its administrators, or the consultant, and the matter must at once be referred to the Regional Medical Officer. Further discussion with the complainant will be suggested, perhaps in the light of the additional views of other consultants, but if this fails the third stage should be set in motion.

---

[12] HC(88)37 at reg. 2(4)(a).
[13] *Select Committee on the Parliamentary Commissioner for Administration. The Powers, Work and Jurisdiction of the Ombudsman* (HC 33–1, Session 1993–94) para. 101.   [14] HC(81)5, para. 19.7.

Stage Three involves an independent professional review of the case. It is designed to deal only with serious cases 'which are not
. . . likely to be the subject of more formal action either by the health authority or through the courts'.[15] In this event, the regional medical officer will arrange for a 'second opinion' on all aspects of the case to be obtained from two independent consultants in active practice in the appropriate specialty or specialties. The independent reviewers should see the clinical records and speak to the doctors concerned with the case. They should also discuss the clinical aspects of the case fully with the complainant. If they consider the complaint unfounded they should seek to allay the complainant's anxieties, and in suitable cases speak to the medical staff involved about ways of avoiding similar problems in the future. The complainant is not entitled to a detailed report of their findings but they should report their actions to the regional medical officer. Short of litigation, there is no further procedure available for clinical complaints.

These provisions call for a number of comments. First, in the financial year ending 1992 over 15,000 Stage One procedures were undertaken in England, of which only 393 continued to the second stage. Of these, 154 were the subject of further independent professional review, of which 64 complaints against clinical judgment were upheld.[16] It would be wrong, therefore, to condemn the system as useless, but it is largely unstructured, so that the Health Service Ombudsman frequently criticizes health authorities for failing to deal with matters promptly; and there are doubts about its fairness and impartiality. The independent review is within the sole judgment of doctors. One does not have to accuse doctors of dishonesty to say that some must feel a sense of allegiance to their colleagues and be reluctant to criticize their judgment when things have gone wrong. What explains the fact, for example, that in 1992–3, '50 per cent of complaints were upheld in the South East Thames Region compared with 6 per cent in the Northern Region.'[17] Even if unconscious bias is not the explanation, patients may well believe that the system is tilted in the doctor's favour. Also, there is no compulsion on doctors to co-operate with the scheme and they may simply reject it. As one

[15] Ibid. para. 26. See p. 236 *supra*.
[16] *The Powers, Work and Jurisdiction of the Ombudsman*, *supra* note 13, at Table 2.   [17] Ibid. para. 108.

commentator has said, since hospital doctors are employees of the
health authority it is 'a strange situation where an employer cannot
require his employee to explain conduct that has resulted in injury
to the clients of the business'.[18]

Secondly, these provisions do not extend to private hospitals in
which there is no guarantee of a procedure under which a clinical
complaint will be investigated.[19] Again, if independent hospitals
contribute their services to the NHS, their engagement should be
made subject to the condition that patients retain all the benefits
they would have if treated in an NHS hospital.

Thirdly, the withdrawal of the complaints procedure from
matters which are likely to become the subject of litigation is very
defensive. It reveals a limit to the principle that the service should
always promote a policy of openness and patients' best interests.
Nevertheless, the policy has received the approval of the Court of
Appeal. In *R* v. *Canterbury and Thanet DHA and SE Thames
RHA*, ex p *F and W*[20] an investigation into allegations of
negligence against a doctor was discontinued after litigation
became probable. The complainants argued that the health
authorities were under a duty to investigate the complaints.
Speaking of HC 81(5) and HC 88(37), the Court said:

> The circular makes it plain that the procedure will not be appropriate
> where litigation is likely. There are obvious reasons for this. The primary
> purpose of the procedure is either to get a second opinion, and therefore a
> change of diagnosis or treatment, or to enable the health authority to
> change its procedures in the light of matters brought to its attention in the
> investigation of the complaint. . . . Secondly, the procedure depends on
> the co-operation of the consultant whose clinical judgment and conduct is
> in question. If the consultant is being or is about to be sued by the
> complainant, it is obvious that the co-operation, which cannot be
> compelled, will not be forthcoming. . . . Thirdly, if the complaints are
> such that a claim for negligence is likely to be made, the matter will
> eventually be fully investigated in court. . . . That is likely to be a far more
> searching inquiry. [21]

---

[18] M. Brazier, *Medicine, Patients and the Law* (Penguin Books, 1992) 207.
[19] Non-clinical matters should have been provided for in the contract, see
Implementing the Patient's Charter, *supra* note 11, annex 3 (discussed above).
[20] [1994] 5 Med LR 132, and comment in [1994] Med LR 359.
[21] Ibid. 140.

This is very much the consultant's view of the matter. An alternative view is that when things have gone wrong there is a need for more, not less, candour between the parties. It would foster the relationship of trust between doctor and patient about which judges speak so often. It might also tend to defuse situations which do not warrant litigation by encouraging an atmosphere of reconciliation and settlement. Present arrangements have the contrary effect.

B. The Health Service Ombudsman[22]

The powers of the Health Service Ombudsman are contained in the Health Service Commissioners Act 1993. He may investigate any allegation that a person: 'has sustained injustice or hardship in consequence of (a) a failure in a service provided by a health service body, (b) a failure of such a body to provide a service which it was the function of the body to provide, or (c) maladministration connected with any other action taken by or on behalf of such a body.'[23]

The health service bodies concerned are RHAs, DHAs, SHAs, NHS Trusts, FHSAs, the Dental Practice Board, and the Public Health Laboratory Service.[24] In addition, he may investigate 'matters arising from arrangements between' health service bodies and independent bodies which agree to provide services for patients.[25] Thus, private hospitals which agree to provide services for NHS patients are also subject to his jurisdiction. As a general rule, the complainant must exhaust his remedies within the health service bodies before turning to the Ombudsman.[26] Matters relating to NHS contracts may be made the subject of investigation,[27] which offers the opportunity for examining the content of agreements between health authorities, as well as the absence of such agreements. However, the Act does not authorize the

---

[22] He refers to himself as 'the Ombudsman'. 'Health Service Commissioner' is his 'Sunday title'. See *The Powers, Work and Jurisdiction of the Ombudsman, supra* note 13, para. 26.
[23] Health Service Commissioners Act 1993, s. 3(1).
[24] 1993 Act, s. 2(1). Uncooperative bodies may be compelled to attend hearings or disclose documents to the Ombudsman. See s. 12(1), 1993 Act.
[25] 1993 Act, s. 7(2)(b).   [26] 1993 Act, ss. 9(5) and (6).
[27] 1993 Act, s. 7(2)(a).

Commissioner 'to question the merits of a decision taken without maladministration by a health service body taken in the exercise of a discretion vested in that body'.[28] Decisions concerning the identification of health service priorities, therefore, would be difficult to challenge, but not impossible. We have already seen him criticize the policy of a health authority to withdraw hospital care from patients with long-term neurological conditions and to make them pay for private nursing care, on grounds of scarce resources. In this case the patient had suffered a serious stroke and still needed full-time nursing care. The Commissioner said that the failure to make long-term care available was unreasonable and constituted a failure by the health authority.[29]

1. Clinical Complaints Excluded

A number of other matters are excluded from his jurisdiction, most important of which are actions taken in connection with the diagnosis of illness, or the care or treatment of a patient 'which in the opinion of the Commissioner, was taken solely in consequence of the exercise of clinical judgment'.[30] In 1992 25 per cent of the complaints which the Ombudsman rejected for investigation concerned clinical judgment.[31] He has been careful, however, not to allow it to be used as a blanket excuse to bar him from investigating cases of patent error. Thus, a failure to diagnose a fracture following inadequate X-rays has been criticized,[32] as has the failure to diagnose the psychosis of a patient who was subsequently left alone and committed suicide.[33] Similarly, he condemned a failure to obtain the consent of a twenty-three year-old woman who had been admitted for an abortion but who, after discussion with her parents, was sterilized without her knowledge;

---

[28] 1993 Act, s. 3(4).
[29] See *Failure to Provide Long Term NHS Care for a Brain-damaged Patient* (HC 197, Health Service Commissioner's Second Report for Session 1993–94) discussed *supra* at p. 11.
[30] 1993 Act, s. 5(1).
[31] See *The Powers, Work and Jurisdiction of the Ombudsman, supra* note 13, para. 110.
[32] *Report of the Health Service Commissioner for 1992–93* (Select Committee on the Parliamentary Commissioner for Administration, HC 42, Session 1993–94) para. 40.
[33] See *Health Service Commissioner* (Annual Report for 1988–89, HC 457, 1989) para. 37.

she only discovered the fact some years later after she had married and wanted a baby.[34] Equally, he accepts large numbers of cases concerning failures in the Independent Professional Review procedures, in which health authorities have failed to answer letters of enquiry, or organize meetings with consultants, or make proper arrangements for a hearing.[35]

Many say that the Ombudsman should not be barred from investigating matters simply because they involve clinical judgment. The House of Commons Select Committee on the Ombudsman believes the present process does not do enough to guarantee impartiality. It said:

questions of clinical judgment demand specialised knowledge and careful consideration. It is therefore essential that any system designed to consider clinical complaints includes the opinions of acknowledged experts in the relevant fields. This does not, however, exclude the possibility of lay involvement. In cases of medical negligence, for example, a judge considers a case with the aid of expert opinion. . . . We recommend that the clinical complaints system introduce a lay element into its procedures.[36]

An obvious candidate for such a function is the Ombudsman himself as the lay member of a final board of Independent Review to whom dissatisfied patients may appeal. No doubt, such a responsibility would place new demands on the office of the Ombudsman and pose other problems which would have to be addressed. On the other hand, although the quality of his work is very highly regarded, the quantity of investigations he is able to deal with is relatively small; around 120 are concluded a year. So long as his contribution were confined to that of a final board of appeal, such an additional role could be possible.[37]

---

[34] See *Report of the Health Service Commissioner 1983–84* (HC 418, Session 1984–85), Case W 415.

[35] See eg *Report of the Health Service Commissioner* (Select Committee on the Parliamentary Commissioner for Administration, HC 388, Session 1992–93) at para. 24.

[36] *The Power, Work and Jurisdiction of the Ombudsman*, supra note 13, para. 109.

[37] See *NHS Complaints Procedures: The Way Forward* (Consumers' Association, 1993).

2. Other Exclusions

Two other exclusions from the Ombudsman's jurisdiction need to be mentioned: cases for which a remedy is available in the courts, and the activities of GPs. Each is discussed in turn. The 1993 Act provides that: 'A Commissioner shall not conduct an investigation in respect of action to which the person aggrieved has or had . . . a remedy by way of proceedings in any court of law unless the Commissioner is satisfied that in the particular circumstances it is not reasonable to expect that person to resort or have resorted to it.'[38]

The logic of the restriction is that payments of compensation can be awarded by the courts alone,[39] and if this is the proper course of action it makes no sense to duplicate work. But many cases do not litigate. Perhaps the plaintiff is unable to obtain legal aid, the facts are too complicated, or the patient is very frail. In matters of this nature the Ombudsman may undertake his own investigation and, should he discover a case which supports litigation, he has no power to stop a complainant commencing legal proceedings for compensation. However, it seems he will not be prepared to assist patients to gather evidence in this way. In one case an investigation was refused concerning a woman who was admitted to hospital having taken an overdose of paracetamol. She was discharged the next day but died at home two days later. Her husband asked for an Independent Professional Review into the case which was refused on the grounds that the case probably involved negligence. The husband turned to the Ombudsman for help but his case was rejected. The Ombudsman said:

the woman's husband realised that the independent consultants had withdrawn because they thought his wife's treatment had been negligent and that the case was suitable for litigation. The husband then tried to find out exactly what it was which had led the independent consultants to their view, but I thought he was going too far when he sought, in effect, precise

---

[38] 1993 Act, s. 4(1).
[39] Although the Ombudsman may award out of pocket expenses wrongfully incurred by patients. See such an award in *Failure to Provide Long-Term NHS Care for a Brain-damaged Patient, supra* note 29, in which the patient's wife had been obliged to pay for private nursing care.

particulars of the negligence which the independent consultants had identified.[40]

Given the queues of cases which wait, both to come before the courts and the Ombudsman, the restriction is sensible so long as legitimate cases are guaranteed some avenue of redress. On the other hand, as legal aid becomes available to fewer and fewer people, and the risks involved in litigation more difficult to contemplate, this category of exclusion must be exercised very carefully.

The second category excluded from the Ombudsman concerns investigations: 'in respect of action taken in connection with any general medical services . . . under the National Health Service Act 1977 by a person providing those services,[41] [and] action taken by a Family Health Services Authority in the exercise of its functions under the National Health Service (Service Committees and Tribunal) Regulations 1992.'[42]

The effect of these exclusions is to remove the conduct of individual GPs from the Ombudsman's review, presumably because they are neither health service bodies nor health service employees. They are private practitioners outside his jurisdiction. If this is the explanation it is unconvincing. GPs agree standard Terms of Service with FHSAs and are subject to standard disciplinary proceedings.[43] As we shall see below, the procedures for investigating general complaints against GPs (as opposed to matters of discipline under the Terms of Service) are extremely weak. There is a strong argument, therefore, supported by both the House of Commons Select Committee[44] and a report commissioned by the Secretary of State for Health,[45] that the conduct of GPs should be brought within the jurisdiction of the Ombudsman, as well as the operation by FHSAs of the disciplinary procedures which may be invoked against them. At present, other than by expensive and distressing actions in the courts (which nobody

---

[40] *Health Service Commissioner's Annual Report* (HC 457, Session 1988–89) para. 27.
[41] 1993 Act, s. 6(1).
[42] 1993 Act, s. 6(3). The regulations are discussed in Chapter 4.
[43] See Section II below.
[44] See *Report of the Health Service Commissioner for 1992–93, supra* note 32, para. 68.
[45] See *Being Heard—The Report of a Review Committee on NHS Complaints Procedures, supra* note 2, para. 322.

favours) there is no adequate system by which complaints can be heard against GPs. As more become fund-holders with financial and managerial interests to balance against those of their patients, an improved system of complaints is desirable.

C. Complaints by NHS Staff

An entirely different matter relates to NHS staff who wish to complain about the system in which they work.[46] To what extent may they do so and how is it possible? Before the introduction of the 1990 reforms the employment contracts used by all district health authororities provided that 'a practitioner shall be free, without the consent of the employing authority, to publish books, articles etc. and to deliver any lecture or speech, whether on matters arising out of his hospital services or not.'[47]

Now, however, DHAs have largely given way to NHS Trusts as the major employers of hospital staff. Under the 1990 Act NHS Trusts have the power 'to employ staff on such terms as the trust thinks fit'.[48] There is anxiety that some have become over-sensitive about the risk to their commercial viability of adverse publicity. Concern has been expressed as to the use of 'gagging' or confidentiality clauses designed to prevent hospital employees from bringing to the notice of the public matters of management or policy. Some have introduced clauses which restrict the freedom of speech previously enjoyed under the old regulations and the Government has been inclined to support them in doing so. This restriction on the right to speak out has caused considerable unease amongst health service employees. The British Medical Journal has fulminated against 'The Rise of Stalinism in the NHS'[49] and the Health Service Ombudsman has received sub-missions about 'a "culture of fear" in the NHS. Staff were unwilling to make complaints and raise concerns they had about standards of service. People were frightened for their jobs. . . .

---

[46] See G. Hunt (ed.), *Whistleblowing in the Health Service* (Edward Arnold, 1995).

[47] *Terms and Conditions of Service for Hospital Medical and Dental Staff* (Department of Health and Social Security, 1986) para. 330.

[48] Sched. 2, para. 16(1)(d) of the National Health Service and Community Care Act 1990. See also M. Siddall, 'Not as Well as Can be Expected', (1992) 142 *New Law Journal* 763.

[49] See the series of articles in 309 *British Medical Journal* 1640 (1994).

Particular concern was expressed about "gagging clauses" in staff contracts of the new NHS trusts.'[50]

NHS guidance provides that 'employees . . . have a duty of confidentiality and loyalty to their employer. Breach of this duty may result in disciplinary action . . .'[51] Does this mean that an employer can insert any clause into a contract of employment, no matter how draconian, as a way of preventing matters being discussed publicly? The law on this matter is not entirely clear and no case has yet tested the power of an NHS employer to restrain its employee in this way. Nevertheless, a number of general propositions can be stated. First, there is a relationship of mutual trust and confidence between all employers and employees and the courts have acted to prevent employees disclosing information to the press on the basis that there is 'a very strong public interest in preserving confidentiality within any organisation, in order that it can operate efficiently, and also be free from suspicion that it is harbouring disloyal employees'.[52] To a large degree, therefore, Trusts arc free to insist that many matters concerning the organization of its business remain confidential, although it is difficult to be precise as to exactly what should fall within this category. As a general rule it would always be wrong to make public any details enabling a particular patient to be identified.[53] Equally, were the patient to agree to the disclosure of such information, the duty would normally cease[54] unless the employer could show some residual claim to confidence. Arguably, outside the area of patient care, the general systems of management, accounting, pay structures, and incentive schemes adopted may all be described as confidential in the contract of employment so that, *prima facie*, during the period of employment the employee is not free to disclose them.[55] On the other hand, it may be argued that

---

[50] *The Powers, Work and Jurisdiction of the Ombudsman*, *supra* note 13, para. 121.

[51] *Guidance for Staff on Relations with the Public and the Media* (EL(93)51, NHSME, 1993), para. 9.

[52] *Science Research Council* v. *Nassé* [1981] 1 All ER 417, 480, *per* Lord Fraser.

[53] See the guidance at para. 8.

[54] 'Where a patient, or a person properly authorised to act on a patient's behalf, consents to disclosure, information to which the consent refers may be disclosed in accordance with that consent.' *Professional Conduct and Discipline: Fitness to Practice* (General Medical Council, 1993), para 77.

[55] See *Printers & Finishers Ltd* v. *Holloway* [1965] 1 WLR 1 and *Littlewoods Organisation Ltd* v. *Harris* [1977] 1 WLR 1472.

this rule, which may be entirely appropriate to the domain of private businesses, may be less suitable in the public sector dedicated to the service of patients.

Secondly, the employer is not free simply to impose a blanket ban which seeks to prevent employees from talking about the Trust. In order to merit protection, the information must be either a trade secret or 'confidential'. The Court of Appeal put the matter as follows:

the information will only be protected if it can properly be classed as a trade secret or as material which . . . is in all the circumstances of such a highly confidential nature as to require the same protection as a trade secret. . . . [A] restrictive covenant will not be enforced unless the protection sought is reasonably necessary to protect a trade secret or to prevent some personal influence over customers being abused in order to entice them away.[56]

If a covenant is found to be unnecessarily broad the general rule is that the court will declare it null and void. It will not attempt to draft a replacement which satisfies the requirements of the law.[57]

Thirdly, there may be circumstances in which the duty of confidentiality is overidden in the public interest; indeed, there may be a duty to disclose information for this purpose. This common law principle has been endorsed in the guidance which accepts that 'the duty of confidence to an employer is not absolute',[58] and imposes on NHS employees 'a duty to draw to the attention of their managers any matter they consider to be damaging to the interests of a patient or client and to put forward suggestions which may improve their care'.[59] The difficulty is in determining what may be disclosed in the public interest. Such a 'duty' has been recognized in a case concerning a doctor who made a psychiatric report on a mental patient, W, which expressed concern as to the patient's mental health and his propensity for

---

[56] *Faccenda Chicken Ltd* v. *Fowler* [1986] 1 All ER 617, 626, *per* Neill LJ.

[57] *Putsman* v. *Taylor* [1927] 1 KB 637.

[58] Para. 10 says: 'In any case involving disclosure of confidential information, it may be claimed that the disclosure was made in the public interest. Such a justification might, in a disputed case, need to be defended and so should be soundly based. As a matter of prudence, then, any employee who is considering making a disclosure of confidential information because they consider it to be in the public interest, should first seek specialist advice.'

[59] Ibid. para. 4.

violence. The question arose: was the patient owed a duty of confidence by the doctor so that the report could not be disclosed to the Home Secretary and the Mental Health Review Tribunal? Scott J said that in these circumstances: 'a doctor called on . . . to examine a patient such as W owes a duty not only to his patient but also to the public. His duty to the public would require him . . . to place before the proper authorities the result of his examination if, in his opinion, the public interest so required. This would be so . . . whether or not the patient instructed him to do so.'[60]

This suggests that the safety of patients and the public is an important ground for overiding the duty of confidence. These are also matters of concern to the professional bodies which impose obligations of their own intended to preserve standards of conduct. Thus, the General Medical Council states that:

it is any doctor's duty, where the circumstances so warrant, to inform an appropriate person or Body about a colleague whose professional conduct or fitness to practise may be called into question or whose professional performance appears to be in some way deficient. Arrangements exist to deal with such problems, and they must be used in order to ensure that high standards of medical practice are maintained.[61]

Nurses are also obliged to 'report to an appropriate person or authority any circumstances in which safe and appropriate care for patients and clients cannot be provided'.[62] In addition, were the complaint to concern allegations of dishonesty amongst employers, it would be unlawful for an employer to suppress the disclosure of information which ought, in the public interest, to be disclosed to those who have a proper interest in receiving it.[63]

Fourthly, it is reasonable to require complaints to be aired internally before they are taken to other bodies and that any such disclosure should be to the appropriate authorities. Obviously, if the circumstances are so urgent that there is insufficient time to undertake an internal enquiry, public disclosure of the information may be justified. Similarly, were the complaint to concern the

---

[60] *W* v. *Egdell* [1989] 1 All ER 1089, 1104, *per* Scott J.

[61] *Professional Conduct and Discipline: Fitness to Practise*, *supra* note 54, para. 63.

[62] See *Code of Professional Conduct* (United Kingdom Central Council for Nursing, Midwifery and Health Visiting, 1992), para. 12.

[63] See *Initial Services Ltd* v. *Putterhill* [1968] 1 QB 396.

abuse of power, or dishonest use of money by senior managers, the matter could not always be disclosed to the employer. Such disclosure must be made responsibly and to the proper authorities. Publication to a newspaper which leads to an inaccurate and exaggerated attack in the national press may be less helpful in bringing about change than raising the matter with one of the professional bodies, the Health Service Ombudsman, or a Member of Parliament. The guidance provides that where a complaint by a member of staff has led to action, he or she should be notified of the measures adopted and, if no action is taken, 'the member of staff should be given a prompt and thorough explanation of the reasons for this'.[64] Where the 'complainant' remains dissatisfied with the response provided a very difficult question has to be asked as to whether the matter should be disclosed in the public interest.

II. PROFESSIONAL DISCIPLINE

Matters of professional discipline may be dealt with by (A) the FHSA, (B) the General Medical Council, and (C) the health authority as employer of the individual concerned.

A. FHSA Discipline of GPs

Complaints about GPs usually arise from patients, although they may be initiated by the relevant FHSA.[65] The purpose of the disciplinary procedure is not to enable patients to express general dissatisfaction with a GP. It is to determine whether there has been a breach by the GP of a specific term, or terms, of his agreement with the FHSA. A study of 1,000 formal complaints showed that they concerned the following matters:[66]

failure to visit	25%
failure to diagnose	20%

---

[64] *Guidance for Staff*, supra note 51.

[65] See the National Health Service (Service Committees and Tribunal) Regs. 1992 (SI 1992, No. 664), reg. 7, as amended by SI 1994, No. 634. The regulations also cover dentists, opticians, and pharmacists.

[66] See C. Owen, 'Formal Complaints Against General Practitioners', *British Journal of General Practice* (1991). Cited in *Being Heard*, supra note 2.

error of prescription	8%
failure to arrange emergency admission	6%
delay in diagnosis	5%
failure to examine	5%
delay in visiting	5%
unsatisfactory attitude	5%
failure to refer for investigation/opinion	5%
poor administration	5%
other	11%

The most common complaints from patients raise issues under the following three provisions of the Terms of Service; first: 'where a decision whether any, and if so what, action is to be taken under these terms of service requires the exercise of professional judgment, a doctor shall not, in reaching that decision, be expected to exercise a higher degree of knowledge and care than . . . that which general practitioners as a class may reasonably be expected to exercise.'[67]

Secondly: 'a doctor shall render to his patients all necessary and appropriate medical services of the type usually provided by general medical practitioners.'[68] And thirdly: 'the services . . . shall be rendered (a) at his practice premises, [or] (b) if the condition of the patient so requires . . . at some other place in the doctor's practice area.'[69]

Complaints are made to the FHSA[70] and may be resolved either informally or formally. Under the informal procedure, the FHSA may seek to settle the matter by means of a conciliation process and it may be that an explanation or an apology will suffice. There are no rules of procedure and the matter may be dealt with in discussion between the parties or by correspondence. The conciliator has no power to impose sanctions and may not make a finding that the doctor has breached his Terms of Service. Thus, if the informal procedure fails, or the complaint is sufficiently serious to make it inappropriate, the formal complaints procedure will be adopted. Informal procedures have great merit in permitting the parties time for reflection and reconciliation but they, too, need regulating. The Health Service Ombudsman upheld a complaint in which the FHSA engaged insufficient lay conciliators,

[67] National Health Service (General Medical Services) Regs. 1992 (SI 1992, No. 635), Sched. 2, para. 3. Note that additional provision is made for doctors who offer specialist services.   [68] Ibid. para.1 2.
[69] Ibid. para. 13.   [70] See ibid., regs. 3 and 4.5.

one of whom lost his temper with a complainant and refused to take any further action in the case. Clearly, this did not contribute to a settlement of the dispute. Considering the case in its annual report, the House of Commons Committee on the Ombudsman said of the FHSA:

the fact that lay conciliators are voluntary makes all the more crucial the effective monitoring of their work . . . the authority is to be criticised for offering a complaints procedure whilst not having in place the resources to operate the procedure effectively. Effective resourcing should take place before the institution of a complaints system, not afterwards.'[71]

By contrast, the formal procedure is regulated in great detail. Notice of the complaint must be given to the FHSA, the principal offices of the RHA, or DHA, within thirteen weeks of the event which is the subject of the complaint[72] and will be referred to the Medical Service Committee for determination (the FHSA's disciplinary committee).[73] Clearly, there will be occasions when the patient is unable through illness to complain, or is simply not aware that anything went wrong until afterwards. In this case complicated rules have to be invoked for the matter to proceed. 'The complaint may nevertheless be investigated if (a) [the committee] is satisfied that the failure to give notice of the complaint . . . was occasioned by illness or other reasonable cause; and (b) the practitioner or the Secretary of State consents to the investigation of the complaint.'[74] Making doctors consent to being made the subject of a complaint against them clearly puts them in an invidious position which is scarcely likely to command the respect of a complainant. The provision has little to recommend it.

Once the matter has been admitted for investigation, the FHSA must refer it to the Medical Services Committee 'as soon as practicable'.[75] A preliminary sifting mechanism enables the chairman of the committee to decide whether the complaint really

---

[71] *Report on the Health Service Commissioner for 1992–93*, *supra* note 32, paras. 28 and 29. The Ombudsman's investigation is limited to the procedures of health authorities. Doctors are not subject to his investigations.
[72] National Health Service (Service Committees and Tribunal) Regs. 1992, *supra* note 65.   [73] Ibid. reg. 4.
[74] Ibid. Sched. 3, para. 1(1). Additional regulations cover the procedure that must be followed by the Secretary of State if the doctor fails to give consent; see ibid. para. 2(1) and (2).   [75] Ibid. Sched. 4, para. 3.

concerns the GP's Terms of Service. If he considers that it does not, then the patient is given fourteen days to submit further evidence to the chairman. For example, if the complaint is simply about rudeness, although perhaps reprehensible, it does not involve the Terms of Service. In this case, the matter may be referred to the full committee without a hearing and the committee may recommend to the FHSA that the complaint be dismissed. Alternatively, the matter may be made subject to a formal hearing before the committee.[76] Both the parties may be represented in the hearing and the doctor will probably be entitled to representation by a professional association (the BMA, the Medical Defence Union, or the Medical Protection Society). Patients may find such expertise more hard to come by. Although lawyers may attend the hearing, they may not address the committee or put questions to witnesses.[77]

After the hearing the committee shall present a report to the FHSA containing details of the evidence of the hearing, the findings of fact, the inferences which ought to be drawn from the facts, and the committee's recommendations as to the action to be taken by the FHSA.[78] The FHSA must then decide for itself whether the doctor has failed to comply with one or more of the Terms of Service.[79] It may decide that no further action be taken. If satisfied a breach has occurred, it may simply warn the doctor to comply with the Terms of Service in future, or impose a number of sanctions. It may recover any expenses incurred by the breach, or recover a sum not exceeding £500 from the doctor's remuneration, or otherwise. In more serious cases it may recommend that the Secretary of State recovers a sum in excess of £500 from the doctor.[80] The result of the determination shall be given to the Secretary of State.[81] In the gravest cases the FHSA may recommend that the continued inclusion of the doctor's name on

---

[76] Ibid. Sched. 4, paras. 3–6.   [77] Ibid. Sched. 4, para. 5(4).

[78] Ibid. Sched. 4, para. 7(1). Previous breaches of the doctor's Terms of Service may also be notified to the FHSA, see para. 4(2).

[79] If it disagrees with the committee's recommendation it must say why. Ibid. reg. 9(2).

[80] The sanctions are contained in ibid. reg. 9(5)(a)–(e). When the committee recommends that a sum in excess of £500 should be recovered, the Secretary of State may seek the advice of the committee as to the proper sum. See ibid., reg. 13(4).   [81] Ibid. reg. 9(9).

the Medical List would be prejudicial to the general medical services and that he should be struck off the list.[82] An appeal procedure is available to the Secretary of State against an adverse · decision of the FHSA;[83] or with respect to the recovery of money,[84] or against being struck off the list.[85]

The formal side of the system is not popular. Patients often confuse it with a general complaints system and both parties find the procedure lengthy, cumbersome, and over-regulated. Its adversarial nature discourages settlement; and the environment of the court room is entirely inappropriate when neither party is entitled to legal representation. It turns the patient into an accuser, to whom it can offer no remedy because its function is only disciplinary. Patients are the conduit through which complaints often reach the FHSA, and so they serve the system well. However the systems fails to recognize that the doctor is entirely at liberty to strike the patient off his own list as a result of a complaint.[86] Patients in rural locations with few practices available should therefore think twice before complaining. All these matters show that the system is badly in need of reform.

B. The General Medical Council

The powers of the FHSA arise out of the quasi-contractual relationship between it and the GP. By contrast, the powers of the General Medical Council (GMC) are statutory and apply to all registered medical practitioners, whether employed by the NHS or privately. Disciplinary powers were first conferred on the GMC in the Medical Act 1858 and are now contained in section 36(1) of the Medical Act 1983. The Act provides that where any registered practitioner

(a) is found by the Professional Conduct Committee to have been convicted in the British Isles of a criminal offence, or

---

[82] National Health Service Act 1977, s. 46. The recommendation is made to 'the Tribunal' which is constituted in accordance with Sched. 9 of the 1977 Act. Its procedure is governed by the Service Committees and Tribunal Regs, *supra* note 65, See also *R* v. *National Health Service Tribunal, ex p City and East London FPC* [1989] 1 Med LR 99.

[83] National Health Service (Service Committees and Tribunal) Regulations 1992, *supra* note 65, reg. 10.   [84] Ibid. reg. 13(7).

[85] Ibid. reg. 27.

[86] These misgivings are discussed in *Being Heard, supra* note 2, 22–5.

(b) is judged by the Professional Conduct Committee to have been guilty of serious professional misconduct, the Committee may if it thinks fit, direct:

(i) that his name shall be erased from the register;

(ii) that his registration in the register shall be suspended . . . during such period not exceeding twelve months as may be specified in the direction;[87] or

(iii) that his registration shall be conditional on his compliance, during such period not exceeding three years as may be specified in the direction, with such requirements so specified as the Committee thinks fit to impose for the protection of members of the public or in his interests.[88]

Part of the GMC's role is to provide advice for members of the medical profession on standards of professional conduct and medical ethics.[89] Such advice is given in *Professional Conduct and Discipline: Fitness to Practise*, known as 'the Blue Book',[90] which details extensive regulation of doctors' conduct. Until recently, for example, there were strict limits to their rights to advertise their practices. This conflicted with the view of the Government which had proposed the 'internal market' with more competition between doctors for patients and also with the Monopolies and Mergers Commission which had published a report concluding that the restriction on advertising operated against the public interest. Indeed, the GMC itself was considering relaxing the rule.[91] Thus, in *Colman* v. *General Medical Council*[92] a doctor who practised 'holistic' medicine which combined the use of medicines with advice about lifestyle, challenged the restriction for being 'inept, illogical and unfair'. He argued, amongst other things, that it unreasonably restricted his freedom to practise his trade ethically and responsibly and, in all the circumstances, was disproportionate to the objective it sought to achieve, namely the preservation of good standards in the profession and the protection of patients.

Despite its sympathy for the doctor, the Court of Appeal said that the doctrine of restraint of trade did not apply to the case

---

[87] See *Taylor* v. *GMC* [1990] 2 Med LR 45.

[88] Medical Act 1983, s. 36. There is an automatic right of appeal by the doctor to the Privy Council, see s. 40.   [89] 1983 Act, s. 35.

[90] GMC, 1993. The Blue Book is regularly updated.

[91] The relaxation was introduced in paras. 97–106 of the Blue Book (1993).

[92] [1990] 1 Med LR 241.

because the restrictions arose, not from an unfair agreement between the parties, but from section 35 of the Medical Act 1983. Lord Donaldson MR said:

Parliament has entrusted the resolution of these competing considerations to the GMC and not to the courts. Accordingly, it is quite beside the point to consider whether I would have reached the same conclusion. It is even possible that the president of the GMC might not do so today, when he has the benefit of the recommendations of the Monopolies and Mergers Commission Report . . . which must cause the GMC to re-examine the guidance contained in the Blue Book.[93]

Having taken this view, he said that the restriction could be only overturned by the courts if it was 'Wednesbury' unreasonable, i.e. so outrageous in its defiance of logic that no sensible person could have arrived at it.[94] The restraint did not fall into such a category. On this test, the courts will permit the GMC considerable latitude in the restrictions it imposes on members of the profession from time to time. Two further ethical principles call for attention.

1. Serious Professional Misconduct

The professional wrongdoing with which the GMC is primarily concerned is described in section 36(1)(b) of the 1983 Act as 'serious professional misconduct.' Until 1969 the principle against misconduct was described as 'infamous conduct in a professional respect'. Some of the older cases on the subject deal with these words and are useful by analogy. In 1894 these word were characterized as follows: 'If it be shown that a medical man, in the pursuit of his profession, has done something with regard to it which would be reasonably regarded as disgraceful or dishonourable, by his professional brethren of good repute and competency, then it is open to the General Medical Council to say that he has been guilty of infamous conduct in a professional respect.'[95]

'Infamous' was said to denote conduct deserving of the strongest reprobation and so heinous as to merit the extreme professional penalty of striking off.[96] Such wrongdoing is not confined to the

[93] [1990] 1 Med LR 253.
[94] The words are taken from those of Lord Diplock in *Council of Civil Service Unions* v. *Minister for the Civil Service* [1985] AC 374, 410.
[95] Allinson v. *General Council of Medical Education and Registration* [1894] 1 QB 750, 760.   [96] Felix v. *General Dental Council* [1960] AC 704, 720.

code of conduct described in the Blue Book and extends to misconduct outside the context of the doctor's medical practice. A veterinary surgeon (governed by similar rules of professional conduct) kept animals on a farm which were allowed to die from inadequate care. He was found guilty by the GMC of conduct disgraceful to a professional man. He argued on appeal that he could not be disciplined for his private activities which had nothing to do with the pursuit of his profession. It was held, however, that the words were not limited in this way. They extended to conduct which would be condemned as disgraceful by his professional colleagues.[97] This is consistent with section 36(1)(b) which covers convictions outside the scope of the doctor's practice.

The provision extends to misconduct which is not negligent. As we have seen, advertising was for a long time considered to be improper, although it may have been done responsibly and helpfully. Improper emotional relationships, even those which occur without sexual misconduct, may amount to serious professional misconduct, because they may damage the trust which should exist between doctor and patient,[98] as may the making of improper and indecent remarks to employees and patients.[99] It seems likely that a practice which has the support of a responsible body of medical practitioners can never be described as 'misconduct'. The question arose in a case in which a doctor adopted an 'unorthodox' policy in relation to patients who were addicted to heroine. Rather than prescribing the usual course of drugs to detoxify the patient, such as methadone, he chose to prescribe valium for self-administration. This was on the basis that, though such treatment may have been addictive, it was more likely than the usual treatment to encourage patients not to return to the more dangerous drugs. Though it could be described as harmful, it did more good than harm. He was found guilty by the Medical Board of Western Australia of 'infamous or improper conduct in a professional respect'.[100] He appealed to the Supreme Court of Australia on the grounds that, though he was in a minority, his

[97] *Marten* v. *Royal College of Veterinary Surgeons' Disciplinary Committee* [1966] 1 QB 1.   [98] See the Blue Book, *supra* note 90, paras. 70 and 71.
[99] *Reza* v. *GMC* [1991] 2 Med LR 255.
[100] *Cranley* v. *Medical Board of Western Australia* [1992] 3 Med LR 94, under the Medical Act 1984 (Western Australia).

practice of 'harm reduction' had the support of a number of distinguished practitioners. The court upheld the doctor's appeal, saying:

> once there is a finding that there is a respectable minority view for a particular treatment it is no part of the task of the tribunal concerned to determine the merits of the particular treatment. The Board may strongly disagree with the merits of the minority view. That is immaterial. . . . What the Board is concerned with is whether there has been improper conduct, and, if a practitioner's method of treatment is approved by a respectable minority of the profession, he will not be guilty of improper conduct.[101]

When will negligence amount to 'serious professional misconduct'? The Blue Book suggests that negligence alone will not necessarily be condemned in this way. The GMC is concerned only with the kind of matters which give rise to actions for negligence 'when the doctor's conduct in the case has involved such a disregard of professional responsibility to patients or such neglect of professional duties as to raise a question of serious professional misconduct.'[102]

In favour of the distinction is the argument that negligence arises in so many forms. Some are worthy of professional condemnation; it is inexcusable for example to leave an anaesthetized patient unattended in an operating theatre.[103] Others, however, are caused by the sort of inadvertence or inexperience[104] which, in many other walks of life, would not create immediate danger, and are 'retrievable' before any loss is inflicted. Negligence is intended not to condemn but to compensate; it is not necessarily a finding that a doctor is a bad or incompetent doctor. It may simply be one isolated instance when an error gives rise to a claim for damages.[105] This ought not to provoke a challenge to the doctor's professional status.

On the other hand, 'serious misconduct' may ignore the problem of the incompetent doctor who is not guilty of misconduct

---

[101] *Cranley* v. *Medical Board of Western Australia* 104.
[102] The Blue Book, *supra* note 90, para. 38.
[103] E.g *R* v. *Adamoko* [1991] 2 Med LR 277.
[104] Eg *Wilsher* v. *Essex AHA* [1987] QB 730.
[105] See *Medicine, Patients and the Law*, *supra* note 18, 139.

but whose standards of practice habitually expose patients to risk. In this case, there may be no worthwhile case in negligence, nor may the matter qualify under the severe test set down by the GMC. In addition:

an NHS employing authority, or private employer, may be able to dismiss a doctor whose performance has been consistently deficient. However, such action does nothing to assist the doctor in improving his or her standard of practice. Furthermore, there is no NHS procedure currently in existence which can prevent an incompetent doctor from continuing in professional practice in another area of the country, either in the NHS or in private practice.[106]

Thus, the GMC has proposed that a new tier of 'performance procedures' be introduced which enable it to take positive action to encourage poor doctors to improve their standards when there is evidence of 'serious deficiency in their performance'.[107] Their proposal is that complaints which fall short of serious misconduct should be dealt with by an Assessment Performance Panel. The panel would assess the standard of care achieved by the doctor and, if necessary, the GMC could insist upon counselling, retraining, and reassessment by a Professional Performance Committee. This would require a supplement to the powers currently available under the Medical Act 1983, which is currently proposed in the Medical (Professional Performance) Bill which has the support of the Government.

2. Confidential Information

An obligation which deserves special mention concerns the disclosure of information gained in confidence. The Blue Book says:

Patients are entitled to expect that the information about themselves or others which a doctor learns during the course of a medical consultation, investigation or treatment, will remain confidential. Doctors, therefore, have a duty not to disclose to any third party information about an

---

[106] *Proposals for New Performance Procedures* (GMC, 1992) para. 4.4. Discussed by M. Stacey, 'Medical Accountability—A Background Paper', in A. Grubb (ed.), *Challenges in Medical Care* (Wiley, 1992).
[107] Ibid. para. 5.6.1.

individual that they have learned in their professional capacity, directly from a patient or indirectly.[108]

The express consent of the patient permits disclosure but the difficult question is: when may the doctor disclose such information without the patient's consent? Inevitably, information about patients being treated in hospital cannot be confined to one doctor; the patient will be treated by a team of doctors and nurses and his or her records will be handled by hospital managers. Nevertheless, the Blue Book requires doctors to restrict such disclosure as far as possible. 'It is for doctors who lead such teams to judge when it is appropriate for information to be disclosed for this purpose. They must leave those whom they authorize to receive such information in no doubt that it is given to them in professional confidence.'[109] This apparent breach of the principle is perhaps based on the supposition that hospital patients impliedly consent to such limited disclosure because they know they will not be dealt with by a single individual. But this presumption should not extend to patients in teaching hospitals whose treatment assists medical training. Such patients should be asked if they consent to their cases being explained to groups of medical students and should be under no obligation to co-operate if they do not wish to do so.[110]

Common sense suggests that close relatives should be kept informed about a patient's progress, even if the patient is unable to consent to such disclosure. Legal and ethical theory, however, provide weak support for such a view unless 'the doctor is satisfied that it is necessary in the patient's best interests to do so.'[111] Sometimes it may be possible to overcome this objection on the ground that the patient's consent may be presumed. But it must often be the case that such a presumption is wrong and the patient would simply not wish his condition to be discussed with relatives. Perhaps disclosure which limited itself to the general condition of

---

[108] *Proposals for New Performance Procedures*, para. 76. This is not only a professional duty, but a legal one. See *R* v. *Egdell* [1990], *supra* note 60, in which the principle was said by Bingham LJ in the Court of Appeal to 'accurately state the general law as it now stands.'

[109] Ibid. para. 79.

[110] The Health Service Ombudsman has taken the same view. See *Health Service Commissioner's Annual Report for 1988–89*, *supra* note 33, para. 80. See also para. 89 of the Blue Book, *supra* note 90.

[111] The Blue Book, *supra* note 90, para. 82.

the patient, with no details of the illness for which he or she is being treated, would be acceptable. The question is very delicate. In one case, the Health Service Ombudsman criticized a hospital for failing to inform relatives that a patient was suffering terminal cancer. Indeed, no criticism was made of the surgeon in the case who said 'it was for the relatives to speak to him if they required information and . . . had they done so he would have given it willingly.'[112] Such a lax view of the doctor's duty of confidence is, however, open to question unless it was based on the patient's own wishes.

Patients whose condition may present a danger to others present particular difficulties. The Blue Book states:

Rarely, cases may arise in which disclosure in the public interest or in the interests of the individual may be justified, for example, [in] a situation in which the failure to disclose appropriate information would expose the patient, or someone else, to a risk of death or serious harm.'[113]

Specific attention has been addressed to the duty to relatives of patients diagnosed as suffering from AIDS or HIV. The GMC advises that the patient should be counselled about the need to inform relatives but that, in principle, confidence ought to be respected if the patient does not wish others to be informed of his or her condition. However, it advises that 'there are grounds for such a disclosure . . . where there is a serious and identifiable risk to a specific individual who, if not so informed, would be exposed to infection'.[114] How far does this exception extend? Does it enable a doctor to inform the police if a patient continues to drive a car while suffering from alcoholism? An analogous question arose in California in the case of *Tarasoff* v. *Regents of the University of California*,[115] in which the defendant hospital knew that a psychiatric patient had violent intentions toward a young woman and failed to alert her to the danger after he had been released from hospital. He murdered her soon thereafter. The defendants were held to owe a duty of care to warn her of his intentions. They knew the likelihood of it happening and the identity of the victim. A special duty thus arose to take steps to avoid such a foreseeable risk and their failure to do so was

---

[112] See *Health Service Commissioner's Annual Report for 1988–89, supra* note 33, para. 50.   [113] Blue Book, *supra* note 33, para. 86.
[114] See *HIV Infection and AIDS: The Ethical Considerations* (GMC, 1993) para. 19.   [115] (1976) 131 Cal Rptr 14 (Cal Sup Ct).

negligent. A similar duty was imposed in *Holgate* v. *Lancashire Mental Hospitals Board*[116] when a dangerous patient who had been compulsorily detained in hospital was given unsupervised leave, during which time he assaulted the plaintiff. Again, the nature of the risk to a particular individual was known. This suggests that the GMC's approach to disclosure is correct in law but it is difficult to know when uncertainties either in respect of the gravity of the risk, or the identity of the subject of it, would negate the duty to inform others.[117] Cases present different mixtures of fact and judges may differ in their responses to them.

C. Health Authorities and NHS Trusts

Quite apart from any complaint initiated by patients, an authority or NHS Trust, may invoke its own disciplinary proceedings against a member of staff. Hospital doctors, nurses, managers, and ancillary staff are employees of the health authorities and Trusts, and are subject to the procedures set down in their contracts of employment. It may be difficult to know, however, what those terms are. Disciplinary procedures are contained in circulars published by the Department of Health which may not be mentioned in individual contracts of employment. In the case concerning Dr Marietta Higgs, for example, the health authority took immediate disciplinary action against her following the report by Lord Justice Butler-Sloss into child abuse in Cleveland. Dr Higgs argued that it was not entitled to do so until it had held its own enquiry into the complaint against her in accordance with a health circular issued by the Department of Health on disciplinary proceedings,[118] the right to which was mentioned in her contract of employment. Her case was dismissed, however, on the ground that her employment contract also provided that rights to disciplinary procedures, including those in the circular, 'shall be binding in honour only and will not give rise to legal obligations'. Hutchison J said of the status of the circular:

the circular tenders guidance as to the procedure which in the Minister's opinion should govern the handling of serious disciplinary charges. It is,

---

[116] [1937] 4 All ER 19.
[117] General threats against children did not create a duty in *Thompson* v. *County of Alameda* 614 P.2d 728 (1980). The difficulty is discussed by M. Jones, *Medical Negligence* (Sweet & Maxwell, 1992) paras. 2.60–2.68.
[118] HM(61)112, which has since been replaced by HC(90)9.

therefore, something to which the Authority may—and no doubt often will—pay regard . . . [But] references to it in contractual documents are not by any means necessarily indicative of an intention to make recourse to it a contractual right.[119]

Thus, neither her contract nor the circular provided a right to an independent hearing of the allegations made against her. Arguably, this is the wrong approach to central guidance in a *national* health service; procedures which affect fundamental employment rights ought to have a common source. However, until the matter is reconsidered by the courts health service employers may, or may not, adhere to the Secretary of State's recommendations and are free to introduce procedures of their own. Bear in mind also the greater tendency for diversity with the introduction of NHS Trusts, which are encouraged 'to employ staff on such terms as the trust thinks fit'.[120] Thus, though the Department of Health recommends the adoption of specific disciplinary procedures, the following discussion of its guidance has to be read subject to the specific terms of individual employees.

The new procedure is contained in *Disciplinary Procedures for Hospital and Community Medical and Dental Staff* (HC(90)19).[121] It contemplates different approaches depending on whether the matter concerns personal conduct, professional conduct, or professional competence. In addition, it distinguishes between three levels of proceedings: the informal, the intermediate, and the formal, depending on the severity of the complaint.

Ordinary cases of personal misconduct do not concern matters of professional skill or judgment. In such a case the disciplinary procedures apply equally to clinical and non-clinical staff and, in the absence of provisions to the contrary, the procedure is set down in the *General Whitley Council Terms and Conditions of Service*.[122] In exceptional cases the authority may immediately dismiss an employee, or suspend him or her from duties. More

---

[119] See *Higgs v. Northern Regional Health Authority* [1989] 1 Med LR 1, 6.

[120] National Health Service and Community Care Act 1990, Sched. 2, para. 16(1)(d). Employees who have been absorbed by NHS Trusts retain their existing rights, see section 6(4), 1990 Act.

[121] *Disciplinary Procedures for Hospital and Community Medical and Dental Staff* (HC(90)19, Department of Health, 1990), which replaces HM(61)112.

[122] DHSS, 1986, section 40, on 'Disciplinary Procedures'.

commonly, the employee will receive a reprimand and a formal warning in writing, signed by the senior officer of the authority, that repetition might result in dismissal.[123] Within seven days of the disciplinary action, the employee should be notified in writing of the reasons for, and the nature of, the disciplinary action taken together with a summary of the facts on which it is based, and of the employee's right of appeal[124] to an appeals committee.

An appeal should normally be lodged within three weeks of receipt of the written notice and the hearing of the appeal should normally take place within five weeks of the employee's notice of appeal. The employee should be given fourteen days' notice of the hearing.[125] The committee consists of not less than three members who have not been directly involved in the proceedings leading to the disciplinary action, one of whom should have special knowledge of the employee's field of work. The employee has the right to appear before the committee and to be represented. Again, one is struck by the adversarial nature of the appeal proceedings, which resemble that of the court room and involve the right to call witnesses, to cross-examine the opponent and their witnesses, to sum up at the end of the case and the right of the appellant, or representative, to speak last.[126] Despite this complex procedure the appeals committee is not itself empowered to determine the case. Instead it must submit a report to the employing authority 'who should thereupon reach a decision on the case'.[127] The health authority appears to be at liberty to do as it pleases with the appeal committee's report and it is not clear precisely what purpose it is supposed to serve. After such a full and formal appeal, one would expect the authority to be under a duty to implement the committee's recommendations, unless there were compelling reasons to the contrary.

Serious cases of professional misconduct arising from medical or dental practice, and cases of professional incompetence concerning the adequacy of those skills and of professional judgment, may

---

[123] Ibid. para. 40(2).
[124] Ibid. para. 40(6). Para. 40(4) speaks of the 'employee's' right of appeal. Arguably, those who have been summarily dismissed are no longer employees and, therefore, lose their right of appeal under these provisions. See *R* v. *Secretary of State for Health and Trent RHA,* ex p *Guirguis* [1989] 1 Med LR 91.
[125] Ibid. para. 40(5).   [126] Ibid. para. 40(8).
[127] Ibid. para. 40(6).

be made the subject of a formal health authority enquiry.[128] Once the chairman of the authority has determined that the available facts appear to warrant an investigation, the doctor should be informed and an investigating panel should be established, normally comprising three people who have no connection with the hospital in which the doctor works. The procedure is very formal. The chairman of the panel is usually a lawyer nominated from a list kept by the Lord Chancellor, who is assisted by an equal number of professional and lay persons. The hearing is designed to establish the facts and make recommendations to the authority as to disciplinary action. The panel itself has no disciplinary power. There is a right to legal representation, to present witnesses in support, and to cross-examine. The circular recommends a strict timetable for each stage of the procedure[129] and the enquiry should be concluded within eight months of the decision that a *prima facie* case exists.

Two alternative procedures exist for less serious cases which do not warrant a full health authority enquiry. For consultants who have repeatedly failed to honour their contractual commitments, an informal procedure exists in which they will be invited to meet a panel established by the Joint Medical Staff Committee. The consultant may be invited to return to meet the panel within six months for review.[130] Secondly, an 'intermediate procedure' is available in cases which warrant action short of dismissal, for which a panel of assessors may be appointed from another region to examine the allegation. If satisfied that the matter does not warrant the formal procedure, it may undertake its own investigations and seek the assistance of other doctors. The panel may make recommendations as to action, but it has no disciplinary powers.[131]

An appeal to the Secretary of State is available to those who consider that they have been unfairly dismissed following a formal inquiry on matters of professional conduct or competence.[132]

---

[128] HC(90)9 para. 5. The circular refers to 'health authorities' only, but it is unlikely that it is intended to apply only to the remaining 10% of hospitals which have not become NHS Trusts. The following assumes it applies to NHS Trusts doctors too.   [129] HC(90)9, para. 17.
[130] HC(90)9, Annex D.   [131] HC(90)9, Annex E.
[132] *Terms and Conditions of Service for Hospital Medical and Dental Staff* (DHSS, 1986) section 190, as revised by HC(90)9, Annex C (HM & D).

Curiously, this elaborate appeal procedure has been held not to be available to those who have been summarily dismissed without the benefit of a formal inquiry. The regulations specifically provide that the disciplinary procedures 'are without prejudice to the right of the Authority to take immediate action (e.g. suspension from duty) where this is required in cases of a very serious nature'.[133]

Why should a devious health authority deprive a doctor of the right to an appeal simply by choosing summary dismissal rather than a formal hearing? The matter was considered by the Court of Appeal who said that, though it may be curious, the rules are clear and there is no right to an appeal in such a case because the contract of employment has ended.[134] The only remedy available to an aggrieved doctor in such a case is an action for unfair dismissal.

---

[133] HC(90)9, Annex B, para. 2.
[134] *R* v. *Secretary of State for Health and Trent RHA, ex p Guirguis* [1989] 1 Med LR 91. See also *Lyndon* v. *Yorkshire Regional Health Authority* 10 BMLR 49 (1993) in which a doctor was suspended under the same provision for alleged incompetence.

8

Ethics in the New NHS

How is the NHS likely to evolve in the future? And what are the tensions that this evolution will bring to the relationship between doctor and patient?

I. FUTURE ORGANIZATION OF THE NHS

The momentum for change in the health service has only just begun. These changes are not necessarily the result of the internal market for health. They arise partly from developments in the science of medicine itself. Four changes will have particular impact on the future organization of the NHS. First, improvements in medical technology mean that patients will spend fewer days occupying hospital beds and there will be a corresponding increase in the treatment of patients as out-patients, and in the community, by GPs and nurses.[1] The concept of the 'general' hospital, with a broad range of services designed to cater for the needs of most patients, will decline. Instead there will be a smaller number of specialist units which maximize the use made of expensive equipment. This implies a movement from secondary to primary care and an increase in the power of GPs both in terms of the numbers of patients they treat and their influence over the distribution of health service resources. Their role as passive partners in the enterprise of health, removed from the reality of hard decisions about costs and benefits, will be eroded. Inevitably, they will be drawn into the debate about priorities in health care.

Secondly, as the power to decide how resources should be spent is decentralized, tension will arise between the duty of the Secretary of State to promote national strategies and objectives and the wishes of local doctors and health managers as to their own goals and aspirations. When those decisions concern sensitive

---

[1] *New Horizons in Acute Care* (National Association of Health Authorities, 1988).

rationing issues, they will provoke arguments about the legitimacy and accountability of the decision-making process. NHS Trust hospitals and GP fund-holders, for example, may be subjected to more regulation as a means of promoting national objectives, rather than local ones. In particular, as the science of assessing health outcomes improves, greater interest will be shown in performance figures of hospitals, surgeons, and GPs. How many operations were performed? What percentage were successful? What are their management costs? (And how, exactly, have the statistics been compiled?) Evidence of this nature may act as a counterbalance to the decentralization of power. Less effective treatments will be discouraged. In this way the old notion of clinical freedom will be subjected to much closer scrutiny and doctors will be expected to justify their decisions, particularly if they depart from the norm. This means an increase in the number and authority of clinical guidelines and, perhaps, national protocols introduced by the Secretary of State as a means of directing the NHS and allocating scarce resources. These measures are intended to improve the service patients receive by making the NHS more effective, but their effect may diminish aspects of care which are currently considered important, such as the idea of clinical priority, candour between doctor and patient, and choice.

Thirdly, the use of a market for health care will not diminish this trend. The use of the word 'market' is undoubtedly contentious and the exact future of the current system of funding is subject to the winds of political change. Equally, both main political parties would endorse the following two principles: (i) that effective care in the NHS is enhanced by the use of some measure of financial incentives which benefit and reward those who achieve most, and (ii) that an entirely unregulated market for health care in the NHS would be largely ineffective and wasteful. The real question, therefore, is not: should we have freedom or regulation in health care? It is one of balance: how much regulation; how much accountability? Political rhetoric obscures this area, but in reality, when so much money is at stake and the consequences of wasting it have such catastrophic consequences for patients, it is crucial to know how resources are used in order to foster quality. Extensive regulation, both of doctors and health authorities, is inevitable regardless of the party in power. But if the relationship is made subject to formal codes of practice, procedures, and accountability, so that its personal context is diminished, some fear that patients may be the losers.

The individual consumer can do little to influence the working of a market based on 'managed competition'. Some units will attract more funds than others and may be able to provide better service, but others could deteriorate. The most vulnerable users may be affected. . . . GPs may refuse to accept patients who are time-consuming or require expensive drugs. Hospitals may prefer to specialise in procedures with few complications that are lucrative. . . . There is a danger that the tradition of public service among doctors and health service workers may be lost.[2]

Fourthly, the distinction between public and private care will become increasingly blurred. Private hospitals may increasingly be able to sell their services to NHS purchasers. Equally, NHS hospitals may need to generate revenue by treating private, fee-paying patients. This will create the need for new lines of control and accountability, with respect both to purchasers of care and patients. In other areas in which public utilities have been bought by private enterprise, official watch-dogs have been created with the aim of ensuring that minimum standards are maintained in the public interest. Bodies analogous to OFGAS and OFWAT (perhaps OFHEALTH or OFFSICK) may be required to regulate standards in the health service,[3] though experience in America suggests that this form of accreditation and regulation is hugely contentious. This need reflects the inescapable fact that competition depends on visible differences of quality between providers. Without them, competition has no effective role to play.

Can we continue to regard the health service as a *national* health service in which central strategy seeks to minimize the effect of inequalities between different hospitals and different regions? Or, given the way in which differences in quality are part of its structure and dynamism, ought we to think in terms of a *federal* health service with more power and authority devolved to individual health authorities? If this is a more accurate description of the service, it raises questions about the plausibility of the Secretary of State's obligation to promote a 'comprehensive health service'. If the words are to retain any meaning amongst the

---

[2] *Quality Standards in the NHS—The Consumer Focus* (National Consumer Council, 1992) 1.
[3] These issues are illuminated by W. Laing, *Managing the NHS—Past, Present and Future* (Office of Health Economics, 1994).

inequalities created by competition, they may serve to indicate a minimum standard, below which care may not fall, but with the hope that many patients will enjoy better. In practical terms, however, it is extremely difficult to describe exactly where such a minimum standard lies and there is a risk that, at least for some, only the common law of negligence will be available to counteract the pressure for doctors to overstretch themselves and provide inadequate treatment. An alternative is to ease the pressure of scarce resources by increasing the types of care for which the patient is obliged to pay. To some extent this is already the case for dental care and prescription medicines, but there is a greater incidence of patients bearing part of the costs of their treatment elsewhere in Europe,[4] and this will be one of the possibilities under considera-tion in the UK.

There seems to be a mismatch between the fact of scarcity in the NHS and the obligations imposed on health service managers and doctors. If patients are increasingly obliged to pay for their care and others are effectively denied care by reason of their age or the cost of hospital treatment, we ought to be more candid about the care which can, and cannot, be provided within the NHS. Although the political difficulties involved in such candour are daunting, patients and insurance companies would be better served if they understood the categories of treatment for which NHS cover could not be guaranteed. When the availability of resources inevitably effects the exercise of medical discretion, what is the future for the traditional idea of clinical freedom?

II. THE FUTURE OF CLINICAL FREEDOM

A. Rationing and the Hippocratic Oath

One of the most pressing problems in medical law concerns the current status of the Hippocratic Oath and the many international codes which have followed it. Under the Oath doctors promise: 'I will follow that system of regimen which, according to my ability

---

[4] See *The Reform of Health Care—A Comparative Analysis of Seven OECD Countries* (OECD, 1992).

and judgment, I consider for the benefit of my patients. . . . Into whatever house I enter, I will go into them [sic] for the benefit of the sick.'

The modern statement of the principle is contained in the Declaration of Geneva, published by the World Health Organisation. It says, *inter alia*, that the 'health of my patient will be my first consideration'. Similarly, the International Code of Medical Ethics provides that: 'a physician shall act only in the patient's best interests when providing medical care which might have the effect of weakening the physical and mental condition of the patient.'[5]

Exactly what counts as a patient's 'best interests' is not, and probably never could be, specified in detail. Patients present doctors with an infinite variety and combination of illnesses and reasonable doctors will naturally differ as to the best way of responding to them. Also, although the Hippocratic Oath presumes that doctors will always promote the best interests of the individual, finite resources have long meant that difficult decisions between patients may sometimes be unavoidable. In all this, however, there is nothing new. Resources have never been infinite and unenviable decisions between patients have always been made, though in a manner less visible in the past. Doctors care for groups of patients and know very well that the use of a bed or operating theatre for one patient may mean that the treatment of another will be delayed or denied altogether. For this reason elderly people have found it more difficult to be referred for surgery,[6] infertility treatment has not always been made available, those suffering mental illness have not always obtained care in hospital, and kidney dialysis has been available to relatively few. In reality, therefore, the idea of absolute clinical freedom may long have been an unaffordable myth.[7] 'It is debatable whether true clinical freedom in fact ever existed and, if it did, whether it should have been allowed. Clinicians should have to justify their clinical actions, either from documented experience, or from the literature.'[8]

[5] See these and other declarations in the appendices to *Medical Ethics Today* (British Medical Association, 1993).

[6] *The Health of the UK's Elderly People* (Medical Research Council, 1994).

[7] See J. Hampton, 'The End of Clinical Freedom', 287 *British Medical Journal* 1237 (1983).

[8] *Clinical Directorates—A Guide for Surgeons* (Royal College of Surgeons, Edinburgh, 1993) 6. 'Clinicians must come to understand why it is in their interest

Indeed, some would go further and say that the whole concept is open to abuse as a means of insulating doctors from the need to justify irrational decisions.

Rationing in the NHS has never been explicitly organised but has hidden behind each doctor's clinical freedom to act solely in the interests of his individual patient. Any conflict of interest between patients competing for scarce resources has been implicitly resolved by doctor's judgments as to their relative needs for care and attention. The clinical freedom to differ widely as to their conception of need has led to inconsistencies of treatment between patients and to the allocation, without challenge, of scarce resources to medical practices of no proven value. It is by no means clear that it is the patient who gains from clinical freedom.[9]

In sharp contrast to the latitude given by the courts, pressure is now being exerted on doctors to comply with clinical practice guidelines, to undertake medical audit of their procedures, and to be prepared to justify substantial differences between them.[10] To what extent will the differing instincts of doctors continue to be supportable? Some have individual patients uppermost in their minds and have always prescribed the best available treatment. Others with an eye on reducing expenditure may try a 'second-best' treatment first, and use the best only if that fails.[11] Modern medical ethics demand that doctors understand the economic impact of their decisions, of what economists call 'opportunity costs', i.e. the range of treatments, the opportunities, that will be forgone if the money to pay for them is diverted elsewhere. Thus, the British Medical Association has said: 'Wastage of resources is unethical because it diminishes society's capacity to relieve suffering through the other uses that could be made of the wasted resources. Doctors working within the NHS need to be aware of

---

to support the clinical director when there is unresolved managerial conflict. Hospitals that fail to achieve efficiency and effectiveness will no longer be attractive, nor indeed viable.' Ibid.

[9] M. Cooper, *Rationing Health Care* (Croom Helm, 1975) 59.

[10] See Chapter 5 above.

[11] This is the recommendation of the Audit Commission in *A Prescription for Improvement: Towards more Rational Prescribing in General Practice* (1994), para. 44: 'Practices should agree a policy that sets out their choice of first, second and third line drugs for key areas of prescribing, particularly where there are major safety considerations.'

cost-effectiveness as well as clinical effectiveness in the care provided for the patient.'[12]

But 'waste' is not a neutral word. Governments, health service managers, doctors and patients all have differing ideas about how resources should be spent. Used as a way of insisting that individual patients receive only the most effective treatment, it may not threaten the idea of clinical freedom. Doctors will be eager to uphold this usage of the word. Many believe the relationship of trust between doctor and patient is precious and that doctors should never compromise their clinical commitment to the individual.[13] The General Medical Council endorses this view and encourages doctors to adhere to their traditional Hippocratic priorities. Recognizing the importance of limited resources, it says: 'The Council endorses the principle that a doctor should always seek to give priority to the investigation and treatment of patients solely on the basis of clinical need.'[14]

By contrast, health economists will stress the need to distribute national resources efficiently and give 'waste' a different meaning. They will stress the 'macro' goals and priorities of health spending. This approach tends to emphasize the clinical benefits to whole communities, rather than to individuals, and could have considerable potential in modifying the relationship between doctors and patients. One set of guidelines, for example, has recommended that the distribution of resources by hospitals and doctors should always be consistent with the policies established by governments at national level so that: 'Health care professionals at the clinical level ought not to make any treatment decision that undermines

[12] *Medical Ethics Today, supra* note 5, 300. See also T. Brennan, *Just Doctoring: Medical Ethics in the Liberal State* (California University Press, 1991) 183: 'I believe physicians should put the beneficence model behind them. Medical ethics as just doctoring requires that physicians consider the political context in which care occurs. This includes consideration by physicians of the need to moderate health care costs. . . . One must openly recognize it as rationing, and must help to ensure that the rationing is fair.'

[13] See R. Veatch, *The Patient-Physician Relation: The Patient as Partner, Part 2* (Indiana University Press, 1991), ch. 19; and A. Relman, 'Dealing With Conflicts of Interest', 313 *New England Journal of Medicine* 749 (1985)

[14] *Contractual Arrangements in Health Care: Professional Responsibilities in Relation to the Clinical Needs of Patients* (General Medical Council, 1992), para. 8. The paragraph acknowledges, at the same time, the need to recognize the effects of medical decision-making on others.

legitimate attempts at a higher level to establish just and efficient use of resources.'[15]

This view is likely to gain ground although it is currently still in its infancy because firm evidence of the cost and effectiveness of medical treatment is unavailable. Its implications, however, are important. Were such an approach to be adopted, doctors would become more openly involved in shaping and implementing social and economic policies and their clinical freedom with respect to individuals would have to be modified as a result. This poses the most clear and coherent threat to the traditional notion of the Hippocratic Oath. On the other hand, in this most delicate and fundamental area of practice, doctors have little training in the principles (whatever they may be) which might assist them. 'Unfortunately, physicians have little experience with the task of bringing moral and social norms to bear on particular disputes and situations. [And] ethicists and jurists are not familiar with the medical and emotional nuances associated with the care of acutely ill and dying patients.'[16]

There is an urgent need for both doctors and the community to address the questions raised by these pressures.

B. Decisions Not to Treat

One of the most difficult issues a doctor may ever have to face concerns the decision not to treat a patient. The decision will always carry implications for the question of resources. Broadly, such a decision may be prompted for reasons that are entirely concerned with the patient's individual circumstances, or they may include considerations of resources. The following considers (1) futile care, (2) the substance and procedures involved in 'do not resuscitate orders' and (3) 'undeserving' patients.

1. Futile Care

Mention has already been made of the idea of 'wasting' resources.

---

[15] *Developing Guidelines for Decisions to Forgo Life-Prolonging Medical Treatment* (The Appleton International Conference, reproduced in the supplement to 18 *Journal of Medical Ethics* (1992)), Part IV, para. 16.
[16] T. Brennan, 'Do-Not-Resuscitate Orders for the Incompetent Patient in the Absence of Family Consent', 14 *Law, Medicine and Health Care* 13.

The courts have considered the matter in the context of futile treatment. What care is 'futile'?[17] In *Airedale NHS Trust* v. *Bland*,[18] a twenty-one year-old patient, Anthony Bland, suffered anoxia (oxygen starvation) after being crushed in the Hillsborough football stadium in 1989. Although he was able to breathe and his heart continued to beat unaided, by 1992 he was in a persistent vegetative state and had no prospect of regaining any degree of consciousness. The hospital sought a declaration that it would be lawful to discontinue artificial feeding, hydration, and other medical treatment in order for him to 'end his life and die peacefully with the greatest dignity and the least pain and distress.'[19]

The House of Lords decided that there was no absolute obligation to keep patients alive regardless of their condition and prospects of recovery. In extreme cases reasonable doctors are entitled to conclude that it is no longer in the patient's best interests that treatment be continued. In these circumstances, treatment can be withdrawn even in the knowledge that the consequence of doing so will be the patient's death. Lord Goff said: 'I cannot see that medical treatment is appropriate or requisite simply to prolong a patient's life when such treatment has no therapeutic purpose of any kind, as where it is futile because the patient is unconscious and there is no prospect of any improvement in his condition. . . . It is the futility of the treatment which justifies its termination.'[20]

Who is to judge futility; doctors or the courts? As a general rule, doctors are advised to seek a declaration from the High Court before terminating treatment to patients in a persistent vegetative state,[21] but this leaves open the question of the grounds on which the decision should be based. The Court of Appeal in *Bland*

---

[17] See R. Veatch and C. Mason Spicer, 'Medically Futile Care: The Role of the Physician in Setting Limits', 13 *American Journal of Law and Medicine* 15 (1992); and D. Callahan, 'Medical Futility, Medical Necessity, The Problem Without a Name', [1991] *Hastings Center Report* July/August 30.

[18] [1993] 1 All ER 821.

[19] Ibid. 824. Note that 'the question is not whether it is in the best interests of the patient that he should die. The question is whether it is in the best interests of the patient that his life should be prolonged by the continuance of this form of medical treatment or care.' See ibid. 869, *per* Lord Goff.

[20] *Airedale NHS Trust* v. *Bland* [1993] 1 All ER 821 at 870. See also Lord Keith, at 861 and Lord Mustill, 896.

[21] See Practice Note [1994] 2 All ER 413, para. 1.

believed that the case provoked moral and ethical issues that were appropriate for the court to decide. They were not exclusively for doctors. Nor, said Hoffmann LJ, 'do I think that the profession would be grateful to the court for leaving the full responsibility for such decisions in its hands'. He continued:

It seems to me that the medical profession can tell the court about the patient's condition and prognosis and about the probable consequences of giving or not giving certain kinds of treatment or care, including the provision of artificial feeding. But whether in those circumstances it would be lawful to provide or withhold the treatment or care is a matter for the law and must be decided with regard to the general moral considerations of which I have spoken. As to these matters, the medical profession will no doubt have views which are entitled to great respect, but I would expect medical ethics to be formed by the law rather than the reverse. . . . This is a purely legal (or moral) decision which does not require any medical expertise and is therefore appropriately made by the court.[22]

And in a subsequent case on similar facts, Sir Thomas Bingham MR said that 'there should not be a belief that what the doctor says is the patient's best interest *is* the patient's best interest' and he insisted that the court should retain the ultimate power and duty to review the doctor's decision in the light of all the facts.[23]

However, the House of Lords in *Bland* took the contrary view. With surprisingly little reference to views expressed in the Court of Appeal on the issue, Lord Keith said that decisions concerning the best interests of patients in continuing to receive treatment should be governed by the views of reasonable doctors. Thus:

a medical practitioner is under no duty to continue to treat such a patient where a large body of informed and responsible medical opinion is to the effect that no benefit would be conferred by continuance. Existence in a vegetative state with no prospects of recovery is by that opinion regarded as not being a benefit, and that, if not unarguably correct, at least forms a proper basis for the decision to discontinue treatment and care: see *Bolam* v. *Friern Hospital Management Committee*.[24]

[22] *Airedale NHS Trust* v. *Bland, supra* note 20, 858, *per* Hoffmann LJ. See also Butler-Sloss LJ, 845.
[23] See *Frenchay NHS Trust* v. *S* [1994] 2 All ER 403, 411 (emphasis in original), although he qualified his view by saying that the courts should be reluctant to contradict a doctor unless 'the court has real doubt about the reliability, or *bona fides*, or correctness of the medical decision in question', 412.
[24] *Airedale NHS Trust* v. *Bland, supra* note 20, 861. The House approved the BMA's guidelines in *Treatment of Patients in Persistent Vegetative State* (1992)

Notice that His Lordship did not confine his decision to patients in a vegetative state. Rather, they were one of a category of patients for whom doctors might reasonably consider that treatment would provide no benefit. Similarly, Lord Browne-Wilkinson, addressing the issue of the non-clinical judgments which doctors bring to this area of practice, said:

Different doctors may take different views both on strictly medical issues and the broader ethical issues which the question raises. . . . The doctor's answer may well be influenced by his own attitude to the sanctity of human life. *In cases where there is no strictly medical point in continuing care*,[25] if a doctor holds the view that the patient is entitled to stay alive, whatever the quality of such life, he can quite reasonably reach the view that the continuation of intrusive care, being the only way of preserving such life, is in the patient's best interests. But, in the same circumstances another doctor who sees no merit in perpetuating a life of which the patient is unaware can equally reasonably reach the view that the continuation of treatment is not for the patient's benefit. Accordingly, on an application to the court for a declaration that the discontinuance of medical care will be lawful, the court's only concern will be to be satisfied that the doctor's decision to discontinue is in accordance with a respectable body of medical opinion and that it is responsible.[26]

He continued: 'In the end it is a matter of personal choice, dictated by his or her background, upbringing, education, convictions and temperament. Legal expertise gives no special advantage here.'[27]

---

which recommend that (i) every effort at rehabilitation should be made for six months, (ii) diagnosis should not be considered confirmed until 12 months, (iii) it should be confirmed by two independent doctors, and (iv) the wishes of the patient's immediate family should be given great weight.

[25] The principle would not, therefore, extend to insulate from liability a Jehovah's Witness consultant who refused to offer a blood transfusion.

[26] *Airedale NHS Trust* v. *Bland, supra* note 20, 833, *per* Lord Browne-Wilkinson, emphasis added.

[27] Ibid. 887. The only cautionary note was sounded by Lord Mustill at 895 who said: 'I venture some reservations about the application of . . . *Bolam* . . . to decisions on "best interests" in a field dominated by criminal law. I accept without difficulty that this principle applies to the ascertainment of the medical raw material such as diagnosis, prognosis and appraisal of the patient's cognitive functions. Beyond this point, however, it may be said that the decision is ethical not medical and there is no reason in logic why on such a decision the opinions of doctors should be decisive.'

Given this latitude, one would expect pressure to extend the concept of 'futility' and the decisions in *Bland*[28] contemplate the possibility of a similar approach being taken in other cases in which the damage is less severe, for example 'the very poor *quality of the life* which may be prolonged for the patient if the treatment is successful';[29] or those suffering the advanced stages of Guillain-Barré syndrome, in which the patient retains some measure of consciousness, but whose brain stem is so damaged that the patient loses all power of movement, including the autonomic reactions of the heart and lungs.[30] Reasoning of this kind has been applied to a baby who was not terminally ill but, whilst retaining some intellectual capacity, suffered spastic quadriplegia, blindness, and deafness. He was unable to react to his environment, and would suffer pain, especially from the mechanical ventilation which was needed from time to time. His 'life would be so afflicted as to be intolerable'[31] and the court ordered, on the recommendation of a consultant, that the local authority responsible for the child be free not to resuscitate the child if he went into crisis.[32] On the other hand, Down's syndrome would not be so awful as to fall into this category,[33] nor the life of a seven year-old victim of meningitis who suffered profound brain-damage as a baby and was unable to interact with his environment.[34]

Clearly, judgments of this nature are highly intuitive and often defy rational analysis. Is it futile to continue to treat those suffering from the advanced symptoms of Alzheimer's disease who are conscious but whose memory and personality have largely been destroyed?[35] Is it futile to treat a ten-year-old suffering

---

[28] Except for Lord Browne-Wilkinson who restricted himself to the facts of *Bland*, *supra* note 20, 884.

[29] Ibid., see Lord Goff at 869, emphasis added. His Lordship considered the case of those brought into hospital and preserved on life support systems.

[30] Ibid., see Lord Goff at 873, and the judgment in *Auckland Area Health Board* v. *A-G of New Zealand* [1993] 1 NZLR 235, to which he paid tribute, 868.

[31] See Re *J (a minor)* [1990] 3 All ER 930, 945.

[32] See also Re *J (a minor)* [1992] 4 All ER 614, no obligation to treat a child with a very short life expectation with comparable afflictions, despite the wishes of the foster mother that treatment be provided.

[33] See Re *B (A Minor)* [1981] 1 WLR 1421.

[34] See Re *Superintendent of Family and Child Service and Dawson* (1983) 145 DLR (3d) 610 (Supreme Court of British Columbia).

[35] See *In the Matter of Claire Conroy* (1985) 486 A 2d 1209 (Supreme Ct, New Jersey). In the absence of her own clear wish that treatment should not be

leukaemia when the chance of a successful outcome is around 2 per cent? In *R* v. *Cambridge DHA,* ex p *B*[35a] the Court of Appeal endorsed the opinion of the responsible health authority that, in the clinical circumstances of the case, treatment need not be provided. What if the chance of success had been 22 per cent? A line must be drawn somewhere. Is it proper for doctors to be given so much discretion in matters which are not primarily clinical? This brings us to the substance and procedure of decisions to withdraw treatment from patients. No doubt, doctors will be available to support both sides of the question. Is it proper that so much discretion should be given to doctors in matters which are not primarily concerned with clinical discretion? This brings us to 'do not resuscitate' orders and the way in which they have been used in practice.

2. Do Not Resuscitate Orders

When are 'do not resuscitate orders' (DNRs) issued and to what procedures are they subject? Decisions to use DNRs in hospital are not uncommon and doctors have candidly identified a number of factors they would consider relevant to such a decision.[36] They make no secret of their differences of opinion. Consider, however, that there are some 18,000 consultants and 30,000 general practitioners in this country. Inevitably, they will represent a vast cross-section of views about non-resuscitation. Religious convictions may play a part in the decisions taken by some, particularly in matters concerning the sanctity of life. The Roman Catholic Church and orthodox Jews oppose the withdrawal of life-support.[37] Others may refuse cardiopulmonary resuscitation to

---

continued (the subjective test, eg in a living will), or the trustworthy evidence of someone else to the same effect (the limited-objective test), or that the burdens of treatment outweighed its benefits (pure-objective test), treatment should not be withdrawn.

[35a] [1995] 2 All ER 129, discussed at 131–33, *supra.*

[36] See generally, L. Blackhall, 'Must We Always Use CPR?', 317 *New England Journal of Medicine* 1281 (1987); B. Lo *et al.,* 'Do Not Resuscitate Orders: A Prospective Study at Three Teaching Hospitals' 145 *Archives of Internal Medicine* 1115 (1985); T. Brennan, 'Ethics Committees and Decisions to Limit Care: The Experience at the Massachusetts General Hospital' 268 *Journal of the American Medical Association* 803 (1985).

[37] See *Bland supra* note 20, *per* Lord Browne-Wilkinson, 879.

elderly patients for fear of causing indignity,[38] or because they have become 'highly dependent on others'.[39] On the other hand, some say that loss of dignity arises from 'the way we care for our sufferers . . . , not from the illness itself'[40] and that the provision of a better environment for elderly patients suffering dementia would prevent the question from arising. For others 'the patient's social environment'[41] is a factor to be taken into account in making the decision, as is the issue of NHS resources.[42] Some would offer haemodialysis to married women with children in preference to a labourer of no fixed abode,[43] but not to those who are under five, or over fifty, or over sixty-five, or too intelligent, or too unintelligent.[44] The literature indicates that a range of highly intuitive factors are used to guide the profession. Inevitably, there will be considerable inconsistency, both between different doctors and in the same doctor from time to time, as to the precise circumstances in which they will be thought appropriate. So long as reasonable doctors can be found to support them, the House of Lords has laid down no standard of its own by which the lawfulness of these differences can be judged.

There is another concern. To what extent can the profession be

---

[38] Ibid. 870. Lord Goff sympathized with such a view. He said: 'it is reasonable also that account should be taken of the invasiveness of the treatment and of the indignity to which . . . a person has to be subjected if his life is prolonged by artificial means.'

[39] R. Gulati, G. Bhan, M. Horan, 'Cardiopulmonary Resuscitation of Old People', [1983] *The Lancet* 267, 269 and J. Henderson, M. Goldacre, M. Griffiths, 'Hospital Care for the Elderly in the Last Year of Life', 301 *British Medical Journal* 17 (1990).

[40] E. Murphy, 'Ethical Dilemmas of Brain Failure in the Elderly', 288 *British Medical Journal* 61 (1984). In one survey, one-third of doctors asked by patients to take active steps to hasten their deaths had done so. See B. Ward & P. Tate, 'Attitudes among doctors to requests for euthenasia' 308 *British Medical Journal* 1332 (1994).

[41] P. Baskett, 'The Ethics of Resuscitation', 293 *British Medical Journal* 189 (1986).

[42] See T. Hope, D. Springings, R. Crisp, ' "Not Clinically Indicated": Patients' Interest or Resource Allocation?', 306 *British Medical Journal* 379 (1993); N. Dudley and E. Burns, 'The Influence of Age on Policies for Admission and Thrombolysis in Coronary Care Units', 21 *Age and Aging* 95 (1992).

[43] See J. Nabarro, 'Selection of Patients for Haemodialysis: Who Best to Make the Choice?', [1967] I *British Medical Journal* 622; and C. Ogg, 'Maintenance Haemodialysis and Renal Transplantation', 4 *British Medical Journal* 412 (1970).

[44] See the illuminating study by T. Halper, *The Misfortunes of Others: End-Stage Renal Dialysis in the United Kingdom* (Cambridge University Press, 1989), particularly 109–28.

sure that its intuition as to the propriety of a DNR is grounded on an accurate assessment of the patient's circumstances? After all, hasty or ill-informed decisions may not be reversible. The issue was considered by the Health Service Ombudsman in a case concerning the emergency admission to hospital of an elderly woman suffering bronchopneumonia.[45] Her son had informed the staff that she was still active and enjoyed a good quality of life. Five days later he noticed that 'not for the 222s' had been noted on her medical record, meaning that if she were to go into crisis the nurses should not telephone the internal emergency number in order to summon help. He was concerned because, by this time, her condition had improved and she was eventually able to go home. He asked the hospital and the DHA about their policy on resuscitation, but failed to receive a satisfactory reply. He referred the matter to the Ombudsman whose report revealed a worrying degree of laxity surrounding decisions not to resuscitate.

There had been a misunderstanding between the medical staff as to the intended duration of the DNR. The doctor originally responsible for the instruction said that he intended it to endure for twenty-four hours only and, since he had not renewed it on the ward round the following day, had impliedly cancelled it. His colleagues, however, had no knowledge of such a system and believed the order remained operative until expressly cancelled. Obviously, such a misunderstanding was extremely dangerous. The Ombudsman found that, at the time, no policy existed to guide doctors in these cases; indeed, that 'production of a policy on such a tricky issue was represented to me as something of a novelty in the National Health Service.'[46] The Ombudsman was so concerned about this apparent lack of agreement as to questions of this nature that he referred the matter to the Chief Medical Officer of the Department of Health who responded by stating that it 'lies with a consultant to ensure that his or her policy [on resuscitation], whether it is written or not, is understood by all staff who may be involved, and in particular by junior staff'.[47]

[45] See *Report of the Health Service Commissioner. (Selected Investigations completed October 1990—March 1991)* (HC 482, 1991) 50.
[46] Select Committee on the Parliamentary Commissioner for Administration, *Reports of the Health Service Commissioner for 1990–91* (HC 44–i, Session 1991–92) 24. At the time, no hospital in the country had such a policy. See ibid.
[47] Letter of the Chief Medical Officer to all the consultants in England on 'Resuscitation Policy', PL/CMO(91)22.

One wonders why more specific guidelines were not suggested. Certainly, one cannot be specific about individual cases in which a DNR would be appropriate. Patients and the conditions they present are different. But it would be possible to indicate the considerations which ought to be taken into account in arriving at such a decision. How often should the DNR be reviewed? Ought relatives to be informed unless the patient wishes otherwise? (They may be able to inform doctors of the patient's own wishes.) To what extent should nurses with day-to-day experience of caring for the patient be involved? How should the patient him or herself be approached about the matter and to what extent should non-clinical matters be considered relevant to the decision?

For the moment the common law generously permits doctors to make choices on the basis of considerations which are not strictly clinical. Recall too that health service managers also influence practice in this area. The case of *Collier*, discussed in Chapter 4, demonstrates that they too have enjoyed freedom from any meaningful review by the courts. It must be said, however, that the grounds for exercising so little supervision over this area are so insubstantial, so unpersuasive, that the matter is bound to be challenged in the future. Both as to matters of substance and procedure, the grounds on which these questions are decided must be subjected to closer examination.

3. 'Undeserving' Patients

What if a patient is the author of his own misfortune? He is obese,[48] or a heavy smoker, or drinker. Ought a patient to be considered for cardiac by-pass surgery whose chosen life-style has contributed to his condition?[49] There is nothing in the Hippocratic Oath about the reciprocal obligations of patients to look after themselves and some doctors have taken a forthright approach to those who refuse to co-operate with the pre-conditions set for surgery.[50] Consider the following:

---

[48] Obesity costs the NHS £200 million per year on treatment and related illnesses according to *Obesity* (Office of Health Economics, 1994)

[49] See M. Underwood and J. Bailey, 'Coronary bypass surgery should not be offered to smokers', 306 *British Medical Journal* 1047 (1993).

[50] See 'Smoker refused operation', *The Times* 8 Oct. 1993.

I have had patients in the past who were intravenous drug users who injected filthy materials into their veins. These materials tend to lodge on the heart valves and cause infections, destroying the valves. For one patient, we replaced his own valve with an artificial one. Later the same month, the patient was readmitted with the same problem, having infected the artificial valve. . . . What does medical ethics demand of me in such a case?[51]

In principle, so long as the decision to refuse treatment can be confined to clinical grounds, namely that the desired medical benefit cannot be achieved because of the patient's behaviour, it may be justifiable. However, there are at least two significant difficulties with this approach. First, how can we isolate the clinical reasons for the refusal from the judgmental or social? Many of us deliberately expose ourselves to risk by driving fast cars, or playing football. Should doctors be able to refuse treatment to accountants and lawyers in the City who choose to work under conditions of great stress and so expose themselves to risk of cardiac disorder? Also, many of us have no real choice in exposing ourselves to danger. Those in the emergency services regularly face danger for the benefit of others and to earn a living. In addition, environmental, genetic, and psychological factors may have an effect which is difficult to quantify.[52] Indeed, there is evidence of a close correlation between social class and poor health, and that socio-economic circumstances play the major part in differences in health between individuals. For example, the problems associated with smoking, drinking, and diet are more prevalent in lower social groups.

[Even] when studies are able to control for factors like smoking and drinking, a sizeable proportion of the health gap remains and factors related to the general living conditions and environment of the poor are indicated. . . . [T]here is also a growing body of evidence that material and structural factors, such as housing and income, can effect health. Most importantly, several studies have shown how adverse social conditions can limit the choice of life-style and . . . living and working

---

[51] T. Brennan, *Just Doctoring, supra* note 12, 176. The author also discusses an AIDS patient who threatened and spat at nurses. See 147–52.

[52] See the discussion in *Choices in Health Care* (Ministry of Welfare, Health and Cultural Affairs, The Netherlands, 1992) 62.

conditions appear to impose severe restrictions on an individual's ability to choose a healthy life-style.[53]

The second problem concerns the interests of third parties. Obviously, a refusal to treat a promiscuous patient with a contagious sexual disease would expose others to risk of infection. This could not be justified on moral or economic grounds. More subtle are the interests of children and other dependents if parents are not treated. Who, in these cases, would really suffer? Ultimately, therefore, except perhaps in a very narrow band of cases in which the patient is unlikely to derive clinical benefit from treatment, the problems involved in making distinctions on these grounds are so difficult that doctors ought not to make them.[54] The General Medical Council has issued particular advice with respect to contagious diseases and says that it is unethical to refuse treatment on the ground that the patient suffers, or may suffer, from a condition which could expose the doctor to personal risk. It continues: 'It is equally unethical for a doctor to withhold treatment from any patient on the basis of a moral judgment that the patient's activities or life-style might have contributed to the condition for which treatment was being sought. Unethical behaviour of this kind may raise a question of serious professional misconduct.'[55]

Is this also an accurate statement of law? Certainly, GPs' Terms of Service do not contemplate the possibility of withholding treatment on the basis of moral judgments, and an NHS Trust or health authority which sought to do so could be challenged for its failure to provide a 'comprehensive health service' under the National Health Service Act 1977. Let us go one step further. Even if we accept that no patient can be described as 'undeserving', are some patients more deserving than others? A young woman has just been run down by a drunken driver. Both are critically hurt. Who should receive treatment in the only intensive care unit available (assuming their injuries are equal), the young woman or the drunk driver? What if the driver is the only bread-winner for

---

[53] M. Whitehead, *The Health Divide*, in *Inequalities in Health* (Pelican, 1988) 305.

[54] See R. Veatch, *The Physician–Patient Relation*, *supra* note 13, ch. 21.

[55] *HIV Infection and AIDS: The Ethical Considerations* (General Medical Council, 1993) para. 7. 'Serious professional misconduct' is discussed at 262–65 *supra*.

his wife and children? Obviously, one's instincts are torn. The circumstances of the accident might sway the decision in favour of the young woman. The interests of third parties, however, incline us in the opposite direction. This is different from the situation in which categories of patient are marked out in advance as 'undeserving' in that it arises from a practical difficulty rather than a deliberate policy. The law finds itself unable to make distinctions of this delicacy about which reasonable people are entitled to disagree, and the court is unlikely to interfere with any such decision.

III. NON-TREATMENT AND THE LAW OF DISCLOSURE

Scarce resources throw new light on the relationship of trust between doctor and patient, and the duty of candour between them. When a doctor decides not to treat a competent patient, should the fact be disclosed to the patient? Failures of communication have always been a major source of complaint from patients. The Audit Commission is critical of the steps taken by hospitals to ensure that patients are kept informed about treatment and the options available to them.[56] Insufficient time is spent talking to patients. Sometimes the circumstances of the discussion, eg in the aftermath of bad news, are such that few patients will be capable of considered questioning; or patients may be informed of the risks and complications of surgery at an inappropriate time. The Commission recommends, for example, that patients awaiting elective surgery should be told about the risks and complications before the decision to operate is made in order to allow time for sensible reflection.

But fifty per cent of the urologists and surgeons in [the study] who treat men with benign prostatic hyperplasia do not mention the risks and complications associated with transuretheral resection of the prostate in the out-patient clinic unless the patient asks about them. Instead, they leave that discussion to the junior doctor who interviews the patient on the ward, to obtain his signed consent just before the operation. This means that the patient first hears of the risks after the decision to operate has been made.[57]

---

[56] See *What Seems to be the Matter: Communication between Hospitals and Patients* (Audit Commission, HMSO, 1993).   [57] Ibid. para. 63.

What are the doctor's duties of disclosure to the patient or relatives? We discuss the cases on the general duty to disclose risks before moving to the specific issue of withholding treatment.

A. The General Duty to Disclose Risks

The doctor's right to treat depends on the patient's consent to treatment. 'Every human being of adult years and sound mind has a right to determine what shall be done with his own body; and a surgeon who performs an operation without his patient's consent commits an assault.'[58]

There are two actions available to a patient who has been treated without consent: trespass to the person and negligence. The less commonly used remedy is the action for trespass to the person (assault and battery) which is available only in circumstances in which the doctor has proceeded with a treatment for which the patient has given no effective consent whatsoever, e.g. where the doctor sterilizes patients who have consented to a caesarian section,[59] an abortion,[60] or the repair of her uterus.[61] Only if the procedure is immediately necessary to save life or preserve health will the doctor be entitled to dispense with the prior obligation to obtain the patient's consent.[62] However, the courts have made clear their reluctance to allow doctors to be pursued by an action in trespass which overlaps with the criminal law.

Trespass ceases to be an appropriate action once the patient has consented to the nature of the operation, even when details of the risks and side-effects have not been adequately disclosed. In this case, the proper ground of complaint is negligence. Thus: 'once the patient is informed in broad terms of the nature of the procedure which is intended, and gives her consent, that consent is

---

[58] *Schloendorff* v. *Society of New York Hospital* (1914) 211 NY 125, 126, *per* Cardozo J. See H. Teff, *Reasonable Care* (OUP, 1994) ch. 6.

[59] E.g. *Hamilton* v. *Birmingham RHB* (1969) 2 *British Medical Journal* 456.

[60] E.g. *Cull* v. *Royal Surrey County Hospital* (1932) 1 *British Medical Journal* 1195.

[61] E.g. *Devi* v. *West Midlands RHA* [1980] CL 687.

[62] E.g. *Marshall* v. *Curry* [1933] 3 DLR 260. During an operation for the repair of a hernia, the surgeon removed a grossly diseased testicle which might have become gangrenous. No assault.

real, and the cause of action on which to base a claim for failure to go into risks and implications is negligence, not trespass.'[63] The majority of medical procedures involve an element of risk. In negligence, therefore, the question is how and how much the doctor ought to tell the patient. The mere signing of a consent form will be worthless if the patient is unable to comprehend any previous explanation of its effect. Hospitals undoubtedly use consent forms in order to protect themselves from legal action, but: 'They will be wholly ineffective for this purpose if the patient is incapable of understanding them, they are not explained to him and there is no good evidence (apart from the patient's signature) that he had understanding and fully appreciated the significance of signing it.'[64]

For this reason, patients who are not told of the real nature of an operation,[65] or who are only told while being sedated before an operation[66] may not be in a position to give consent to risks. What of the extent of the discussion required of doctors? The leading case is that of *Sidaway* in which a patient agreed with the advice of her doctor that she should have a laminectomy to her spine to relieve pain caused by the oppression of nerve roots. She was not informed that the surgery carried an unavoidable risk, even when performed carefully, of interfering with blood vessels around the spine. The likelihood of such an event was less than 2 per cent and the risk was of temporary or permanent immobility. In the most serious case, the patient would suffer partial paralysis. In the event, this most serious risk materialized. The plaintiff's complaint was that she ought to have been informed about these risks and that, had she known about them, she would have chosen more conservative treatment (say) by analgesics which carried less risk. Their Lordships, though expressing differing views, agreed that the matter is largely, though not entirely, within the discretion of the medical profession. Lord Bridge said:

[63] *Chatterton* v. *Gerson* [1981] 1 All ER 257, 265. Apparent consent may be vitiated by fraud, e.g. doctors who offer treatment for AIDS which they wrongly claim to be effective. See *Sidaway* v. *Royal Bethlem Hospital Governors* [1984] 1 All ER 1018, 1026, *per* Lord Donaldson MR.

[64] *Re T (adult: refusal of medical treatment)* [1992] 4 All ER 649, 663, *per* Lord Donaldson MR.

[65] See *Coughlin* v. *Kuntz* [1990] 2 WWR 737.

[66] See *Beausoleil* v. *La Communauté des Soeurs de la Charité de Providence* (1964) 53 DLR (2d) 65.

the issue whether non-disclosure in a particular case should be condemned as a breach of the doctor's duty of care is an issue to be decided primarily on the basis of expert medical evidence, applying the *Bolam* test. . . . But even in a case where . . . no expert in the relevant medical field condemns the non-disclosure as being in conflict with accepted and responsible medical practice, I am of opinion that the judge might in certain circumstances come to the conclusion that disclosure of a particular risk was so obviously necessary to an informed choice on the part of the patient that no reasonably prudent medical man would fail to make it.[67]

Similarly, Lord Templeman said that, notwithstanding medical discretion, there was no doubt that a doctor ought to draw the attention of the patient to dangers which may be special in kind or magnitude or special to the patient.[68] More cautiously, Lord Diplock inclined to the view that 'the *Bolam* test of medical negligence should be applied'[69] since the issues of disclosure of risks and the standard of care in treatment concerned the same exercise of professional skill and should be governed by the same test. But he too stopped short of declaring the matter to be wholly within the discretion of doctors because some categories of patient would be entitled to information sufficient to enable them to decide for themselves whether or not to go ahead with the treatment. He said:

When it comes to warning about risks, the kind of training and experience that a judge will have undergone at the Bar makes it natural for him to say (correctly) *it is my right to decide* whether any particular thing is done to my body, and I want to be fully informed of any risks there may be involved of which I am not already aware from my general knowledge as a highly educated man of experience, so that *I may form my own judgment* as to whether to refuse the advised treatment or not.[70]

Thus, the matter does not lie within the absolute discretion of the doctor. This is more clearly the case when a patient asks the doctor for specific information. Lord Diplock continued: 'No doubt, if the patient in fact manifested this attitude by means of questioning, the doctor would tell him whatever it was the patient wanted to know.'[71] His Lordship used the example of judges, but

---

[67] *Sidaway, supra* note 63, 662. Lord Keith agreed.   [68] Ibid. 665.
[69] Ibid. 659.   [70] Ibid. 659, emphasis added.
[71] Ibid. Lord Bridge agreed, saying at 661: '. . . when questioned specifically by a patient of apparently sound mind about risks involved in a particular treatment proposed, the doctor's duty must . . . be to answer both truthfully and as fully as the questioner requires.'

it must also be true of other educated and experienced people. It must be true of doctors who seek medical advice; it could extend to nurses, barristers, and a host of professional and other people. Curiously, however, in subsequent cases the Court of Appeal has been reluctant to explore the extent to which the judgment in *Sidaway* permits the court to impose its own standards of disclosure on doctors. Rather, it has adopted a passive and uncritical approach to medical discretion. In *Blyth* v. *Bloomsbury Health Authority*[72] the plaintiff was a qualified nurse and a health worker in London. She was prescribed the long-acting contraceptive drug, Depo-Provera. Having previously reacted very badly to a contraceptive drug, she had good reason to ask specific questions of her doctor about Depo-Provera on this occasion; and her training enabled her to understand the information she sought. She alleged that she was not given an adequate warning of the side-effects of the drug and would have chosen other means of contraception had her questions been answered properly. Rejecting her claim, the Court of Appeal said that doctors were entitled, within the boundary set by *Bolam*, to determine how much information should be disclosed to patients, even to the extent of deciding if and how specific questions should be answered. Kerr LJ said 'I am not convinced that the *Bolam* test is irrelevant even in relation to the question of what answers are properly to be given to specific enquiries'.[73]

This result is particularly surprising given the entirely elective nature of the treatment given. When there is no medical 'need' for treatment, why should the doctor be presumed to know what is best? However, the Court of Appeal adopted the same view in a case of a failed sterilization operation. In *Gold* v. *Haringey Health Authority* the plaintiff argued that, given the non-therapeutic nature of the operation, she should have been free to choose for herself what was best. Her claim was dismissed on the ground that it was a matter of professional discretion.[74] Does this mean doctors can lie to patients in order, for example, to allay their fears? In 1954 Lord Denning said this was permissible. The case concerned a broadcaster who had a toxic thyroid gland. She was concerned about the risk which an operation presented to her voice and was

[72] [1993] 4 MedLR 151.   [73] Ibid. 157. Neill LJ agreed: 160.
[74] See *Gold* v. *Haringey Health Authority* [1987] 2 All ER 888.

assured that there was none. The reassurance was well intended but misleading and the plaintiff's voice was damaged in the operation so that she was no longer able to broadcast. Lord Denning said that although her doctor had told a lie, other doctors were not prepared to criticize him, and nor would the court.[75]

This uncritical application of the *Bolam* test to the duty of disclosure seems wrong, both in principle and under the tests expounded by their Lordships in *Sidaway*. Certainly, in Canada[76] and Australia[77] it has been rejected as an inappropriate means of assessing a patient's consent to treatment because:

> there is a fundamental difference between, on the one hand, diagnosis and treatment and, on the other hand, the provision of clear information to the patient. . . . Because the choice to be made calls for a decision by the patient . . . it would be illogical to hold that the amount of information to be provided by the medical practitioner can be determined from the perspective of the practitioner alone or, for that matter, of the medical profession.[78]

Why should English judges be so indulgent toward the different *styles* of practice that doctors adopt, their differences of 'bedside manner'? Some may consider themselves to be in partnership with the patient so that decisions concerning the risks and benefits of treatment, or non-treatment, would be discussed candidly for a shared view to be reached of the clinical and the personal sides of the case. Others, however, may practice in a more detached manner. They may regard themselves more as skilled assessors, engaged to offer professional advice about a technical problem, but not to enter discussion about personal preferences. Alternatively, doctors may consider themselves to be 'healers' whose job is to make people better. They would not normally expect to discuss the risks and benefits of other treatments, or to

---

[75] See *Hatcher* v. *Black*, *The Times* 2 July 1954. Contrast his view in *Chapman* v. *Rix* (1994) 5 Med LR 239, 248, in which he said that such an approach was understandable but should never prejudice the right of patient to receive proper treatment.

[76] See *Reibl* v. *Hughes* (1980) 114 DLR (3d) 1; and G. Robertson, 'Informed Consent Ten Years Later: The Impact of *Reibl* v. *Hughes*' (1991) 70 *Canadian Bar Review* 423.

[77] *Rogers* v. *Whitaker* (1992) 109 ALR 625, [1990] 1 Med LR 463.

[78] Ibid., 632.

explain the reasoning for their clinical decision.[79] Lord Scarman in his dissenting judgment in *Sidaway* adopted a more demanding view of the duty to disclose information and there is a feeling that 'it must now only be a matter of time'[80] before English law adopts a presumption of openness and candour between doctor and patient similar to that applied in Australia and Canada. Indeed, such an approach has been adopted in a recent case concerning a patient suffering from a rectal prolapse. The doctor failed to warn his patient that the operation to remedy the condition could cause erectile and bladder dysfunction. The operation was not essential, because the patient had learned how to manage the problems which the condition presented. Nevertheless, it was performed and the damage occurred. The patient said that had he been told of those risks he would have refused the operation. The doctor was able to find colleagues who would not have made such disclosure in these circumstances. This support notwithstanding, the judge said: 'although some surgeons may still not have been warning patients similar in situation to the plaintiff of the risk of impotence, that omission was neither reasonable nor responsible.'[81]

Thus, the failure was held to have been negligent on the court's own assessment of the facts of the case.

B. Disclosure of Non-treatment

Against this general background, how does the law apply to decisions to withhold treatment? The cost of medical intervention is being more accurately quantified, doctors are being made aware of the cost implications of their decisions, they are often responsible for the management of specific budgets, and patients are becoming aware of the difficult choices which have to be made between deserving cases. What then is the doctor's duty of disclosure when treatment is denied for financial reasons?

A strong pragmatic case can be made that an obligation to disclose the reasons for failing to treat a patient in these

[79] See the discussion in R. Veatch, *The Patient–Physician Relation, supra* note 13, 11–15.
[80] See I. Kennedy and A Grubb, *Medical Law: Text with Materials* (Butterworths, 2nd edn.) 200.
[81] *Smith* v. *Tunbridge Wells HA* [1994] 5 Med LR 334, 339.

circumstances ought to be imposed. A patient refused access to care on economic grounds for whom treatment could provide valuable medical benefit should be able to consider whether he or she could obtain the treatment privately. That opportunity may be denied unless the reasons for the decision not to treat are made clear. Or, the patient might wish to become involved in modifying the way in which the system of priorities has been set, or to raise the matter with his MP.

Some patients may have their own resources for obtaining medical care. . . . Others may choose to invest their energies in trying to change rationing policies rather than passively accepting [them]. In any event, many patients may have personal or professional priorities and commitments that would change in the light of full, truthful information about their medical conditions and treatment options. To deny such patients such information is to compromise the exercise of personal autonomy, the *raison d'être* of the informed consent doctrine.[82]

Also, as a matter of principle, the law of disclosure is intended to promote the relationship of trust and confidence between doctor and patient. 'The relationship . . . is based on the concept of partnership and collaborative effort. Ideally decisions are made through frank discussion, in which the doctor's clinical expertise and the patient's individual needs and preferences are shared, to select the best option.'[83] Unless medical decisions based on economic considerations are disclosed to the patient the relationship risks substantial erosion. The need is made more urgent because the system of buying care in the internal market may introduce conflicts of interest between doctor and patient.[84] Fundholding practices, with an obligation of 'managing the allotted sum effectively and efficiently',[85] may be under pressure to preserve their allowances, or wish to change the patterns of their treatment altogether (say) by targeting particular categories of patient in

[82] F. Miller, 'Denial of Health Care and Informed Consent in English and American Law' 18 *American Journal of Law and Medicine* 38, 71 (1992).

[83] *Medical Ethics Today*, *supra* note 5; 1.

[84] T. Brennan, 'An Ethical Perspective on Health Insurance Reform', 19 *American Journal of Law and Medicine* 46, 66 (1993).

[85] See Sched. 2, para. 5 of the National Health Service (Fund-holding Practices) Reg. 1993, SI 1993, No. 567. Failure to do so entitles the Regional Health Authority to remove the recognition as a fund-holding practice. See ibid. and Part IV of the Regulations.

favour of others. And NHS Trust hospitals may wish to maximize revenue from referrals by focusing on particular categories of treatment, or patient, at the expense of others.

When hospital treatment can no longer be provided to a satisfactory standard as a result of inadequate resources, the Medical Defence Union advises its members as follows:

Should the level of medical or support services reach a critical point, [doctors] may have to use their judgment and not expose patients to a particular hazard. This may mean postponing investigations, admissions or courses of treatment. It will certainly mean giving full details to individual patients as their consent may not be valid if they have not been told of the risks which may arise from poor facilities.[86]

Take the case of a doctor who is concerned with cost. He recommends a course of action to his patient which he knows is not the best available, though he believes it will be effective. He knows, however, that if he were treating himself, or a member of his own family, he would certainly choose the best available treatment. Ought the fact to be disclosed? Two cases suggest that the doctor is under an obligation to inform a patient of the range of treatment options available. In *Haughian* v. *Paine*[87] the Saskatchewan Court of Appeal considered a case very similar to *Sidaway*. The plaintiff was not warned of the inevitable risks which attended a laminectomy and suffered disability. Departing from the majority in the House of Lords, the court held that the patient ought to have been given the opportunity to consider the merits of conservative treatment which avoided surgery. Under the obligation of disclosure there was the duty 'to advise the appellant of the consequences of leaving the ailment untreated and the duty to advise of alternate means of treatment'.[88] It is the duty to advise of alternate treatment which is of interest. Presumably, such a duty would include the obligation to discuss treatment which is not available under the NHS for reasons of cost, so that the patient could decide what action to take in the light of that information. No such argument has been considered in the English courts, but it has an appealing logic if the duty of trust and confidence is to be preserved.

A more onerous duty was imposed by a majority of the Supreme

[86] *Medical Defence Union, Annual Report, 1988* 22.
[87] 37 DLR (4th) 624 (1987).   [88] Ibid. 639.

Court of California in *Truman* v. *Thomas*[89] to inform patients of the dangers of *not* consenting to a cervical smear. The patient said that she could not afford the costs involved. Her cancer of the cervix remained undiagnosed until it became inoperable and from which she died. It was not sufficient simply to offer his advice; given the patient's symptoms the doctor 'has the additional duty of advising of all the material risks of which a reasonable person would want to be informed before deciding not to undergo the procedure'.[90] This too signals a duty to disclose all the information needed for a patient to do what is best. On the other hand, the dissenting opinion of Clark J recognized the practical and economic implications of the decision. He said such an onerous duty 'will result in reduced care for others. Requiring physicians to spend a large portion of their time teaching medical science before practising it will greatly increase the cost of medical diagnosis—a cost ultimately paid by an unwilling public'.[91]

This difference of opinion highlights precisely the potential for conflict between the rights and expectations of individual patients and the needs of the community. Equally, were the rights of the individual to be completely subsumed on grounds of medical cost, the nature of the doctor–patient relationship would change radically. Arguably, if doctors are to be put in the position of rationing care, they should not have to make such decisions in the course of their day-to-day practice and the extent that they affect individuals should be known to both doctor and patient. This means that patients should have access to the guidelines which recommend when treatment should not be offered in order both to preserve the confidence which ought to exist between them and to enable alternative steps to be taken if the patient so desires.

No English case has gone this far. If an operation is cancelled for reasons associated with resources, is the patient entitled to know why so that, if needs be, they can challenge the decision or take steps to find treatment elsewhere? If the patient belongs to a low-priority category for reasons of their own life-style (e.g. smokers and drinkers), or the category of referring GP (e.g. not a fund-holder), should the patient be told? Should the patient be entitled to know that a decision has been made to use a less expensive, or less effective, method of treatment? In principle, there ought to be

---

[89] (1980) 611 P. 2d 902. [90] Ibid. 906. [91] Ibid. 910.

a presumption that patients would prefer to know about the non-technical aspects of their treatment, or non-treatment. The *Patient's Charter* does not recognize such a general right,[92] except in accident and emergency units which have to conduct a system of triage as a means of prioritizing between patients. It says: 'Every patient attending an accident and emergency department should be seen immediately and their need for treatment clinically assessed by an appropriately qualified person. . . . Departments categorise patients in different ways. What is important is that patients understand the process and the reasons why they may have to wait longer than others.'[93]

Is there any good reason for affording those in emergency units greater rights to information than those whose needs are 'urgent', or those on standard waiting lists? No convincing distinction can be made between these cases.

Perhaps there was once a time when doctors had fewer patients,[94] when they could spend longer at their bedsides, were trusted and respected by families and communities, and when 'Doctor's orders' possessed real authority. In such circumstances, there is less need for patients' rights and charters; the harmony between the parties makes them unnecessary. Whatever the reason, this is not now the case. The relationship is now described as an equal partnership.[95] We are less deferential, more litigious, and more concerned about quality. The momentum of these changes, however, is to incline the system of medical care toward an environment more familiar to lawyers.[96] The system of funding in the NHS depends on 'contracts'; *The Patient's Charter*[97] creates

[92] Although it does say that 'your operation should not be cancelled on the day you are due to arrive in hospital. However, this could happen because of emergencies or staff sickness. If exceptionally, your operation has to be postponed twice you will be admitted to hospital within one month of the date of the second cancelled operation.' See *Patient's Charter* (Department of Health, 1991) 14.

[93] *The Patient's Charter News* (Issue no. 1, March 1992) 2.

[94] Statistics suggest the contrary. 'The number of GPs has grown by 23% since 1978/79 and as a result, average patient list sizes have fallen by nearly 17%.' R. Robinson, D. Evans, M. Exworthy, *Health and the Economy* (National Association of Health Authorities and Trusts, 1994) 24.

[95] See R. Veatch, *The Patient–Physician Relation, supra* note 13.

[96] See, in the American context, D. Hadorn, 'Emerging Parallels in the American Health Care and Legal-Judicial Systems', 18 *American Journal of Law and Medicine* 73 (1992).

[97] Department of Health, 1994. See also *Implementing the Patient's Charter* (HSG(92)4, NHSME, 1992).

specific expectations for the patient, and targets for hospitals and GPs; the mechanisms for making complaints are more structured and formal; doctors are increasingly influenced by clinical guidelines; and of course the number of legal authorities produced by litigation increases.

In this environment, 'partnership' is a euphemism. It masks the potential for conflict and inequality in the relationship.[98] Nowhere is the potential more patent than in decisions affected by resources: whether treatment is recommended and whether the patient should know about decisions based on scarcity. There is a need, therefore, to recognize the circumstances in which doctors may find themselves in conflict with the best interests of their patients and to ask whether they also owe allegiance to other patients which allows them to compromise the treatment of any individual patient. Central to the problem is this question: should the doctor be regarded as the patient's advocate? If resources threaten to compromise the doctor's clinical discretion, should he or she be expected to argue the clinical merits of the case before those who are withholding facilities? And, in the interests of the trust that exists between them, should the doctor be entirely candid with the patient as to the result? Or is the better analogy that of a manager? Here, the doctor has obligations to more than one patient at a time. It would be foolish to devote so much time to a single patient that others suffer avoidable harm. Thus, he must allocate his time and resources in a way that recognizes the interests of the majority, even if in doing so an individual receives second-best treatment.

Logic suggests that the second of these choices is unavoidable. It arises from the nature of the doctor's enterprise and must have been true since the time of Hippocrates. Increasingly, doctors are encouraged to manage resources, whether as GP fund-holders or clinical directors in hospitals. Perhaps the scientific theory of QALYs will never exactly represent the way in which doctors will make decisions about resources, but it makes a useful point. If this is right, however, there will be no sense of trust between doctor and patient, no partnership between them, and no ethics unless

---

[98] See S. Woolf, 'Conflict Between Doctor and Patient', 16 *Law, Medicine and Health Care* 197 (1988).

doctors accept the need for candour.[99] The Supreme Court of Canada has offered some support for such an approach in *Norberg* v. *Wynrib*[100] in which McLachin J developed the notion of a fiduciary relationship between patient and doctor, similar to that which exists between guardian and child, man and wife, lawyer and client, and confessor and penitent. She said:

the doctor–patient relationship shares the peculiar hallmark of the fiduciary relationship—trust, the trust of a person with inferior power that another person who has assumed superior power and responsibility will exercise that power for his or her good and only for his or her best interests.[101]

English common law has yet to commit itself on the issue of candour in the matter of resource allocation. The present law contained in *Sidaway* leans away from absolute candour, and the tendency of the common law system is to introduce change hesitantly and only in the light of persuasive argument. Without a development of this kind, however, there is a danger of the relationship becoming more cynical, defensive, and subject to distrust. In addition, there is a need for greater public understanding of the implications of scarce resources. One of the most immediate sources of information in this respect is the medical profession. These factors suggest that the changes to the law of disclosure introduced in Australia and Canada should also be instituted here.

There is something more. Resources may be managed by doctors, but they are equally the responsibility of health service administrators and managers. They should share a similar commitment to openness with patients. The Royal Commission in 1979 believed it was important that the lay public should be involved in the process of setting priorities and that the professional advice on which policies and priorities are based should be made public.[102] A similar view has been voiced by the Government today. It says: 'Patients and the public will be given greater scope to influence health services in their community. Health authorities will be

---

[99] See T. Brennan, 'An Ethical Perspective on Health Insurance Reform', *supra* note 84, 47–74 (1993).   [100] (1992) 92 DLR (4th) 449.
[101] Ibid. 486.
[102] *Royal Commission on the Health Service* (Cmnd. 7615, 1979), para. 6.7.

expected to increase the involvement of local people in developing strategies to meet local needs.'[103]

This will be a cause for concern because it has implications when things go wrong. It reveals another potential conflict for managers keen to preserve resources against claims for damages. But this is the acid test of the commitment to patients.

IV. PATIENT CONFIDENTIALITY

A major principle in medical law and ethics concerns the confidences which pass from patient to doctor. The principle assumes that candour assists doctors to promote their patients' best interests and has its origins in the Hippocratic Oath, which states: 'Whatsoever things I see or hear concerning the life of men, in my attendance on the sick or even apart therefrom, which ought not to be noised abroad, I will keep silence thereon, counting such things to be as sacred secrets.'

As we saw in Chapter 7, the common law recognizes a similar duty of confidence between doctor and patient,[104] as does the General Medical Council in its 'Blue Book' on professional discipline which provides that patients are entitled to expect that information disclosed during medical consultations will remain confidential and not be disclosed to third parties.[105] Of course, as we have also seen, this general principle is subject to exceptions which allow, for example, for third parties to be protected from serious risk of danger from a patient.[106] In addition, there are half a dozen statutes which specifically oblige aspects of a patient's medical records to be disclosed for statistical purposes.[107] The idea of the 'confidential relationship' between doctor and patient, however, is under threat. One of the threats comes from the fact

---

[103] *Managing the New NHS: Functions and Responsibilities in the New NHS* (NHS Executive, 1994) para. 3.4

[104] See *W* v. *Egdell* [1990] 1 All ER 835 and 265–68, *supra*.

[105] *Professional Conduct and Discipline: Fitness to Practise* (General Medical Council, 1993), para. 76.

[106] Exceptional circumstances in which such confidences may be disclosed are provided in paras 81–91 of the 'Blue Book'. See generally I. Kennedy and A. Grubb, *Medical Law*, *supra* note 80, ch. 9.

[107] See e.g. National Health Service (Notification of Births and Deaths) Regs. 1982 (SI 1982, No.286), Public Health (Infectious Diseases) Regs. 1988 (SI 1988, No.1546, Abortion Regs. 1991 (SI 1991, No. 499).

that more and more information about patients is stored electronically and consequently is easily copied from one place to dozens of others by the stroke of a key. This practical problem has been addressed by the Data Protection Act 1984, discussed in Chapter 5. But another institutional threat has been introduced by the pressures of the internal market for health.

Health service managers are encouraged to maximize the performance of the activities for which they are responsible. In doing so, they will naturally need to know how different departments have discharged their duties and, in particular, the success with which different doctors have treated patients, so that those parts of the system, or doctors, which perform badly can be encouraged to improve their standards. They must also identify the existence of risks in the system and reduce them wherever possible so as to reduce dangers to patients and minimize liability to pay large sums in damages. In one sense these are laudable aims which patients will welcome. So long as the information on which action is taken is reliable, it is good that shoddy or out-of-date performance should be identified and prevented. However, this objective also has serious implications for the confidences which pass between doctor and patient. Obviously, in order for action of this nature to be possible, managers will need to have access to the information about the patients for whom the doctor has been responsible, the nature of the illnesses with which they were presented, the relative degree of difficulty associated with each one, and so on. This is the case in hospital, but it may be the same in general practice. Doctors who wish to refer a patient to a hospital as an 'extra contractual referral' have to obtain the consent of their district health authority in order to do so, and, in so doing, explain the reasons why such a referral is necessary. What is the status of the relationship of confidence in these circumstances?

One way of avoiding a breach of confidence is to conceal from managers the identities of the individual patients concerned. If the relevant health records are made anonymous, for example by replacing names with numbers, the problem could be circumvented.[108] But this solution has serious limitations. First, such a

---

[108] This is the solution proposed to requests for extra contractual referrals in *Guidance on Extra Contractual Referrals* NHSME, 1993), paras. 21–3 which

system would probably be administered by managers themselves. Secondly, if managerial action were contemplated against a doctor for poor performance, such a procedure would surely need to protect the interests of doctors by requiring that the files concerned should be examined properly in a way which identified patients by reference to their names. Thirdly, patients would often be included amongst such small categories of analysis that it would not be difficult to discover their identities.

These are matters of concern to the British Medical Association. It takes the view that the principle of confidentiality remains an important guarantee to patients. It says there is: 'a strong public interest in enforcing the medical duty of confidentiality. In the absence of guarantees that their secrets will be protected, patients may withhold information important to their health care and possibly to the wellbeing of others, including health professionals.'[109]

Similarly, although the General Medical Council recognizes the need for disclosure to other doctors for good *clinical* reasons,[110] it makes no such concession in respect of managers for non-clinical reasons. These misgivings may be particularly relevant to those with diseases which attract social disapprobation, or those whose illnesses are caused by the illegal use of drugs. NHS managers, however, take a different view.

Draft guidelines on managerial rights of access to patients' records state: 'In general, personal health records should not be disclosed to any person who is not directly concerned with the particular patient's care unless: [a] the patient has expressly consented; or [b] disclosure of information on a 'need to know basis' is essential for the maintenance of the public health and functioning of the NHS.'[111]

The basis for this view of the rights of managers to patient's records is that 'patients implicitly authorise that their records . . .

concedes that there will be cases in which there is a need to know the patient's identity; see para. 25.

[109] *Medical Ethics Today, supra* note 5; 38.
[110] See the 'Blue Book', paras. 82–4.
[111] *Confidentiality, Use and Disclosure of Personal Health Information* (Department of Health draft guidance, 1994), para. 4.6.

will be used by the NHS and Department of Health for wider purposes which are essential to the delivery of high quality health care to themselves and the population as a whole'.[112] But such an assumption is questionable. The NHS has around one million personnel and, increasingly, engages private contractors to assist it. Should it be assumed without question that, no matter what my reason for seeking medical help in hospital, I consent to my records being disclosed in this way? Such a broad assumption seems unreasonable. Indeed, the presumption may be precisely to the contrary: that I wish the matter to remain confidential unless I expressly say otherwise. An alternative argument might be advanced that the tangible records kept by GPs belong to the FHSA, and those of hospital doctors belong to the NHS Trust or DHA which employs them. They are free, therefore, to do with them as they please. In the Court of Appeal, however, Sir Roger Parker has disapproved such a contention:

> I regard as untenable the proposition that, at common law, a doctor or health authority has an absolute property in medical records of a patient, if this means . . . that either could make what use of them they chose. Information given to a doctor by a patient or a third party is given in confidence and the absolute property rights are therefore necessarily qualified by the obligations arising out of the situation.[113]

Thus, the common law certainly imposes limits on the right to disclose confidences between patient and doctor, although the precise location of those limits for the NHS is undecided. The courts may be persuaded to adopt a more relaxed view of the doctor–patient relationship, which acknowledges that confidences may be disclosed to managers for managerial purposes. Arguably, however, until they do so the common law requires doctors to explain to patients that information disclosed during consultation or treatment may have to be disclosed within the NHS for reasons that are not pertinent to their own treatment, and to obtain the patient's consent to such a possibility. Presumably, those who do not wish their confidences to be disclosed in this way are entitled to have their wishes respected without their rights to treatment being affected.

---

[112] Ibid. para. 4.9.
[113] *R* v. *Mid Glamorgan FHSA*, ex p *Martin* [1994] 5 Med LR 383, 398.

Postscript

The Health Authorities Bill is before Parliament and, subject to approval, is scheduled to come into force on 1 April 1996. It does not seek to change the position of patients, doctors, or NHS Trusts. Its scope is limited to the authorities responsible for purchasing health care. It will abolish regional health authorities, district health authorities, and family health service authorities (special health authorities are retained). In their place will be 'Health Authorities' which, together with the National Health Service Executive, will assume responsibility for the strategic and operational provision of services to patients. Thus, in place of the current obligation to establish RHAs, DHAs, and FHSAs, the Bill proposes to amend the 1977 Act by providing that: 'It is the duty of the Secretary of State by order to establish . . . authorities to be called Health Authorities.'[1]

The principle reasons for the changes are as follows.

A. Abolition of Regional Health Authorities

With the development of the internal market for health, decision-making power in the NHS has devolved towards local purchasers of health care. Thus, it is perceived that the role of RHAs has diminished to such an extent that their functions can be reduced, the authority abolished, and the residual responsibilities absorbed by the NHSE. The Government said:

RHAs have played an important role in the management of the NHS for many years and the decision to abolish them has not been taken lightly. However, the development of the health reforms has already brought about a shift of responsibility toward local purchasers and providers, and there is no longer a need for 14 separate statutory bodies at an

---

[1] Clause 1, Health Authorities Bill.

intermediate level. The [NHSE] will take on those functions of the RHAs which remain the responsibility of central management.[2]

The responsibilities to be retained by central government have been outlined by the Minister of State for Health, who said that the following should be the responsibility of the NHSE: national screening programmes for breast and cervical cancer, cancer registries, various other functions which cannot be provided by individual authorities (say, because they are relatively uncommon and expensive) and which need to be provided by groups of authorities co-ordinated by one 'lead' authority under central guidance, and matters of education and training. In addition, the Minister provided a list of other functions to be supervised centrally:

performance management of health authorities and NHS trusts; approving general practitioner fundholding applications and the setting of GP fundholding budgets; regulation of the internal market; implementation of information management and technology strategy . . . ; capital allocation to providers, supporting . . . consortia of health authorities . . . ; medical work force planning and GP vocational training; public consultation in the establishment of NHS trusts . . . ; and emergency planning.[3]

One advantage of these changes is the savings in administrative costs which they may achieve. Opposition focused on the loss of an independent voice in the service, capable of making strong representations to government on behalf of regional communities.

B. Abolition of DHAs and FHSAs

The proposal to merge DHAs and FHSAs is less controversial. Many such mergers have already taken place on an informal basis. DHAs and FHSAs sometimes refer to themselves jointly as 'Health Commissions' in which they co-operate closely with one another. In the past, DHAs were concerned with the provision of hospital (secondary) services and FHSAs for GP (primary) services. Under the reformed system power and influence in the

---

[2] *Managing the New NHS* (Department of Health, 1993), para. 20.
[3] *Health Authorities Bill* (Select Committee A, Fifth Sitting, 7 February 1995), cols. 146–7.

system devolve to GPs with responsibility for both primary and secondary services and it is artificial to separate responsibility for the two.

The Bill also reduces the number of purchasing authorities. At present there are 111 DHAs and 92 FHSAs. The Bill gives the Secretary of State power to determine the boundaries of the new health authorities and the government proposes they should number between 80 and 90. The larger size of these authorities raises questions concerning the ease with which individuals will be able to gain access to them and to express views.

Obviously, the number of amendments which the new Act will require to be made to previous legislation is vast. The Bill contains only ten clauses, which are contained in four pages. However, its consequential amendments to other statutes run to a further fifty pages which alter the names of the various health authorities mentioned in them. This process of amendment, alteration, deletion, and substitution to the National Health Service Act 1977 has now been going on since 1980. The Act has been changed so many times that it is now simply inaccessible without the aid of sophisticated up-dating services which are not generally available. This is an area of considerable public concern which ought to be resolved by enacting a comprehensive statute. The 1977 Act, together with the changes of the past fifteen years, should be consolidated into one new Act.

Select Bibliography

1. DEMAND AND SUPPLY IN HEALTH CARE

J. Appleby, *Financing Health Care in the 1990's* (Open University Press, 1992).
C. Gudex, *QALYS and their use by the Health Service* (University of York, 1986).
D. Hunter, *Rationing Dilemmas in Health Care* (National Association of Health Authorities and Trusts, 1993).
W. Laing, *Financing Long-Term Care: the Critical Debate* (Age Concern, 1993).
G. Mooney, *Economics, Medicine and Health Care* (Harvester Wheatsheaf, 2nd ed., 1991).
G. Mooney, K. Gerard and C. Donaldson, *Priority Setting and Purchasing—Some Practical Guidelines* (National Association of Health Authorities and Trusts, 1992).
Royal Commission on the National Health Service (Cmnd. 7615, 1979).

2. EVOLUTION OF THE NATIONAL HEALTH SERVICE

A. Culyer, A. Maynard and J. Posnett, *Competition in Health Care— Reforming the NHS* (Macmillan Press, 1990).
A. Enthoven, *Reflections on the Management of the Health Service—An American looks at incentives to efficiency in health services management in the UK* (Nuffield Provincial Hospitals Trust, 1985).
A. Glennerster, M. Matsaganis and P. Owens, *A Foothold for Fund holding—A Preliminary Report on the introduction of GP fundholding* (King's Fund Institute, 1992).
C. Ham, *Management and Competition in the Health Service* (Radcliffe Medical Press, 1994).
Health Care Systems in Transition, the Search for Efficiency (OECD, 1990).
J. Le Grand and W. Bartlett (eds.), *Quasi-Markets and Social Policy* (Macmillan, 1993).
R. Robinson and J. Le Grand, *Evaluating the NHS Reforms* (King's Fund Institute, 1994).
P. Strong and J. Robinson, *The NHS Under New Management* (Open University Press, 1990).

3. LEGAL REGULATION OF HEALTH CARE

G. Annas, S. Law, R. Rosenblat, and K. Wing, *American Health Law* (Little Brown and Co., 1990).

M. Brazier, *Medicine, Patients and the Law* (Penguin Books, 1992).

B. Furrow, T. Greaney, S. Johnson, T. Jost and R. Schwartz, *Health Law* (West Publishing Co., 1995).

I. Kennedy, *Treat Me Right* (Oxford University Press, 1988).

I. Kennedy and A. Grubb, *Medical Law—Text with Materials* (Butterworths, 2nd ed., 1994).

J. Mason and A. McCall Smith, *Law and Medical Ethics* (Butterworths, 4th ed., 1994).

Medical Ethics Today, Its Practice and Philosophy (British Medical Association, 1993).

M. Jones, *Medical Negligence* (Sweet & Maxwell, 1991).

H. Teff, *Reasonable Care* (Oxford University Press, 1994).

4. RESOURCES AND THE EVOLUTION OF CLINICAL CARE

T. Brennan, *Just Doctoring: Medical Ethics in the Liberal State* (California University Press, 1991).

D. Callahan, *Setting Limits: Medical Goals in an Aging Society* (Simon and Schuster, New York, 1990).

Choices in Health Care (Government Committee on Choices in Health Care, The Netherlands, 1992).

R. Gillon, *Philosophical Medical Ethics* (Wiley, 1986).

A. Grubb (eds.), *Choices and Decisions in Health Care* (Wiley, 1993).

M. Henwood, *Through a Glass Darkly: Community Care and Elderly People* (King's Fund Institute, 1992).

F. Honnigsbaum, *Who Shall Live? Who Shall Die?—Oregon's Health Financing Proposals* (King's Fund College, 1993).

I. Illich, *Limits to Medicine* (Penguin, 1978).

R. Veatch, *The Patient–Physician Relation* (Indiana University Press, 2 vols., 1991).

M. Whitehead, *Inequalities in Health* (Pelican Books, 1988).

5. RELATION OF CLINICIANS AND MANAGERS IN THE HEALTH SERVICE

Audit Commission, *A Prescription for Improvement—Toward More Rational Prescribing in General Practice* (Audit Commission, HMSO, 1994).

J. Ayres, 'The Use and Abuse of Medical Practice Guidelines', in 15 *Journal of Legal Medicine* 421 (1994).

T. Brennan, 'Practice Guidelines and Malpractice Litigation: Collision or Cohesion', in 16 *Journal of Health, Politics, Policy and Law* 67 (1991).

J. Butler, *Patients, Policies and Politics* (Open University Press, 1992).

T. Folmer Anderson and G. Mooney (eds.), *The Challenge of Medical Practice Variations* (Macmillan, 1990).

D. Eddy, 'Variations in Clinical Practice: The Role of Uncertainty', in 3 *Health Affairs* 74 (1984).

S. Harrison, D. Hunter *et al.*, *Just Managing: Power and Culture in the National Health Service* (Macmillan, 1992).

D. Hunter, 'Doctors as Managers, Poachers turned Gamekeepers', in 35 *Social Science and Medicine* 557 (1992).

W. Laing, *Managing the NHS—Past, Present and Future* (Office of Health Economics, 1994).

6. ACCOUNTABILITY AND COMPLAINTS IN THE HEALTH SERVICE

Accountability in the Health Service (British Medical Association, 1994).

Acting on Complaints (Department of Health, 1995).

Being Heard—Report of a Review Committee into NHS Complaints Procedures (Department of Health, 1994).

Code of Conduct and Accountability (Department of Health, 1994).

Ensuring Effective CHCs in the New Structure (Association of Community Health Councils for England and Wales, 1994).

A Health Standards Inspectorate (Association of Community Health Councils for England Wales, 1993).

G. Hunt (ed.), *Whistleblowing in the Health Service* (Edward Arnold, 1995).

Local Authorities and the Health Service (Association of Metropolitan Authoritics, 1994).

Index

freedom to enter and leave relation-
    ship 157–9
home visits 150–1
meaning 148
obligations to 148–52
primary care centres, use of 151
severing relationship 158–9
Dwarfism 6

Economic logic in health care 19–38
Efficiency trap 41–2
Elderly patients
    QALY principle 26–7
Emergencies
    general practitioners, and 152–7
Employees
    vicarious liability for 95
Enthoven, A.
    National Health Service, on 42
Ethics in the new NHS 273–307
Executive letters 190–3
    legitimacy 190–1
    mandatory 192
    rights, and 193
Extra contractual referrals 186–9
    costs 189
    funds for 187–8
    grounds for refusal 188–9

Family Health Service Authority
    abolition 310–11
    complaints to 257–8
    discipline of GPs 256–60
        formal procedure 258
        reference to Medical Services
            Committee 258–9
    relationship with general practitioner
        146–8
Federal health service 275–6
Fund-holders 212–23
    accountability 212–23
    'allotted sum' 213–15
        comparison 215–16
        exceeding 218–20
        overspending 218–20
        priorities 217–18
        savings from 215–18
    consortia 220–3
        benefits 221–2
        costs 221–2
        influence of GPs 222
    gate-keeping role 220

Funding providers of health care
    63–76
Funding purchasers of health care
    59–63
    GP fund-holders 62–3
    health authorities 60–2
        allocation of resources 60–2
        weighted capitation formula 60–1
Funding the NHS 59–76
Futile care 280–5
    extension of concept 284–5
    judgment of futility 281–2
    personal choice, and 283
    reasonableness, and 282
Future organization of NHS 273–6

General Medical Council 260–8
    advice on professional conduct and
        ethics 261
    confidential information 265–8
        AIDS 267–8
        close relatives, and 266–7
        dangerous patients 267
        HIV 267–8
        nature of duty 265–6
    disciplinary powers 260–8
    role 261
    serious professional misconduct
        262–5
        improper conduct 263–4
        'infamous' 262–3
        negligence, and 264–5
        performance procedures 265
General practitioners 145–59
    assignees 155–7
    deputy, responsibility as 153–4
    discipline by FHSA 256–60
    emergencies 152–3
    Family Health Service Authority,
        and 146–8
    independent contractors, as 147
    Medical List 147
    obligations to patients not on list
        152–7
    remuneration 147
    terms of service 145–59
    unavailability 148
    violent patients 155–7
Genetic treatment 5–6
GP fund-holder
    funding purchasers, as 212–13
GP fund-holding practices 40–1
Griffiths Report 165–6